Microsoft® Excel® & Access™ Integration with Office 2007

Michael Alexander and Geoffrey Clark

1807
WILEY
2007

Wiley Publishing, Inc.

Microsoft® Excel® & Access™ Integration with Office 2007
Published by
Wiley Publishing, Inc.
10475 Crosspoint Boulevard
Indianapolis, IN 46256
www.wiley.com

Copyright © 2007 by Wiley Publishing, Inc., Indianapolis, Indiana

Published simultaneously in Canada

ISBN: 978-0-470-10488-0

Manufactured in the United States of America

10 9 8 7 6 5 4 3 2

For general information on our other products and services or to obtain technical support, please contact our Customer Care Department within the U.S. at (800) 762-2974, outside the U.S. at (317) 572-3993 or fax (317) 572-4002.

Library of Congress Control Number: 2007007062

About the Authors

Mike Alexander is a Microsoft Certified Applications Developer (MCAD) with over 14 years experience developing Office solutions for a wide array of Companies and industries. He currently lives in Frisco, Texas, where he works as a Senior Program Manager for a top technology firm. He is the author of several books on data analysis using Excel and Access, and he is the principal behind `DataPigTechnologies.com`, a site that offers free tutorials on Excel and Access.

Geoff Clark holds an MBA from Duke University's Fuqua School of Business where he graduated as a Fuqua Scholar in 2000. After business school, Geoff joined McKinsey & Company in Charlotte, NC, as an associate management consultant. It was at McKinsey & Company where Geoff began applying advanced Microsoft Excel and Access techniques to aid clients in analytical problem solving and fact-based decision making. After his stint in management consulting, Geoff served as director of marketing analytics with a $700 million environmental services firm. Currently, he is a manager at a major technology outsourcing company and develops office applications to enable enterprise-wide metrics and change initiatives. Geoff lives in Plano, TX, with his wife and son.

Credits

Acquisitions Editor
Katie Mohr

Development Editor
Kelly Talbot

Technical Editor
Ed Ferrero

Production Editor
Angela Smith

Copy Editor
Travis Henderson

Editorial Manager
Mary Beth Wakefield

Production Manager
Tim Tate

**Vice President and Executive
Group Publisher**
Richard Swadley

**Vice President and Executive
Publisher**
Joseph B. Wikert

Project Coordinator
Kristie Rees

Graphics and Production Specialists
Denny Hager
Stephanie D. Jumper
Jennifer Mayberry
Barbara Moore
Ronald Terry

Quality Control Technicians
John Greenough
Brian H. Walls

Proofreading and Indexing
Aptara

Anniversary Logo Design
Richard Pacifico

Contents

Acknowledgments

We would like to express our deepest thanks to Katie Mohr and Kelly Talbot, for all the hours of work put into making this book as clear as it can be. Thanks also to Ed Ferraro for saving us from embarrassment as he worked to correct our mistakes and suggest numerous improvements in our examples and text. Any errors you may find here are ours, not his. We would also like to thank the brilliant team of professionals who helped bring this book to fruition. Finally, a special thank you goes out to our families for putting up with all the time we spent away on this project.

Introduction

Since Office 2000, Microsoft has marketed the Office suite as a set of interoperable applications that easily enable integration of multiple processes. For most users, however, Office is still a suite of individual applications. Excel is used for spreadsheet analysis and reporting whereas Access is used for database functions—and that's it. Indeed, most mainstream training courses and documentation are often dedicated to one application or another, often providing very little information on the concept of integration.

In fact, it seems that most Office users tend to fall in one of two camps: Excel users and Access users. Very few people operate comfortably in both camps. Even fewer realize the full integration potential of these powerful Office applications.

Microsoft Excel reigns supreme among spreadsheet applications. In the corporate world, Excel is a ubiquitous and nearly universal application. This popularity has come with a severe downside as most business analysts have constrained themselves to just one tool for all their analytical and reporting needs — Excel. What's the problem with that? Well, Excel is not designed to do many of the activities we try to make it do — like integrating disparate data sources and performing complex, multi-stage data processing. Rather than explore the functionality of other Office applications (namely Access), analysts instead engage in hand-to-hand combat with their data, creating complex workarounds and inefficient processes.

As a relational database application, Microsoft Access enables integration of disparate data sources and multi-step data manipulation that would be cumbersome or even impossible to do in Excel. However, Access has its limitations in the business community. First, it does not have a fraction of the popularity that Excel has. Chances are that nearly everyone in your company, from the president to the recent graduate new hire, has some working knowledge of Excel. How many company presidents have an Access database on their laptops, or would know what to do with it if they did? Furthermore, training for Access has rarely targeted the community of business analysts, choosing instead to cater to database and application builders. How will a working knowledge of user-subforms or knowing how to set up a contact database help a struggling analyst synthesize financial data from three different legacy IT systems? Understandably, the business analyst community of Excel power users have stuck with the tools they know and steered clear of those they do not.

In so doing, however, they have left a lot of potential productivity off the table. It is our aim with this book to help the Excel user (and the Access user) harness that productivity by using and integrating both Excel and Access. Through integration, Access gains the benefit of flexible presentation layer and versatile analysis capabilities in Excel; Excel gains the benefit of relational database structure and robust querying tools in Access. Integrating both applications can yield incredible productivity gains and enable penetrating business analyses.

What this book will highlight is that there are powerful functionalities in both Excel and Access that can help you go beyond the one dimensional world of either spreadsheet or database. This book will liberate you from the daily grind of routine data practices and help you to explore all the functionality that exists when Excel and Access are brought together.

Although both of these applications are powerful tools on their own, combining the functionality of Excel and Access opens up a whole new world of possibilities

What to Expect from This Book

In this book, you will find a comprehensive review of the wide range of integration techniques that can be performed using Excel and Access. Through step-by-step instruction, you will explore the benefits of integrating Excel and Access, the differences and similarities between Excel and Access, and some of the common pitfalls of moving and analyzing data across applications. After reading this book, you will be able to:

- Easily move data between Excel and Access
- Store Excel data in a structured, relational database
- Use Excel pivot tables with Access data
- Report Access data using the Excel presentation layer
- Move data between Excel and Access using VBA, ADO and SQL

- Automate redundant processes using VBA to save time and increase productivity
- Simplify integration tasks using XML
- Integrate Excel data into other Office applications

Skills Required for This Book

In order to get the most out of this book, you have the following skills:

- Some experience working with data and familiarity with the basic concepts of data analysis such as working with tables, aggregating data, and performing calculations.
- Experience using Excel with a strong grasp of concepts such as table structures, filtering, sorting and using formulas.
- Some basic knowledge of Access, enough to know it exists and to have opened a database once or twice

How This Book Is Organized

This book is organized into two parts: Basic Integration Techniques and Advanced Integration Techniques.

Part I: Basic Integration Techniques

Part I of this book is dedicated to those integration techniques that can be accomplished via the Excel and Access user interfaces. This part includes Chapters 1 through 6. Chapters 1 through 4 will teach you how to get your Excel data into Access as well as how to leverage the many Access utilities to go beyond the functionality found in Excel. Chapter 5 demonstrates the best ways to use Access data in Excel. Chapter 6 introduces you to the world of macros, demonstrating automation techniques from both an Excel and Access point of view.

Part II: Advanced Integration Techniques

Part II of this book is dedicated to automating your integration processes via VBA (Visual Basic for Applications) code. Chapter 7 provides a high level introduction to VBA. Chapter 8 covers the various methods of moving data between Excel and Access using VBA. In Chapter 9, you will learn how to control and manipulate Excel from Access and vice versa. Chapter 10 introduces you to the world of XML; discussing several ways XML can help you simplify your integration tasks. Finally, Chapter 11 rounds out this book with a look into the various ways you can integrate Excel with Word, PowerPoint and Outlook.

Companion Database

The examples demonstrated throughout this book can be found in the companion database. This sample database is located at www.wiley.com.

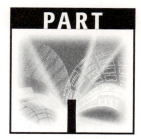

Basic Integration Techniques

Getting Excel Data into Access

The business world is split between Access users and Excel users. Access users tend to be the database guys and the techie application builders. Everybody else uses Excel. If you work in corporate America, you are probably conversant in the language of Excel. You can send even the most seasoned of senior vice presidents a spreadsheet-style report and trust she will know what to do with it. Send that same VP an Access file and ask her to run a crosstab query, and you've relegated your career to the cubicle farm.

Simply put, Excel has few equals when it comes to performing large numbers of calculations based on other cells and then presenting that information in a widely acceptable and familiar format. However, as a relational database application, Access is a powerful tool that gives the user the ability to integrate disparate data sources to perform analysis and reporting that would be cumbersome or even impossible to do in Excel. Integrating both applications brings the best of each to bear on a plethora of business analyses. Yet few professionals in corporate America and elsewhere have the experience necessary to accomplish this.

Our goal is to introduce the power of Microsoft Access to Excel users of all skill levels. We want to show you how integrating Access and Excel can improve and expand your abilities in data analysis and reporting beyond what is possible by simply using Excel. In so doing, you will become an indispensable team member with a very rare set of skills.

This chapter explores the first steps in integrating these two Microsoft Office applications for data analysis. The first section describes the relevant differences between Access and Excel for the Access uninitiated. The remaining sections include a hands-on exercise on getting Excel data into Access and is followed by tips and tricks about how to optimize your new database's performance.

Differences Between Access and Excel

Before you dive in to bringing Excel data into Access, take a closer look at each application. Specifically, you need a better understanding of just what the utility is of each application and how they are different. You'll start by examining different categories of spreadsheets in Excel.

Different Types of Excel Spreadsheets

Not all spreadsheets are created equal. Intuitively, you probably already know this. Before importing Excel data into Access, however, you should familiarize yourself with the different types of worksheets.

At the risk of oversimplification, Excel worksheets (not applications) come in three fundamental forms: the Excel report, the Excel flat data file, and the Excel indexed list. Only the last two types are compatible with Access. To ensure your Excel data is in the proper format to be used in Access, you must understand these three types of spreadsheets.

The Excel Worksheet in Report Format

The Excel report is a means of formatting and displaying data, often for managers or other users. A good Excel report makes judicious use of empty space for formatting, summarizes data where appropriate, and clearly marks data fields. In Excel, the spreadsheet can be used both for data storage and for data reporting. A spreadsheet in report format may make a good report, but it does not make a good Access table. The Access table is a repository of data. Other Access objects, like queries, forms, and reports, need to refer to data in these tables to generate useful summaries and reports.

Take, for example, the spreadsheet in Figure 1-1. This worksheet makes for a pretty good report, but it's not in a format that can be imported into Access.

For starters, the geographical region information does not have its own column. Region information is found in the Treatment Type column. If you want to import an Excel worksheet into Access, the worksheet must be in a row by column format. This means every data field must have its own unique column.

	A	B	C	D	E	F
1	TREATMENT TYPE	TREATMENT TECHNOLOGY		4 WEEK INTERVAL	8 WEEK INTERVAL	12 WEEK INTERVAL
2	SOUTH REGION					
3	Earwig eradication					
4		Bugkiller formula EWI34		$ 84.50	$ 112.75	$ 150.50
5		Green treatment		$ 104.50	$ 132.75	$ 170.50
6		Vacuum		$ 124.50	$ 152.75	$ 190.50
7	Termite treatment					
8		Bugkiller formula TT56		$ 124.50	$ 152.75	$ 190.50
9		Green treatment		$ 164.50	$ 192.75	$ 230.50
10		Vacuum		$ 180.75	$ 209.00	$ 246.75
11	RolleyPolley Roundup					
12		Bugkiller formula RPR45		$ 84.50	$ 112.75	$ 150.50
13		Green treatment		$ 104.50	$ 132.75	$ 170.50
14		Vacuum		$ 124.50	$ 152.75	$ 190.50
15	NORTH REGION					
16	Earwig eradication					
17		Bugkiller formula EWI34		$ 92.00	$ 120.25	$ 158.00
18		Green treatment		$ 112.00	$ 140.25	$ 178.00
19		Vacuum		$ 132.00	$ 160.25	$ 198.00
20	Termite treatment			$ 7.50	$ 7.50	$ 7.50
21		Bugkiller formula TT56		$ 132.00	$ 160.25	$ 198.00
22		Green treatment		$ 172.00	$ 200.25	$ 238.00
23		Vacuum		$ 188.25	$ 7.50	$ 7.50

Figure 1-1: An Excel spreadsheet in report format

The worksheet in Figure 1-1 also has blank columns and cells in the data. Column C is blank. Additionally, there are blank cells in every row of the report. For proper importing into Access, the data must be *contiguous*, meaning in one solid block with no extraneous rows or columns.

There are columns that house more than one type of information. This issue is a bit more subtle, but look more closely at columns D, E, and F. Each column is telling us something about price *and* something about service term (notice the column labels contain information on service term). A good data source for importing to Access will have columns that contain one unique type of data. For example, in a proper table, these three columns would be replaced with two columns — one for service price and one for service term.

The Excel Worksheet in Flat File Format

Flat files are data repositories organized by row and column. Each row corresponds to a set of data elements called a *record*. Each column is called a *field*. A field corresponds to a unique data element in a record. Figure 1-2 contains the same data as the report in Figure 1-1 in the flat file format.

Notice that every data field has a column and every column corresponds to one and only one data element. Furthermore, there is no extra spacing and each row, or record, corresponds to a unique set of information. However, notice that there is no single field that uniquely identifies a record. In fact, in many of these records, you would have to specify four separate fields before you could uniquely identify the record (Region, Treatment Type, Treatment Technology, Service Interval)!

	A	B	C	D	E
1	REGION	TREATMENT TYPE	TREATMENT TECHNOLOGY	SERVICE INTERVAL	PRICE
2	SOUTH	Earwig eradication	Bugkiller formula EWI34	4	$84.50
3	SOUTH	Earwig eradication	Bugkiller formula EWI34	8	$112.75
4	SOUTH	Earwig eradication	Bugkiller formula EWI34	12	$150.50
5	SOUTH	Earwig eradication	Green treatment	4	$104.50
6	SOUTH	Earwig eradication	Green treatment	8	$132.75
7	SOUTH	Earwig eradication	Green treatment	12	$170.50
8	SOUTH	Earwig eradication	Slow suffocation	4	$124.50
9	SOUTH	Earwig eradication	Slow suffocation	8	$152.75
10	SOUTH	Earwig eradication	Slow suffocation	12	$190.50
11	SOUTH	Termite treatment	Bugkiller formula TT56	4	$84.50
12	SOUTH	Termite treatment	Bugkiller formula TT57	8	$112.75
13	SOUTH	Termite treatment	Bugkiller formula TT58	12	$150.50
14	SOUTH	Termite treatment	Green treatment	4	$104.50
15	SOUTH	Termite treatment	Green treatment	8	$132.75
16	SOUTH	Termite treatment	Green treatment	12	$170.50
17	SOUTH	Termite treatment	Flame thrower	4	$124.50
18	SOUTH	Termite treatment	Flame thrower	8	$152.75
19	SOUTH	Termite treatment	Flame thrower	12	$190.50
20	SOUTH	RolleyPolley Roundup	Bugkiller formula RPR45	4	$124.50
21	SOUTH	RolleyPolley Roundup	Bugkiller formula RPR45	8	$152.75
22	SOUTH	RolleyPolley Roundup	Bugkiller formula RPR45	12	$190.50
23	SOUTH	RolleyPolley Roundup	Green treatment	4	$164.50
24	SOUTH	RolleyPolley Roundup	Green treatment	8	$192.75

Figure 1-2: An Excel worksheet in flat file format

As convenient as flat files can be, they aren't the most efficient way to store data in Access. Flat files come with their own set of drawbacks:

- Flat files often contain redundant data (that is, data that is duplicated multiple times). This naturally makes for unnecessarily large datasets.

- Flat files often contain irrelevant data columns. These columns are typically holdovers from another process that no one wants to delete.

- Flat files often contain blank or empty data elements. Because flat files are typically a mish mash of many subjects in one data table, it is not uncommon to have holes in the data.

TIP Chapter 2 discusses some of the drawbacks of flat files in the section "Understanding the Concept of Relational Databases."

The Excel Worksheet in Indexed List Format

The indexed list is the type of spreadsheet most compatible with importing into Access. Excel users who employ VLOOKUP or HLOOKUP functions are already implicitly aware of the indexed list concept. The reference list used in these functions must always be an indexed list. An indexed list shares properties with the flat file format in that it is contiguous and organized by row and column. It is different in two very important ways, however. First, the indexed list contains information about one and only one subject. Second, an indexed list has one column with non-repeating data that uniquely identifies each record. Take a look at our data in an indexed list format in Figure 1-3.

The indexed list shown here is all about one subject: product pricing. The field called Product Number uniquely identifies each service offering and service interval combination. Notice how information about the Region, Treatment Type, and Treatment Technology no longer exists in this table. That is because the Product Number field is now used as an index to represent these elements. In a properly designed database structure, the Region, Treatment Type, and Treatment Technology might be stored in their own separate indexed lists with the subjects focused on things such as Service Descriptions and Region Hierarchy.

Don't worry if these concepts don't sink in at first glance. As you move through Chapter 2 and start working with some data in Access, you will intuitively grasp these concepts. As you will learn in Chapter 2, indexed lists will make database design more elegant and your analysis less prone to errors.

	A	B	C
1	PRODUCT NUMBER	SERVICE INTERVAL	PRICE
2	1064	8	$132.75
3	1085	12	$150.50
4	1085	4	$164.50
5	1135	12	$246.75
6	1165	4	$124.50
7	1213	12	$170.50
8	1218	8	$152.75
9	1261	4	$124.50
10	1287	4	$180.75
11	1303	12	$170.50
12	1320	8	$192.75
13	1329	4	$104.50
14	1351	8	$152.75
15	1414	12	$230.50
16	1453	12	$190.50
17	1493	4	$84.50
18	1607	4	$84.50
19	1685	8	$132.75
20	1689	8	$209.00
21	1709	4	$104.50
22	1808	12	$190.50
23	1854	12	$150.50

Figure 1-3: An Excel worksheet in indexed list format

The Access Table

Now that you have reviewed what type of Excel data format is compatible with Access, let's take a brief look at where the Excel data will be going — the Access table. Access contains many objects that are very useful in manipulating and presenting data. The table is where the data is stored. Queries, forms, reports, and other Access objects ultimately reference data in an Access table.

The Table in the Datasheet View

In the sample files for this book, you will find a sample Access database. Open this database. When the database is open, go up to the application ribbon, select the Create tab, and then click the Table command button. A new table similar to the one illustrated in Figure 1-4 is activated in Datasheet view.

You will notice how similar the table is to a blank Excel spreadsheet. Both are organized by row and column. As with an Excel flat file and indexed list, each row corresponds to a record of data and each column corresponds to a field or a unique data element within the record.

As you can imagine, one way to create a table in Access is to start entering data in the Datasheet view. You can enter new data fields by entering data in the cells and pressing the Tab key. Enter a new record by pressing Enter. This method of entry will work if you need to get very small Excel lists into Access. However, there are much more efficient and powerful methods such as importing and linking, which you will explore later in this chapter.

The Table in the Design View

At the far left end of the Access ribbon, you will see the View icon. Click the View icon and select Design from the drop down menu. After being prompted to save and name the table, you will see the Design view (see Figure 1-5).

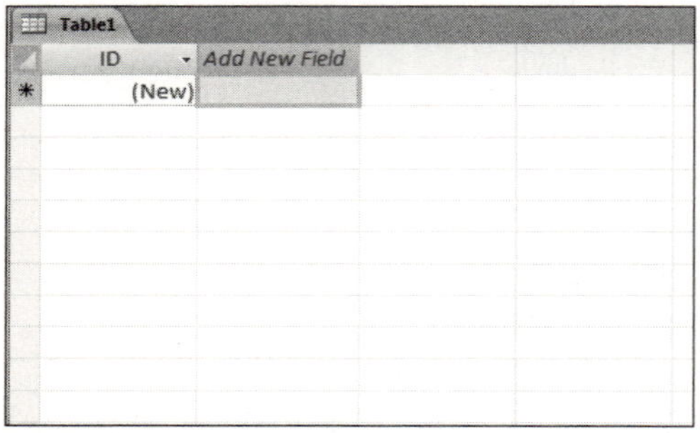

Figure 1-4: The Access table in the Datasheet view

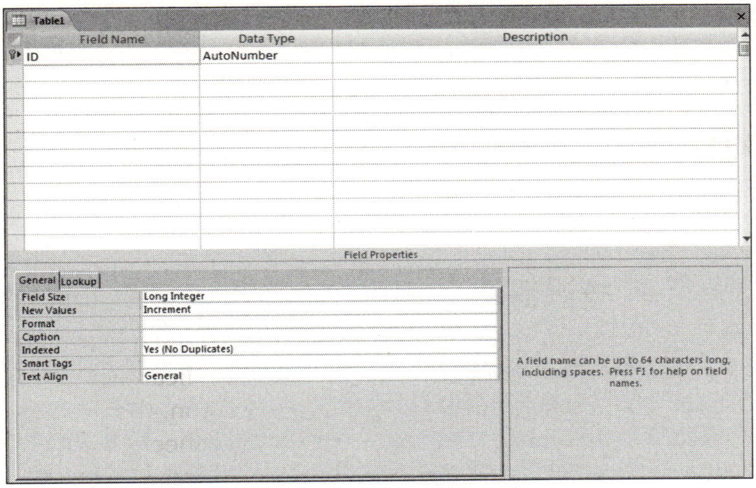

Figure 1-5: The Access table in the Design view

Here you can change the properties of the fields in the table: the field name, the data type (which characterizes what kind of information exists in the field), and a description (where you can manually enter a more descriptive word or phrase about the field).

Different Types of Data

Ten data types can be defined in Access. You will probably use just a few of them. However, this section includes a brief description of all the types in case you are relatively new to Access. The 10 data types are: Text, Memo, Number, Date/Time, Currency, AutoNumber, Yes/No, OLE Object, Hyperlink, and Attachment.

- **Text:** Text is the most common data type you will use in Access. Technically, any combination of letters, numbers, and characters is text — even spaces! Keep in mind that any number stored as text cannot be used in a calculation. Examples of numbers commonly stored as the Text data type are customer numbers, product SKUs, or serial numbers. Obviously, you would never perform any calculations on these types of numbers. The Text data type is limited to a maximum of 255 characters.

- **Memo:** The Memo field allows you to store text data that exceeds the 255-character limit of the text field.

- **Number:** The Number field is a numeric data type that is actually several data types under one heading. Use this data type with fields that might be summed or otherwise modified through arithmetic operations.

After selecting the Number data type in the Design view of the table, go to the Field Size field at the top of the Field Properties menu. Selecting this menu will give you the following choices: Byte, Integer, Long Integer, Single, Double, Replication ID, and Decimal. The most common field sizes of the Number data type are Long Integer and Double. Long Integer should be selected if the numbers are whole numbers (no decimals). Double should be selected if decimal numbers need to be stored in that field.

- **Date/Time:** The Date/Time data type is used to record the exact time or date that certain events occurred. The posting date of a transaction and the exact time a service call was placed are perfect examples of fields where the Date/Time data type is most useful.

- **Currency:** The Double field size of the Number data type can also be used for currency fields, but the Currency data type is ideal to store all data that represents amounts of money.

- **AutoNumber:** This data type is a Long Integer that is automatically created for each new record added to a table, so you will never enter data into this field. The AutoNumber can be one mechanism by which you can uniquely identify each individual record in a table, but it is best practice to use a unique record identifier that already exists in your data set.

- **Yes/No:** There are situations where the data that needs to be represented is in a simple Yes/No format. Although you could use the Text data type for creating a True/False field, it is much more intuitive to use Access's native data type for this purpose.

- **OLE Object:** This data type is not encountered very often in data analysis. It is used when the field must store a binary file, such as a picture or sound file.

- **Hyperlink:** When you need to store an address to a web site, this is the preferred data type.

- **Attachment:** You can use attachments to store several files, and even different types of files, in a single field. The Attachment field is new for Access 2007 and stores data files more efficiently than using other fields like the OLE Object field.

Different data types and field sizes can get overwhelming, but don't worry. When you import your data from Excel, Access will choose a default type for you. Most of the time, the default type is correct. If it's not, however, you have the opportunity to change it when importing or when you data is already in Access.

Table and Field Naming Conventions

There are important conventions and limitations when it comes to naming your access database tables and fields within those tables. The maximum length of a field name is 64 characters. Although you should give your fields descriptive names to clarify what the field represents, try using considerably less than the 64-character limit. In addition, your field name cannot include a period (.), an exclamation point (!), an accent grave (`), or brackets ([ ]).

> **TIP** It's good practice not to put any spaces in field or table names. When constructing queries or referring to tables in VBA code, spaces in the field names can lead to problems. If you need to indicate a space in your field name, use the underscore character (_).

Bringing Your Excel Data into Access

From the prior section, you know that your Excel data must be in flat file or indexed list format to be compatible with Access. Once you have your Excel data in the correct form, you can start bringing that data into Access. This section introduces the many ways of getting Excel data into Access.

Importing a Worksheet into a New Table

Open Microsoft Access and select the Blank Database icon as demonstrated in Figure 1-6. On the right, you see an input box used to name your new database.

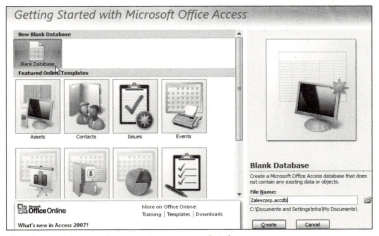

Figure 1-6: Menu for creating a new database

NOTE By default, all new databases are automatically created in the My Documents directory (in Vista, the default directory is the Documents directory). You can select a different location for your database by clicking the folder icon next to the input box containing the name of the database.

When you click the Create button, you will have an empty database. At this point, start by bringing in employee data. The employee data you need comes from Human Resources. They export it from their HR system into an Excel file and make some manual adjustments to it each month. You can take a look at the data in the Excel file EmployeeMaster (see Figure 1-7).

TIP The `ExcelMaster.xlsx file` can be found within the sample files for this book installed under `C:\Integration`.

The data looks to be in indexed list format with Employee Number uniquely identifying each record. Now let's import our worksheet to a new Access table with the Access Import Spreadsheet Wizard. To begin importing an Excel spreadsheet, simply click the External Data tab and then click the Excel icon above the import section. If you are familiar with earlier versions of Access, you will remember that this functionality was buried several layers deep within the File menu.

Now browse for the file you want to import and then select the option Import the source data into a new table in the current database. Figure 1-8 shows you what the wizard should look like now.

	A	B	C	D	E	F	
1	Employee_Number	Last_Name	First_Name	Employee_Status	Hire_Date	Last_Date_Worked	Job_Title
2	104	WIBB	MAURICE	A	4/11/1994		SERVICE
3	1044	BLECKMAN	PHILLIP	A	6/24/1992		SERVICE
4	1050	VALLOFUIRTE	LOUIS	I	11/20/1996	10/8/2004	SERVICE
5	1054	STEMPFL	JOHN	A	7/5/1977		SERVICE
6	106	CESTENGIAY	LUC	A	4/15/1996		SERVICE
7	113	TRIDIL	ROCH	A	10/24/1988		SERVICE
8	1130	RIID	RUSSELL	A	2/27/1986		SERVICE
9	1135	FERNEM	ROBERT	A	10/9/1990		TEAMLEA
10	1156	RACHERDS	PATRICK	A	8/24/1987		SERVICE
11	1245	HERPIR	JAMES	A	10/10/1994		SERVICE
12	1336	RACHTIR	CHARLES	A	3/24/1986		SERVICE
13	1344	ZAMMIRMAN	CHAD	A	1/5/1998		SERVICE
14	1416	CERMACHEIL	KEVIN	A	9/12/1990		SERVICE
15	142	CETE	GUY	A	10/26/1998		SERVICE
16	1435	HIGHIS	MICHAEL	A	7/20/1992		SERVICE
17	145	ERSINEILT	MIKE	A	9/28/1998		SERVICE
18	1462	GIFFIY	SHAWN	I	4/20/1998	1/26/2005	SERVICE
19	1464	GRANTHEM	PETER	A	7/5/1988		TEAMLEA
20	1465	PRZISLEWSKI	BRIAN	A	8/30/1994		SERVICE
21	1536	GLUISEN	JOSEPH	A	5/7/1986		SERVICE
22	1544	TERRIS	ANGELO	I	5/26/1998	6/15/2004	SERVICE
23	1564	BEWIN	BRANDON	I	1/21/1998	2/20/2004	SERVICE
24	160006	BEICHERD	SHANE	I	7/27/2003	7/9/2004	SERVICE

Figure 1-7: Employee data in Excel

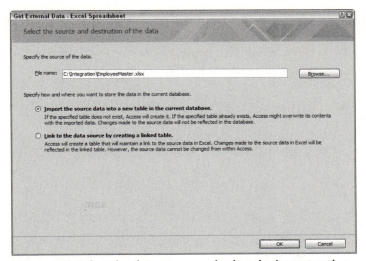

Figure 1-8: Select the data source and select the import option.

Click the OK button to activate the Import Spreadsheet Wizard shown in Figure 1-9. The first box in the Import Spreadsheet Wizard allows you to specify the worksheet or range you want to import. If your workbook has more than one worksheet, all worksheets will be listed here. In this case, there is only one worksheet. Select the target worksheet and click the Next button.

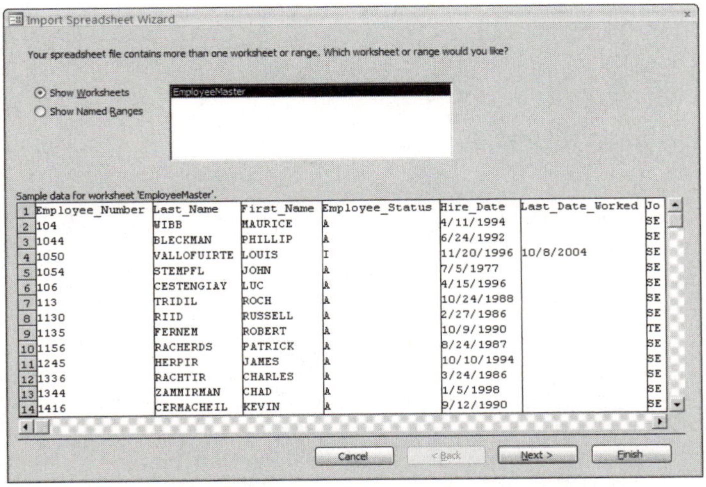

Figure 1-9: Identify the worksheet or range you want to import.

The next screen allows you to select whether the source data has headings at the tops of the columns (see Figure 1-10). As you can see, you simply check the check box if your source data has headings. Click the Next button to move on.

The next screen allows you to specify the data type for each field (see Figure 1-11). This setting allows you to tell Access whether the given field is a number, text, currency, date, or so on. The idea is to select each field and check to make sure the data type for that field is correct. In addition, you can specify whether any given field is to be indexed. When you index a field, Access creates a kind of organizational mapping of the field allowing for faster querying and grouping.

The best way to illustrate indexing is by an analogy. Imagine you had a file cabinet with 10,000 folders, each dedicated to a specific customer. Now imagine these files were in random order. To access the customer name Schnogg's Accounting Service, you would have to pore through every customer file until you found it. Now imagine finding the file if your customer folders were organized (or *indexed*) alphabetically.

When you sort or filter on a non-indexed field, Access will search every record until the correct record is found. Indexing a field in Access is conceptually identical to alphabetizing the file system. Indexing a field makes Access create an organizational scheme for that field such that it can be found much more rapidly.

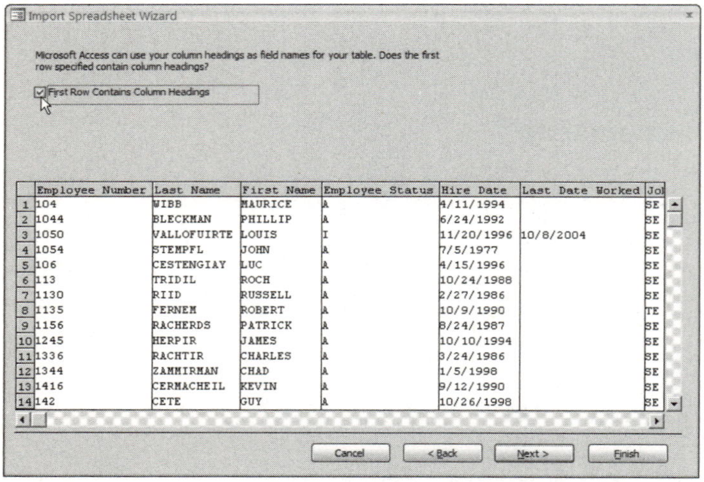

Figure 1-10: Specify whether your data source comes with headings.

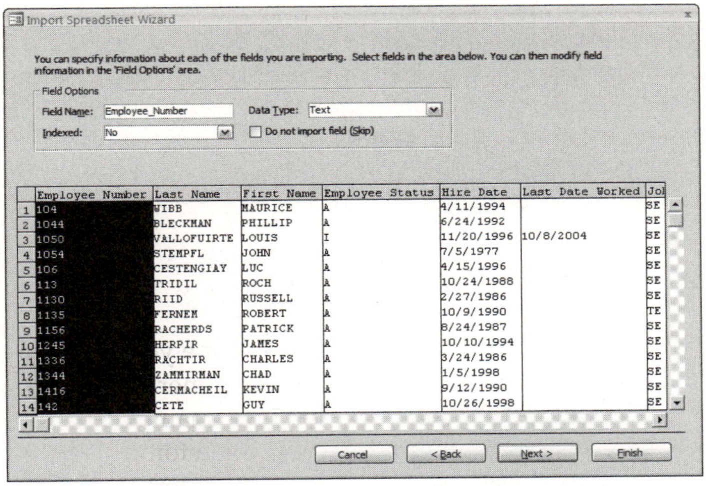

Figure 1-11: Apply data types and indexing to your fields

TIP You may wonder why you would not index all your fields. Wouldn't that make your queries run faster? The answer is an emphatic *no!* Indexing is a good idea on fields you expect to filter or join to another table. Indexing is not a good idea for fields you expect to perform calculations on. You should also be aware that while indexing can improve the performance for some types of analysis, other types could actually be slowed by using indexed fields. The relevance and importance of indexing fields will become clearer as we discuss different Access query types in Chapter 2.

The next screen allows you to select the primary key (see Figure 1-12). A primary key is a data field that uniquely identifies each record in a data set. Each table in a properly designed relational database should contain information about one entity, and each record should be uniquely identified by one field. That one field is called the primary key. In this example, the Employee_Number field contains unique numbers; one for each unique employee represented.

Sometimes the Excel data you import will be in flat file format and will not have one field that uniquely identifies each record. In these cases, the Import Spreadsheet Wizard will default to assigning an Autonumber primary key for you.

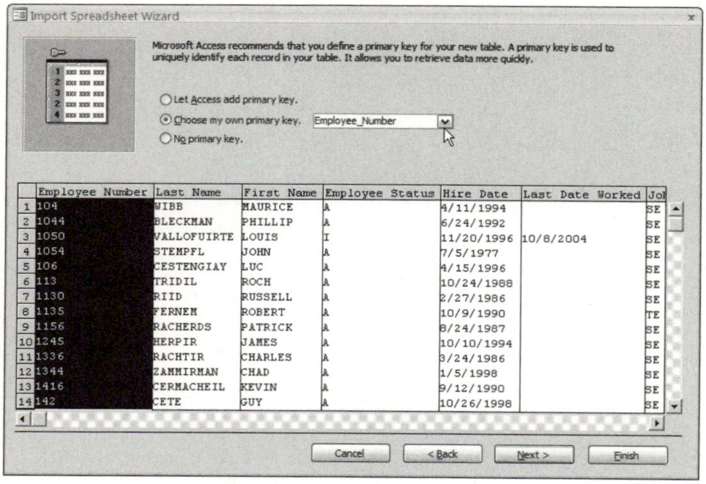

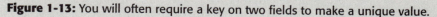

Figure 1-12: Define which field will be your primary key.

A WORD ON CREATING COMPOUND KEYS

Sometimes a flat file will have two or more fields that together uniquely identify a record. In these cases you will need to create what is called a compound key. Take the table shown here in Figure 1-13, for example. This table contains both an invoice number and a product number. There are duplicate values for each field when looked at separately. A sales rep may have sold multiple products to a customer on the same invoice. By combining the invoice and product number, however, you can create a compound primary key that is truly unique for each record.

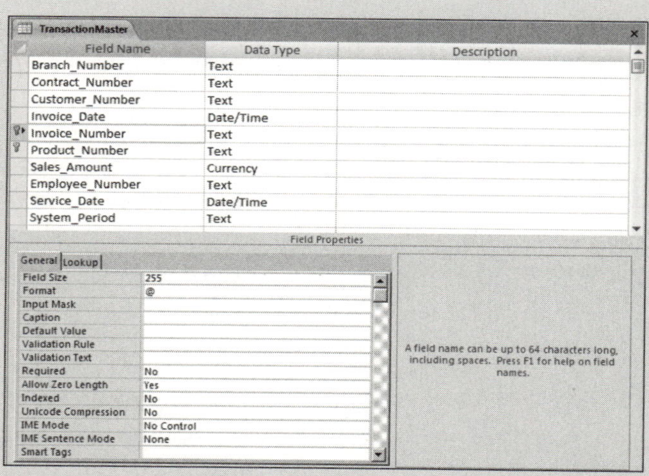

Figure 1-13: You will often require a key on two fields to make a unique value.

> If you need a compound key, import your data without specifying a key in the Import Spreadsheet Wizard. Then when your table is created, view your table in the Design view. When in Design view, select the fields that together make up your compound key, right-click, and select the primary key icon from the drop-down menu. Close the table and save your changes.

The last screen of the Import Spreadsheet Wizard asks to you name your new table (see Figure 1-14). By default, the name of your new table is the name of your imported worksheet, but you can change the name to suit your needs. At this point, you can click the Finish button to start the import.

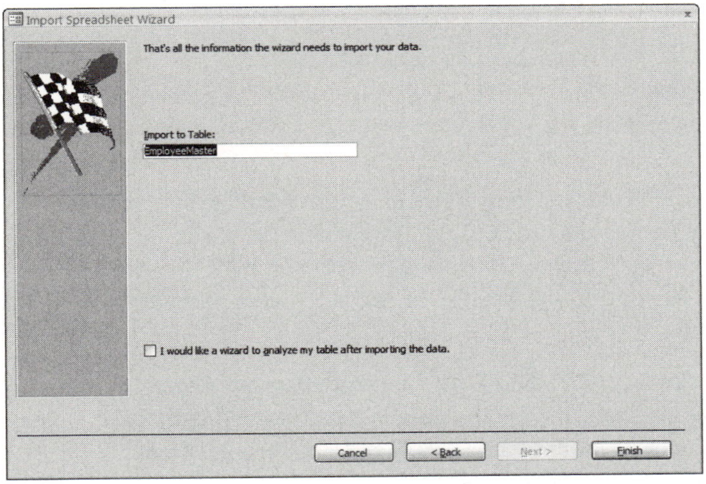

Figure 1-14: Name your imported table and click the Finish button.

NOTE It's important to note that naming your import table the same name as an existing table in your database causes Access to give you a warning that you are about to overwrite your existing table. Be careful that you do not inadvertently overwrite an existing table with a careless table name choice.

After your data has been imported, you see a dialog box that asks whether you want to save your import steps (see Figure 1-15). This is a new feature in Access 2007, allowing you to save time when the same dataset must be routinely imported. As you can see in Figure 1-15, clicking the Save import steps check box allows you to save your import steps as a named task that can be used whenever you need. To recall a saved import task, simply click the Saved Imports command button under the External Data tab in the Access ribbon.

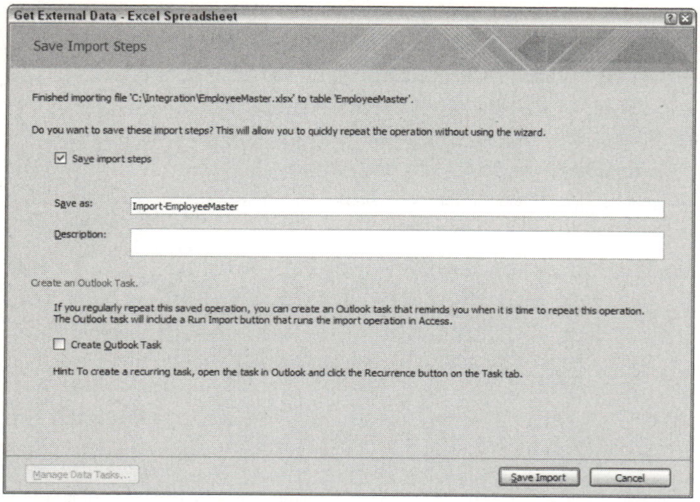

Figure 1-15: You now have the option of saving your import steps.

TIP Another quick way to create a new table in Access from Excel is to drag and drop between the two applications. Open Access and Excel and arrange the windows so you can see both applications. Now simply highlight the selected Excel range you want to import and drag it into Access. You've immediately created an Access table.

Be aware that this action actually moves the data from Excel to Access. The data will no longer be in Excel! To copy the data instead of moving it, hold down the Ctrl key on your keyboard while you drag from Excel to Access.

Linking an Excel Worksheet to Access

Sometimes the Excel data you want to incorporate into Access is going to change frequently. Perhaps the Excel data you need is owned by someone else and is updated daily. Does it make sense to import that data into a new Access table every time it changes? What if you do not know when it changes, yet it is critical to have the most up-to-date information for your analysis? In these situations it makes more sense to get your Excel data by linking a worksheet.

Linking data is different from importing data in that Access references the linked data in its original location. Importing data brings a local copy of the information into the Access database. Any changes made to the local copy in

Access do not affect the original spreadsheet. Likewise, any changes made to the original spreadsheet after importing are not reflected in the Access table.

Conversely, a linked Excel sheet exists in real time. Changes made to the sheet in the original Excel file are reflected in Access upon refresh. However, you cannot make changes to the Excel data through Access. Linking is a one-way street of data flow.

As with the prior example, start by selecting the External Data tab and then select the Import Excel icon. In the Get External Data dialog box, browse for the Location_Master.xlsx file. This time, select the option Link to the data source by creating a linked table (see Figure 1-16). Click the OK button to continue.

This launches the Link Spreadsheet Wizard shown in Figure 1-17. You will notice it looks nearly identical to the Import Spreadsheet Wizard. As with the Import Spreadsheet Wizard, the idea is to go through each screen of the wizard, answering the questions posed and clicking the Next button. The last step in the wizard gives you the option to name your linked table. Again, the default name is the worksheet name or named range. Click the Finish button to apply the link.

NOTE When linking to a data source, you can't specify data types, indexing, or primary keys. Therefore, you can't see those selections in the Link Spreadsheet Wizard.

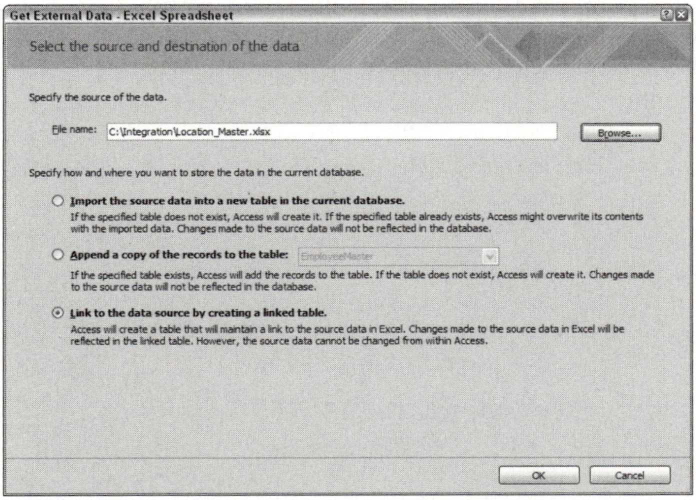

Figure 1-16: To link to a data source, select the Link option.

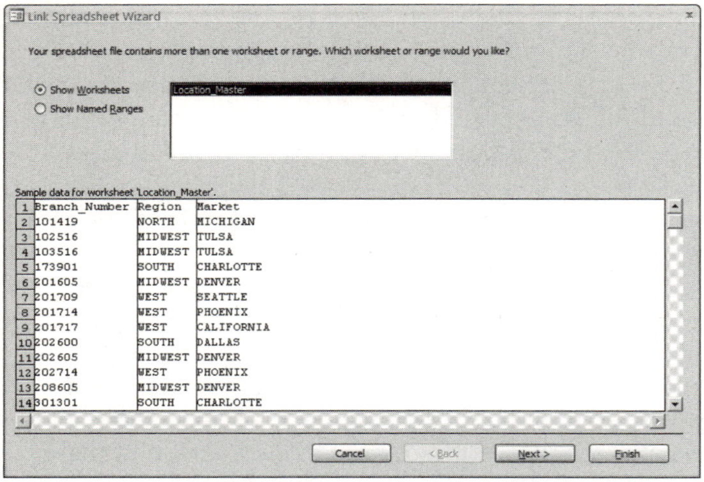

Figure 1-17: The steps in this wizard are nearly identical to those of the Import Spreadsheet Wizard.

Figure 1-18 illustrates the difference in the icons between imported tables and linked tables. Notice that tables linked to an Excel data source have an Excel icon.

Earlier you learned that a linked Excel table incorporates changes from the Excel file to Access but does not allow changes from Access back to Excel. To test this, open the linked table in Access by double-clicking the linked Excel table icon. Next, try to change the data by replacing branch number 101313 with 999999. When you try to enter the first 9, you hear an alert. Look in the bottom-left corner of the screen, and you will see the warning "This Recordset is not updateable" (see Figure 1-19).

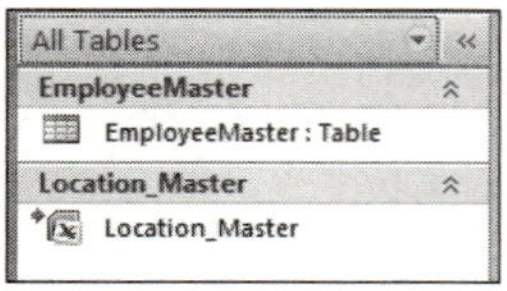

Figure 1-18: A linked table has a different-looking icon than an imported table.

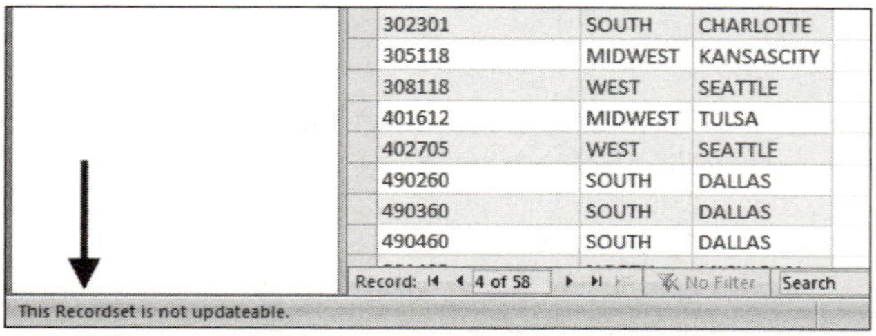

Figure 1-19: You cannot update a linked Excel table through the Access interface.

Now that you've proven that you cannot update the Excel spreadsheet through Access, test whether Access sees changes made to the source data. Close the Location_Master table in Access by clicking the X in the upper-right corner of the table window. Open Excel, locate the Location_Master worksheet and open it. Now try the same exercise of changing branch 101419 to 999999. Save and close the Excel file. Now open up the Access linked table Location_Master to verify that our change carried through (see Figure 1-20).

NOTE You may be wondering why anyone would link to an Excel file when they can't change the data in Access. Well, the primary utility of a linked table is to get the latest data from a source that changes often without having to import the data repeatedly. Imagine you have an Excel file updated nightly. If you were to use that file in your Access queries or reports, linking to that source would allow you to get the latest changes without importing the data every day.

If the structure of the data source for your linked table changes, you will have to refresh your link in order to get those structural changes. For example, if you were to add a column to the Location_Master Excel file, you would not be able to see that change in Access until you refresh the link to the Location_Master Excel file. To do so, use the Linked Table Manager. The linked table manager can be found under the Database Tools tab in the Access ribbon.

When you click the Linked Table Manager button, the dialog box shown in Figure 1-21 activates, displaying all the linked tables in the current database. In this case, you'll see one linked table: the Location_Master table. Select the check box beside the linked table and click the OK button. Your data has been successfully refreshed!

Location_Master		
Branch_Nun ▾	Region ▾	Market ▾
999999	NORTH	MICHIGAN
102516	MIDWEST	TULSA
103516	MIDWEST	TULSA
173901	SOUTH	CHARLOTTE
201605	MIDWEST	DENVER
201709	WEST	SEATTLE
201714	WEST	PHOENIX
201717	WEST	CALIFORNIA
202600	SOUTH	DALLAS

Figure 1-20: Updates to the linked Excel table carry through to Access.

IMPORTING OR LINKING TO NON-EXCEL DATA

You may want to import and analyze non-Excel data and then send it to Excel after analysis in Access. One of the most common data types for import is text-delimited data. Delimited text is simply text where the individual fields in a record are separated by a specific character like a tab, comma, or space.

Fortunately, Access recognizes delimited text and even allows you to choose the specific character that separates fields. To get delimited text into Access, simply choose Text file from the External Data ribbon and walk through the same process you would when importing or linking to an Excel file.

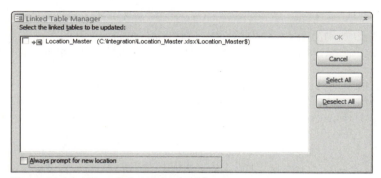

Figure 1-21: View of the Linked Table Manager

Appending an Excel Worksheet to an Existing Table

The last topic on importing Excel data to Access is how to use the Append function in the Get External Data dialog box. When you append data to a table, you essentially add records to the end of the table. This is useful when you have a process where records for a specific table are added over time (for example, if new employees come into an organization and need to be added to the EmployeeMaster table).

Select the External Data tab and click the import Excel icon. Browse for the file that contains the records you want to add. In the Get External Data dialog box, select the option Append a copy of the records to the table and specify the table to which you would like to append your new records. In Figure 1-22, you can see that new employee records from an Excel file called NewEmployees are appended to the EmployeeMaster table.

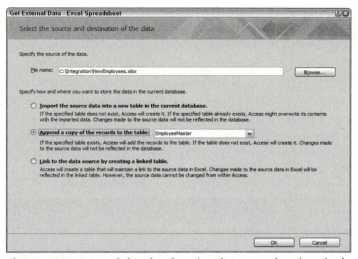

Figure 1-22: Append data by choosing the append options in the Get External Data dialog box.

Clicking the OK button activates the Import Spreadsheet Wizard. As with importing and linking data, the idea is to go through each screen of the wizard, answering the questions posed and clicking the Next button. When you get to the last screen, click the Finish button to trigger the append action.

Potential Errors When Using the Append Import Wizard

It's important to note that you may encounter some potential errors when appending data. Unfortunately, Access is not very clear when it does not like some portion of the append process. The most likely consequence of an append error is simply not being able to get your data into Access. The wizard spits out an error and does not let you continue with the import. Let's review some of the most common error messages, the underlying problem, and what is required to fix it.

- **Type Conversion Failure:** This error occurs when the data type of a value in the records you are trying to append does not match the data type of the field to which you are appending. For example, suppose you originally imported a transaction file and changed the default data type of the Invoice Number field to Number. Now suppose that invoice numbers in your organization start coming in as alphanumeric (such as INV20231). When you append additional data to your transaction table, you will receive an error because you are trying to put a text field into a field designated for numbers.

- **Key violations:** Key violations occur when you try to append a field with duplicate values to a field designated as a primary key. A primary key is a data field that uniquely defines a record in a data set. In other words, a primary key cannot have duplicates. Access will not let you append a field that has duplicate data to a field designated as a primary key.

- **Lock violation:** If the table you are trying to append to is open, Access will not allow you to append the new records until you close the table. Make sure the table you are appending to is closed before starting the Append Import Wizard.

USING COMPACT AND REPAIR

Access has a size limit of about 2 GB. When an Access database gets close to this limit, performance will degrade rapidly. Additionally, the risk of database corruption increases as well. Properly designed Access Database applications should rarely approach this size limit. I have used Access databases that perform tons of query operations on several million record transaction tables and have rarely approached this limit. The most common cause of approaching this size limit is from not doing proper maintenance to the database.

When you delete a large table of data in Access, you may think you are automatically reducing the size of the Access file. In fact, you are not. Access does not automatically release the storage space associated with a deleted table. Let's say you import a million row transaction table to your Access database only to realize that you forgot to import several relevant fields. Conscious of the size limits in Access, you delete the table and import another table with all the appropriate fields. Even though you have deleted the first table, Access still has not released the space and your file size has doubled. Another cause of this database bloat occurs when performing a series of action queries, making numerous intermediate tables for a final analysis. Even if those intermediate tables are deleted, Access is still allocating space for them.

The solution to this problem is to routinely compact and repair your database. Press the Office File icon and select Manage, Compact and Repair Database (see Figure 1-23).

Figure 1-23: Using the Compact and Repair Database Utility in Access

How often you perform this operation really depends on how frequently you add and then delete tables from your database. The best practice is to compact and repair your Access database at least every time you open or close it. This action can be automated for you by selecting the file icon and then selecting the Access Options button at the bottom of the menu. This opens the Access Options dialog box. By selecting the Current Database menu item from the list on the left and checking the Compact on Close check box, you will ensure your database is compacted and repaired at least every time you close the application.

Summary

Getting your Excel data into Access is the first step in leveraging the powerful utilities and functionality of Access. Outside of manually entering data into your Access tables, there are three basic ways of getting Excel data into your Access processes: importing, linking, and appending.

Importing data allows you to create a table in Access that you can control and use to run queries, build reports, and perform any other Access-related task. Linking data creates a connection to your Excel file, allowing you to instantly see any changes made to your source file without having to take further action. The primary utility of a linked table is to get the latest data from a source that changes often, without having to import the data repeatedly. Appending data allows you to add records to the end of the table. This is useful when you have a process where the records for a specific table are added over time. Now that you understand the different ways of getting your data into Access, you can effectively use whichever one best suits your needs in a given situation.

CHAPTER 2

Analyzing Excel Data with Access Queries

The previous chapter discusses how to get data into Access. Now it's time to do something with that data. Once you have your data stored in Access tables, you can turn your focus to one of the more useful features of Access: Queries.

By definition, a query is a question. For the purposes of this chapter, it is a question about the data that is stored in tables. Although most Excel users have heard of Access queries, few have been able to relate to them. The primary reason is that in Excel, the concept of querying data is a bit nebulous as it can take the form of different functionalities in Excel. That is to say, there is no such object called a query in Excel. Instead, you have things like formulas, AutoFilters and PivotTables. Consider this; in Excel, when you use AutoFilter, a VLookup formula, or Subtotals, you are essentially running queries against some set of data to achieve an answer Access queries revolve around the same concept.

In this chapter, you will explore the world of Access queries, discovering the various ways you can create analyses from your data.

Introduction to Access Queries

When you are working with data, it is often preferable to work with smaller sets of data at a time. Although your tables may contain all the records pertaining to a particular entity, you may need to extract or evaluate only a subset of that data. This is where Select queries come in handy. As the name applies, a Select query enables you extract or select data based on criteria you provide.

Creating Your First Select Query

Access provides a graphical interface that is easy to use and quite user friendly. Microsoft calls this graphical interface the Query Design view, although many Access users refer to it as the *query grid*. In Query Design view, tables and columns are represented visually, making it easy to visualize the question you would like to ask of the data.

To start your first Select Query, go up to the application ribbon in Access and select the Create tab. From here, select Query Design as demonstrated in Figure 2-1.

The Show Table dialog box now opens on top of a blank query grid, as shown in Figure 2-2.

Figure 2-1: Activate the Query Design view in Access.

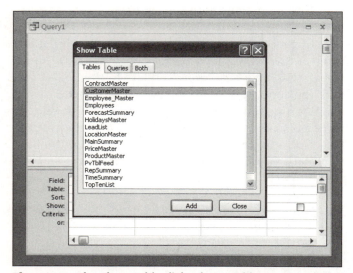

Figure 2-2: The Show Table dialog box enables you to select the tables or queries you will query.

As you can tell from the first dialog box you see, the first thing you must determine is from which tables you need to retrieve data. The Show Table dialog box enables you to select one or more tables. As you can see in Figure 2-2, there are also tabs for Queries and Both. One of the wonderful features of queries is that you are not limited to just querying directly from the table. You can create queries of other queries.

For your first query, select the CustomerMaster table. You can do this by either by selecting the table in the list and clicking the Add button or by double-clicking the table name in the list. After you have selected the table from which you want to retrieve data, you can close the Show Table dialog box and select the fields of that table that you would like to retrieve.

The Query Design view is divided into two sections. The top half shows the tables or queries from which the query will retrieve data. The bottom half (often referred to as the query grid) shows the fields from which the query will retrieve data.

You will notice in Figure 2-3, that the CustomerMaster table shown at the top half of the Query Design view lists all the fields but has an asterisk at the top of the list. Selecting the asterisk is tantamount to telling Access to select all the fields in the table. It is essentially a time-saver, allowing you to select all fields without explicitly calling each field by name.

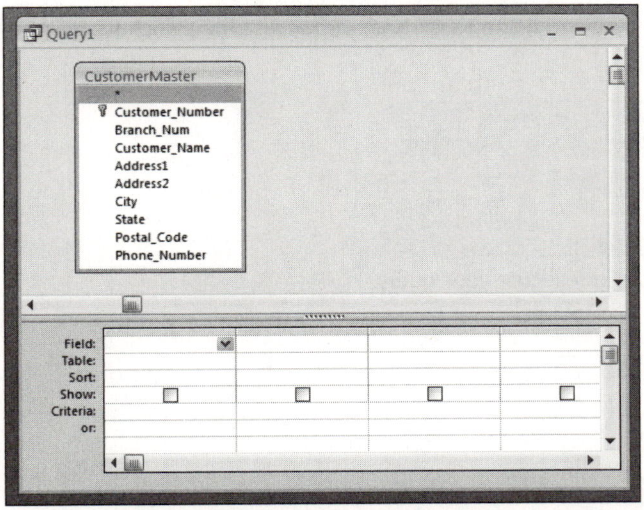

Figure 2-3: The asterisk is the traditional database symbol, which means that all fields from that table will be in the output.

For this example, you will select the following three fields: Branch_Num, Customer_Name and State and add them to the query grid (the bottom half of the Query Design view). You can either double-click each field to add each to the query grid, or drag each field down to the query grid. Figure 2-4 shows you how your query should look after selecting your selected fields.

At this point, you have all you need to run the query. To run the query, click the Run button located on the Design tab shown here in Figure 2-5.

As you can see in Figure 2-6, the output from a query looks similar to a regular Access table after it is open.

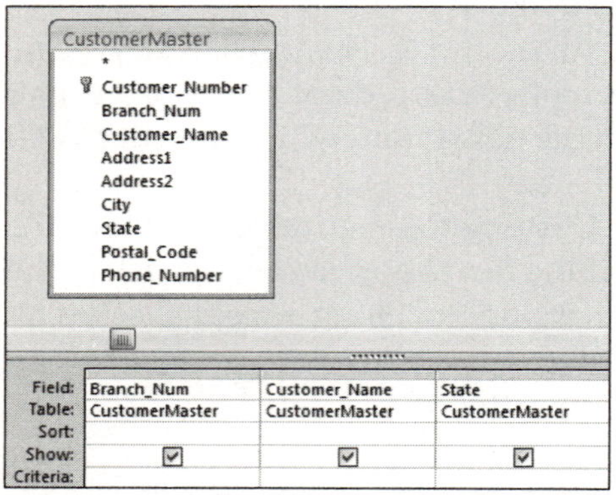

Figure 2-4: The lower half, or query grid, shows the output fields of the select query.

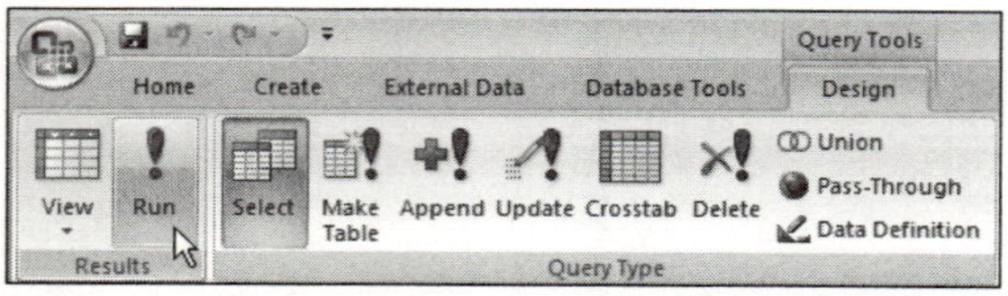

Figure 2-5: Click the Run button to execute your query.

Branch_Num	Customer_Name	State
301301	CORRUL Corp.	GA
301301	ANYTHA Corp.	GA
301301	RHFUSU Corp.	GA
301301	MUUZEO Corp.	GA
301301	NABCO Corp.	GA
301301	UNESTU Corp.	GA
301301	ALTUC Corp.	GA
301301	TORAEA Corp.	GA
301301	CARTUM Corp.	GA
301301	ATLANT Corp.	GA
301301	HALLSG Corp.	GA
301301	ATLANT Corp.	GA
301301	VALCAN Corp.	GA
301301	PRATT Corp.	GA
301301	PLANTU Corp.	GA

Figure 2-6: The Datasheet view of the query shows the results of the query.

NOTE To return to the Query Design view, simply go up to the Home tab in the Access ribbon and click View → Design View.

One thing you should keep in mind is that the results of a Select query are not located in a separate table. The results are directly from the table, from which it is querying. This is analogous to running an AutoFilter on a table in Excel. When you change a value in the results of your Select query, you will be changing the value in the source table.

Sorting Query Results

Just as a table can be sorted in Excel, you can tell Access to sort one or more columns in your query results in ascending or descending sort. In the query grid, you notice the Sort row of the grid. This is where you can choose to sort any of the columns shown in the query grid. If you choose to sort multiple columns, the query will sort the results in order of left to right.

To help demonstrate sorting with a query, go to the State column of the query you just built and click your mouse on the Sort section. As shown in Figure 2-7, a down box appears, allowing you to select either Ascending or Descending for that particular column.

Select Ascending and rerun the query. When you previously ran the query, the states were in no particular order. After setting the sort order of the State column to ascending, you will notice that your results are now in alphabetical order by state.

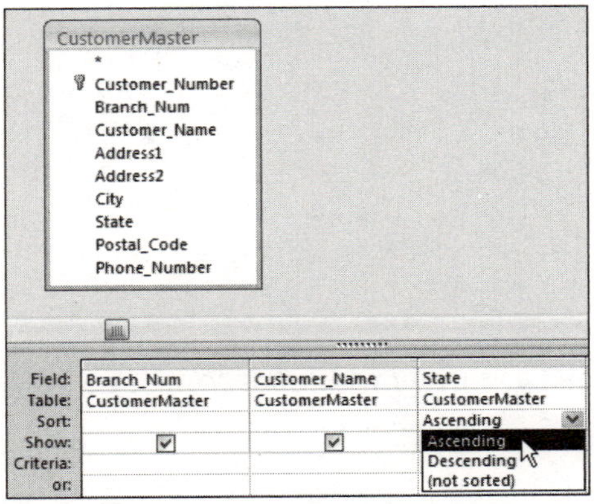

Figure 2-7: The query grid provides the sort order options for a column.

Filtering Query Results

In many cases, you may want to filter your query to retrieve only the specific records to analyze. In Access, filtering a query is often referred to as *setting criteria* for the query; note the Criteria row in the query grid. This is where you will enter the value or values, with which you would like to filter or evaluate the query. When you enter your criteria in the Criteria row of the query grid, only those records that meet your criteria are returned in the query output.

In the example shown in Figure 2-8, your manager wants to see the list of customers from California. Since California is designated by "CA" that is what you will enter in the Criteria row of the State column.

> **NOTE** You will notice that when entering text in the query grid, you must enclose the text string with quotation marks. You can either type the quotation marks yourself or simply type your text and click another part of the query grid. Access will automatically place quotation marks around your criteria if the field you are filtering is textual.

When you run your query, you will notice that fewer records are returned. A quick scan of the results verifies that indeed only records with CA in the State column were returned, as shown in Figure 2-9.

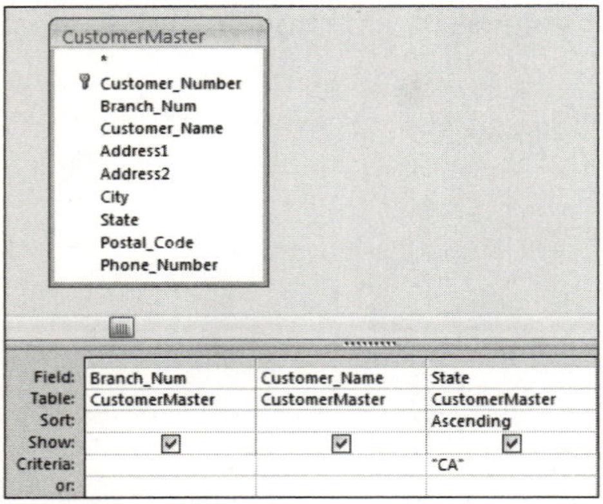

Figure 2-8: The Criteria section is where you enter a value for which you want to filter the data.

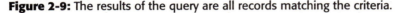

Branch_Num	Customer_Name	State
701717	SULUSZ Corp.	CA
501717	HULAXH Corp.	CA
501717	DANRED Corp.	CA
501718	FUDUSA Corp.	CA
701715	CALSAN Corp.	CA
701715	ANTUS Corp.	CA
701715	HORRAS Corp.	CA
201717	LAMUTA Corp.	CA
501717	CATYOF Corp.	CA
501717	DAOLAC Corp.	CA
201717	TUQQAA Corp.	CA
803717	RUTSI Corp.	CA
201717	JUSDAN Corp.	CA
701717	SAORUZ Corp.	CA
701715	MEESE Corp.	CA

Figure 2-9: The results of the query are all records matching the criteria.

Querying Multiple Tables

One of the major benefits of using Access is that it is a relational database. This means that you can specify a relationship between two seemingly unrelated data sources, allowing you to query multiple tables at one time.

For example, the query shown in Figure 2-10 joins CustomerMaster table with the TransactionMaster table to create a dataset that shows both customer information and transaction information.

You will notice that the CustomerMaster table contains information about customers, while the TransactionMaster table contains information about invoice transactions. The fields that are populating the query grid come from both tables, allowing you to see data from two tables in one consise query result.

Before you jump into creating your own multi-table queries, it's important to understand this concept of joining tables.

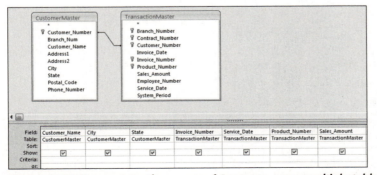

Figure 2-10: You can use the power of Access to query multiple tables at once.

Understanding the Concept of Relational Databases

To the average Excel user, it doesn't make sense that the CustomerMaster table contains only customer information, whereas the TransactionMaster contains only transaction information. After all, why would you not have the customer information in the same table the transaction information is stored?

The reason this doesn't make sense to most Excel users is because they are adept at working with data that has been stored in flat-file format. The flat-file organizes data into rows and columns. Let's look at a typical example of a flat file. Figure 2-11 shows a typical flat-file list of invoices.

To get the customer information for each invoice, there are several fields for customer specific information: Customer Name, Address, City, and so on. Since most firms sell to customers more than once, for each invoice the same customer information has to be repeated. Duplicate information is one of the main drawbacks of the flat-file format.

What is wrong with duplicate data? Besides the hard drive space and memory that is wasted on redundant data, the major issue arises when that data needs to be updated. The example in Figure 2-11 shows several invoices for CORRUL Corp. You can see that the information about the customer has to be repeated for each instance of an invoice. Imagine a scenario where the customer information might change. For example, the customer acquires new office space and you want to reflect this change of location in your data. You have to update the change in several different places. You need to ensure that every invoice correctly maps back to its relevant customer information.

Although there are excellent functions that find and replace data in Excel, there is still a danger that you might not make all the updates correctly. Whenever you are changing the same duplicated information there is always the risk of introducing unintentional errors. This could significantly affect your data analysis. For example, imagine that customer, CORRUL Corp. moved not just to a different address, but a different city. Figure 2-12 demonstrates how easy it is to incorrectly update the data.

Customer_Name	Address1	City	State	Invoice_Number	Invoice_Date	Sales_Amount
CORRUL Corp.	13 HUSSLUY MALL RD	CARROLLTON	GA	27812618	12/16/2004	$140.09
CORRUL Corp.	13 HUSSLUY MALL RD	CARROLLTON	GA	26507793	7/8/2004	$112.39
CORRUL Corp.	13 HUSSLUY MALL RD	CARROLLTON	GA	25251995	1/28/2004	$112.39
CORRUL Corp.	13 HUSSLUY MALL RD	CARROLLTON	GA	26507793	7/8/2004	$140.09
CORRUL Corp.	13 HUSSLUY MALL RD	CARROLLTON	GA	26940942	9/3/2004	$112.39
CORRUL Corp.	13 HUSSLUY MALL RD	CARROLLTON	GA	26940942	9/3/2004	$140.09
CORRUL Corp.	13 HUSSLUY MALL RD	CARROLLTON	GA	27378702	10/29/2004	$112.39
CORRUL Corp.	13 HUSSLUY MALL RD	CARROLLTON	GA	27378702	10/29/2004	$140.09
CORRUL Corp.	13 HUSSLUY MALL RD	CARROLLTON	GA	27812618	12/16/2004	$112.39
CORRUL Corp.	13 HUSSLUY MALL RD	CARROLLTON	GA	26078955	5/12/2004	$112.39
CORRUL Corp.	13 HUSSLUY MALL RD	CARROLLTON	GA	25656619	3/25/2004	$140.09
CORRUL Corp.	13 HUSSLUY MALL RD	CARROLLTON	GA	25251995	1/28/2004	$140.09
CORRUL Corp.	13 HUSSLUY MALL RD	CARROLLTON	GA	25656619	3/25/2004	$112.39
CORRUL Corp.	13 HUSSLUY MALL RD	CARROLLTON	GA	26078955	5/12/2004	$140.09
ANYTHA Corp.	4556 CUNSTATASAUN F	ATLANTA	GA	27314610	10/20/2004	$194.05
ANYTHA Corp.	4556 CUNSTATASAUN F	ATLANTA	GA	27535362	11/16/2004	$194.05
ANYTHA Corp.	4556 CUNSTATASAUN F	ATLANTA	GA	27096178	9/28/2004	$194.05

Figure 2-11: Data is usually stored in an Excel spreadsheet using the flat-file format.

Customer_Name	Address1	City	State	Invoice_Number	Invoice_Date	Sales_Amount
CORRUL Corp.	4120 DUNNALLY AVE SW	ATLANTA	GA	27812618	12/16/2004	$140.09
CORRUL Corp.	4121 DUNNALLY AVE SW	ATLANTA	GA	26507793	7/8/2004	$112.39
CORRUL Corp.	4122 DUNNALLY AVE SW	ATLANTA	GA	25251995	1/28/2004	$112.39
CORRUL Corp.	4123 DUNNALLY AVE SW	ATLANTA	GA	26507793	7/8/2004	$140.09
CORRUL Corp.	4124 DUNNALLY AVE SW	ATLANTA	GA	26940942	9/3/2004	$112.39
CORRUL Corp.	4125 DUNNALLY AVE SW	ATLANTA	GA	26940942	9/3/2004	$140.09
CORRUL Corp.	4126 DUNNALLY AVE SW	ATLANTA	GA	27378702	10/29/2004	$112.39
CORRUL Corp.	4127 DUNNALLY AVE SW	ATLANTA	GA	27378702	10/29/2004	$140.09
CORRUL Corp.	4128 DUNNALLY AVE SW	ATLANTA	GA	27812618	12/16/2004	$112.39
CORRUL Corp.	4129 DUNNALLY AVE SW	ATLANTA	GA	26078955	5/12/2004	$112.39
CORRUL Corp.	4130 DUNNALLY AVE SW	ATLANTA	GA	25656619	3/25/2004	$140.09
CORRUL Corp.	4131 DUNNALLY AVE SW	ATLANTA	GA	25251995	1/28/2004	$140.09
CORRUL Corp.	4132 DUNNALLY AVE SW	ATLANTA	GA	25656619	3/25/2004	$112.39
CORRUL Corp.	13 HUSSLUY MALL RD	CARROLLTON	GA	26078955	5/12/2004	$140.09
ANYTHA Corp.	4556 CUNSTATASAUN R	ATLANTA	GA	27314610	10/20/2004	$194.05
ANYTHA Corp.	4556 CUNSTATASAUN R	ATLANTA	GA	27535362	11/16/2004	$194.05
ANYTHA Corp.	4556 CUNSTATASAUN R	ATLANTA	GA	27096178	9/28/2004	$194.05

Figure 2-12: The last record of CORRUL Corp. was not correctly updated to the new address.

If the City data is not properly updated everywhere, then you will not get accurate results when you attempt a by city filter/analysis. Some of the invoice records could reflect the incorrect state locations of the customer. The attributes of data can and often do change, if these changes are not accurately recorded, our data analysis is providing an incorrect picture of the actual situation.

Would it not be more logical and efficient if you could write the name and information of the customer only once somewhere? Instead of having to write the same customer information repeatedly, would it not be more productive to have some form of customer reference number? This is the idea behind the relational database concept. A relational database typically contains separate, carefully designed lists of data that can be relate to each other by using identifiers.

Creating a Query that Joins Two Tables

Imagine that you want to see the customer transactions from Colorado. A quick examination of the TransactionMaster table reveals there is no State field on which you can filter. However, you see there is a Customer_Number field. The Customer_Number field can be used to join to the CustomerMaster table.

Start a new query and in Design view and add both the TransactionMaster table and the CustomerMaster table. To join the two tables, simply click the Customer_Number field in one of the tables and drag it over to the Customer_Number field in the other table. The idea is to draw an imaginary line between the two as illustrated in Figure 2-13.

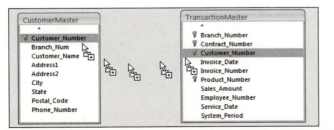

Figure 2-13: Draw an imaginary line between the two Customer_Number fields.

As you can see in Figure 2-14, Access automatically joins the field names from the two tables in Query Design view.

From here, you can simply fill in the query grid, selecting the fields that you need to appear in the query output, and specifying the criteria by which the results are to be filtered (see Figure 2-15).

As you can see in the results shown in Figure 2-16, invoice data matched with its appropriate customer data. Although there is repeating data, as with the flat-file examples, there is a significant difference. The repeating data is being read from a single source, the CustomerMaster table. If a value were to change in the CustomerMaster table, that changed value would persist in the query results, effectively overcoming potential update errors inherent with duplicate data.

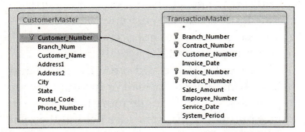

Figure 2-14: Fields from two tables are visibly joined in the Query Design view.

Field:	Customer_Name	City	State	Invoice_Number	Service_Date	Product_Number	Sales_Amount
Table:	CustomerMaster	CustomerMaster	CustomerMaster	TransactionMaster	TransactionMaster	TransactionMaster	TransactionMaster
Sort:							
Show:	☑	☑	☑	☑	☑	☑	☑
Criteria:			"CO"				
or:							

Figure 2-15: Specify the fields and criteria for the query.

Customer_Name	City	State	Invoice_Number	Service_Date	Product_Number	Sales_Amount
ANTUSM Corp.	MONTROSE	CO	25515555	2/18/2004	16000	$119.87
ANTUSM Corp.	MONTROSE	CO	25515556	2/18/2004	30300	$144.60
ANTUSM Corp.	MONTROSE	CO	25931820	4/19/2004	16000	$119.87
ANTUSM Corp.	MONTROSE	CO	25931821	4/19/2004	30300	$144.60
ANTUSM Corp.	MONTROSE	CO	26360917	6/10/2004	16000	$119.87
ANTUSM Corp.	MONTROSE	CO	26360918	6/10/2004	30300	$144.60
ANTUSM Corp.	MONTROSE	CO	26792217	8/11/2004	16000	$119.87
ANTUSM Corp.	MONTROSE	CO	26792218	8/11/2004	30300	$144.60
ANTUSM Corp.	MONTROSE	CO	27226481	10/4/2004	16000	$119.87
ANTUSM Corp.	MONTROSE	CO	27226482	10/4/2004	30300	$144.60
ANTUSM Corp.	MONTROSE	CO	27663573	11/22/2004	16000	$119.87
ANTUSM Corp.	MONTROSE	CO	27663574	11/22/2004	30300	$144.60
MUNTRU Corp.	MONTROSE	CO	25466918	2/18/2004	16000	$119.87
MUNTRU Corp.	MONTROSE	CO	25879599	4/7/2004	16000	$119.87
MUNTRU Corp.	MONTROSE	CO	26307363	6/2/2004	16000	$119.87
MUNTRU Corp.	MONTROSE	CO	26737966	8/4/2004	16000	$119.87
MUNTRU Corp.	MONTROSE	CO	27172731	9/30/2004	16000	$119.87
MUNTRU Corp.	MONTROSE	CO	27610249	11/16/2004	16000	$119.87

Figure 2-16: The results of the query have successfully brought together and matched data from two separate tables.

Using Operators to Further Refine Your Queries

You can filter for multiple criteria on any given field by using operators. The following operators enable you to combine multiple values in different logical contexts so you can create complex queries.

Mathematical Operators

Access recognizes the most common mathematical operators (=, +, -, *, /, >, <) and enables you to use them in your queries. Later in this chapter, you will discover how you can use these operators to actually perform calculations in your queries.

Or

The Or operator specifies that either condition can be true. Multiple criteria values for one field can either be separated on different criteria lines or combined in one cell with the use of the Or operator. For example, Figure 2-17 demonstrates how to filter for both Colorado and California by typing **"CO"** or **"CA"** in the Criteria field.

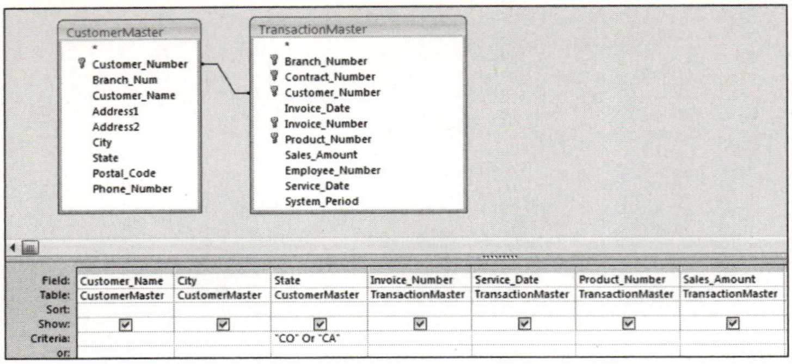

Figure 2-17: Using the Or operator

Between

The Between operator tests for a range of values. For example, Figure 2-18 demonstrates how you can filter for all invoices between 4/20/2004 and 11/19/2004.

> **NOTE** You will notice that when entering a date in the query grid, you must enclose the date in pound signs (hash marks). In most cases, Access will automatically place the pound signs around your criteria if the field you are filtering is a date.

Like

The Like operator tests for string expression matching a pattern. For example, you can filter for all records with a customer number that begins with the numbers 147 by typing **Like "147*"** in the Criteria field (see Figure 2-19). The asterisk acts as a wild card character, which can signify any character or combination of characters.

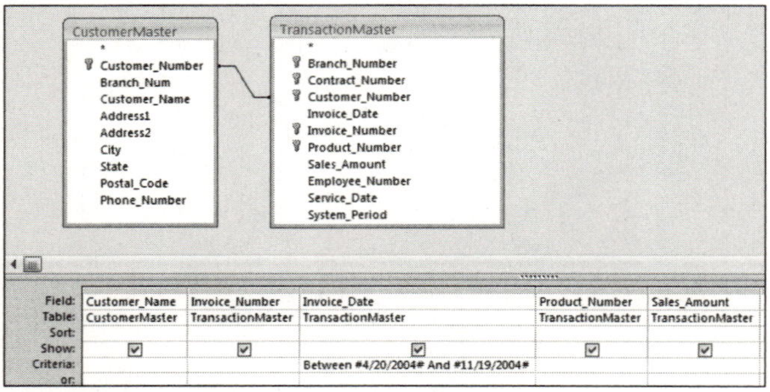

Figure 2-18: Using the Between operator

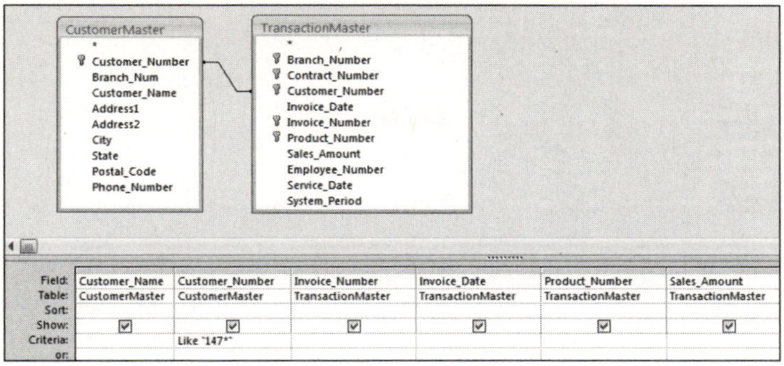

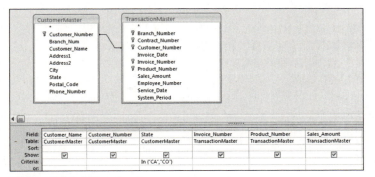

Figure 2-19: Using the `Like` operator

In

The `In` operator essentially works in a similar fashion as the `Or` operator, evaluating all records against values that are contained as arguments within the parentheses. This operator comes in handy as a time-saver when you have more than a handful of criteria to evaluate. Figure 2-20 demonstrates how to filter for both California and Colorado by using the `In` operator.

Not

Opposite of the `In` operator, the `Not` operator filters for all records not matching the arguments within the parentheses. Figure 2-21 demonstrates how to filter for all transactions that did not come from either California or Colorado.

Figure 2-20: Using the `In` operator

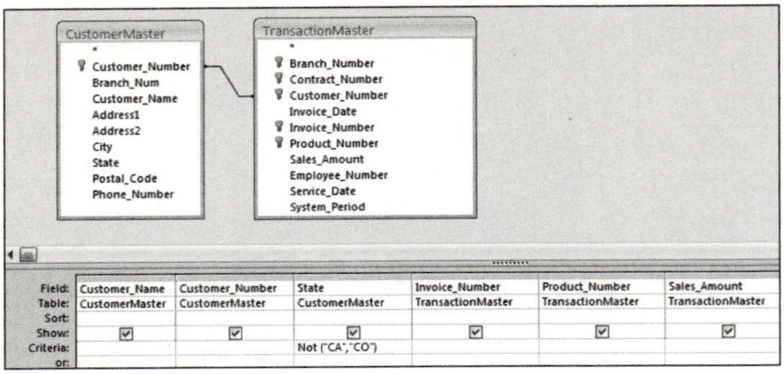

Figure 2-21: Using the `Not` operator

Is Null

Oftentimes, you will have fields that contain empty values. These values are considered *null* — a value of nothing. The `Is Null` operator filters all records that have the database value Null in the Criteria field. See Figure 2-22.

Exporting Query Results

Now that you have covered the basics of creating queries, you need to be able to export these results back to Excel or another format. The simplest way to do this in Access is to right-click the query name in the Navigation pane after it has been saved. Select Export and choose the appropriate file type. The query takes a snapshot of the data at that moment in time and saves the results in the requested format.

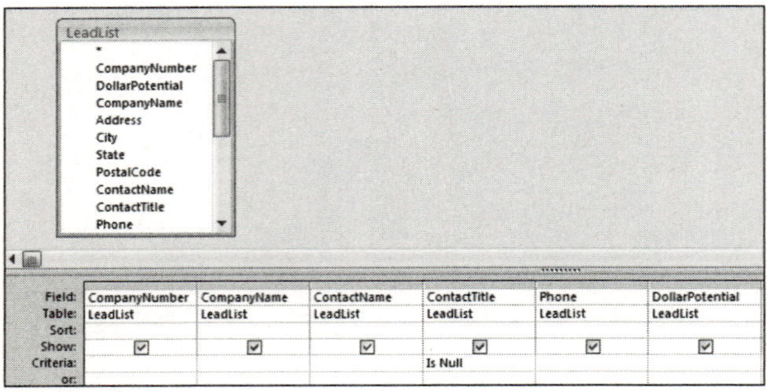

Figure 2-22: Using the `Is Null` operator

Do you want to output your query results to Excel without saving them anywhere?

After creating a query, you can select a set of records and quickly bring those to Excel without the need to save the query or create a temporary file.

First, you select the rows or columns you are interested in. Next you click the highlighted square around the chosen cells (as shown in Figure 2-23), and you drag them directly onto an Excel spreadsheet.

The data you selected is output to a spreadsheet with labels. Figure 2-24 demonstrates how this looks. This nifty trick allows you to do some on-the-fly analysis between Access and Excel without saving a gaggle of temporary files.

NOTE You can also use the old reliable copy-and-paste technique to copy data from Access to Excel.

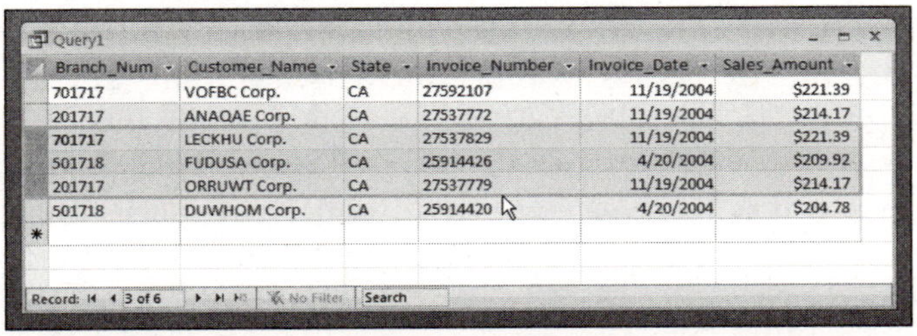

Figure 2-23: Clicking the orange border around a set of selected cells enables you to drag them directly into an Excel spreadsheet.

Figure 2-24: Your data has been output to Excel!

Using Aggregate Queries

An Aggregate query, sometimes referred to as a *group-by* query is a type of query that you can build to help you quickly group and summarize your data. With a Select query, you can only retrieve records as they appear in your data source. However, with an Aggregate query, you can retrieve a summary snapshot of your data that will show you totals, averages, counts, and more.

Aggregate Query Basics

To get a firm understanding of what an Aggregate query does, take the following scenario as an example. You have just been asked to provide the sum of total revenue by period. In response to this request, start a query in Design view and bring in the System_Period and Sales_Amount fields as shown in Figure 2-25. If you run this query as is, you will get every record in your dataset instead of the summary you need.

To get a summary of revenue by period, you need to activate Totals in your design grid. To do this, go up to the ribbon, select the Design tab, and then click the Total button. As you can see in Figure 2-26, after you have activated Totals in your design grid, you will see a new row in your grid called Total. The Total row tells Access which aggregate function to use when performing aggregation on the specified fields.

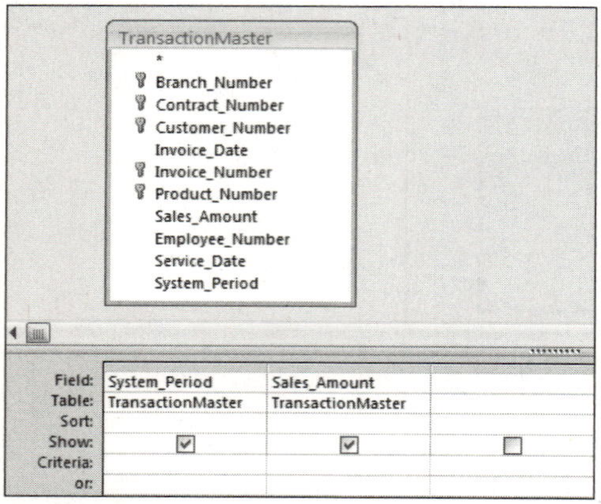

Figure 2-25: Running this query returns all the records in your dataset, not the summary you need.

You will notice that the Total row contains the words Group By under each field in your grid. This means that all similar records in a field are grouped to provide you with a unique data item. You cover the different aggregate functions in-depth later in this chapter.

The idea here is to adjust the aggregate functions in the Totals row to correspond with the analysis you are trying perform. In this scenario, you need to group all the periods in your dataset, and then sum the revenue in each period. Therefore, you will need to use the `Group By` aggregate function for the System_Period field, and the `Sum` aggregate function for the Sales_Amount field.

Since the default selection for Totals is the `Group By` function, no change is needed for the System_Period field. However, you will need to change the aggregate function for the Sales_Amount field from `Group By` to `Sum`. This tells Access that you want to sum the revenue figures in the Sales_Amount field, not group them. To change the aggregate function, simply click the Total drop-down list under the Sales_Amount field, shown in Figure 2-27, and select Sum. At this point, you can run your query.

As you can see in Figure 2-28, the resulting table gives a summary of your dataset, showing total revenue by period.

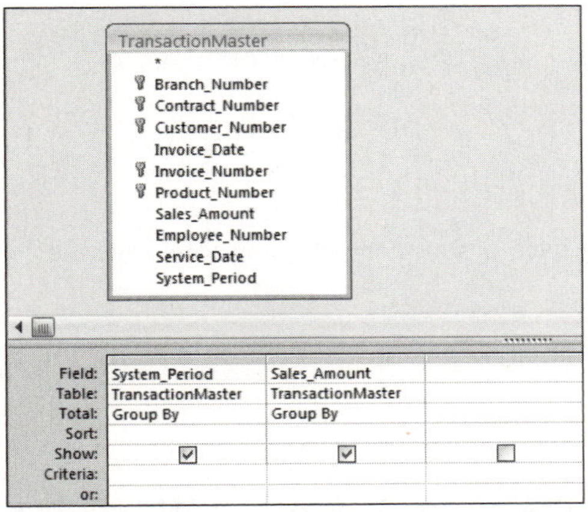

Figure 2-26: Activating Totals in your design grid adds a Total row to your query grid that defaults to Group By.

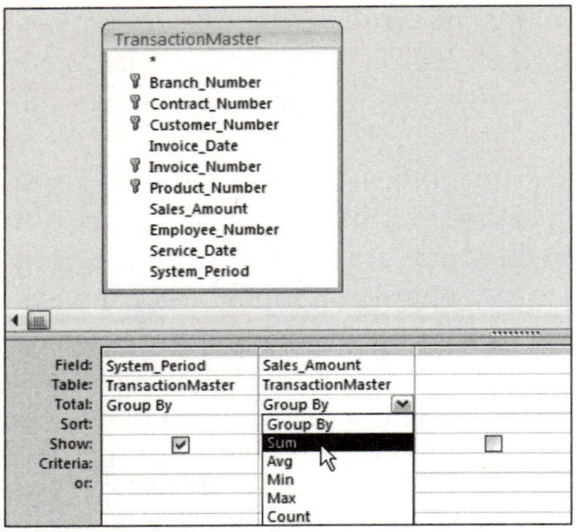

Figure 2-27: Change the aggregate function under the Sales_Amount field to Sum.

System_Period	SumOfSales_Amount
200401	$681,865.93
200402	$1,116,917.74
200403	$657,612.02
200404	$865,499.74
200405	$925,803.97
200406	$868,931.46
200407	$640,587.94
200408	$1,170,263.89
200409	$604,552.87
200410	$891,255.01
200411	$949,606.37
200412	$887,666.43

Figure 2-28: After you run your query, you have a summary showing total revenue by period.

About Aggregate Functions

In the example shown in Figure 2-27, you selected the `Sum` aggregate function from the Totals drop-down list. Obviously, you could have selected any one of the 12 functions available. Indeed, you will undoubtedly come across analyses where you will have to use a few of the other functions available to you. In this light, it is important to know what each one of these aggregate functions implicates for your data analysis.

Group By

The Group By aggregate function aggregates all the records in the specified field into unique groups. Here are few things to keep in mind when using the Group By aggregate function.

- **Access performs the Group By function in your aggregate query before any other aggregation.** If you are performing a Group By function along with another aggregate function, the Group By function will be performed first. The example shown in Figure 2-28 illustrates this concept. Access groups the System_Period field before summing the Sales_Amount field.

- **Access treats multiple Group By fields as one unique item.** To illustrate this point, create a query that looks similar to the one shown in Figure 2-29. As you can see after running the query, Access counted all the transactions that were logged in the 200401 System_Period.

  Now return to Query Design view and add Product_Number as shown in Figure 2-30. This time, Access treats each combination of System_Period and Product Number as a unique item. Each combination is grouped before the records in each group are counted. The benefit here is that you have added a dimension to your analysis. Not only do you know how many transactions per Product_Number were logged in 200401, but also if you add up all the transactions, you will get an accurate count of the total number of transactions logged in 200401.

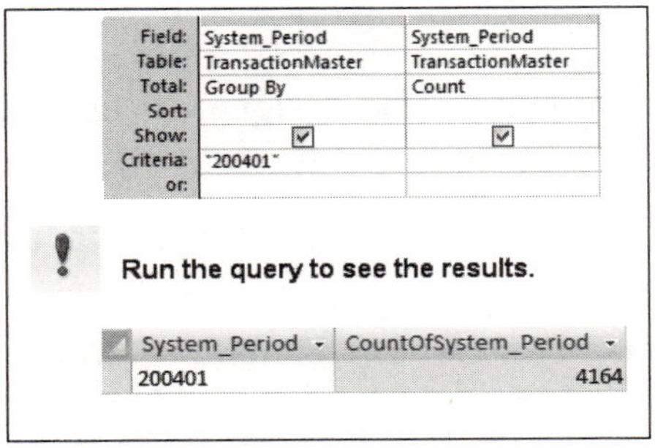

Figure 2-29: After you run this query, you will have a summary showing you that there are 4164 records in System_Period 200401.

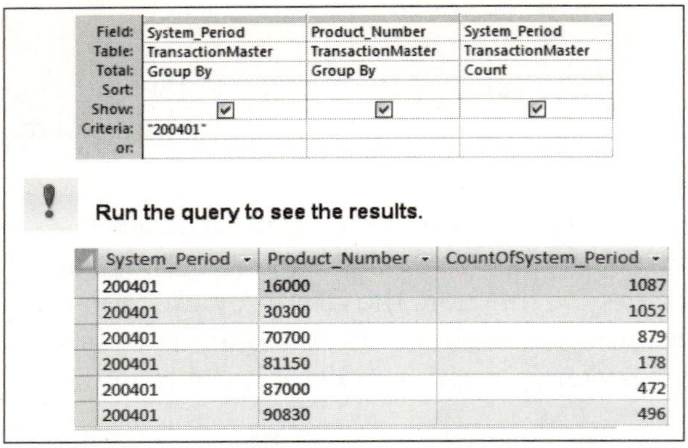

Figure 2-30: This query results in a few more records, but if you add up the counts in each group, they will total to 4,164.

- **Access sorts each Group By field in ascending order.** Unless otherwise specified, any field tagged as a Group By field will be sorted in ascending order. If your query has multiple Group By fields, each field will be sorted in ascending order starting with the left-most field.

Sum, Avg, Count, StDev, Var

These aggregate functions all perform mathematical calculations against the records in your selected field. It is important to note that these functions exclude any records that are set to null. In other words, these aggregate functions ignore any empty cells.

Sum

Sum calculates the total value of the all the records in the designated field or grouping. This function only works with the following data types: AutoNumber, Currency, Date/Time, and Number.

Avg

Avg calculates the Average of all the records in the designated field or grouping. This function only works with the following data types: AutoNumber, Currency, Date/Time, and Number.

Count

Count simply counts the number of entries within the designated field or grouping. This function works with all data types.

StDev

StDev calculates the standard deviation across all records within the designated field or grouping. This function only works with the following data types: AutoNumber, Currency, Date/Time, and Number.

Var

Var calculates the amount by which all the values within the designated field or grouping vary from the average value of the group. This function only works with the following data types: AutoNumber, Currency, Date/Time, and Number.

Min, Max, First, Last

Unlike other aggregate functions, these functions evaluate all the records in the designated field or grouping and return a single value from the group.

Min

Min returns the value of the record with the lowest value in the designated field or grouping. This function only works with the following data types: AutoNumber, Currency, Date/Time, Number, and Text.

Max

Max returns the value of the record with the highest value in the designated field or grouping. This function only works with the following data types: AutoNumber, Currency, Date/Time, Number, and Text.

First

First returns the value of the first record in the designated field or grouping. This function works with all data types.

Last

Last returns the value of the last record in the designated field or grouping. This function works with all data types

Expression, Where

One of the steadfast rules of aggregate queries is that every field must have an aggregation performed against it. However, there will be situations where you will have to use a field as a utility. That is, use a field to simply perform a calculation or apply a filter. These fields are a means to get to the final analysis you are looking for, rather than part of the final analysis. In these situations, you use the `Expression` function or the `Where` clause. The `Expression` function and the `Where` clause are unique in that they don't perform any grouping action, per se.

Expression

The `Expression` aggregate function is generally applied when you are utilizing custom calculations or other functions in an aggregate query. `Expression` tells Access to perform the designated custom calculation on each individual record or group separately.

Create a query in Design view that looks like the one shown in Figure 2-31. Note that you are using two aliases in this query, Revenue for the Sales_Amount field and Cost for the custom calculation defined here. Using an alias of Revenue gives the sum of Sales_Amount a user-friendly name.

TIP   An alias is an alternate name you can give to a field to make it easier to read the field's name in the query results. To create an alias, simply preface the field with the text you would like to see as the field name, followed by a colon (as demonstrated in Figure 2-31).

Now you can use [Revenue] to represent the sum of Sales_Amount in your custom calculation. The `Expression` aggregate function ties it all together by telling Access that [Revenue] * . 33 will be performed against the resulting sum of Sales_Amount for each individual System_Period group. Running this query returns the total Revenue and Cost for each System_Period group.

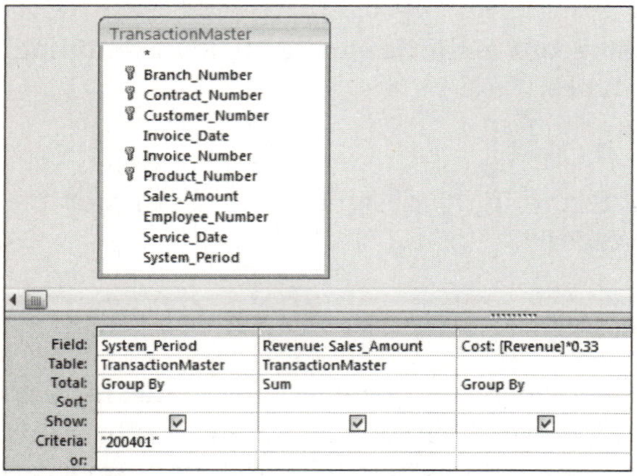

Figure 2-31: The `Expression` aggregate function allows you to perform the designated custom calculation on each System_Period group separately.

Where

The `Where` clause enables you to apply a criterion to a field that is not included in your aggregate query, effectively applying a filter to your analysis. To see the `Where` clause in action, create a query in Design view that looks like the one shown in Figure 2-32.

As you can see in the Total row, you are grouping Product_Number and summing Sales_Amount. However, System_Period has no aggregation selected because you only want to use it to filter out one specific period. You have entered "200401" in the criteria for System_Period. If you run this query as is, you will get the following error message: "You tried to execute a query that does not include the specified expression 'System_Period' as part of an aggregate function."

To run this query successfully, click the Total drop-down list for the System_Period field and select Where from the selection list. At this point, your query should look similar to the one shown in Figure 2-33. With the `Where` clause specified, you can successfully run this query.

> **NOTE** Notice in Figure 2-33 that the check box in the Show row it is not selected for the System_Period. This is because fields that are tagged with the Where clause cannot be shown in an aggregate query. Therefore, this check box must remain cleared. If you select the Show check box of a field with a `Where` clause, you will get an error message stating that you cannot display the field for which you entered Where in the Total row.

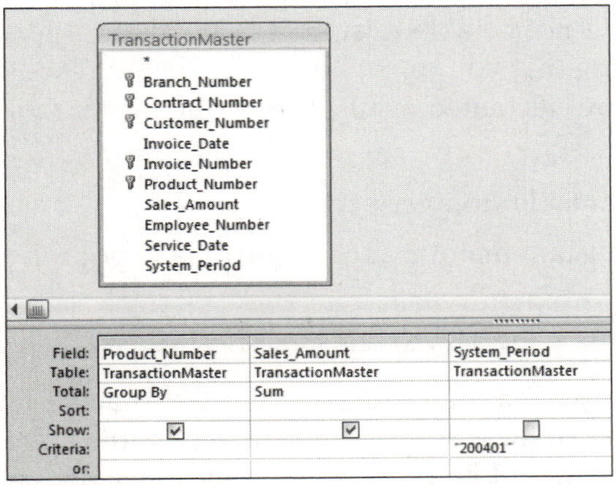

Figure 2-32: Running this query causes an error message because you have no aggregation defined for System_Period.

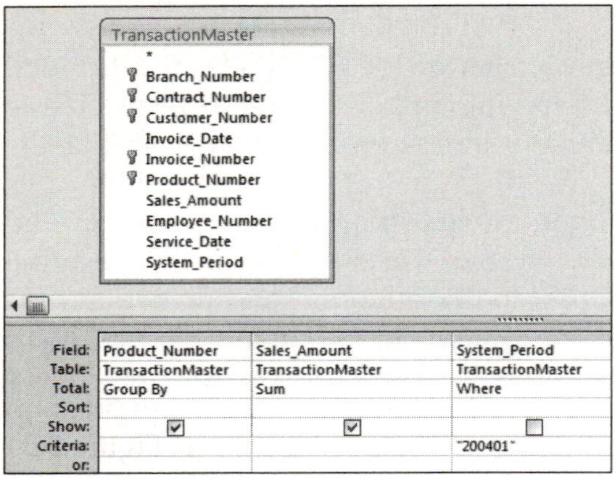

Figure 2-33: Adding a Where remedies the error and allows you to run the query.

Using Calculations in Your Analysis

If you are an Excel user trying to familiarize yourself with Access, one of the questions you undoubtedly have is, "Where do the formulas go?" In Excel, you have the flexibility to enter a calculation via a formula directly into the dataset you are analyzing. You do not have this ability in Access. So the question is, where do you store calculations in Access?

As you have already learned, things work differently in Access. The natural structure of an Access database forces you to keep your data separate from your analysis. In this light, you will not be able to store a calculation (a formula) in your dataset. Now, it is true that you can store the calculated results as hard data, but using tables to store calculated results is problematic for several reasons.

- Stored calculations take up valuable storage space.
- Stored calculations require constant maintenance as the data in your table changes.
- Stored calculations generally tie your data to one analytical path.

Instead of storing the calculated results as hard data, it is a better practice to perform calculations in real time, at the precise moment when they are needed. This ensures the most current and accurate results, and does not tie your data to one particular analysis.

Common Calculation Scenarios

In Access, calculations are performed by using *expressions*. An expression is a combination of values, operators, or functions that are evaluated to return a separate value to be used in a subsequent process. For example, 2+2 is an expression that returns the integer 4, which can be used in a subsequent analysis. Expressions can be used almost anywhere in Access to accomplish various tasks; in queries, forms, reports, data access pages, and even in tables to a certain degree. In this section, you learn how to enhance your Access queries by building real-time calculations using expressions.

Using Constants in Calculations

Most calculations typically consist of hard-coded numbers or *constants*. A constant is a static value that does not change. For example, in the expression [Price]*1.1, 1.1 is a constant; the value of 1.1 will never change. Figure 2-34 demonstrates how a constant can be used in an expression within a query.

In this example, you are building a query that analyzes how the current price for each product compares to the same price with a 10 percent increase. The expression, entered under the alias Increase, multiplies the price field of each record with a constant value of 1.1, calculating a price that is ten percent over the original value in the Price field.

Using Fields in Calculations

Not all your calculations require you to specify a constant. In fact, many of the mathematical operations you will carry out are performed on data that already resides in fields within your dataset. You can perform calculations using any fields formatted as number or currency.

For example, in the query shown in Figure 2-35, you are not using any constants. Instead, your calculation will be executed using the values in each record of the dataset. This is similar to referencing cell values in an Excel formula.

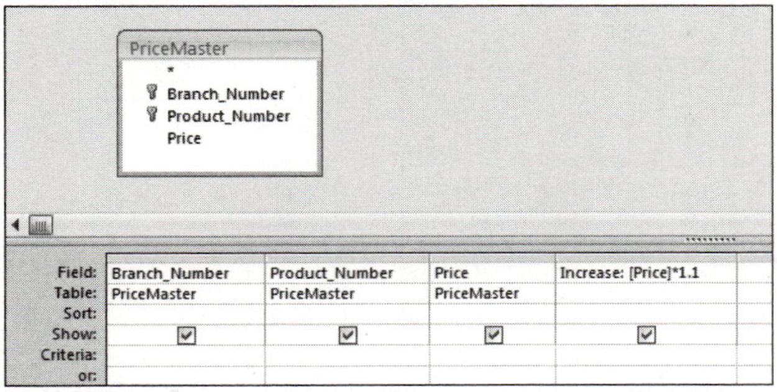

Figure 2-34: In this query, you are using a constant to calculate a 10 percent price increase.

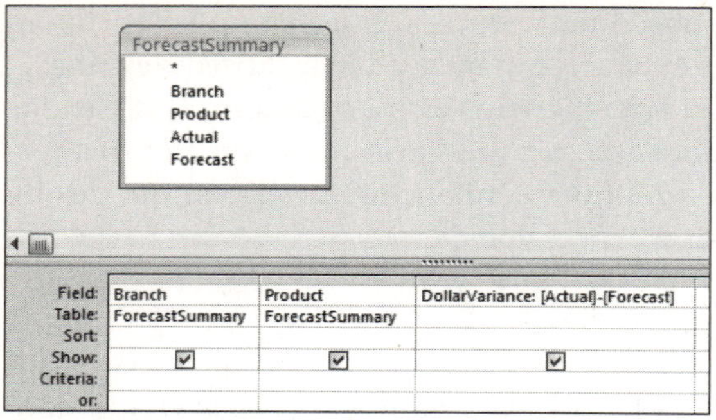

Figure 2-35: In this query, you are using two fields in a Dollar Variance calculation.

Using the Results of Aggregation in Calculations

Using the result of an aggregation as an expression in a calculation enables you to perform multiple analytical steps in one query. In the example in Figure 2-36, you are running an aggregate query. This query executes in the following order:

1. The query first groups your records by branch number.

2. The query calculates the count of invoices and the sum of revenue for each branch.

3. The query assigns the aliases you have defined respectively (Invoice-Count and Rev).

4. The query then uses the aggregation results for each branch as expressions in your AvgDollarPerInvoice calculation.

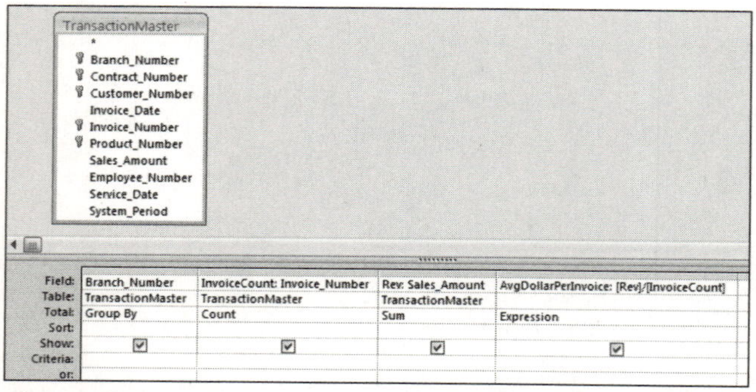

Figure 2-36: In this query, you are using the aggregation results for each branch number as expressions in your calculation.

Using the Results of One Calculation as an Expression in Another

Keep in mind that you are not limited to one calculation per query. In fact, you can use the results of one calculation as an expression in another calculation. Figure 2-37 illustrates this concept.

In this query, you are first calculating an adjusted forecast and then using the results of that calculation in another calculation that returns the variance of Actual versus Adjusted Forecast.

Performing Simple Date Calculations

Have you ever noticed that you can perform calculations in Excel with dates? Well, you can do the same in Access. This is thanks to the Office-wide system of storing dates called the *1900 system.* In the 1900 system, every possible date starting from January 1, 1900 is stored as a serial number. For example, January 1, 1900 is stored as 1; January 2, 1900 is stored as 2; and so on. You can take advantage of this system to perform calculations with dates.

Figure 2-38 shows one of the simplest calculations you can perform on a date. In this query, you are adding 30 to each invoice date. This effectively returns the invoice date plus 30 days, giving you a new date.

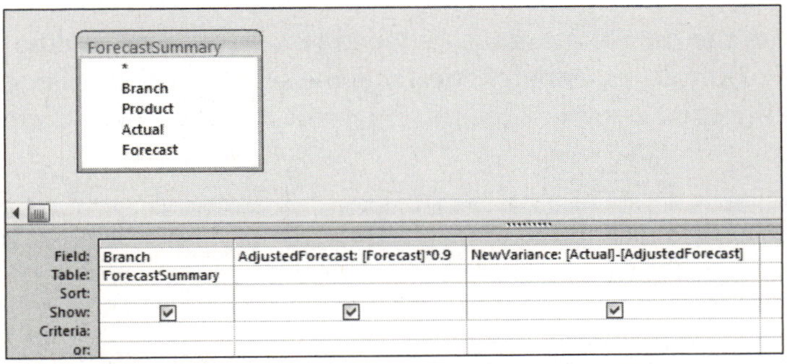

Figure 2-37: This query uses the results of one calculation as an expression in another.

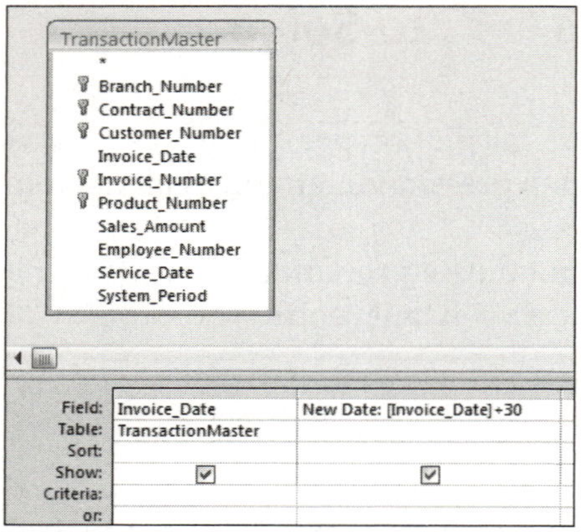

Figure 2-38: You are adding 30 to each invoice date, effectively creating a date equal to the invoice date plus 30 days.

CAUTION To be calculated correctly dates must reside in a field that is formatted as a Date/Time field. If you enter a date into a Text field, the date will continue to look like a date, but Access will treat it like a string. The end result is that any calculation done on dates in this Text-formatted field will fail. Ensure that all dates are stored in fields that are formatted as Date/Time.

You can also calculate the number of days between two dates. The calculation in Figure 2-39, for example, essentially subtracts the serial number of one date from the serial number of another date, leaving you the number of days between the two dates.

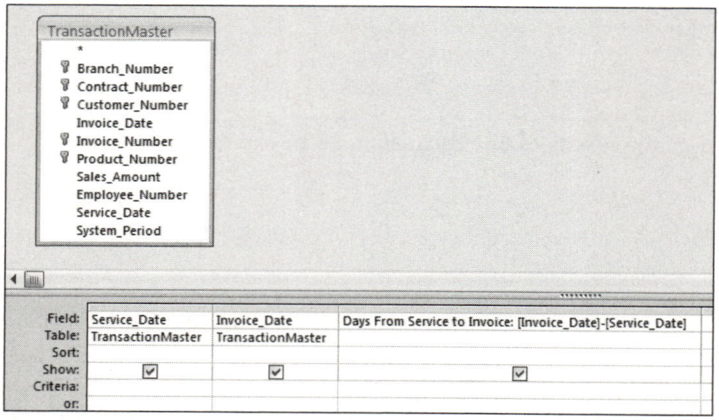

Figure 2-39: In this query, you are calculating the number of days between two dates.

Leveraging Access Query Wizards to Solve Common Excel Problems

Access comes with a handful of useful query wizards; each focused on helping you solve a specific problem. Although there are ways to manually duplicate the functionality that these wizards provide, the time and effort saved by using these wizards make exploring them a worthwhile endeavor.

The Find Duplicates Query Wizard

Duplicate records are absolute analysis killers. The effect duplicate records have on your analysis can be far-reaching, corrupting almost every metric, summary, and analytical assessment you produce. It is for this reason that finding and removing duplicate records should be your first priority when you receive a new dataset.

Although Excel 2007 comes with new functionality to remove duplicate data, the drawback is that Excel does not give you the opportunity to review the records that will be removed. Therefore, what you get is a nail-biting process that leaves you wondering what exactly was deleted from your dataset. One minute you have 1000 records, then all of a sudden you have 250 records; meanwhile you're wondering what just happened?

An alternative to removing duplicates in Excel is the Access Find Duplicates Query Wizard. This wizard isolates all records you define as duplicates, then allows you to review them before deleting them.

To start this wizard, go to the application ribbon and select the Create tab. There you find the Query Wizard button, which activates the New Query dialog box shown in Figure 2-40. From there, you can select Find Duplicates Query Wizard and then click the OK button.

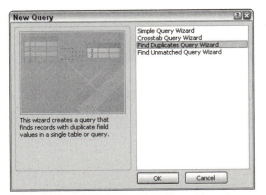

Figure 2-40: Select the Find Duplicates Query Wizard and then click the OK button.

At this point, you must select the particular dataset you will use in your Find Duplicate query. Notice you can use queries as well as tables. Select the LeadList table, as shown in Figure 2-41.

Next, you must identify which field, or combination of fields, best defines a unique record in your dataset. In the example shown in Figure 2-42, the CompanyNumber field alone defines a unique record. Click Next.

The next step, shown in Figure 2-43, is to identify any additional fields you would like to see in your query. Click the Next button.

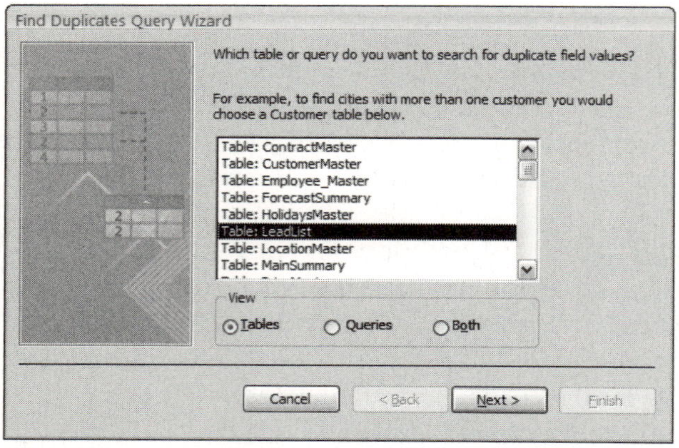

Figure 2-41: Select the dataset in which you want to find duplicates, then click Next.

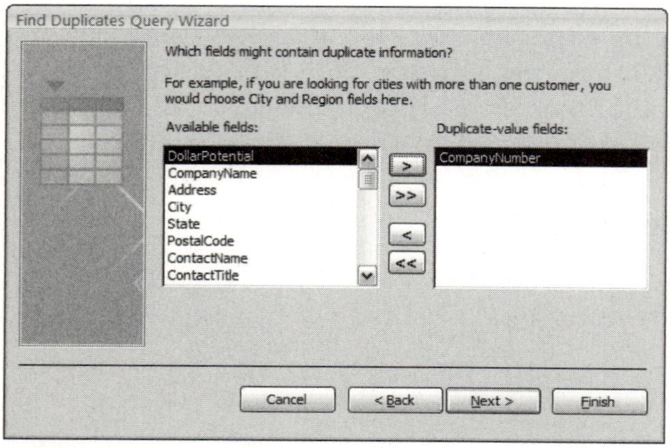

Figure 2-42: Select the field or fields that make up a unique record in your dataset.

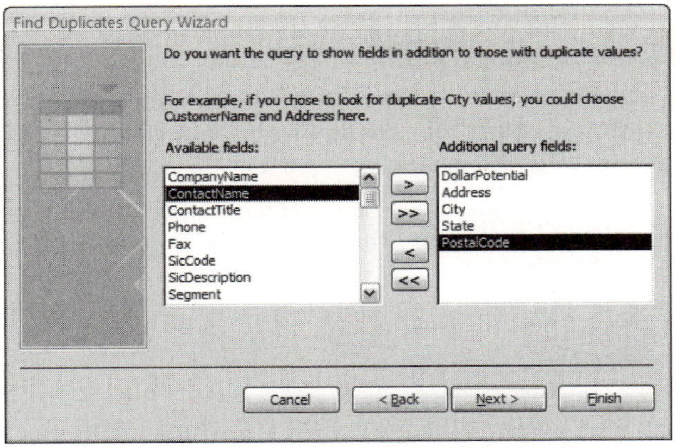

Figure 2-43: Select the field or fields you want to see in your query.

In the final step, shown in Figure 2-44, finish off the wizard by naming your query and clicking the Finish button.

When you click Finish, your new Find Duplicates query will immediately open for your review. Figure 2-45 shows the resulting query.

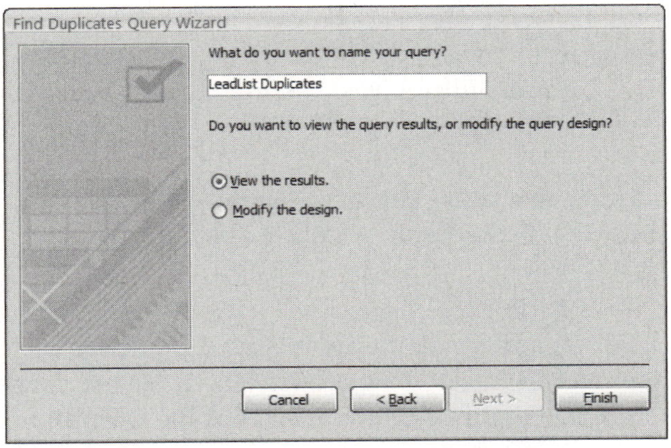

Figure 2-44: Name your query and click Finish.

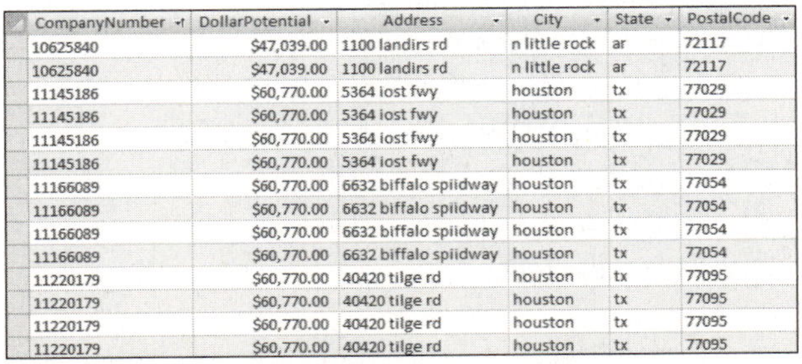

CompanyNumber	DollarPotential	Address	City	State	PostalCode
10625840	$47,039.00	1100 landirs rd	n little rock	ar	72117
10625840	$47,039.00	1100 landirs rd	n little rock	ar	72117
11145186	$60,770.00	5364 iost fwy	houston	tx	77029
11145186	$60,770.00	5364 iost fwy	houston	tx	77029
11145186	$60,770.00	5364 iost fwy	houston	tx	77029
11145186	$60,770.00	5364 iost fwy	houston	tx	77029
11166089	$60,770.00	6632 biffalo spiidway	houston	tx	77054
11166089	$60,770.00	6632 biffalo spiidway	houston	tx	77054
11166089	$60,770.00	6632 biffalo spiidway	houston	tx	77054
11166089	$60,770.00	6632 biffalo spiidway	houston	tx	77054
11220179	$60,770.00	40420 tilge rd	houston	tx	77095
11220179	$60,770.00	40420 tilge rd	houston	tx	77095
11220179	$60,770.00	40420 tilge rd	houston	tx	77095
11220179	$60,770.00	40420 tilge rd	houston	tx	77095

Figure 2-45: Your Find Duplicates query

NOTE **The records shown in your Find Duplicates query are not only the duplications-- they include one unique record plus the duplication. For example, in Figure 2-45, you will notice that there are four records tagged with the CompanyNumber 11145186. Three of the four are duplicates that can be removed, while one should remain as a unique record.**

Removing the duplicates can be as easy as manually deleting records from your Find Duplicates query.

The Find UnMatched Query Wizard

A common analysis that many Excel users often need to perform is comparing two datasets. For example, Figure 2-46 contains two datasets that need to be compared to determine which customers generated revenue in 2004, but did not generate revenue in 2005.

This is unofficially called the VLookup shuffle. This is where you would pull out all the `VLookup`, `Index`, and `Match` formula tricks you can muster. The problem is that any number of things can go wrong, causing you to get an error. You could make an error in your formula, your dataset may not be contiguous, you could unintentionally sort your dataset incorrectly, and the list goes on.

The Access Find Unmatched Query is designed to do this type of analysis. The first step is to bring the two datasets into Access. Name the two datasets 2004_Revenue and 2005_Revenue, respectively.

TIP **The Excel file that contains the two tables shown in Figure 2-46 can be found in the sample files that come with this book. The file is called** `Chapter 2-Find Unmatched Sample.xlsx`**.**

Next, go to the application Ribbon and select the Create tab. Find the Query Wizard button to activate the New Query dialog box. There, select Find Unmatched Query Wizard as shown in Figure 2-47 and then click the OK button.

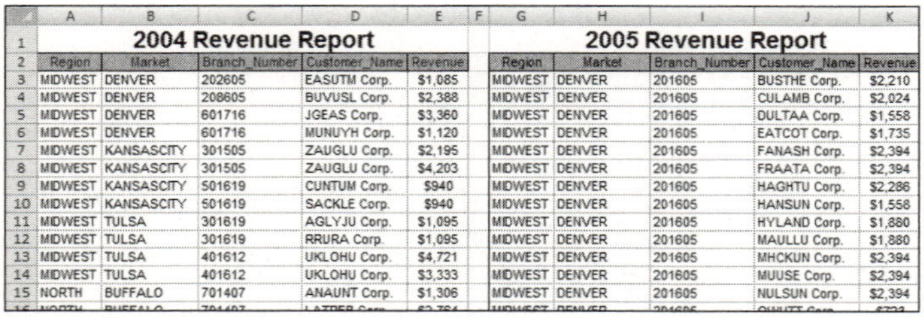

	A	B	C	D	E	F	G	H	I	J	K
1	2004 Revenue Report						2005 Revenue Report				
2	Region	Market	Branch_Number	Customer_Name	Revenue		Region	Market	Branch_Number	Customer_Name	Revenue
3	MIDWEST	DENVER	202605	EASUTM Corp.	$1,085		MIDWEST	DENVER	201605	BUSTHE Corp.	$2,210
4	MIDWEST	DENVER	208605	BUVUSL Corp.	$2,388		MIDWEST	DENVER	201605	CULAMB Corp.	$2,024
5	MIDWEST	DENVER	601716	JGEAS Corp.	$3,360		MIDWEST	DENVER	201605	DULTAA Corp.	$1,558
6	MIDWEST	DENVER	601716	MUNUYH Corp.	$1,120		MIDWEST	DENVER	201605	EATCOT Corp.	$1,735
7	MIDWEST	KANSASCITY	301505	ZAUGLU Corp.	$2,195		MIDWEST	DENVER	201605	FANASH Corp.	$2,394
8	MIDWEST	KANSASCITY	301505	ZAUGLU Corp.	$4,203		MIDWEST	DENVER	201605	FRAATA Corp.	$2,394
9	MIDWEST	KANSASCITY	501619	CUNTUM Corp.	$940		MIDWEST	DENVER	201605	HAGHTU Corp.	$2,286
10	MIDWEST	KANSASCITY	501619	SACKLE Corp.	$940		MIDWEST	DENVER	201605	HANSUN Corp.	$1,558
11	MIDWEST	TULSA	301619	AGLYJU Corp.	$1,095		MIDWEST	DENVER	201605	HYLAND Corp.	$1,880
12	MIDWEST	TULSA	301619	RRURA Corp.	$1,095		MIDWEST	DENVER	201605	MAULLU Corp.	$1,880
13	MIDWEST	TULSA	401612	UKLOHU Corp.	$4,721		MIDWEST	DENVER	201605	MHCKUN Corp.	$2,394
14	MIDWEST	TULSA	401612	UKLOHU Corp.	$3,333		MIDWEST	DENVER	201605	MUUSE Corp.	$2,394
15	NORTH	BUFFALO	701407	ANAUNT Corp.	$1,306		MIDWEST	DENVER	201605	NULSUN Corp.	$2,394

Figure 2-46: Comparing tables in Excel is no easy feat.

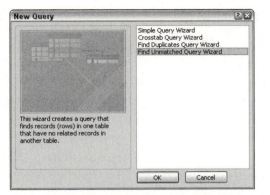

Figure 2-47: Select the Find Unmatched Query Wizard and then click the OK button.

At this point, you must select the particular dataset that contains the data you want to return. Remember, you want to see all customers that generated revenue in 2004 that did not generate revenue in 2005. Therefore the 2004_Revenue table contains the records you need (see Figure 2-48).

Next, you must select the table you want to evaluate against. In this case, you select 2005_Revenue as demonstrated in Figure 2-49.

The next step in the wizard requires that you identify which field you want to use to do the matching. In this example, you want to use the Customer_Name field (see Figure 2-50).

You are almost done. In the next step, you select the fields you want to see in the results of your query. After you move over all the fields, your dialog box should look like the one in Figure 2-51.

Figure 2-48: Select the dataset that contains the records you want returned.

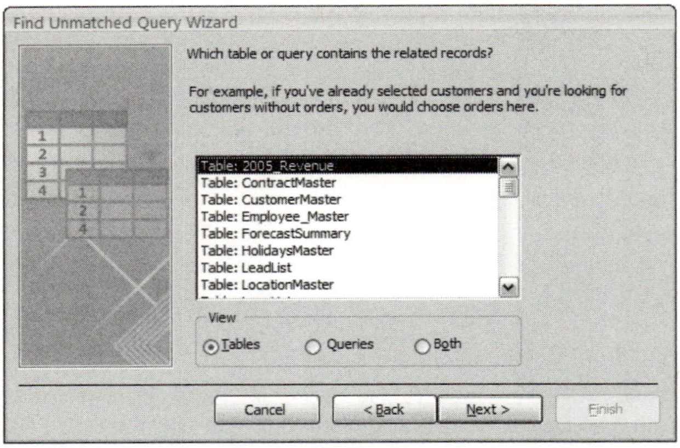

Figure 2-49: Select the dataset against which you want to evaluate.

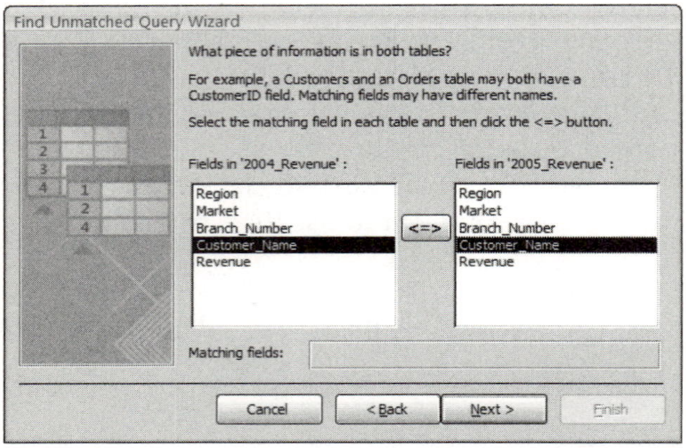

Figure 2-50: Select the field that will be used to perform the match.

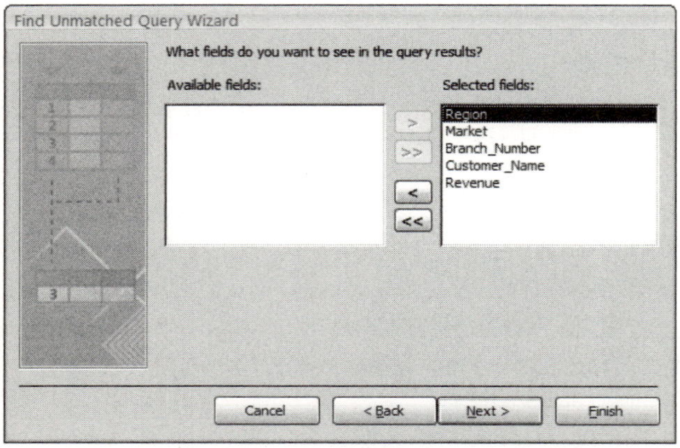

Figure 2-51: Select all the fields you want represented in the query results.

In the final step, shown in Figure 2-52, finish off the wizard by naming your query and clicking the Finish button.

When you click Finish, your new Find Unmatched query immediately opens for your review. Figure 2-53 shows there are 59 customers that generated revenue in 2004, but did not generate revenue in 2005.

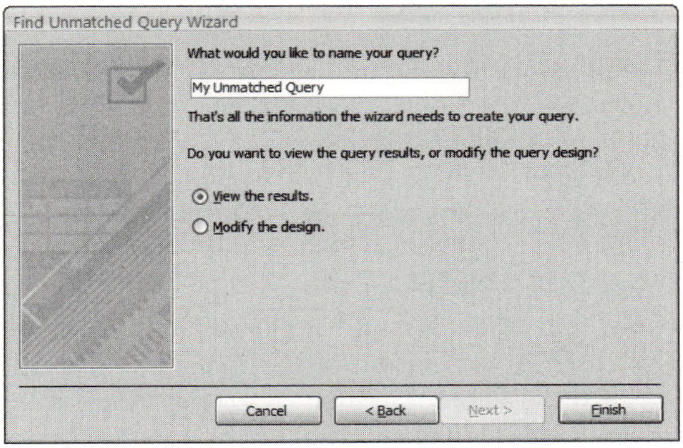

Figure 2-52: Name your query and click Finish.

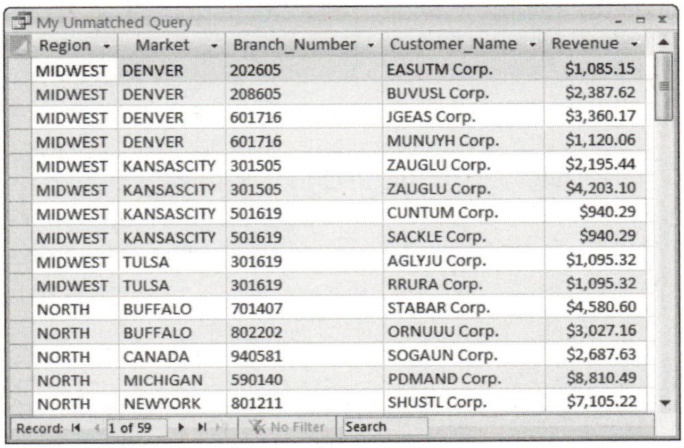

My Unmatched Query

Region	Market	Branch_Number	Customer_Name	Revenue
MIDWEST	DENVER	202605	EASUTM Corp.	$1,085.15
MIDWEST	DENVER	208605	BUVUSL Corp.	$2,387.62
MIDWEST	DENVER	601716	JGEAS Corp.	$3,360.17
MIDWEST	DENVER	601716	MUNUYH Corp.	$1,120.06
MIDWEST	KANSASCITY	301505	ZAUGLU Corp.	$2,195.44
MIDWEST	KANSASCITY	301505	ZAUGLU Corp.	$4,203.10
MIDWEST	KANSASCITY	501619	CUNTUM Corp.	$940.29
MIDWEST	KANSASCITY	501619	SACKLE Corp.	$940.29
MIDWEST	TULSA	301619	AGLYJU Corp.	$1,095.32
MIDWEST	TULSA	301619	RRURA Corp.	$1,095.32
NORTH	BUFFALO	701407	STABAR Corp.	$4,580.60
NORTH	BUFFALO	802202	ORNUUU Corp.	$3,027.16
NORTH	CANADA	940581	SOGAUN Corp.	$2,687.63
NORTH	MICHIGAN	590140	PDMAND Corp.	$8,810.49
NORTH	NEWYORK	801211	SHUSTL Corp.	$7,105.22

Record: 1 of 59 No Filter Search

Figure 2-53: Your Find Unmatched query

Crosstab Queries

A Crosstab query is a special kind of aggregate query that summarizes values from a specified field, and groups them in a matrix layout by two sets of dimensions, one set down the left side of the matrix and the other set listed across the top of the matrix. Crosstab queries are perfect for analyzing trends over time, or providing a method for quickly identifying anomalies in your dataset.

In Excel, PivotTables give you the equivalent functionality to Crosstab queries in Access. Indeed, the power of PivotTables far surpasses that of Crosstab queries. So, what's the benefit of Crosstab queries?

Well for one, you can perform your analysis right in Access, without the need to export back and forth to Excel. Another reason is that the results of a Crosstab query are much less memory and disk space intensive than the pivot cache required to create a PivotTable. When you initiate the creation of a PivotTable, Excel takes a snapshot of your dataset and stores it in a pivot cache, a special memory subsystem in which your data source is duplicated for quick access. You can think of a pivot cache as a container that stores the snapshot of the data source. The pivot cache holds the full contents of your dataset in order for the PivotTable to be both dynamic and interactive. Meanwhile, because a Crosstab query is static in nature, it does not require a memory container like the pivot cache. This enables you to create a view of your data that takes up much less space than the source data.

So if you are interested in creating compact analyses that are easy to read but won't result in an Excel file that is 20 megabytes, then Crosstab queries are something to think about.

To activate the Crosstab Query Wizard, go to the ribbon and select the Create tab. Here, select the Query Wizard button. This brings up the New Query dialog box shown in Figure 2-54. Select Crosstab Query Wizard from the selection list and then click the OK button.

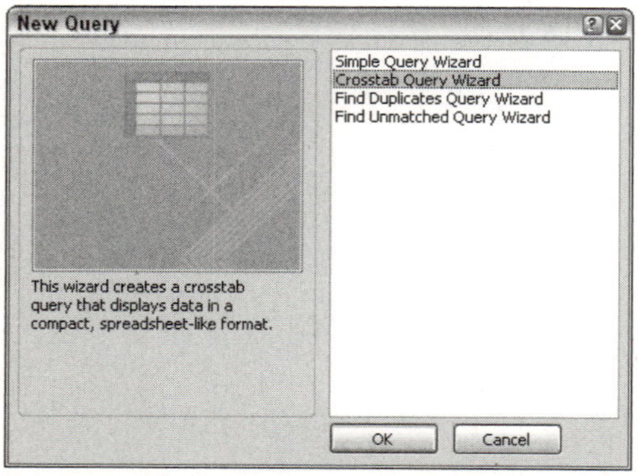

Figure 2-54: Select Crosstab Query Wizard from the New Query dialog box.

The first step in the Crosstab Query Wizard is to identify the data source you will be using. As you can see in Figure 2-55, you can choose either a query or a table as your data source. In this example, you will be using the Trasaction-Master table as your data source. Select TransactionMaster and then click the Next button.

The next step is to identify the fields you would like to use as the row headings. Select the Product_Number field and click the button with the > symbol on it to move it to the Selected Items list. At this point, your dialog box should look like Figure 2-56. Notice the Product_Number field is shown in the sample diagram at the bottom of the dialog box.

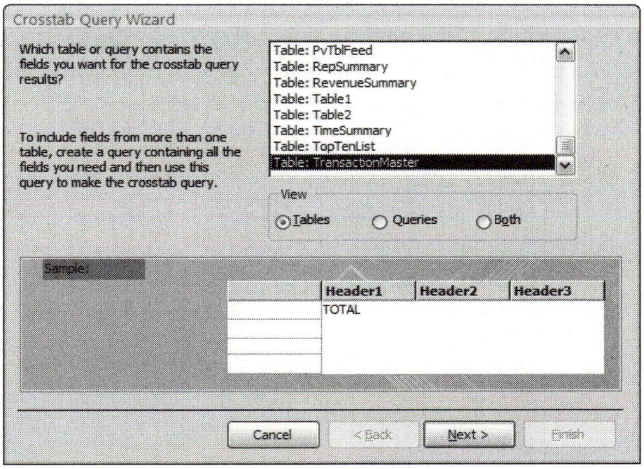

Figure 2-55: Select the data source for your Crosstab query.

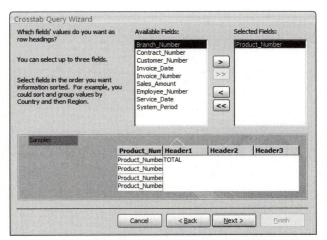

Figure 2-56: Select the Product_Number field, then click the Next button.

You can select up to three fields to include in your Crosstab query as row headings. Remember that Access treats each combination of headings as a unique item. That is, each combination is grouped before the records in each group are aggregated.

The next step is to identify the field you would like to use as the column heading for your Crosstab query. Keep in mind, there can be only one column heading in your Crosstab. Select the Invoice_Date field from the field list. Again, notice in Figure 2-57 that the sample diagram at the bottom of the dialog box updates to show the Invoice_Date.

NOTE If the field being used as a column heading includes data that contains a period (.), an exclamation mark (!), or a bracket ([or]), those characters will be changed to an underscore character (_) in the column heading. This does not happen if the same data is used as a row heading. This behavior is by design, as the naming conventions for field names in Access prohibit use of these characters.

If your column heading is a date field, as the Invoice_Date is in this example, you will see the step shown here in Figure 2-58. In this step, you have the option of specifying an interval to group your dates by. Select Quarter here and notice that the sample diagram at the bottom of the dialog box updates accordingly.

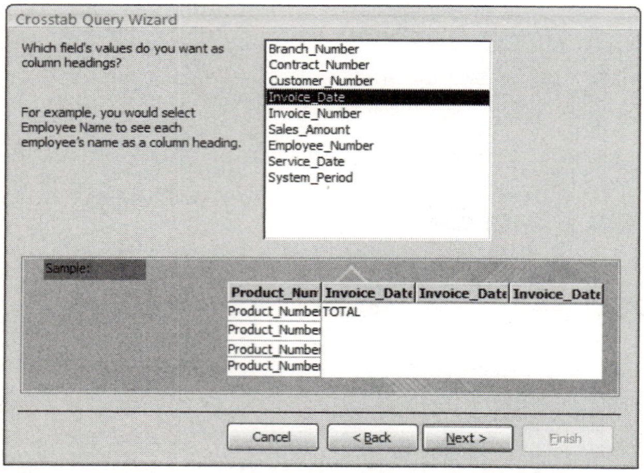

Figure 2-57: Select the Invoice_Date field, then click the Next button.

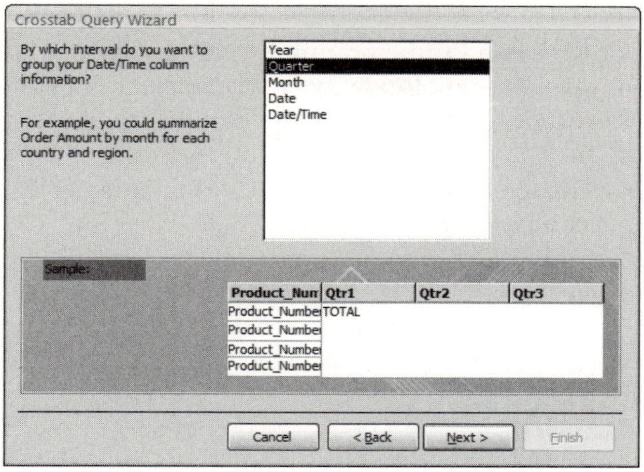

Figure 2-58: Select Quarter, then click the Next button.

You're almost done. In the second to last step, shown in Figure 2-59, you identify the field you want to aggregate, and the function you want to use. Select the Sales_Amount field from the Fields list and then select Sum from the Functions list.

Note that the Yes, include the row sum check box is selected by default to ensure that your Crosstab query includes a Total column that contains the sum total for each row. If you do not want this column, clear this check box.

If you look at the sample diagram at the bottom of the dialog box, you will get a good sense of what your final Crosstab query will do. In this example, your Crosstab calculates the sum of the Sales_Amount field for each Product_Number by Quarter.

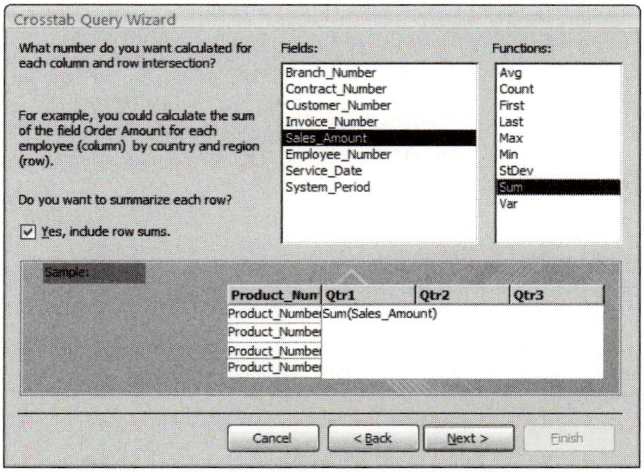

Figure 2-59: Select the Sale_Amount and Sum, and then click the Next button.

The final step, shown in Figure 2-60, is to name your Crosstab Query. In this example, you are naming your Crosstab Product Summary by Quarter. After you name your query, you have the option of viewing your query or modifying the design. In this case, you want to view your query results, so click the Finish Button.

In just a few clicks, you have created a powerful look at the revenue performance of each product by quarter (see Figure 2-61).

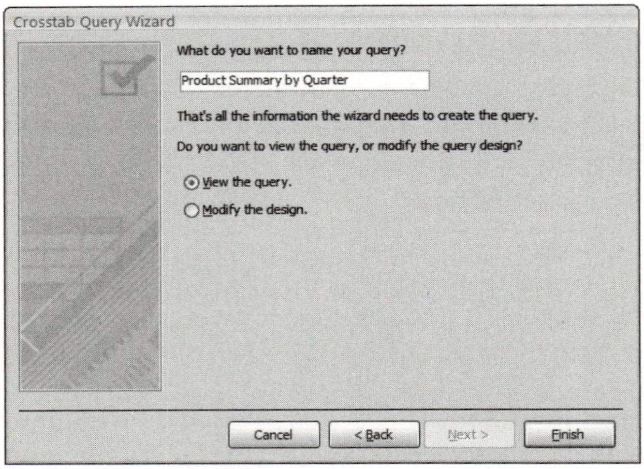

Figure 2-60: Select Finish to see your query results.

Product_Number	Total Of Sales_Amount	Qtr 1	Qtr 2	Qtr 3	Qtr 4
16000	$2,361,161.41	$563,800.21	$621,715.87	$600,810.41	$574,834.92
30300	$2,627,798.02	$612,496.21	$691,440.40	$674,592.20	$649,269.21
70700	$2,178,932.11	$533,128.55	$567,392.96	$552,382.16	$526,028.44
81150	$1,138,595.78	$257,218.54	$290,074.98	$297,252.21	$294,050.05
87000	$1,190,911.60	$288,795.91	$310,668.86	$303,084.76	$288,362.07
90830	$1,276,790.55	$293,195.50	$325,277.88	$329,788.62	$328,528.56

Figure 2-61: A powerful analysis in just a few clicks

Summary

A query is a question about the data stored in tables. The results of a query are separate from the data. If the data in the table is changed and the query run again, you would most often get different results. The most common query is the select query. With a select query, you can extract a dataset or individual data items. You can also utilize the built-in operators to apply filters and sorting to your queries.

Aggregate queries allow you to quickly group and summarize data, aggregating the returned dataset into totals, averages, counts, and more.

Utilizing some basic query fundamentals, you can leverage the powerful analytic tools and wizards in Access to solve some of the most common data issues in Excel. For example, the Find Duplicates Query Wizard allows you to effectively pinpoint and manage duplicates. The Find Unmatched Query Wizard allows you to easily compare two datasets and extract those records that don't match. Finally, the Crosstab Query Wizard enables you to create data summaries that are compact, flexible, and perfect for quickly identifying anomalies in your dataset.

CHAPTER 3

Sprucing Up Excel Data with Access Reports

If you are an Excel user, you are no doubt familiar with creating Excel reports that include sorting, layout, and formatting. In this chapter, you learn that Microsoft Access 2007 has some very slick functionality for reporting as well. In fact, it has utilities that can take your report building way beyond the limits of Excel by incorporating slicker formatting, external graphics, and data-driven custom letters.

If you are familiar with creating reports in Access, don't be too quick to skip over this chapter. Access 2007 has changed enough of the report building interface to warrant a look. It's the aim of this chapter to introduce both Excel and Access users to the powerful new aspects of report building in Access 2007.

A Closer Look at the Access Report

In this section, you create your first Access report and explore ways to view that report. You'll find that after walking through this section, you will have enough grounding to start building your own slick Access reports.

Creating Your First Report

The first step in creating a report in Access is to define the data source for the report. The data used in any Access reports can come from either a table or a query. One of the easiest ways to define a data source for a report is to build a query that is specifically designed to feed your report.

For your first report, create the query you see in Figure 3-1 and save it as TopReps. As you can see, you are combining transaction data and employee data to return a listing of the service representatives by sales revenue.

Now, with your newly created query selected, select the Create tab in the ribbon and click the Report command button as demonstrated in Figure 3-2.

Within a few seconds, Access produces a report that looks similar to the one illustrated in Figure 3-3. As easy as that, you have created your first Access report.

Close the report and you will see a message, shown in Figure 3-4, asking whether you want to save your changes. Clicking the No button essentially leaves you with no report. Clicking the Yes button activates a dialog box where you can name your new report. Access defaults the name of the report to the same name as its source. In this case, the name TopReps is fine.

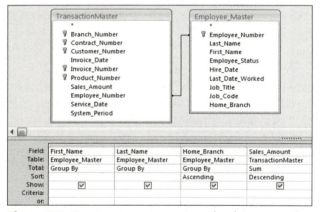

Figure 3-1: Create a query to serve as the data source for your report and name it TopReps.

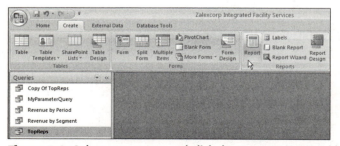

Figure 3-2: Select your query and click the Report command button.

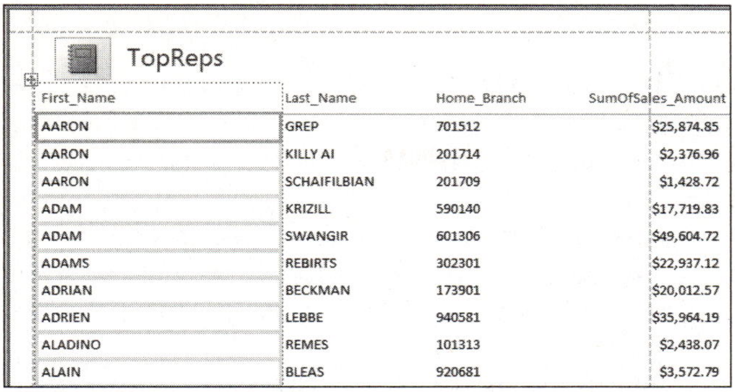

First_Name	Last_Name	Home_Branch	SumOfSales_Amount
AARON	GREP	701512	$25,874.85
AARON	KILLY AI	201714	$2,376.96
AARON	SCHAIFILBIAN	201709	$1,428.72
ADAM	KRIZILL	590140	$17,719.83
ADAM	SWANGIR	601306	$49,604.72
ADAMS	REBIRTS	302301	$22,937.12
ADRIAN	BECKMAN	173901	$20,012.57
ADRIEN	LEBBE	940581	$35,964.19
ALADINO	REMES	101313	$2,438.07
ALAIN	BLEAS	920681	$3,572.79

Figure 3-3: You have created your first Access report.

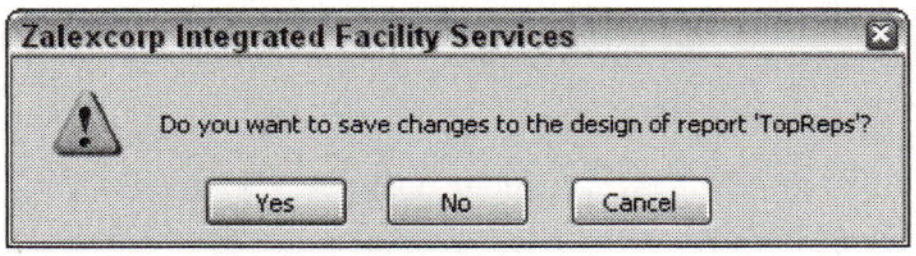

Figure 3-4: Be sure to save your report.

Viewing Your Report

At this point, you will see your newly created report in the Navigation pane (see Figure 3-5). Simply double-click the report name to open it.

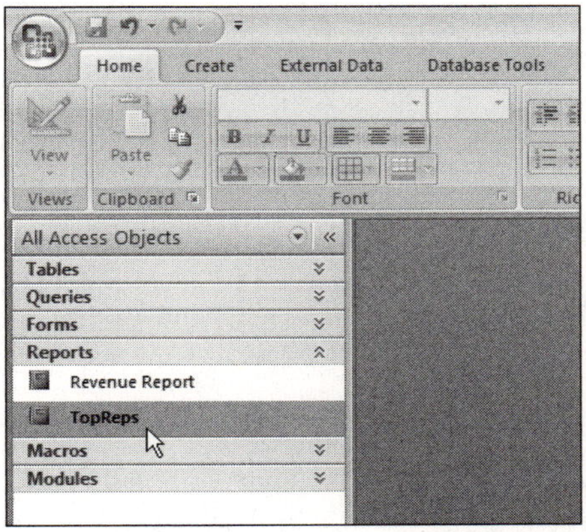

Figure 3-5: All reports are displayed in the Navigation pane.

Report View

By default, your reports open in Report view. The Report view lets you view and interact with your report as the report user would. You can't edit the data, labels, or layout in Report view. However, Access 2007 offers some interesting new functionality in Report view.

In prior versions of Access, the Report view was much like a PDF file or Print Preview mode — you could see the report but there was no interactivity whatsoever. Access 2007 enables you to apply filters to your reports in real time.

For example, select any branch number in the Home_Branch field and right-click. As you can see in Figure 3-6, a context menu activates giving you several filter options. This allows anyone using this report to select their branch and instantly have a customized report!

Layout View

The Layout view is new for Access 2007 and it will make life much easier for the Access novice. In Layout view, you can change elements of the report layout and grouping, while seeing how your report will be displayed to the user.

To get to Layout view, you would open your Access report and select View → Layout View in the Home tab as demonstrated in Figure 3-7.

When your report is in Layout view, you can do a great deal of formatting, grouping, and ordering. The idea is that you can select any component of the report by simply clicking that component. In Layout view, you can do things such as change the report title, change the data labels, resize columns, remove individual fields, or add new fields. Take some time here to walk through a simple example of how you can apply some formatting to your report via the Layout view.

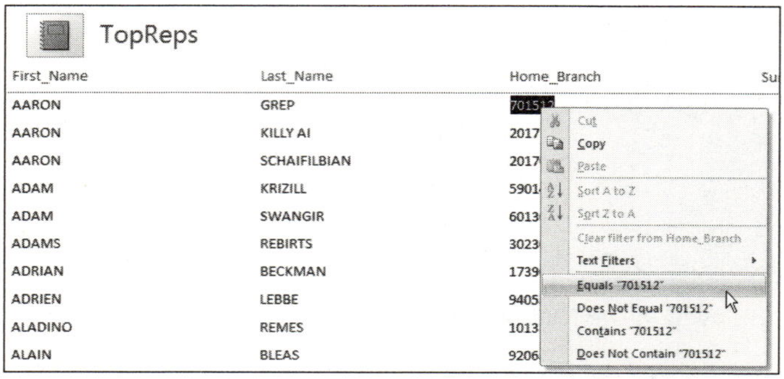

Figure 3-6: Access 2007 allows you to filter your reports in Report view.

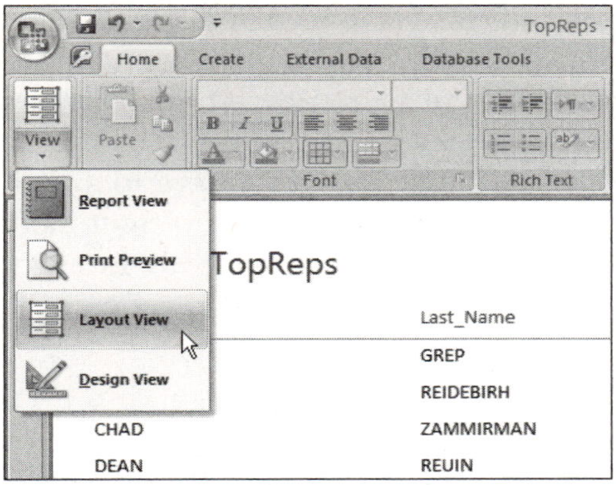

Figure 3-7: Switching to Layout view

With your report open in Layout view, select the report detail by clicking the white space to the left of the data rows. To make sure you have correctly selected the proper section, click the Property Sheet command button found in the Arrange tab. This activates the Property Sheet pane shown in Figure 3-8 on the right. The Section Type in this pane should read Detail.

NOTE You can use the Section Type drop-down menu in the Property Sheet pane to select the appropriate report section.

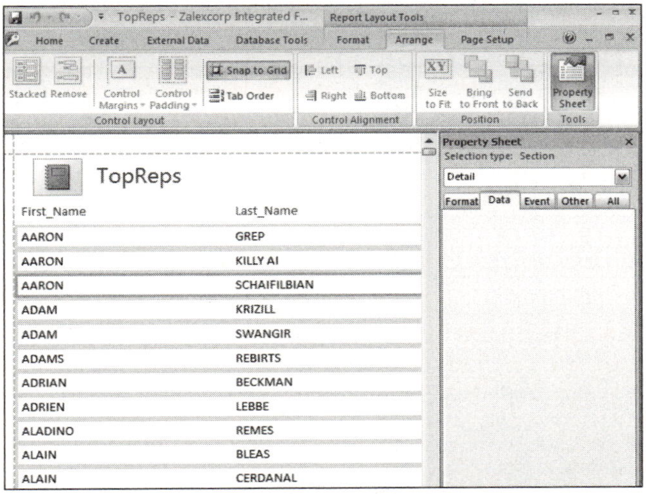

Figure 3-8: Select the Detail section of the report.

With the detail section selected, turn your attention to the Property Sheet pane. You will see several tabs that organize many different actions you can take. Select the Format tab and change the AutoHeight property to No, then change the Height property to .5" (see Figure 3-9).

Note that your changes take effect in real time. You don't have to switch back to Report view to see the effect of your change; it shows up right there live on your screen. As you can see, the Layout view is a relatively intuitive and user-friendly way to manipulate your reports.

Design View

The Design view allows you to design your report in the traditional grid interface. For the Access novice, deciphering a report in Design view can be a little intimidating. However, when you understand the basics of the Design view, creating reports will become much more intuitive and simple. To get to Design view, open your Access report and select View → Design View in the Home tab.

Opening the TopReps report in Design view brings up the screen shown in Figure 3-10.

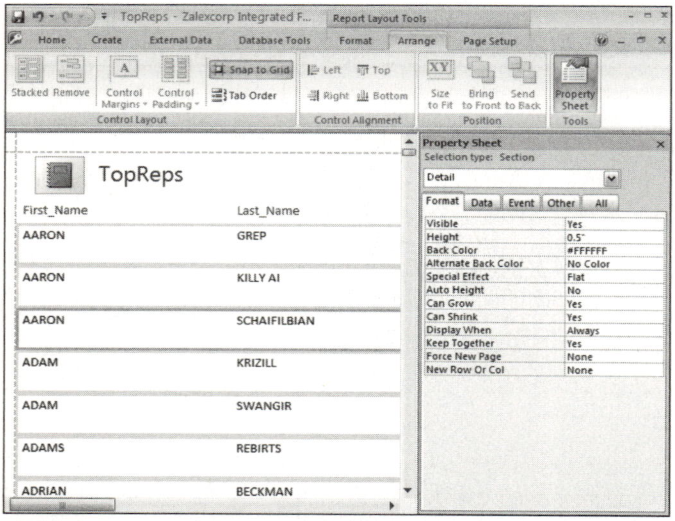

Figure 3-9: You can easily change the properties of your report in Layout view.

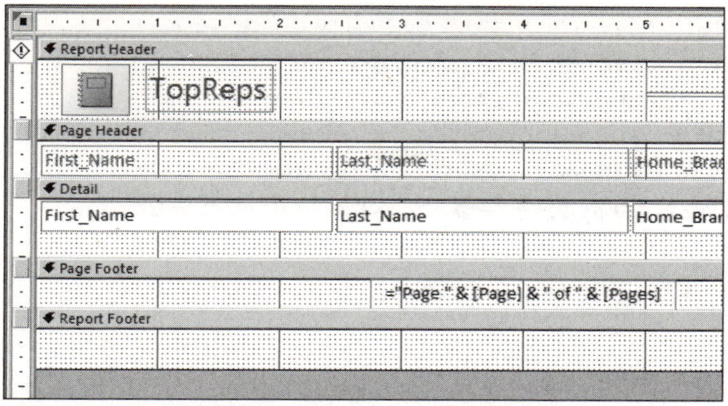

Figure 3-10: The TopReps report in Design view.

Note this report has five distinct sections: Report Header, Page Header, Detail, Page Footer, and Report Footer. These sections are typically the sections you will see when you initially create your reports in Access. The following sections explore what each section is designed to do.

Report Header

The Report Header section typically contains a label that serves as the main title for your report. Just like a header in Word, anything placed in the header section of the Access Design view shows up at the top of your report. As you can see, Access includes an auto logo along with a report title — therefore that logo also shows up at the top of your report. It's important to note that items in the Report Header section need not be simple labels. They can be data driven as well, such as page numbers, the current date, or virtually any other data element.

Page Header

The Page Header section typically contains labels that serve as the heading for each page in your report. Again, items in the Page Header section need not be simple labels. They can be data fields, page numbers, a date indicator, or virtually any other data element.

Although it's not evident in this view, you can have different sub-header types. In each instance the header section gives you a place for data that will repeat only once at the top of each logical section, be it report, page, or grouping. You will explore sub-headers and grouping later in this chapter.

TIP You can hover the cursor over the bottom boundary of any section and the cursor changes to a resizing arrow. Simply drag the bottom boundary up or down and you resize that section of your report. Resizing the sections effectively changes the distance between the sections, allowing you to reduce the white space in your report, expand a section to make room for additional fields, or simply create a bit more space to move around easier while working in a particular section.

Detail

The Detail section houses the actual data of your report. As you can see, each data field in your report is represented by a single text box. You can manipulate the content and formatting of any given field by right-clicking on a field and selecting Properties. This activates the Property Sheet pane, shown in Figure 3-11 on the right. This pane enables you to easily edit and format the chosen field simply by adjusting the properties found here.

Page Footer

The Page Footer section is virtually identical to the Page Header section. The only difference is that labels and data in the footer section come at the end of each page view in the report. Common data elements in the footer include page number, date, and labels. The report shown in Figure 3-10 earlier has a data-driven page number field inserted in the footer section.

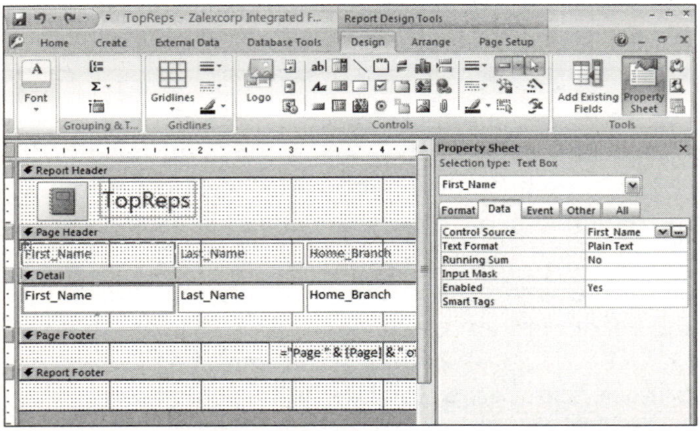

Figure 3-11: Use the Property Sheet pane to adjust the properties of any given field.

ADDING REPORT ELEMENTS TO YOUR HEADERS AND FOOTERS

It's always handy to have your report headers and footers display information about your report, especially page numbering and report dates. Although Access does apply these report elements by default, you may want to manually create these elements or change their format and content.

You can apply these elements using the Insert Page Numbers and Date & Time command buttons found in the Controls group of the Design tab (see Figure 3-12).

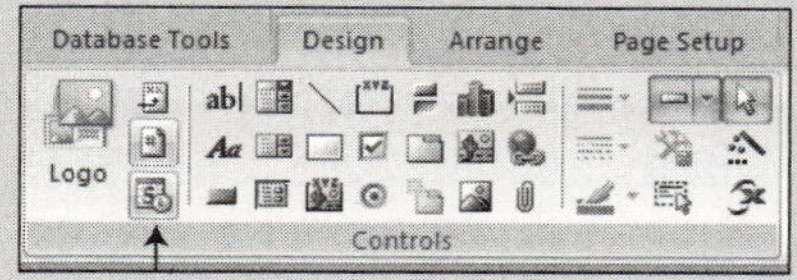

Figure 3-12: You can apply report elements using the Insert Page Numbers and Date & Time command buttons.

Each of these command buttons opens a dialog box that enables you to configure the report element to suit your needs. For example, Figure 3-13 illustrates the Insert Page Numbers dialog box used to configure the format of the report's page numbering.

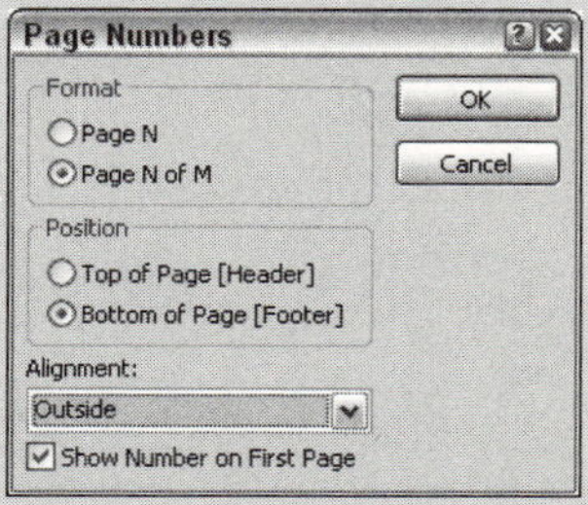

Figure 3-13: The Insert Page Numbers dialog box

Report Footer

The Report Footer section is virtually identical to the Report Header section. The only difference is that labels and data in the footer come at the end of the report. Common data elements in the footer include page number, date, and labels.

Creating and Modifying Grouped Reports

This section explores the power of Access reports by illustrating grouping, sorting, and totaling techniques. You will look at a set of specific example reports, using both the Design and Layout views to complete them.

Grouping

Grouping your report is one of the easiest and most powerful ways to make slick, useful Access reports. Although your TopReps report contains some useful information, grouping the report can tailor it to your target user. Let's assume that your target users will be upper management and branch managers. Each set of users will want to see a rank ordering of service representatives organized by branch.

You can do this by modifying the TopReps report in Layout view. Start by opening the TopReps report in Layout view. Next select the Formatting tab from the ribbon and click the Group and Sort menu item. The Group, Sort, and Total pane show up on the bottom of your screen (see Figure 3-14).

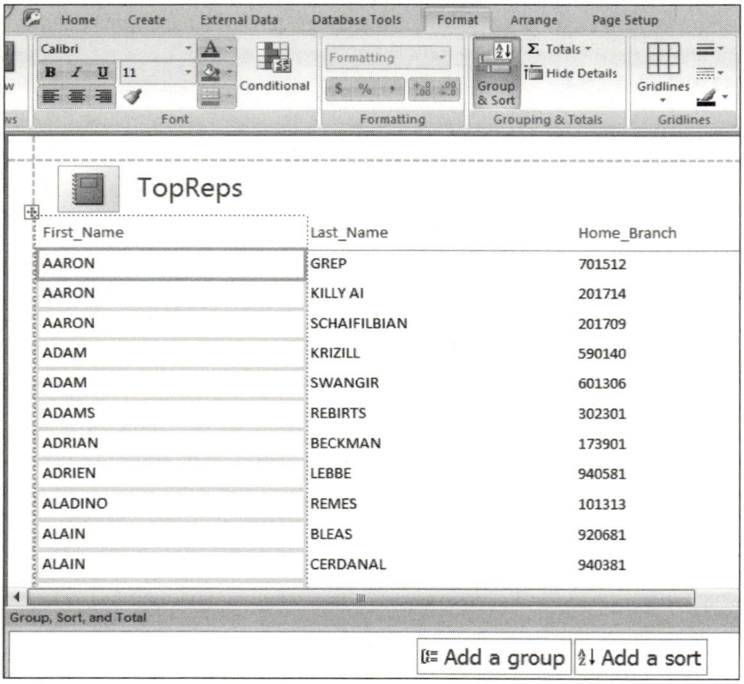

Figure 3-14: The Group, Sort, and Total pane in Layout view

Note that there are two menu items in the Group, Sort, and Total pane —
Add a group and Add a sort. Select the Add a group item. This displays a
drop-down menu asking which field you want to group by (see Figure 3-15).
Select Home_Branch.

At this point, you can switch to Report view to get a better feel for what your
clients will see (see Figure 3-16).

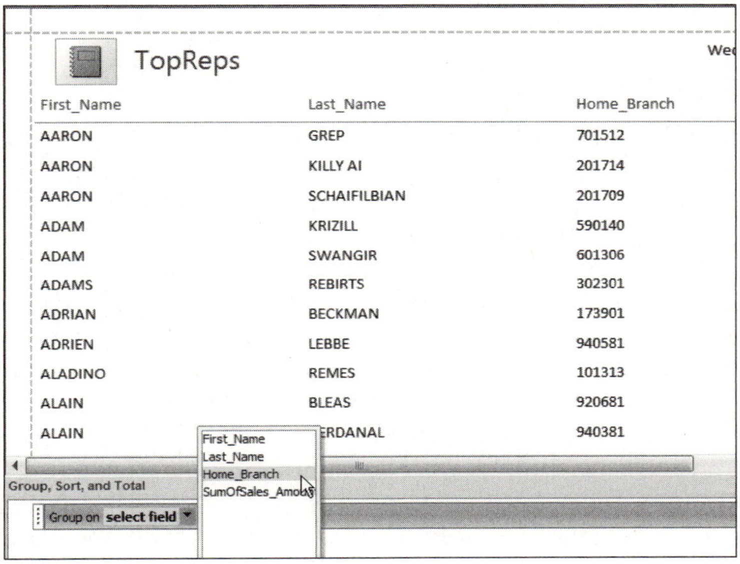

Figure 3-15: You want to group by the Home_Branch field.

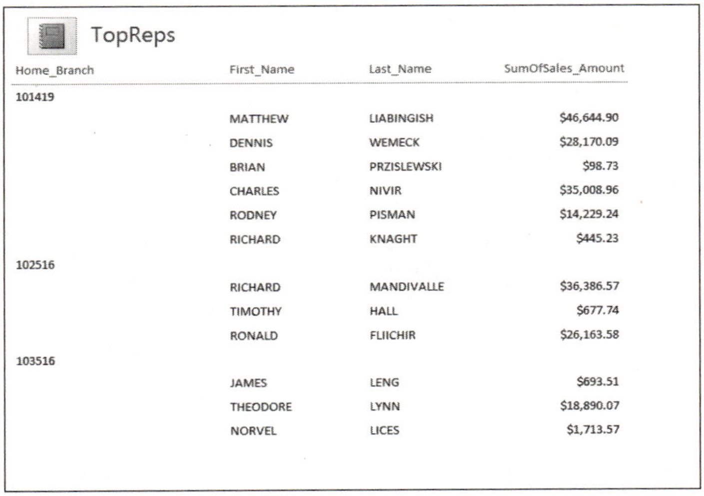

Figure 3-16: Your grouping has been applied.

First, notice how Access moved your grouping field, Home_Branch, to the far left of the report. Also notice that the service rep names and their respective sales amounts appear to be associated with one particular home branch. In addition, that home branch is listed only once instead of repeatedly for each of the branch's service reps. This report is looking better, but we imagine that the branch and upper management might want to see a rank ordering of service reps along with a sales total for each branch. This is where Sorting and Totaling come in.

Sorting and Totaling

Fortunately, the Access Layout view makes sorting and totaling very easy and intuitive. Switch back to Layout view and take a closer look at the Group, Sort, and Total pane. As you can see in Figure 3-17, this pane now shows you the grouping has been applied to this report.

The first line of the Group, Sort, and Total pane tells you that Access is grouping the report first by Home_Branch and sorting Home_Branch in Ascending order (with A on top). The second line is indented slightly. This is how Access displays the sorting and grouping hierarchy within the report. If you want to manipulate anything related to the top group and sort, Home_Branch, then you need to work with the menu items on the top line. For additional grouping or sorting underneath Home_Branch, you would work with the menu items in the second line.

In this example, you want to add a group total for each Home_Branch and sort service reps underneath Home_Branch. Start by sort sales reps according to sales revenue. Select the Add a sort menu item. As you can see in Figure 3-18, this activates a drop-down menu asking you to select the field by which you want to sort. Choose the SumofSales_Amount field.

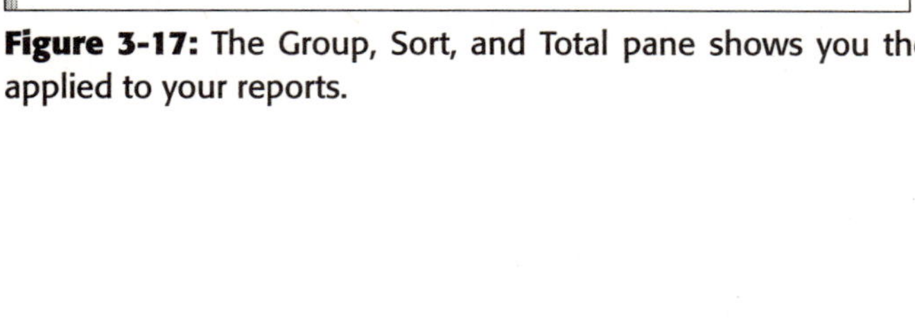

Figure 3-17: The Group, Sort, and Total pane shows you the groupings that have been applied to your reports.

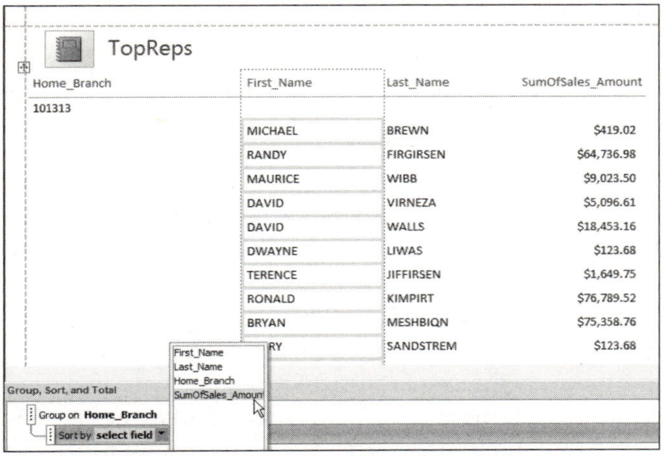

Figure 3-18: Choose the field you want to sort by.

You'll notice that a new line appears in the Group, Sort, and Total pane. This line represents the sorting you just applied. Because the sales amount must be sorted in descending order, you will need to change the sort direction as demonstrated in Figure 3-19.

At this point, the service reps in each home branch should be sorted in descending order by revenue. The final step is to add a sales total to each home branch. That is to say, you want to display a total after each home branch group that represents the sum revenue for all the service reps in that branch.

In Layout view, go to the Group, Sort, and Total pane and select the More drill-down button for the Home_Branch grouping (see Figure 3-20).

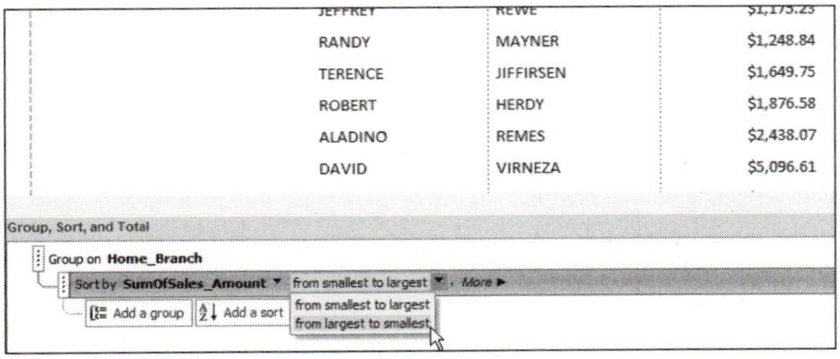

Figure 3-19: Change the sort direction by using the drop-down selectors.

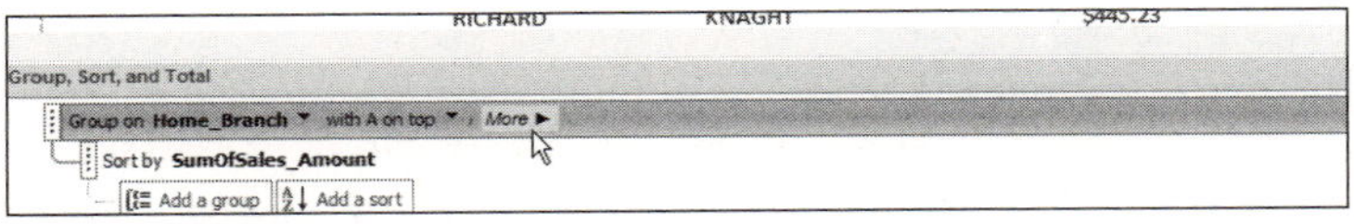

Figure 3-20: Select the More drill-down button.

As promised, you see more options for your grouping. One of these options is the totals option, which is set by default to with no totals. Click on the drop-down selector for the totals option, as demonstrated in Figure 3-21, to activate the Totals dialog box.

The Totals dialog box can be a bit tricky. The top menu item is the Total on selection box. You choose a field to total on from this list. Notice the default selection is the first field in your report, First_Name. If you were to leave the default selection, then your report would total the count of each First_Name in our Home_Branch grouping.

For this exercise, you don't care about the count of service reps in this grouping. You want sales revenue to be totaled. Select the SumofSales_Amount field from the Total on the drop-down menu (see Figure 3-22).

Access now gives you more options in the Type drop-down menu. The default value in the Type drop-down menu is Sum. This is what you need, but keep in mind there are other options for summarizing the grouped sales data from this menu, including average, maximum value, minimum value, and several others.

Keep the Sum selection in the Type drop-down menu and click the Show in group footer check box at the bottom of the list. This tells Access to display the total in the group footer section of the report. At this point, your Totals dialog box should look similar to the one shown in Figure 3-23.

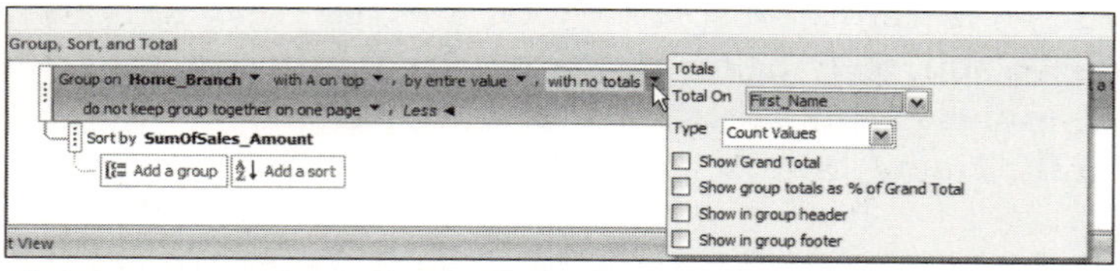

Figure 3-21: Activate the totals context menu.

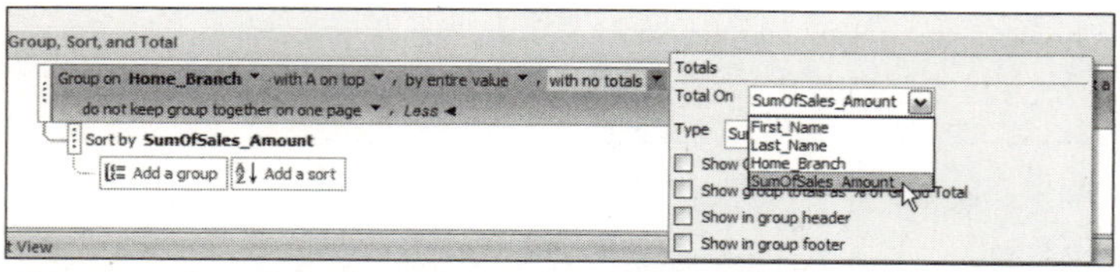

Figure 3-22: Select the field you need to total on.

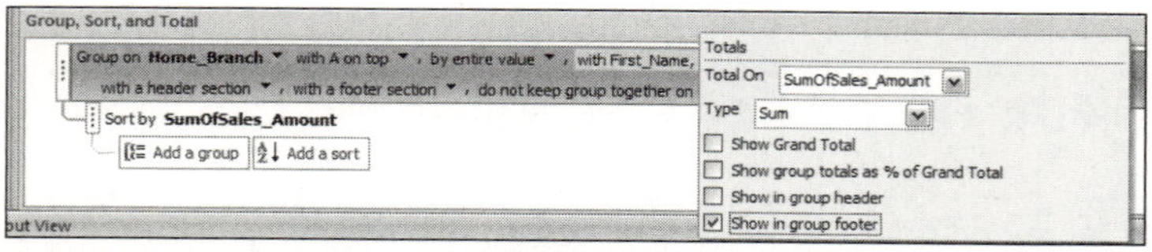

Figure 3-23: Your completed Totals dialog box is set.

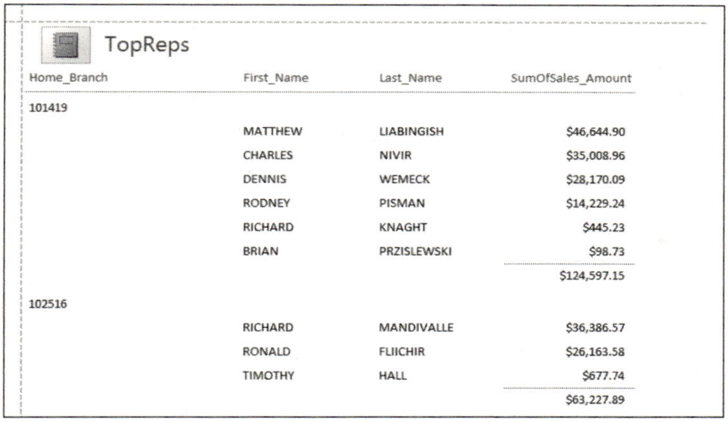

Figure 3-24: Your report now has a level of depth and analysis it did not have before.

Take a moment to save your report, then switch to Report view. Figure 3-24 illustrates what the grouping, sorts, and totals look like for a couple of branches. With a just few clicks of the mouse, you've added a level of depth and analysis to your report, making it much easier read and comprehend.

Customizing Reports with Formatting

This section introduces a series of slick formatting techniques to make your reports more readable and to highlight certain results. Specifically, you will cover page layout techniques and techniques to draw attention to specific report records.

Page Layout Techniques

You will find that you often have to customize your report's layout to ensure that it prints properly and it's easy to read. Let's take a moment to walk through few of these techniques

Solving Page Break Issues

A common problem in grouped, multi-page reports occurs when users go to print. Very often, a page break occurs during the middle of a grouping or even right after a group heading, making it difficult for the user to read. Fortunately, there is an easy fix in the Access Layout view. Before you get to that fix, look at the report shown in Figure 3-25. As you can see, the header for branch 102516 starts at the very end of page one. Page two has all the data for 102516 but no header.

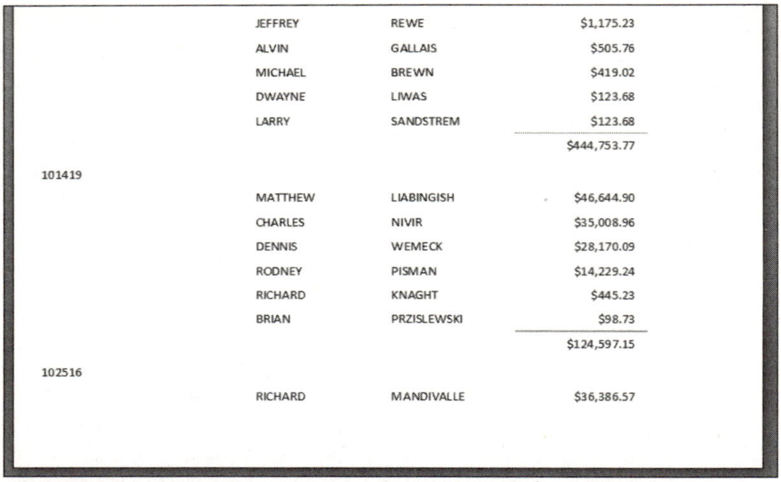
JEFFREY REWE $1,175.23
ALVIN GALLAIS $505.76
MICHAEL BREWN $419.02
DWAYNE LIWAS $123.68
LARRY SANDSTREM $123.68
$444,753.77
101419
MATTHEW LIABINGISH $46,644.90
CHARLES NIVIR $35,008.96
DENNIS WEMECK $28,170.09
RODNEY PISMAN $14,229.24
RICHARD KNAGHT $445.23
BRIAN PRZISLEWSKI $98.73
$124,597.15
102516
RICHARD MANDIVALLE $36,386.57

Figure 3-25: You can see any page break problems in Print Preview.

To avoid this issue in your report, you will need to tell Access to keep your groups together on one page. To do this, open your report in Layout view and expand the sub-menu for the Home_Branch grouping under the Group, Sort, and Total menu. When expanded, you will see an option labeled do not keep group together on one page. Using the drop-down selector, change that option to keep the whole group together on one page (see Figure 3-26).

Examine your report in Print Preview, and you will see that your groupings are no longer split by page breaks.

Multi-Column Report Layout Example

In all prior examples, your reports contained individual columns of data that were repeated only once per report page. What if you wanted a report with two or three columns of the same data on a report page?

To illustrate this concept, you will walk through the creation of a specific type of report called an Alpha Roster.

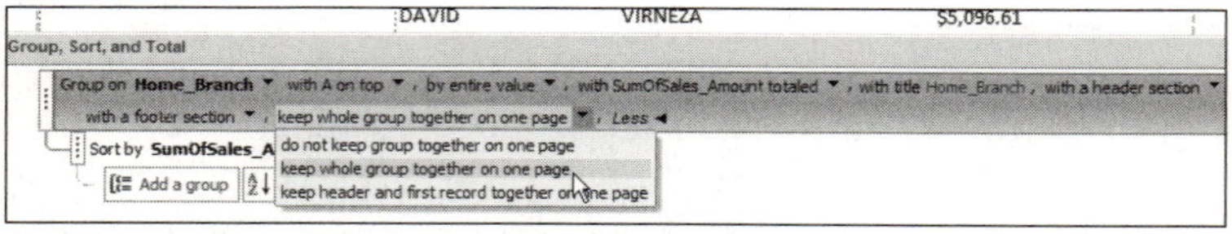
DAVID VIRNEZA $5,096.61
Group, Sort, and Total
Group on Home_Branch with A on top, by entire value, with SumOfSales_Amount totaled, with title Home_Branch, with a header section
with a footer section, keep whole group together on one page, Less
Sort by SumOfSales_A
do not keep group together on one page
keep whole group together on one page
keep header and first record together on one page
Add a group

Figure 3-26: Avoid page break issues by choosing to keep your groups together.

An Alpha Roster is a fancy name for an alphabetically grouped and sorted report, usually for addresses, contact information, or something similar. For this exercise, you will create an Alpha Roster for company employees. The report will be grouped by the first letter of the employee's last name and sorted alphabetically.

Adding a Data Source with the Query Builder

To create this report, go to the Create tab of the Access Ribbon and select Report Design. When in Design view, ensure the Property Sheet pane is activated by right-clicking inside the white area of the report and selecting Properties (you can also select F4 on your keyboard).

Instead of using a predesigned external query, you will create the source for your report on-the-fly using the Query Builder. Make sure the Selection Type drop-down menu in the Property Sheet pane is set to Report. Now select the Data tab and click the ellipsis button (the button with the three dots) next to the Record Source property (see Figure 3-27).

Clicking this button invokes the Query Builder, which you can use just as you if you were building a standard query. At this point, you can create the query shown in Figure 3-28. As you want to make an alphabetical listing of employees, you will choose the most relevant pieces of data for your record source — first and last name, branch number, and job title.

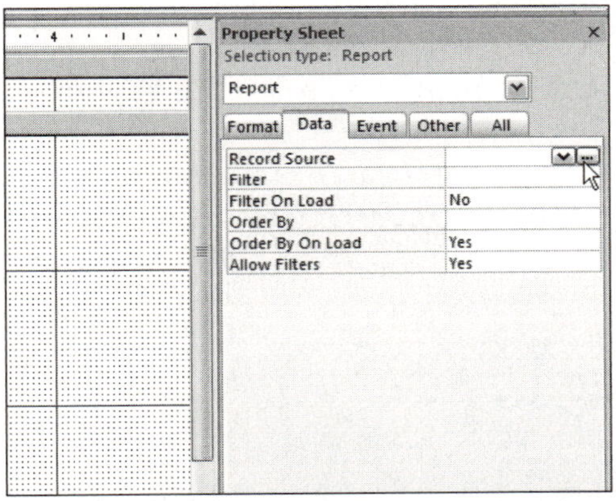

Figure 3-27: Click the ellipsis button to build the data source using the Query Builder.

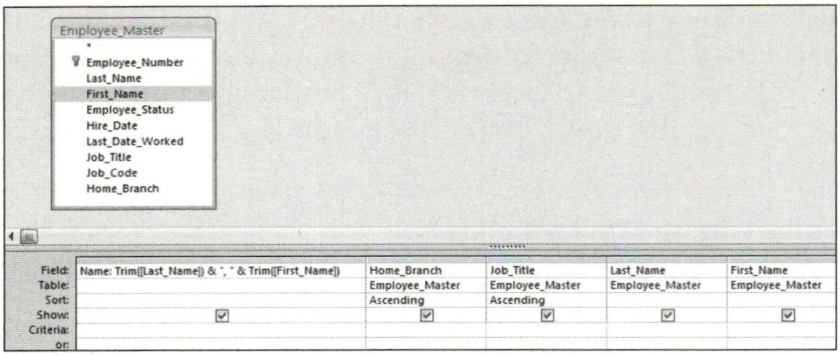

Figure 3-28: Query design for Employee Roster

> **NOTE**   Note the special syntax in the first column of the query. We have
> introduced two neat and simple operations you can easily do in Access. First is
> the TRIM function. This function cuts out all extra blank spaces at the
> beginning or end of a text string. This is useful in working with data that comes
> from a data warehouse or other legacy system as it often has extra spaces
> before or after the text string. The second operation is the ampersand (&) which
> is a quick way of concatenating text strings in Access fields. In effect, the syntax
> combines the Last_Name and First_Name fields into a combine field that looks
> like the following: Last_Name, First_Name.

Now you must save your query to ensure it remains as the report record
source. Click the close button from the Design menu and select the Yes button
when presented with the message box shown in Figure 3-29.

For a quick check, go to the Property Sheet pane and examine the Record-
Source property of your report to make sure it contains your newly created
query.

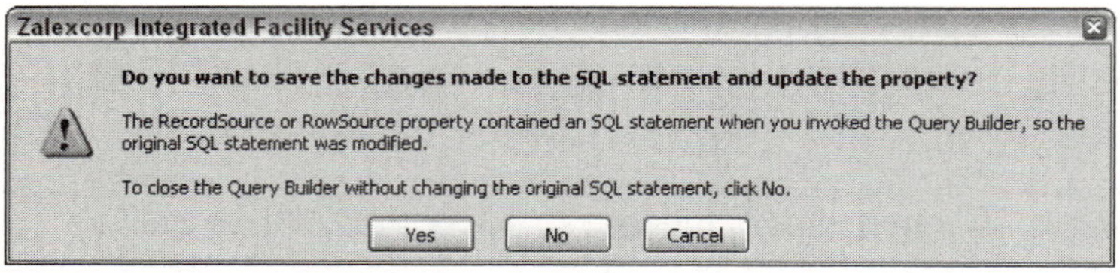

Figure 3-29: Be sure to save your changes by clicking the Yes button when asked to save
your query.

Building the Report in Design View

From the Design tab of the ribbon, click the Add Existing Fields button. This opens the Field List pane. The idea is to drag the fields you want on your report. Drag the fields you need over to the detail section of your report as demonstrated in Figure 3-30.

Now you have the basic data elements for your employee roster. Before you continue, position your data fields and clean up your labels until they look like Figure 3-31.

TIP For quick-and-easy positioning of data and labels, highlight your fields and labels, go to the Arrange tab on the ribbon and select Stacked. Access automatically aligns and distributes your labels and data into a neat block.

Remember that you want your report grouped and sorted alphabetically. So naturally, the next step is to add a grouping. From the Design tab on the ribbon, click the Group and Sort icon. You see the same Group, Sort, and Total menu you saw earlier. From this menu, group on the Name field by clicking the Add Group button and selecting Name.

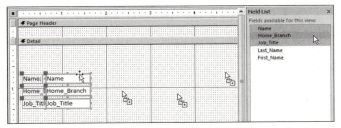

Figure 3-30: Drag the appropriate fields to the Detail area.

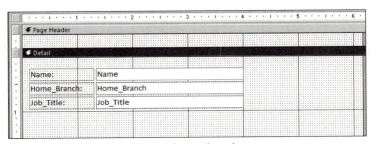

Figure 3-31: Employee Roster in Design view

Next, order your grouping with A on top. Expand the menu by clicking the More button, and select the third drop-down menu with the default value by entire value (see Figure 3-32). This menu gives different options for how to group by the Name field. Select to group by first character of the Name field.

Now you have a grouping that bundles all the employees with the same first letter of their last names. Things are starting to come together now, but you still aren't quite done. You need a field that explicitly shows the report users what grouping (what letter of the alphabet) they are viewing. For this, you must add a field to the group header section.

In the Design tab, click the Text Box control as demonstrated in Figure 3-33.

Place the new Text Box in the group header section of the Name field. (see Figure 3-34).

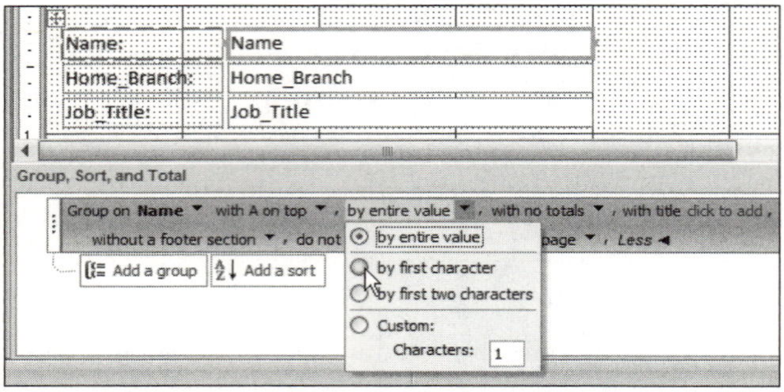

Figure 3-32: Group report by first character

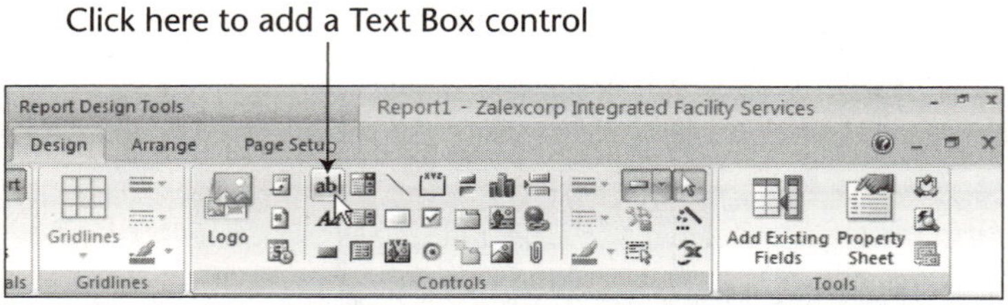

Figure 3-33: Click the Text Box control to add a new Text Box.

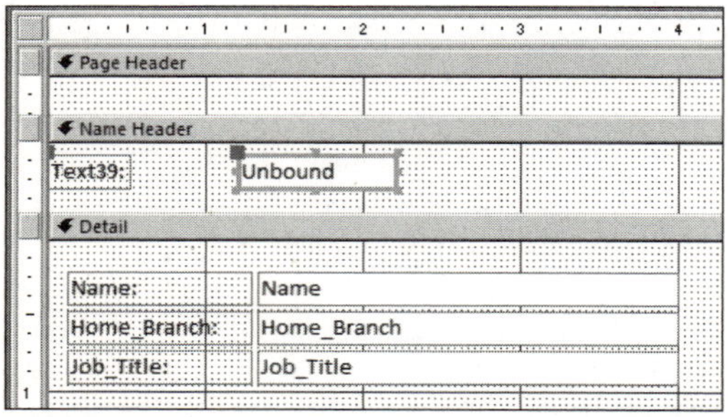

Figure 3-34: Place the Text Box in the header section for the Name field.

Type the following in your new text box:

```
=LEFT([Last_Name],1)
```

The LEFT function parses out the leftmost characters of a text string. It requires one argument, which specifies the number of characters to parse. The preceding code returns the single leftmost character in the Last_Name text string. Now take a moment to look at your report in Report view. At this point, your report should look similar to Figure 3-35.

You are almost done. Switch back to Design view, and give your newly created group header Text Box some formatting that will set it off much better.

Also, you should change the column layout of the report to make better use of our report space. Go to the Page Setup tab from the Access ribbon and select the columns icon. Change the settings for Grid display, Column size, and Column layout so they look like Figure 3-36.

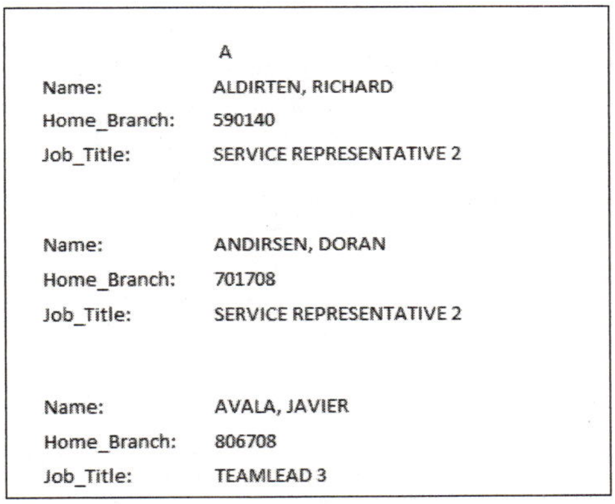

Figure 3-35: Draft of alphabetically sorted Employee Roster

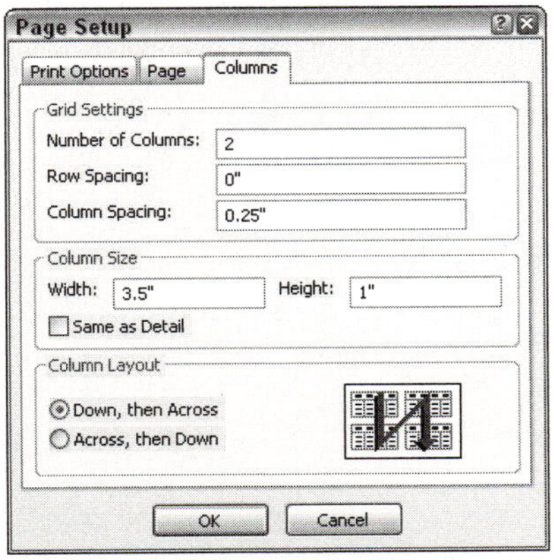

Figure 3-36: Columns menu from Page Setup

The Grid display tells Access that you want two columns per sheet instead of the default, which is one column. You also need to adjust the column width in the Column Size section such that your multiple columns will actually fit on the page. Here the column width is changed to 3.5". Last, you need to tell Access that the data should be organized first by going down the page and then starting another column when the end of the page is reached. At this point, you can switch to Print Preview to have a look at your final report (see Figure 3-37).

You now have a useful and nicely formatted report. For practice, modify this report to group employees by branch number and then create another report where they are grouped by job title. Once you create a master grouped report like this, it is very quick and easy to create additional reports with different groupings.

Formatting Techniques

Now let's examine a few other nifty formatting options. First, we will cover some formatting tips to make your reports easier to read. Then we will explore how to highlight specific results using conditional formatting in reports.

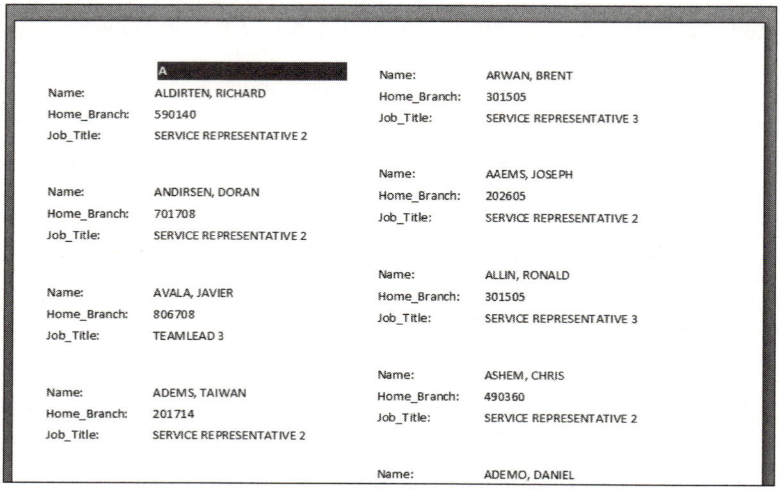

Figure 3-37: Final Employee Roster report in Print Preview mode

Formatting to Make Reports More Readable

Often on list reports like your TopReps report, it's easier on the user's eyes to have rows with alternating background colors. That way, reading across a row is not so problematic. In addition, numbering the service reps within the group could be helpful so that the user can see at a glance the total service reps by branch and the rank order of a particular rep. In older versions of Access, this could be accomplished only with some non-intuitive text box formatting. For 2007, Microsoft made many of these pieces of functionality much more accessible.

Let's start with alternating background colors on your group details. To apply alternating background colors, open the TopReps report in Layout view and activate the Property Sheet pane. In the Property Sheet pane, select Detail from the Selection Type drop-down menu. At this point, all the detail in your report should be highlighted.

Now select the Format tab and find the Alternate Back Color property. There, you use the drop-down selector to choose the Alternate Row item as demonstrated in Figure 3-38.

If you examine the report now, you'll see some nice subtle shading that off-sets every other row in the group detail section.

To add a running count for each group, switch over to Design view. Go to the Design tab and click on the Text Box control button (Figure 3-33 demonstrates how). Place the new Text Box in the detail section of your report (see Figure 3-39).

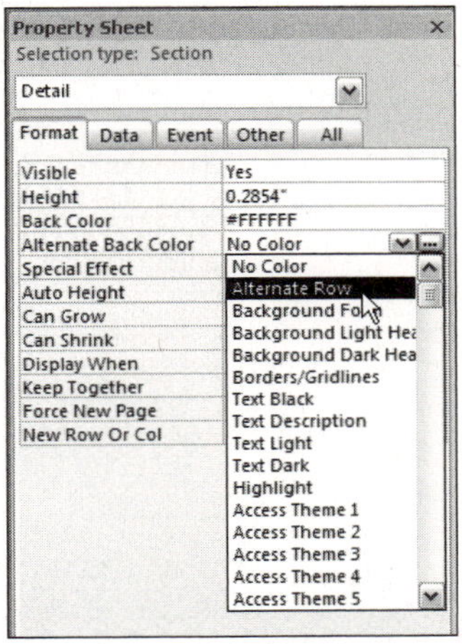

Figure 3-38: Selecting alternating background color by row

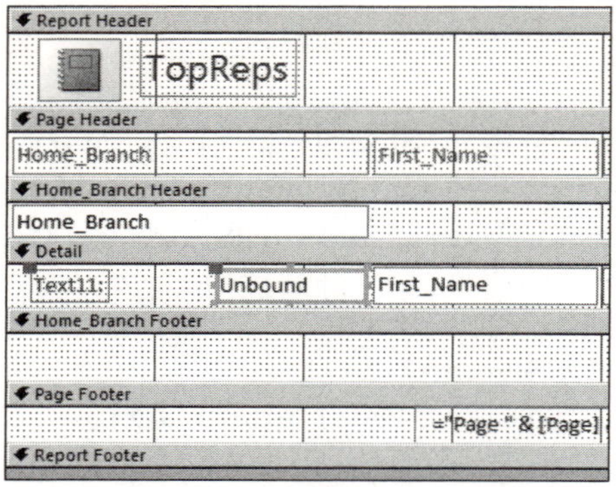

Figure 3-39: Adding a Text Box control to the detail section

Now you must modify the properties of your newly created Text Box. Click on the new Text Box, go to the Property Sheet pane, and select the Data tab. In the Control Source property, enter **=1**. Next, set the Running Sum property to Over Group. Figure 3-40 illustrates what the Property Sheet pane should look like after these changes are made.

In essence, you've told Access that the value of this text box control will be 1. However, you have also told Access to change the property of this text box such that it will contain a running count of each record in the group. Clean up the formatting a bit by removing the label from your text box, changing your title, and changing the column labels so they are a bit more intelligible. Your final report will look similar to the one shown in Figure 3-41.

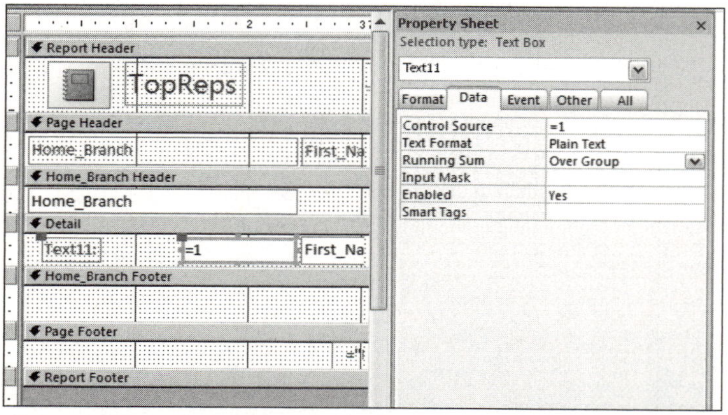

Figure 3-40: Use the Property Sheet pane to create a running count in the detail of your report.

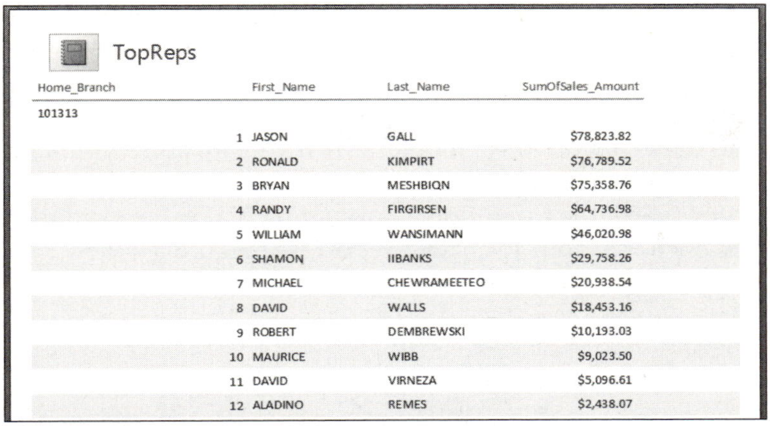

Home_Branch		First_Name	Last_Name	SumOfSales_Amount
101313				
	1	JASON	GALL	$78,823.82
	2	RONALD	KIMPIRT	$76,789.52
	3	BRYAN	MESHBIQN	$75,358.76
	4	RANDY	FIRGIRSEN	$64,736.98
	5	WILLIAM	WANSIMANN	$46,020.98
	6	SHAMON	IIBANKS	$29,758.26
	7	MICHAEL	CHEWRAMEETEO	$20,938.54
	8	DAVID	WALLS	$18,453.16
	9	ROBERT	DEMBREWSKI	$10,193.03
	10	MAURICE	WIBB	$9,023.50
	11	DAVID	VIRNEZA	$5,096.61
	12	ALADINO	REMES	$2,438.07

Figure 3-41: Final TopReps report in Report view

Formatting to Highlight Specific Results

Quite often, you will want to highlight specific records in your report to draw the users' attention. For example, you may want to highlight those service reps that fall in the top or bottom 10 percent of all service reps. How would you do that if your service reps are grouped and sorted by branch? Access's conditional formatting functionality makes this easy.

Open your TopReps report in Design view and select SumofSales_Amount in the Detail section of the report. Next, select the Conditional button found in the Design tab under the Font group. This activates the Conditional Formatting dialog box shown in Figure 3-42.

The idea here is to add certain conditions that if met, will get a certain formatting. Suppose that in this scenario, you want to highlight any Sales_Amount field that is above $26,000 or below $200.

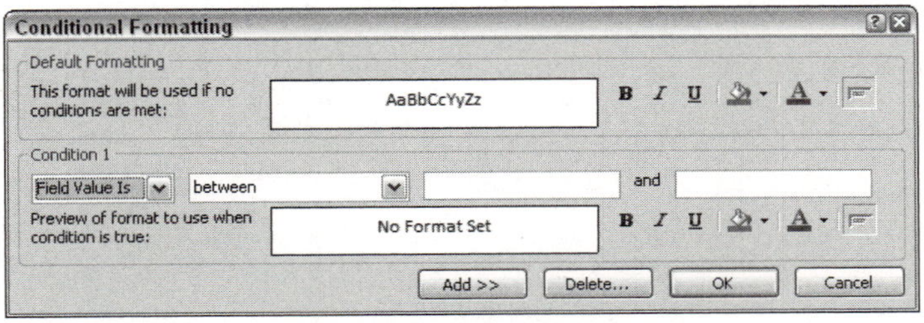

Figure 3-42: The Conditional Formatting dialog box

In the first condition, set the operator to greater than and type the value **$26,000**. Then set the format to a green background and the font to white and bold. Click the Add button to add a second condition. In the second condition, set the operator to less than and type the value **$200**. Then set the format to a red background and the font to white and bold. When you are done, your dialog box should look similar to Figure 3-43.

Click the OK button to exit the Conditional Formatting dialog box, and then switch to Print Preview to see your formatted report (see Figure 3-44).

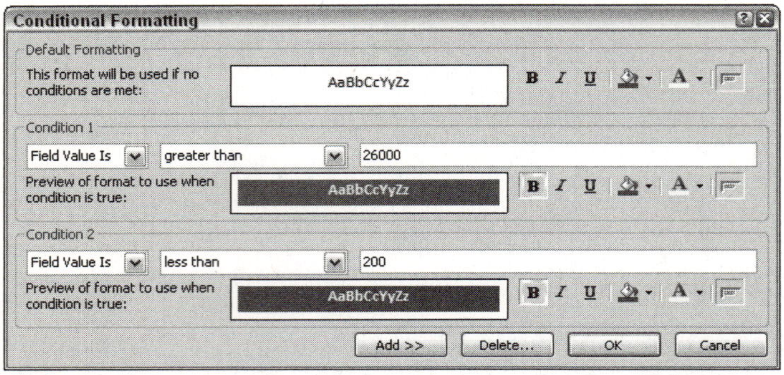

Figure 3-43: You are highlighting any Sales_Amount field that is above $26,000 or below $200.

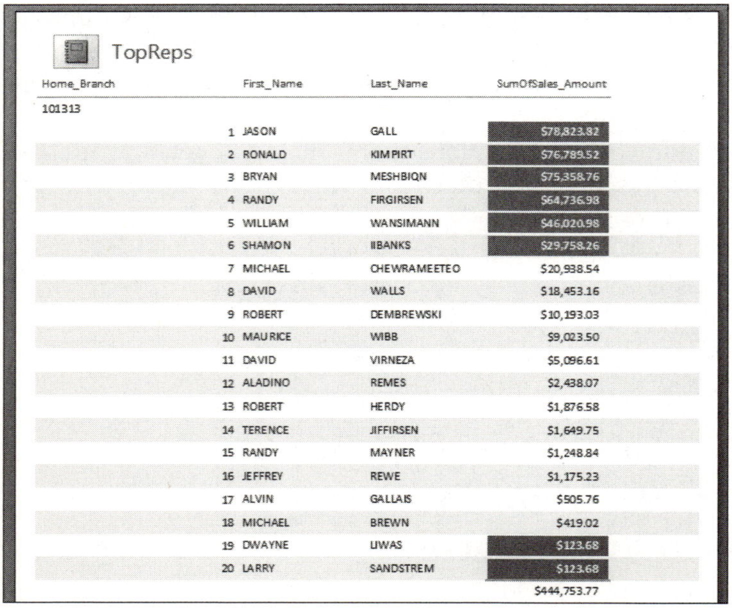

Figure 3-44: Conditionally formatted TopReps report in Print Preview

Creating an Individualized Customer Letter

In this section, you pull together what you have learned in this chapter to produce a form letter that is tailored to each customer. This is similar to using mail merge in Microsoft Word, only there is no need to launch Word here. This is an exercise easily completed with the power of Access and Access reports.

Developing the Report Data Feed

In this walk-through, you will send a thank-you letter to your customer base for their patronage of your company. You also need to make the letter a bit individualized by addressing the customer by name and by including their sales history over the past six months.

Obviously, this means you need customer name, address, and contact information. You will also need transaction-level detail such as product description and sales amount. This enables you to include each customer's sales history in his or her own personalized form letter. When you have an idea of what fields you may need in your letter, you can start designing your source query. Create the query you see in Figure 3-45.

The CustomerMaster table houses customer name, address, and contact information. The TransactionMaster table contains the sales detail needed, specifically the product description, the date of service, and the sales amount on each date of service. ProductMaster contains easy-to-read product descriptions. Note that you are aggregating and summing the records by the Sales_Amount field. This enables you to summarize your data by Service Date. Save your query and name it MailMergeFeed. Close your query.

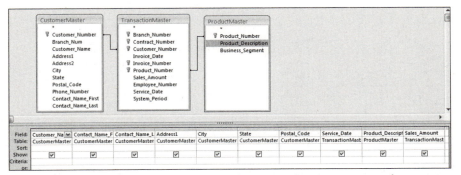

Figure 3-45: Create this query to serve as the source for your customer letter.

> **NOTE** It's generally a good idea to test the query you will use as the source for your reports and customer letters. This enables you to see exactly what results are being returned, giving you the opportunity to adjust for errors in the query.

Initial Design of the Report

Create a new report in Design view by clicking Report Design in the Create tab of the Access ribbon. Activate the Property Sheet pane and select Region in the Selection Type drop-down menu. Next, click the Data tab and select the MailMergeFeed query you just created from the drop-down list (see Figure 3-46).

Now click the Add Existing Fields command button under the Design tab. Add all fields to the report's Detail section as shown in Figure 3-47.

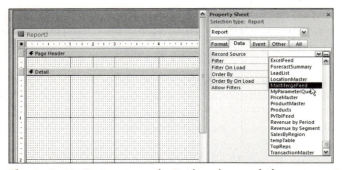

Figure 3-46: Start a report in Design view and choose your MailMergeFeed query as the source.

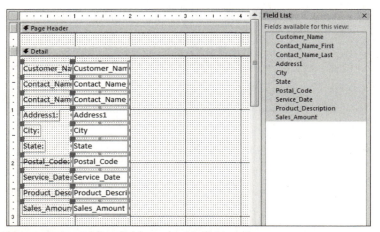

Figure 3-47: Adding fields to the MailMerge Report

At this point, you have the beginnings of your individualized customer letters. Of course, you will need some sort of grouping on this report to individualize it by customer. Since each letter will be specific to one customer name and address, it's natural that you would add a Customer_Name grouping.

Take a moment to think a bit about what information should go into the group header and what should go into the group detail. As the group header information will be repeated for every change in grouping, it makes sense that you would want your customer name and address information in that section. The detail section, then, would house customer-specific transaction information. So first, create a grouping on the Customer_Name field. Your report should look similar to Figure 3-48.

Now move all information that uniquely identifies that customer into the newly created Customer_Name group header. In addition, delete the default data labels that Access added and position the address information so it looks suspiciously like the top of a letter (see Figure 3-49).

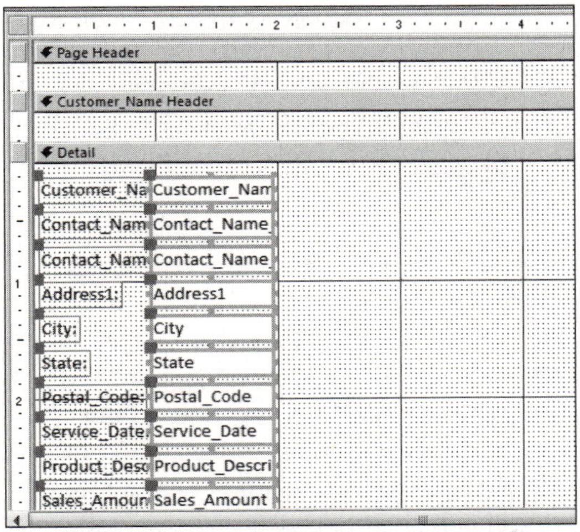

Figure 3-48: Add a Customer_Name group to your report.

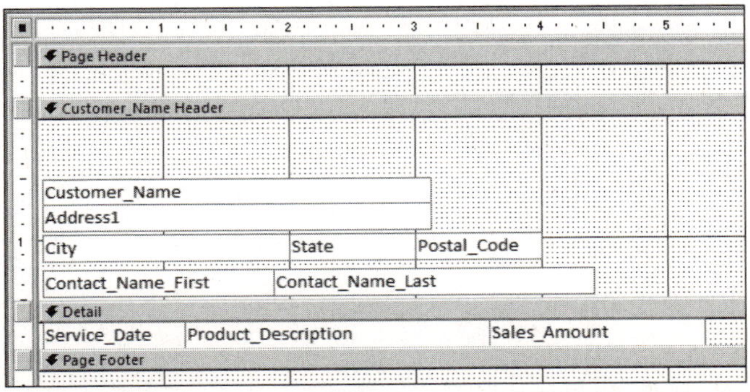

Figure 3-49: Position your fields to make it look more like a standard letter.

If you were to look at this report in Report view, you would see that your letter is starting to shape up, but the address looks funny. This is because you have three separate fields (City, State, and Postal_Code) that should be brought together to make a clean address line. To fix this problem, add a new Text Box control from the Control group under the Design tab. Then enter the following syntax to your newly added Text Box:

```
=Trim([City]) & ", " & Trim([State]) & "   " & [Postal_Code]
```

Here, you are joining the three fields using ampersand (&) operators. Notice that you are also adding a comma and a few spaces wrapped in quotes. This ensures your address is formed in the widely accepted City, State, and Postal-Code format. You are also using the `Trim` function to remove any excess spaces. Once you have this Text Box built, you can delete the City, State, and PostalCode fields.

Add another Text Box control and this time, enter the following syntax:

```
="Attn: " & Trim([Contact_Name_First]) & " " & Trim([Contact_Name_Last])
```

This joins the first name field and the last name field preceded with the string *Attn:* (followed by a space). Again, after you have created this Text Box, you can delete the Contact_Name_First and Contact_Name_Last fields. At this point, your report should look similar to Figure 3-50.

NOTE You may be wondering why you would not simply use an existing field to merge City, State, and Postal_Code. Well, if you try to add functions to a control that has been added with the Add existing fields menu, you will get an "Invalid control source" or "Circular reference" error. The problem is that Access uses the field name as the name of the control. So if you have a field named LastName, then the Add existing fields command will create a text box named LastName. If you then use the LastName field in a function within this text box, you get an ambiguous reference. If you need to create a custom field that contains a function, it's generally easiest to add a new Text Box control from the Control group under the Design tab. That way you can ensure your custom report functions are error free.

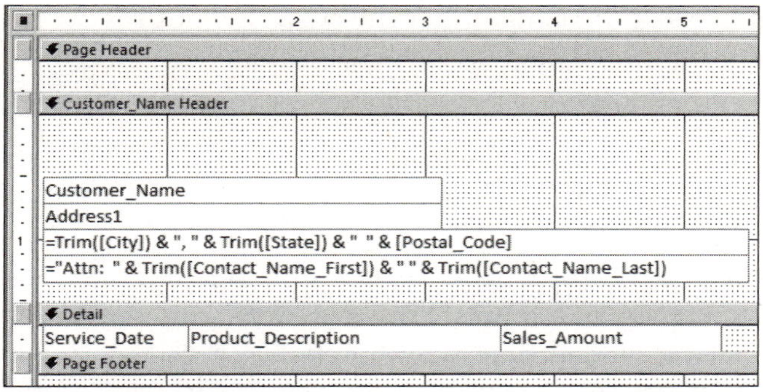

Figure 3-50: You have added your own custom fields to clean up the address block.

Your next steps involve a bit of formatting to get this report looking more like a letter.

1. Start by working on your detail section first.

   a. Position Service_Date, Product_Description, and SumofSales_Amount so they are on one line and just touching each other. Make sure you give each field enough horizontal space so the data isn't cut off in the Report view.

   b. Select each field, and go to the Formatting tab of the properties window. Select Solid from the Border Style line. This gives the transaction detail a table-like look.

   c. Reposition the fields and resize the detail section so the bottom and top are just even with the report fields. This turns your transaction data into a contiguous table if there are multiple lines.

2. Now turn your attention to the Customer_Name header section of the report. The goal is to make the report look more like a letter, so do the following:

   a. Stretch out the vertical spacing of the Customer_Name header and position the address and contact information near the middle.

   b. Position the customer address and contact information fields so they are aligned with one another on the left and have no vertical space between them.

   c. Add some labels to the very bottom of the group header section for Service_Date, Product_Description, and SumofSales_Amount. Be sure to make the labels clear and descriptive. Position the labels so they are horizontally aligned with the respective data in the detail section and so the bottom label edge is just touching the bottom of the group header boundary. Add some background formatting to the labels to set them off from the detail.

    d. Add a Text Box control and a label under the customer address information so you can put some text that individually addresses your customer. At this point, your report should look similar to Figure 3-51.

3. You can't have a letter without a signature section, and you can't have a signature section without a Group footer. Let's add that now.

    a. Select the Group and Sort button from the Design tab to open the Group, Sort, and Total Menu. Expand the Company_Name menu and change without a footer section to with a footer section as shown in Figure 3-52.

    b. Expand the footer section until it's about the same vertical height as the group header section. Add some text for a proper sign-off and some spacing for a signature. Figure 3.53 gives you an idea of some of the information you may want to include.

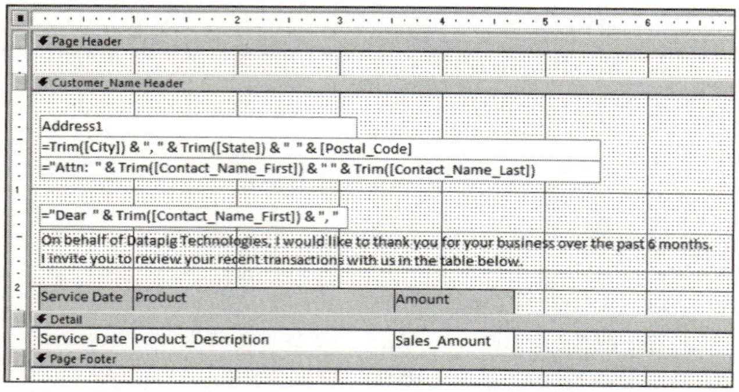

Figure 3-51: Making the group header section look like a letter

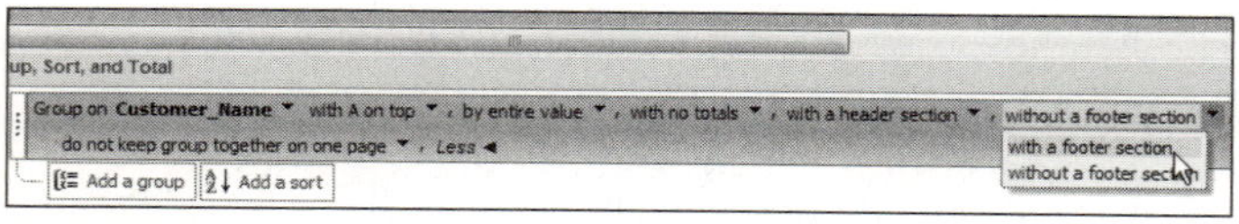

Figure 3-52: Add a Company_Name group footer section

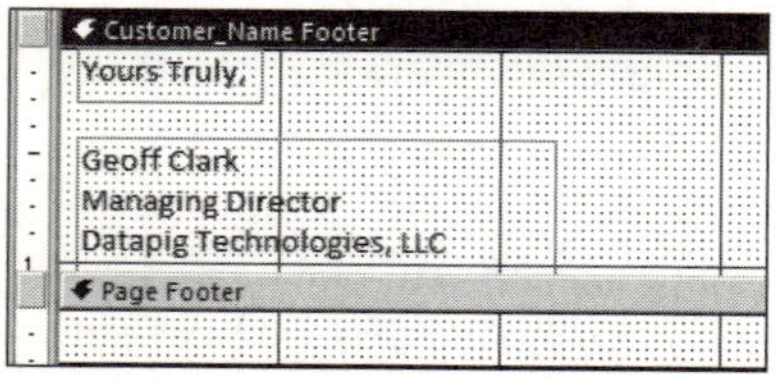

Figure 3-53: Adding some signature information

As you can see in Report view, your letter is starting to look like a professional document. Let's add a few finishing touches to make our letter really slick.

Adding Finishing Touches for a Professional Look

In this last section, you add a few finishing touches that will give your letter a more professional look and feel.

First you can add a logo to create a company letterhead look and feel. You can use your company logo or any graphic you happen to have. Inserting the logo is as simple as selecting the Logo command button from the Control group of the Design tab, browsing for your file, and selecting Open when you've found it. Access 2007 supports all manner of graphics files, so it doesn't matter whether your image is a JPEG, BMP, PNG, or GIF file. Go ahead and add a logo using any image you may have and place it in the top-right section of the Customer_Name header section.

You can also add a personal signature to your letter. With a scanner or even an electronic fax account (simply fax yourself a page with your signature on it) you can easily get a graphics file of your signature. In your favorite graphics editor, crop the signature to just the image you need and save it as an image file. Now insert the image of your signature right after your name using the Image command button from the Controls group under the Design tab. Be sure to resize the image if you need to.

You can add a date field at the top of your letter by inserting a Date and Time control from the Control group of the Design tab (refer to Figure 3-12). That way your letter is automatically updated with the current date, and you won't need to worry about changing it if you mail it at a later date.

Finally, to prevent your letters from running together when you print them, activate the Group, Sort, and Total menu and verify that the option keep whole group together on one page is selected for your Customer_Name grouping. Also, you will need to force a new page after every customer. To do this, simply right-click anywhere inside the Customer_Name footer section (where you put your signature info) and select Properties. This activates the Property Sheet pane. Select the Format tab and change the Force New Page property to read After Section as shown in Figure 3-54.

You're done! Switch to Print Preview to see your professional-looking letters (see Figure 3-55). At this point, you can print and mail these letters to your customers, or you can save this template and customize it for other letters you might need to send — at a fraction of the effort.

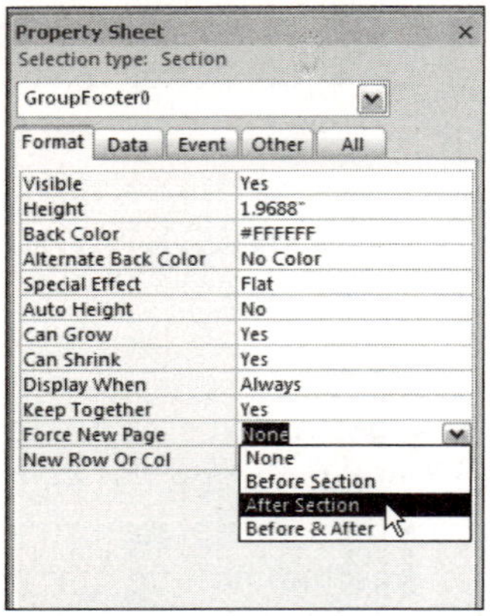

Figure 3-54: Forcing a new page prevents your letters from running together.

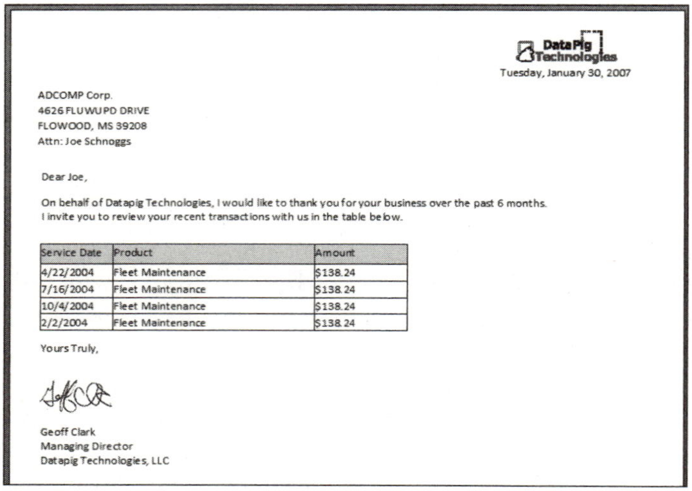

Tuesday, January 30, 2007

ADCOMP Corp.
4626 FLUWUPD DRIVE
FLOWOOD, MS 39208
Attn: Joe Schnoggs

Dear Joe,

On behalf of Datapig Technologies, I would like to thank you for your business over the past 6 months.
I invite you to review your recent transactions with us in the table below.

Service Date	Product	Amount
4/22/2004	Fleet Maintenance	$138.24
7/16/2004	Fleet Maintenance	$138.24
10/4/2004	Fleet Maintenance	$138.24
2/2/2004	Fleet Maintenance	$138.24

Yours Truly,

Geoff Clark
Managing Director
Datapig Technologies, LLC

Figure 3-55: Your customized letter

Summary

Access reports enable you to build professional looking reports from the data in your Access database. You can use both tables and queries as the source for your Access reports. With Access reports, you can create PDF-style reporting, complete with grouping, sorting, and conditional formatting. You can also use your Excel data to easily create Alpha Rosters, invoices, or data-driven custom letters. In fact, the convenience and productivity improvements you can gain from Access reports are only limited by your creativity and initiative!

CHAPTER 4

Using PivotTables and PivotCharts in Access

In this chapter, you will discover that you can apply your knowledge of Excel PivotTables to Access, creating both PivotTable and PivotChart analyses. You will learn how to leverage these powerful tools to change the way you analyze your Access data and the way you create your Excel exports.

TIP This chapter focuses on using the power of PivotTables and PivotCharts in Access. We assume that you are familiar with both the mechanics and the benefits of using PivotTables and PivotCharts in Excel. If you are new to PivotTables altogether, consider picking up *Pivot Table Data Crunching for Microsoft Office Excel 2007* by Bill Jelen, Michael Alexander (ISBN: 978-0-7897-3601-7).

Working with PivotTables in Access

A PivotTable is one of the most robust analytical tools found in Excel. With a PivotTable, you can group, summarize, and perform a wide variety of calculations in a fraction of the time it takes by hand. The most impressive functionality of a PivotTable is the ability to interactively change its content, shape data, and alter its overall utility. You can drag and drop fields, dynamically change your perspective, recalculate totals to fit the current view, and interactively drill down to the detail records.

If PivotTables are your passion and the reason you use Excel, then you had better lean in close as we tell you a secret. You have the power of PivotTables at your fingertips right there in your Access database. That's right. Access comes with its own version of the PivotTable, allowing you to customize your analysis on-the-fly without re-writing your queries or turning to code.

PivotTables in Access?

For years, PivotTables could only be found in Excel. The closest equivalent to this functionality in pre-2000 versions of Access was the traditional Crosstab query, which didn't come close to the analytical power of PivotTables. The first attempts at an Access PivotTable came with Access 2000 where users had the ability to embed an Excel PivotTable report inside of a form. Unfortunately, this feature was a bit clunky and left users with an interface that felt clumsy at best. However, Access 2000 also introduced a promising new technology in the form of Office Web Components. Office Web Components allowed users to create interactive web pages with functionality normally found only in Excel. One of these components was the PivotTable Component. Although this component did expose PivotTable functionality to Access, the fact that it was limited for use only on Data Access Pages (ASP-and HTML-based web pages), made it an impractical tool for day-to-day data analysis.

With the release of Office XP, Microsoft gave Access users the ability to use the PivotTable and PivotChart components in both the Query and Form environments. This finally allowed for practical data analysis using PivotTables in Access. Alas, this functionality remained relatively untouched by many users, as it was relatively difficult to find in previous versions.

In Access 2007, the PivotTable and PivotChart components still exist and have been brought to the forefront. So the only question for you is, why should you get excited about using PivotTables in Access?

From a data analysis point of view, PivotTables and PivotCharts are some of the most powerful data-crunching tools found in Access today. Consider these capabilities:

- You can create multi-dimensional analyses that far surpass the limitations of traditional Crosstab queries.
- You can interactively change your analysis without re-writing your query.
- You can dynamically sort, filter, group, and add custom calculations with a few clicks of the mouse.
- You have drill-down capabilities that enable you to collapse and expand analytical details without writing code.
- You can perform more of your analysis in Access instead of spending time exporting raw data back and forth to Excel.

The Anatomy of a PivotTable

Figure 4-1 shows an empty PivotTable. As you can see a PivotTable is comprised of four areas. Because how you choose to utilize these areas defines both the utility and the appearance of your PivotTable, it's important to understand the functionality of each area.

The Totals and Detail Area

The Totals and Detail Area, highlighted in Figure 4-2, is the area that calculates and supplies the details for your report. You can recognize this area by the phrase Drop Totals or Detail Fields Here. This area tends to be confusing for first time users because it has a dual role. First, it displays aggregate totals such as Sum of Revenue, Count of Units, and Average of Price. Second, it stores detailed row data that is exposed upon expansion of Row and Column fields.

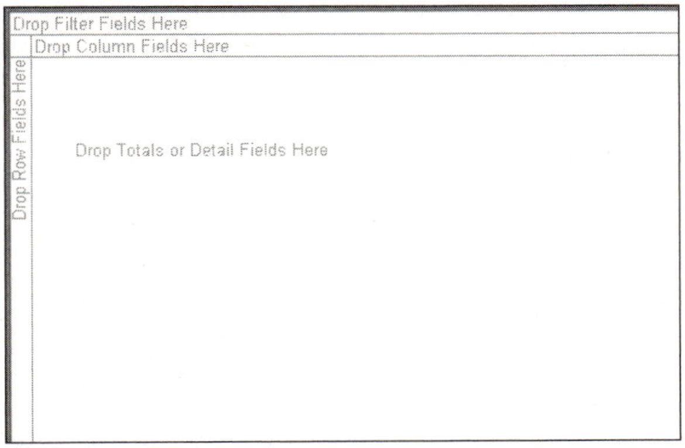

Figure 4-1: An empty PivotTable in Access

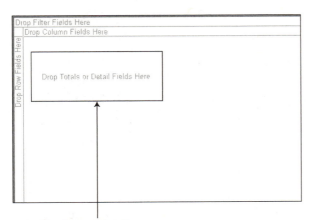

Totals and detail area

Figure 4-2: The Totals and Detail area calculates fields and stores record details.

The Row Area

The Row Area, highlighted in Figure 4-3, creates the headings down the left side of the PivotTable. You can recognize this area by the phrase Drop Row Fields Here. Dropping a field into the Row Area displays each unique value in that field down the left side of the PivotTable. The types of data fields that you would drop here would be things you would want to group and categorize (for example, locations, customer names, and products).

The Column Area

The Column Area, highlighted in Figure 4-4, makes up the headings that span across the top of the PivotTable. You can recognize this area by the phrase Drop Column Fields Here. Dropping a field into the Column Area will display each unique value in the field in a column-oriented perspective. The Column Area is ideal for showing trending over time. Some examples of fields you would drop here would be Months, Periods, and Years.

Row area

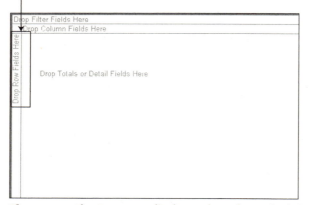

Figure 4-3: The Row area displays values down the left side of the PivotTable.

Column area

Figure 4-4: The Column area displays values across the top of the PivotTable.

The Filter Area

The Filter Area, highlighted in Figure 4-5, allows for dynamic filtering of your PivotTable based on a value in a field. You can recognize this area by the phrase Drop Filter Fields Here. The fields dropped here are things you would want to isolate and focus on, such as locations, employee names, and products.

Creating a Basic PivotTable

Start by building the query you see in Figure 4-6, and then go to the Design tab and select View → PivotTable View.

At this point, you see an empty PivotTable, shown in Figure 4-7 and a list of fields that are in your dataset.

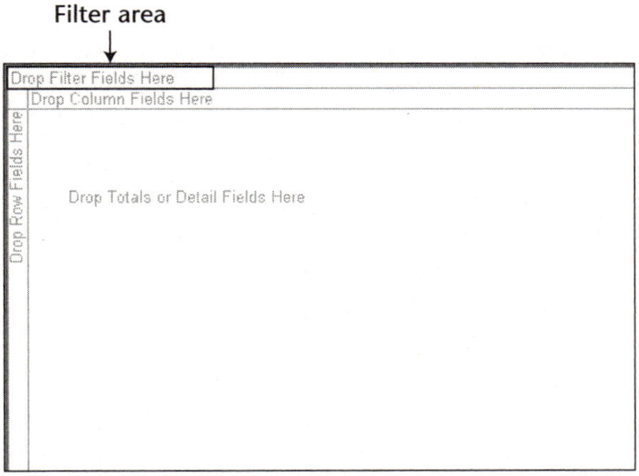

Filter area

| Drop Filter Fields Here |
| Drop Column Fields Here |

Drop Row Fields Here

Drop Totals or Detail Fields Here

Figure 4-5: The Filter area allows you to filter your PivotTable.

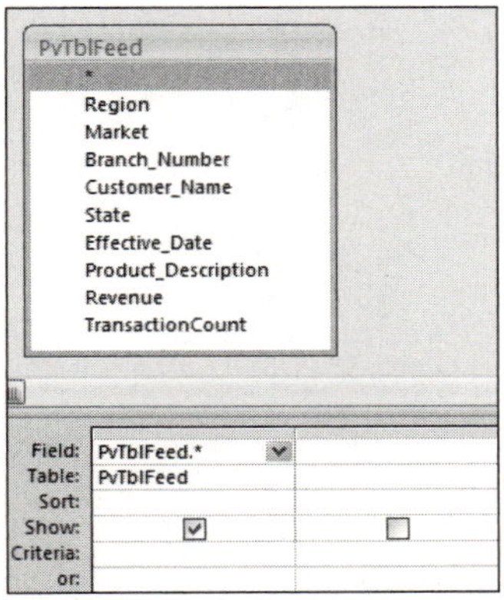

PvTblFeed

Region
Market
Branch_Number
Customer_Name
State
Effective_Date
Product_Description
Revenue
TransactionCount

Field:	PvTblFeed.*	
Table:	PvTblFeed	
Sort:		
Show:	☑	☐
Criteria:		
or:		

Figure 4-6: Build your query and then switch to PivotTable view.

Figure 4-7: Use the field list to build your PivotTable.

The idea is to drag the fields you need into the PivotTable's drop areas. How do you know which field goes where? To answer this question, consider two things: what are you measuring, and how do you want it presented. The answer to the first question will tell you which fields in your data source you will need to work with, and the answer to the second question will tell you where to place the fields. For example, if you want to measure the amount of revenue by region, you automatically know that you will need to work with the Revenue field and the Region field. In addition, you want regions to go down the left side of the report and revenues to be calculated for each region. Therefore, you know that the Region field will go into the Row area, whereas the revenue field will go into the Detail area.

Now that you know what you need, start by selecting the Region field from your field list and drag it to the Row area as shown in Figure 4-8.

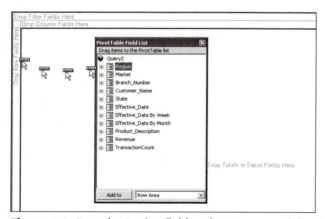

Figure 4-8: Drag the Region field to the Row area of the PivotTable.

TIP If you accidently close out your PivotTable field list, simply right-click inside the PivotTable and select Field List to reactivate it.

Next, select the Revenue field, then select Data Area from the drop-down list box at the bottom of the PivotTable field list as shown in Figure 4-9. Click the Add To button.

NOTE Why not just drag the Revenue field to the Detail Area? The reason is that the PivotTable Web Component requires that you view detail data before you add totals. So if you simply drag the Revenue field to the data area, the PivotTable will not display the sum of revenue, instead it would display the detailed revenue for reach record in your dataset.

Keep in mind that in order to use the method shown in Figure 4-9, the field you are adding must be a numeric or currency field.

At this point, your PivotTable should look like the one shown in Figure 4-10. You can add some dimension to this report by the dragging the Product-Description field to the column area. As you can see in Figure 4-11, with this you now have a cross tabular view of revenue by region and product.

Now add the Market field to the Row area and drag the Region field to the Filter area (the area that reads Drop Filter Fields Here). Your PivotTable should look like the one shown in Figure 4-12. With just a few clicks, you not only have a totally new perspective on the same data, but you can now filter by region.

Figure 4-9: Add the Revenue field using the field drop-down list.

Drop Filter Fields Here		
	Drop Column Fields Here	
Region ▾	Sum of Revenue	
MIDWEST	$1,848,890.66	
NORTH	$2,779,015.40	
SOUTH	$3,141,451.17	
WEST	$3,004,832.22	
Grand Total	$10,774,189.46	

Figure 4-10: You have created your first PivotTable report.

	Product_Description ▾		
	Cleaning & Housekeeping Services	Facility Maintenance and Repair	Fleet Maintenance
Region ▾	Sum of Revenue	Sum of Revenue	Sum of Revenue
MIDWEST	$174,518.08	$463,078.85	$448,800.61
NORTH	$534,284.19	$606,748.65	$610,791.49
SOUTH	$283,170.17	$846,508.06	$1,046,229.86
WEST	$146,623.34	$444,825.85	$521,976.06
Grand Total	$1,138,595.78	$2,361,161.41	$2,627,798.02

Drop Filter Fields Here

Figure 4-11: Drag the ProductDestription field to the Column area of the PivotTable.

Region ▾			
All			
	Product_Description ▾		
	Cleaning & Housekeeping Services	Facility Maintenance and Repair	Fleet Maintenance
Market ▾	Sum of Revenue	Sum of Revenue	Sum of Revenue
BUFFALO	$66,844.23	$69,568.80	$86,461.34
CALIFORNIA	$37,401.55	$281,203.86	$337,224.62
CANADA		$294,258.33	$273,175.05
CHARLOTTE	$170,341.83	$223,346.86	$245,119.74
DALLAS	$18,807.34	$136,844.19	$156,152.05
DENVER	$12,563.96	$160,325.12	$170,188.42
FLORIDA	$20,448.86	$410,039.45	$556,003.84
KANSASCITY	$65,439.45	$132,119.42	$133,170.10
MICHIGAN	$243,451.28	$65,079.56	$66,408.19
NEWORLEANS	$73,572.13	$76,277.55	$88,954.24
NEWYORK	$223,988.68	$177,841.95	$184,746.91
PHOENIX	$96,685.78	$125,522.50	$150,788.58
SEATTLE	$12,536.02	$38,099.49	$33,962.86
TULSA	$96,514.67	$170,634.31	$145,442.10
Grand Total	$1,138,595.78	$2,361,161.41	$2,627,798.02

Figure 4-12: Adding the Market field and dragging the Region field to the Filter area allows you to analyze market revenue for a specific region.

A WORD ABOUT DRAGGING FIELDS FROM ONE AREA TO ANOTHER

When you are dragging fields from one area of a PivotTable to another, your cursor will turn into a mini PivotTable. That is to say, your cursor turns into an icon that represents your PivotTable. As you move your cursor from one area of your actual PivotTable to the next, you will notice that different parts of the icon will be shaded. The shaded area corresponds to the area over which you are currently hovering. This enables you to easily discern in which area you are about to drop your field. The key to telling which area you are hovering over is to watch the shaded area of the cursor as shown in Figure 4-13.

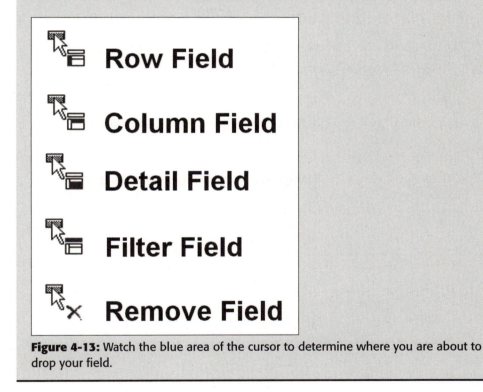

Figure 4-13: Watch the blue area of the cursor to determine where you are about to drop your field.

TIP If you need to remove a field from your PivotTable, an alternative to dragging it off is to right-click the field name and select Remove.

Creating an Advanced PivotTable with Details

This section demonstrates how you can incorporate record details into your PivotTable, effectively building an analysis that can drill down to the record level. First create the PivotTable shown in Figure 4-14 by following these steps:

1. Start by building the query shown earlier in Figure 4-6, then go up to the Design tab and select View → PivotTable View.

2. Drag the Market and Product_Description fields to the Row area of the PivotTable.

3. Select the Revenue field, then select Data Area from the drop-down box at the bottom of the PivotTable field and click the Add To button. Now your PivotTable should look like Figure 4-14.

   Take a moment and look at what you have so far. You've created a basic analysis that reveals the amount of revenue by product for each market. Now you can enhance this analysis by adding customer details to the PivotTable. This enables you to drill into a product segment and view all the customers that make up that product's revenue.

4. Select the Customer_Name field, then select Detail Data from the drop-down box at the bottom of the PivotTable field and click the Add To button.

5. Select the Effective_Date field, then select Detail Data from the drop-down box at the bottom of the PivotTable field and click the Add To button.

6. Select the Revenue field, then select Detail Area from the drop-down list box at the bottom of the PivotTable field and click the Add To button.

Drop Filter Fields Here		
		Drop Column Fields Here
Market ▾	**Product_Description** ▾	**Sum of Revenue**
⊟ BUFFALO	Cleaning & Housekeeping Services	$66,844.23
	Facility Maintenance and Repair	$69,568.80
	Fleet Maintenance	$86,461.34
	Green Plants and Foliage Care	$34,830.18
	Landscaping/Grounds Care	$65,464.84
	Predictive Maintenance/Preventative Maintenance	$127,309.32
	Total	$450,478.72
⊟ CALIFORNIA	Cleaning & Housekeeping Services	$37,401.55
	Facility Maintenance and Repair	$281,203.86
	Fleet Maintenance	$337,224.62
	Green Plants and Foliage Care	$830,422.28
	Landscaping/Grounds Care	$248,343.46
	Predictive Maintenance/Preventative Maintenance	$520,155.87
	Total	$2,254,751.64
⊟ CANADA	Facility Maintenance and Repair	$294,258.33
	Fleet Maintenance	$273,175.05
	Green Plants and Foliage Care	$15,965.46
	Landscaping/Grounds Care	$76,751.57
	Predictive Maintenance/Preventative Maintenance	$116,097.37
	Total	$776,247.78

Figure 4-14: Build the PivotTable shown here.

At this point, it looks as though your PivotTable hasn't changed. However, if you click the plus sign next to any one of the products segments, you will now see the customer details for every customer that contributed to that segment's total revenue (see Figure 4-15).

TIP You can drill into all details at one time by right-clicking the field names and selecting Show Details. Conversely you can hide the details by right-clicking the field names and selecting Hide Details.

CAUTION Incorporating record details into your PivotTables is a technique that should be limited to smaller datasets. Because the PivotTable component opens a separate ADO recordset for each cell it contains, accessing a large amount of details through your PivotTable can lead to performance issues. If you absolutely need to view all row and column details for a large dataset, you should consider using a Query or a Form.

Saving Your PivotTable

It's important to remember that when you are building your analysis with a PivotTable, you are actually working with a query in a PivotTable view. Therefore, when you save your analysis it will save as a query. You will notice that the next time you open the query it will open in Datasheet view. This doesn't mean your PivotTable is lost. Just switch back to PivotTable view to see your PivotTable.

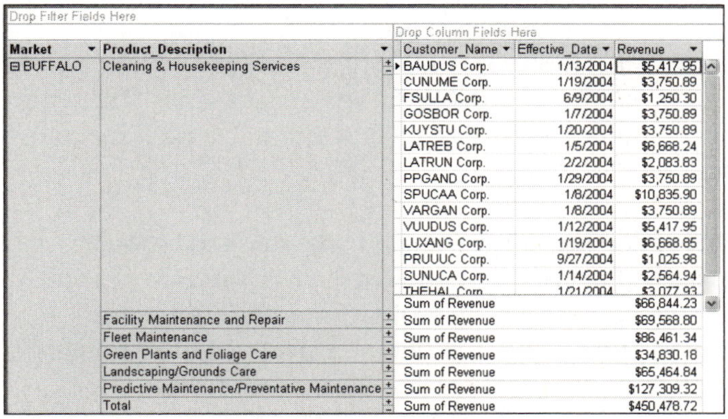

Figure 4-15: You now have the capability to drill down into the details that make up your revenue totals.

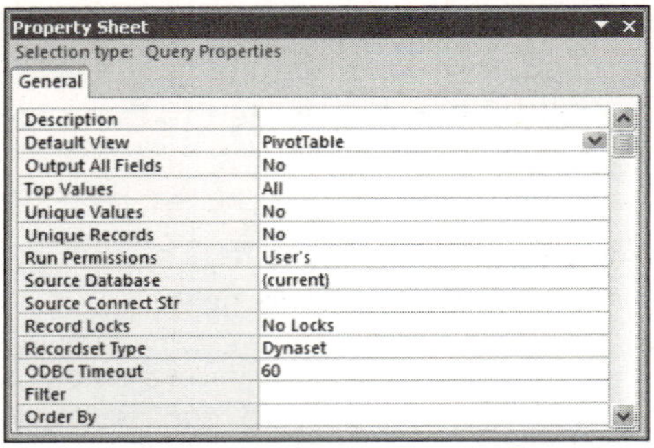

Figure 4-16: Change the Default View property to PivotTable.

If you want your query to run in PivotTable view by default, just change the Default View property of the query. To do this, open your query in Design view. Once in Design view, you will see a button called Property Sheet in the Design tab under the Show/Hide group. Select the Property Sheet button. This activates the Property Sheet dialog box shown in Figure 4-16. Change the Default View property to PivotTable. The next time you open your query, it will open in PivotTable view.

Sending Your Access PivotTable to Excel

When you are happy with your Access PivotTable analysis, you may want to share your PivotTable with the world. You can distribute your Access-made PivotTable via Excel. To do so, open your query in PivotTable view. Then go to the Design tab and click the Export to Excel button. This sends your PivotTable to Excel where you can format it and mail it out as a professionally made analysis.

The nifty thing about this technique is that only the pivot cache is sent to Excel. That is to say, the raw data behind the PivotTable is not sent to the workbook to be placed in a separate sheet. This means a smaller file size and a cleaner looking workbook.

TIP What if you wanted your users to have access to the raw data as well? Because Access only transfers the PivotTable and not the raw data, are you out of luck? No. To get the raw data, simply double-click the bottom-right-most Grand Total value of your PivotTable. This drills into the pivot cache and outputs the raw data that makes up your PivotTable onto a separate worksheet.

PivotTable Options

You will often find that the PivotTables you create need to be tweaked to get the result you're looking for. In this section, you will cover some of the Pivot-Table options you can adjust to enhance your analysis. To prepare for the examples in this section, create the PivotTable shown in Figure 4-17 by following these steps:

1. Start by building the query you see in Figure 4-6, and then select View → PivotTable View from the Design tab.

2. Drag the Region, Market, and Customer_Name fields to the Row area of the PivotTable.

3. Select the Revenue field, then select Data Area from the drop-down list box at the bottom of the PivotTable field and click the Add To button.

4. Select the TransactionCount field, then select Data Area from the drop-down box at the bottom of the PivotTable field and click the Add To button.

Region	Market	Customer_Name	Sum of Revenue	Sum of TransactionCount
⊟ MIDWEST	⊟ DENVER	ADOMSC Corp.	$1,190.30	6
		ADVANC Corp.	$1,709.64	12
		ALLAAN Corp.	$625.25	4
		ALLFAN Corp.	$448.02	4
		ALPANE Corp.	$4,578.26	25
		ALUXAN Corp.	$1,139.76	8
		AMPRUT Corp.	$448.02	4
		AMPUST Corp.	$5,592.04	30
		AMUSYS Corp.	$937.88	6
		ANAQAE Corp.	$1,172.20	8
		ANATUD Corp.	$4,644.84	24
		ANCLEM Corp.	$716.28	6
		ANDALU Corp.	$997.29	7
		ANDART Corp.	$2,421.99	17
		ANDUQU Corp.	$1,318.73	9
		ANDUSS Corp.	$448.02	4
		ANFANA Corp.	$434.06	4
		ANGUSS Corp.	$1,318.73	9

Figure 4-17: Build the PivotTable shown here.

Expanding and Collapsing Fields

It's always difficult to perform an effective analysis on a large volume of data. So when you are analyzing a large amount of data in a PivotTable such as the one shown in Figure 4-17, it's helpful to see small chunks of data at a time.

To facilitate this need, Access enables you to expand or collapse detail easily by clicking on the plus and minus signs shown in the PivotTables. You can also expand or collapse all values in a field at once. For example, right-click the Market field and select Collapse. As you can see in Figure 4-18, all the customer details for each market are now hidden, which makes this PivotTable easier to read. Now you can analyze the customer detail for one market at time clicking on the plus sign for that market.

Changing Field Captions

Access often attempts to name aggregated fields with its own name such as Sum of TransactionCount. You can imagine how titles like this can be confusing for the consumer. You can customize your field captions by changing the Caption property of the field.

To demonstrate this, right-click the Sum of TransactionCount field heading and select Properties. This activates the Properties dialog box shown in Figure 4-19. Click the Captions tab and enter Count of Transactions in the Caption input box. Close the dialog box and your changes will immediately take effect.

Drop Filter Fields Here				
			Drop Column Fields Here	
Region ▾	**Market** ▾	**Customer_Name** ▾	Sum of Revenue	Sum of TransactionCount
⊟ MIDWEST	⊞ DENVER		$645,584.10	4231
	⊞ KANSASCITY		$574,899.15	3784
	⊞ TULSA		$628,407.41	4417
	Total		$1,848,890.66	12432
⊟ NORTH	⊞ BUFFALO		$450,478.72	2625
	⊞ CANADA		$776,247.78	4981
	⊞ MICHIGAN		$678,708.11	3689
	⊞ NEWYORK		$873,580.79	4808
	Total		$2,779,015.40	16103
⊟ SOUTH	⊞ CHARLOTTE		$890,514.49	5389
	⊞ DALLAS		$467,086.11	3392
	⊞ FLORIDA		$1,450,397.76	11486
	⊞ NEWORLEANS		$333,452.80	1920
	Total		$3,141,451.17	22187
⊟ WEST	⊞ CALIFORNIA		$2,254,751.64	13617
	⊞ PHOENIX		$570,254.17	3222
	⊞ SEATTLE		$179,826.42	1053
	Total		$3,004,832.22	17892
Grand Total			$10,774,189.46	68614

Figure 4-18: Collapsing fields makes your PivotTables easier to read.

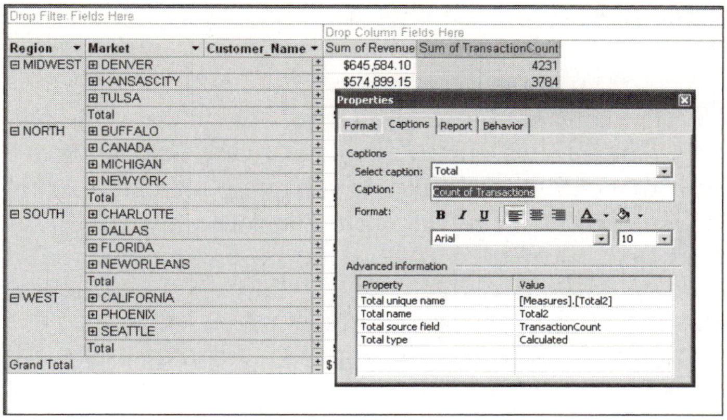

Figure 4-19: You can change a field's name by setting the Caption property of the field.

Sorting Data

By default, PivotTables are initially sorted in ascending order. However, you may prefer to present your data in an order that makes more sense in your situation. To change the sort order of a particular field or aggregation, simply right-click the chosen field or aggregation and select Sort, and then select Sort Ascending or Sort Descending.

Grouping Data

A particularly useful feature in PivotTables is the ability to create a new layer of analysis by grouping and summarizing unrelated data items. Imagine that you need to group the products shown in Figure 4-20 into two segments: outside services and inside services. Green Plants and Foliage Care and Landscaping/Grounds Care need to be classified as Outside Services, whereas the rest would be considered Inside Services.

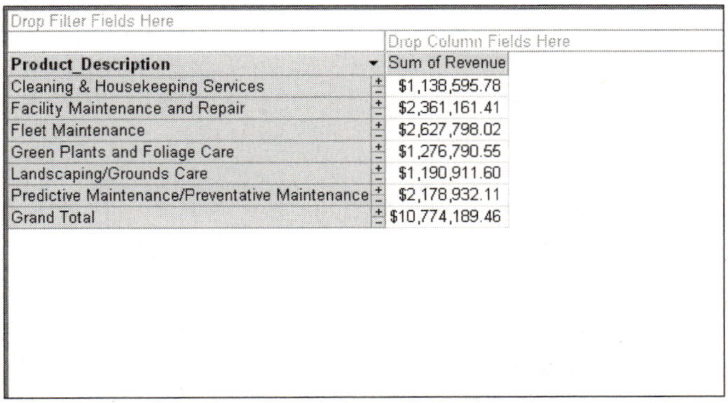
Drop Filter Fields Here

Drop Column Fields Here

Product_Description	Sum of Revenue
Cleaning & Housekeeping Services	$1,138,595.78
Facility Maintenance and Repair	$2,361,161.41
Fleet Maintenance	$2,627,798.02
Green Plants and Foliage Care	$1,276,790.55
Landscaping/Grounds Care	$1,190,911.60
Predictive Maintenance/Preventative Maintenance	$2,178,932.11
Grand Total	$10,774,189.46

Figure 4-20: You need to group these products into two groups.

To accomplish this task, hold down the Ctrl key on your key board and select both Green Plants and Foliage Care and Landscaping/Grounds Care. Then right-click and select Group Items as shown in Figure 4-21.

At this point, your PivotTable should look similar to the one shown in Figure 4-22. As you can see, you have essentially created a new field with two data items: Group1 and Other. All that's left to do now is to change the captions on these newly created objects to reflect their true meaning. To change the caption of a grouped field, simply right-click the field name and select Properties. This activates the Properties dialog box where you can click the Caption tab and edit the Caption input box.

Figure 4-23 illustrates what the final report with a new Product Segment field should look like.

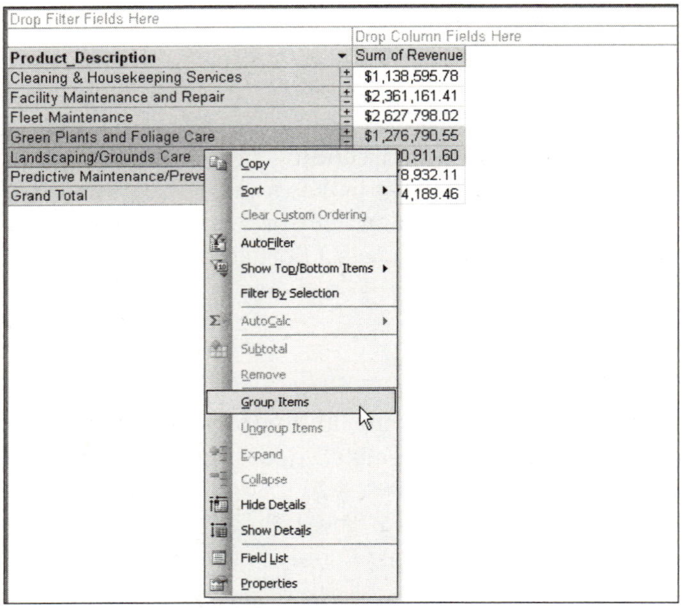

Figure 4-21: You need to group these products into two groups.

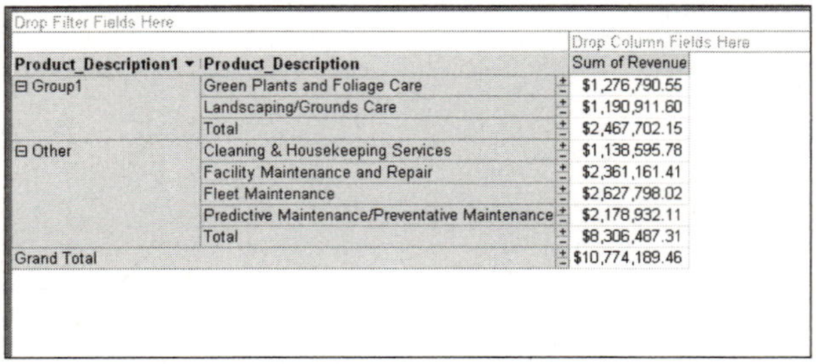

Figure 4-22: You need to group these products into two groups.

Drop Filter Fields Here			
		Drop Column Fields Here	
Product Segment ▾	**Product_Description**	Sum of Revenue	
⊟ Outside Services	Green Plants and Foliage Care	±	$1,276,790.55
	Landscaping/Grounds Care	±	$1,190,911.60
	Total	±	$2,467,702.15
⊟ Inside Services	Cleaning & Housekeeping Services	±	$1,138,595.78
	Facility Maintenance and Repair	±	$2,361,161.41
	Fleet Maintenance	±	$2,627,798.02
	Predictive Maintenance/Preventative Maintenance	±	$2,178,932.11
	Total	±	$8,306,487.31
Grand Total		±	$10,774,189.46

Figure 4-23: In just a few clicks, you have added another layer to your analysis.

One last note about grouping data. If you activate your field list and drill in to the Product_Description field, as shown in Figure 4-24, you will notice that your newly created grouping is listed there as a sub field. This means you can treat this field as any other in your field list. To delete your grouping, right-click its entry in the field list and select Delete.

Drop Filter Fields Here		
	Drop Column Fields Here	
Product_Description	▾	Sum of Revenue
Cleaning & Housekeeping Services		
Facility Maintenance and Repair		
Fleet Maintenance		
Green Plants and Foliage Care		
Landscaping/Grounds Care		
Predictive Maintenance/Preventative Maintenance		
Grand Total		

PivotTable Field List ✕
Drag items to the PivotTable list
- ❤ PivotTableView
- ⊟ 📊 **Totals**
  - 📊 **Sum of Revenue**
- ⊞ Region
- ⊞ Market
- ⊞ Branch_Number
- ⊞ Customer_Name
- ⊞ State
- ⊞ Effective_Date
- ⊞ Effective_Date By Week
- ⊞ Effective_Date By Month
- ⊟ **Product_Description**
  - Product Segment
  - **Product_Description**
- ⊞ Revenue
- ⊞ TransactionCount

| Add to | Row Area | ▾ |

Figure 4-24: To delete your grouping, find it in the PivotTable Field List, then right-click and select Delete.

Using Date Groupings

Notice that in Figure 4-25, you see a field called Effective_Date and directly underneath that field you see Effective_Date by Week and Effective_Date by Month. Unlike Excel where you would have to explicitly create date groupings, Access automatically creates these groupings for any field that is formatted as a date field.

Figure 4-26 illustrates how you can simply drag these date groupings onto your PivotTable just as you would any other field.

NOTE One drawback to using the Access-provided date groupings is that you can't separate them. For instance, you cannot drag the Year grouping into the Column area then drag the Month grouping into the Row area.

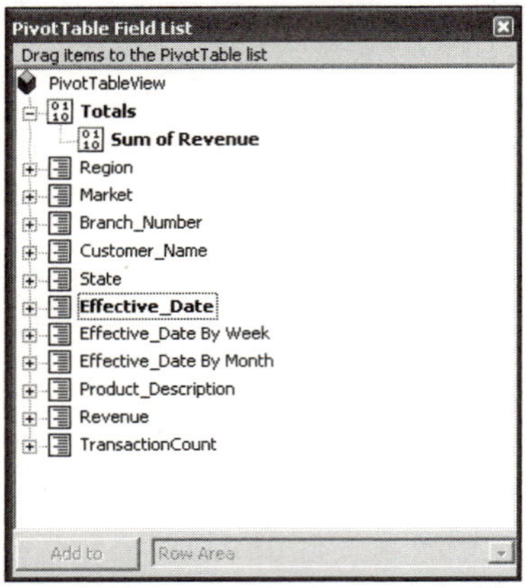

Figure 4-25: Access automatically creates date groupings for any field that is formatted as a date field.

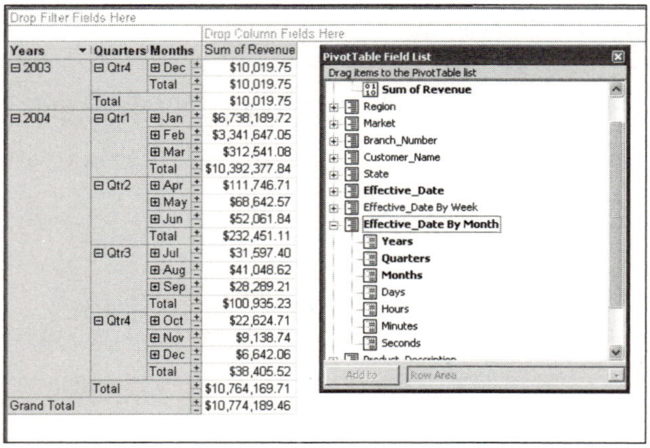

Figure 4-26: Date Groupings in action

Filtering for Top and Bottom Records

Filtering your PivotTable to show the top or bottom Nth records can be done with just a few clicks of the mouse. In the example illustrated in Figure 4-27, you have a list of customers and want to limit the list to the top ten customers by sum of revenue. Right-clicking the Customer_Name field heading exposes a shortcut menu where you select Show Top/Bottom Items → Show only the Top → 10.

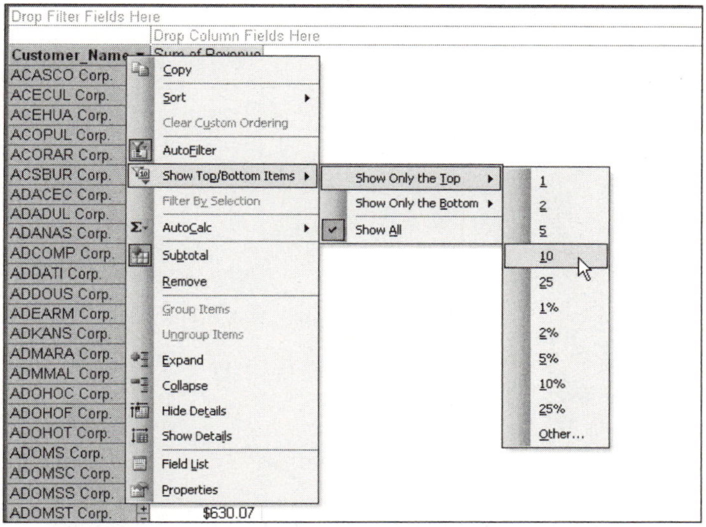

Figure 4-27: This is an example of how easy it is to filter the top 10 customers.

As you can see in Figure 4-27, the filtering options also include the ability to filter by percent of records. You can remove the applied filter by right-clicking the field heading and selecting AutoFilter.

TIP There are actually two methods you can use to remove an applied filter from a field:

■ **Method 1: Right-click the field heading and select AutoFilter**

■ **Method 2: Right-click the field heading and select Show Top/Bottom Items → Show All.**

Method 1, highlighted above, has an added advantage in that it will enable you to reapply the last known filter to the field at any time by right-clicking the field heading and selecting AutoFilter. Method 2, on the other hand, clears the filter settings altogether.

Adding a Calculated Total

When you create a PivotTable, you may find it useful to expand your analysis by performing calculations on summary totals. To demonstrate this, create the PivotTable shown in Figure 4-28. This analysis calculates total revenue and total count of transactions. Upon reviewing these results, you determine that you need to get an average dollar per transaction.

Go to the Design tab and select Formulas → Create Calculated Total. This sets off two events. First, a new field called New Total appears in your PivotTable as shown in Figure 4-29. Second, the Properties dialog box for this field activates.

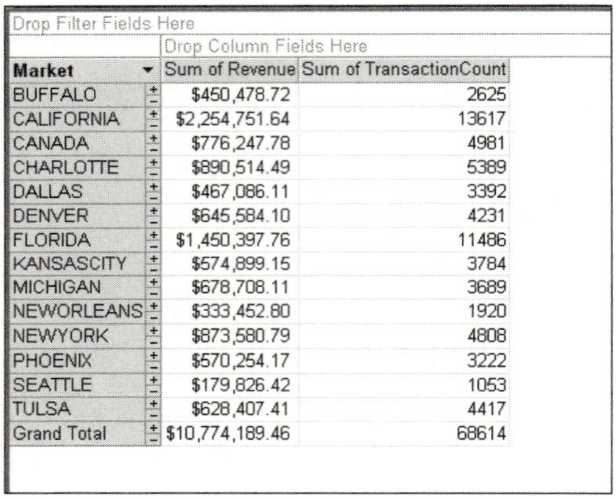

Drop Filter Fields Here

Drop Column Fields Here

Market	Sum of Revenue	Sum of TransactionCount
BUFFALO	$450,478.72	2625
CALIFORNIA	$2,254,751.64	13617
CANADA	$776,247.78	4981
CHARLOTTE	$890,514.49	5389
DALLAS	$467,086.11	3392
DENVER	$645,584.10	4231
FLORIDA	$1,450,397.76	11486
KANSASCITY	$574,899.15	3784
MICHIGAN	$678,708.11	3689
NEWORLEANS	$333,452.80	1920
NEWYORK	$873,580.79	4808
PHOENIX	$570,254.17	3222
SEATTLE	$179,826.42	1053
TULSA	$628,407.41	4417
Grand Total	$10,774,189.46	68614

Figure 4-28: You need to calculate the average dollar per transaction for each market.

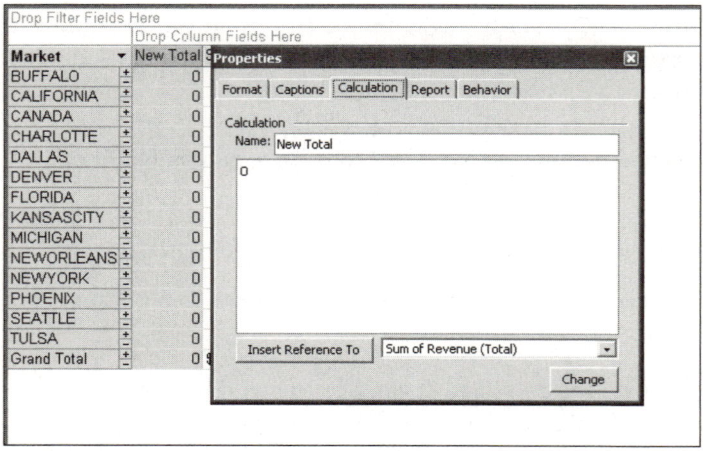

Figure 4-29: Adding a new calculated total creates a new field in your PivotTable.

The idea is to enter the calculation you need into the dialog box:

1. Enter **Dollars per Transaction** into the Name input box.
2. Delete 0 from the large input box below Name.
3. Select Sum of Revenue (Total) from the drop-down list box, then click the Insert Reference To button.
4. Type / to indicate division.
5. Select Sum of TransactionCount (Total) from the drop-down list box, then click the Insert Reference To button.

   At this point, your dialog box should look similar to Figure 4-30.
6. Click the Change button.
7. Go to the Format Tab and select Currency from the Number input box.

As you can see in Figure 4-31, your new calculation looks and acts like any other Totals field in your PivotTable.

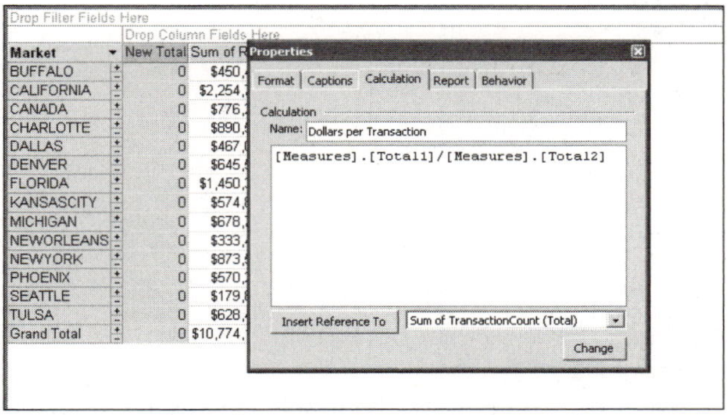

Figure 4-30: Your dialog box should look like this.

Drop Filter Fields Here

Drop Column Fields Here

Market	Dollars per Transaction	Sum of Revenue	Sum of TransactionCount
BUFFALO	$171.61	$450,478.72	2625
CALIFORNIA	$165.58	$2,254,751.64	13617
CANADA	$155.84	$776,247.78	4981
CHARLOTTE	$165.25	$890,514.49	5389
DALLAS	$137.70	$467,086.11	3392
DENVER	$152.58	$645,584.10	4231
FLORIDA	$126.28	$1,450,397.76	11486
KANSASCITY	$151.93	$574,899.15	3784
MICHIGAN	$183.98	$678,708.11	3689
NEWORLEANS	$173.67	$333,452.80	1920
NEWYORK	$181.69	$873,580.79	4808
PHOENIX	$176.99	$570,254.17	3222
SEATTLE	$170.78	$179,826.42	1053
TULSA	$142.27	$628,407.41	4417
Grand Total	$157.03	$10,774,189.46	68614

Figure 4-31: You have enhanced your analysis with a calculated total.

To adjust the calculation behind your calculated total, right-click the field heading and select Properties. This opens the Properties dialog box where you can change the calculation in the Calculation tab.

To delete your calculated total, right-click its entry in the field list, shown in Figure 4-32, and select Delete.

NOTE You can also create Calculated Detail Field using the same steps illustrated previously. However, it's generally a better idea to perform calculations on details in the actual query as opposed to a PivotTable. This way, the Microsoft ACE database (ACE is the Access 2007 replacement for Microsoft Jet) performs the calculation instead of the PivotTable component, making your PivotTable view perform better.

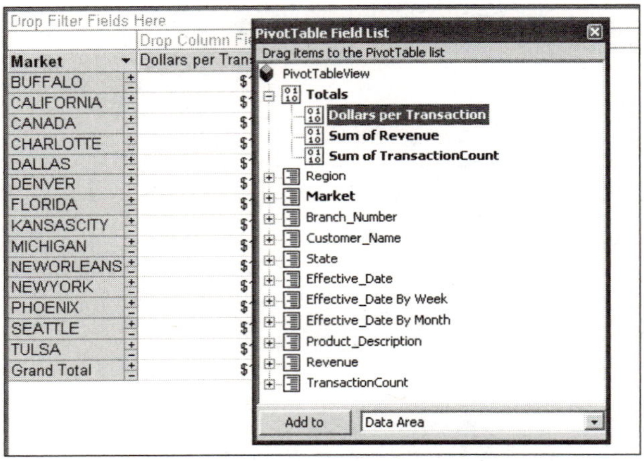

Figure 4-32: To delete your calculated total, find it in the PivotTable Field List, then right-click it, and then click Delete.

Working with PivotCharts in Access

A PivotChart is essentially a PivotTable in chart form. Once you learn the basics of using a PivotTable, a PivotChart will feel quite intuitive. There are, however, slight differences in the anatomy of a PivotChart. Figure 4-33 shows an empty PivotChart where you can see four distinct areas. Just as in Pivot-Tables, how you choose to utilize these areas defines both the utility and the appearance of your PivotChart.

The Data Area

The Data area, highlighted in Figure 4-34, is the area that calculates and supplies the data points for your chart. You can recognize this area by the phrase Drop Data Fields Here.

The Series Area

The Series area, highlighted in Figure 4-35, is the area that typically makes up the y axis of your chart. You can recognize this area by the phrase Drop Series Fields Here. This area is equivalent to the Column area of a PivotTable. In other words, if you create a PivotTable and switch to PivotChart view, the fields in the Column area of the PivotTable will become the y axis series.

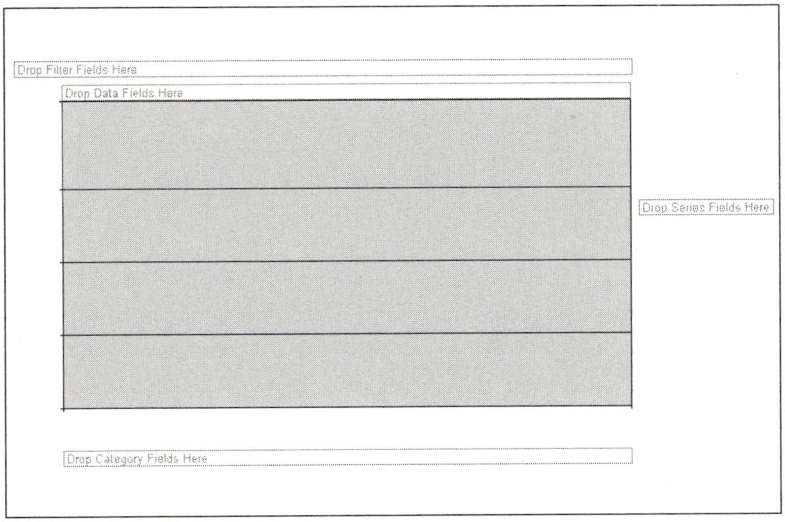

Figure 4-33: An empty PivotChart in Access

Data Area

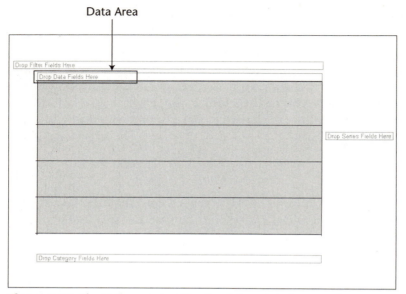

Figure 4-34: The Data area supplies the data points for your chart.

Y Axis

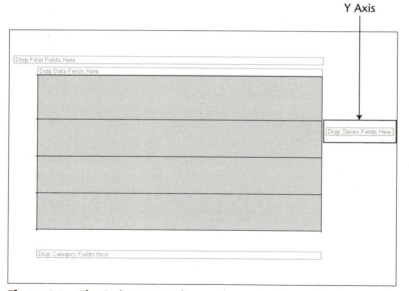

Figure 4-35: The Series area makes up the *y* axis of your chart.

The Category Area

The Category area, highlighted in Figure 4-36, is the area that makes up the x axis of your chart. You can recognize this area by the phrase Drop Category Fields Here. This area is equivalent to the Row area of a PivotTable. In other words, if you create a PivotTable and switch to PivotChart view, the fields in the Row area of the PivotTable will become categories in the x axis.

The Filter Area

The Filter Area, highlighted in Figure 4-37, allows for dynamic filtering of your PivotChart based on a value in a field. You can recognize this area by the phrase Drop Filter Fields Here. This area is identical to the Filter area of a PivotTable.

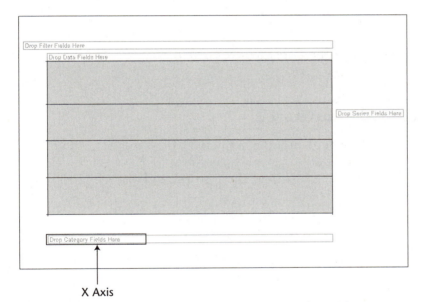

X Axis

Figure 4-36: The Category area makes up the x axis of your chart.

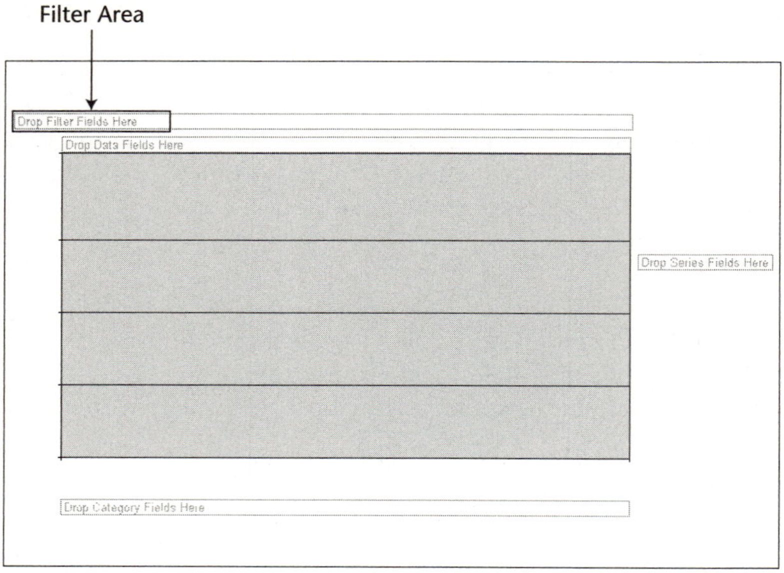

Filter Area

Figure 4-37: The Filter area allows you to filter your PivotChart.

Creating a Basic PivotChart

To create a PivotChart, start by building a query in Design view, as shown in Figure 4-38, then go to the Design tab and select View → PivotChart View.

At this point, you see an empty PivotChart, shown in Figure 4-39 and a list of fields that are in your dataset

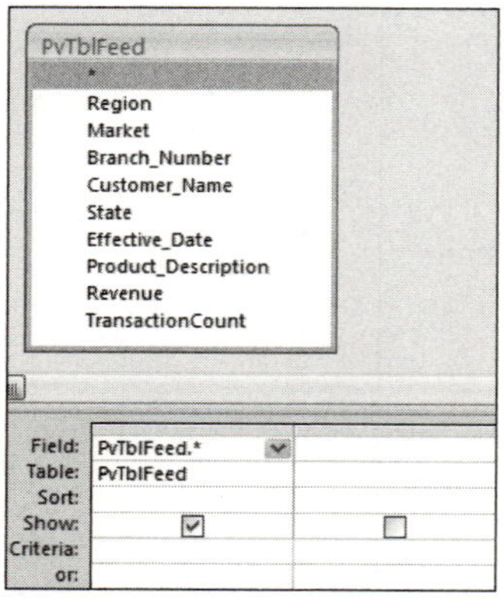

Figure 4-38: Build your query then switch to PivotChart view.

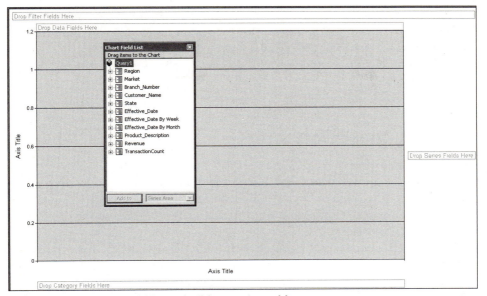

Figure 4-39: Use the field list to build your PivotTable.

Just as in a PivotTable, the idea is to drag the fields you need into the PivotChart's drop areas. Build a basic chart by dragging the Revenue field to the Data area, then the Market field to the Category Area. Finally drag the Region field to the Filter Area. Your completed chart should look like the one illustrated in Figure 4-40.

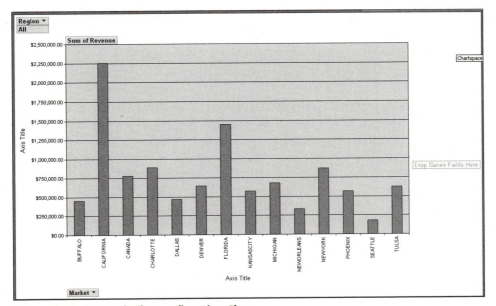

Figure 4-40: You've built your first PivotChart.

NOTE You may notice that the PivotCharts produced by Access are not as polished as the ones Excel produces. This is because Access uses the old Office Web Component technology that was primarily designed for reporting on the Web. Excel, on the other hand, uses the slick new graphics engine that comes with Office 2007.

Formatting Your PivotChart

The key to formatting a PivotChart in Access is to remember that everything revolves around property settings. Each object on the chart has its own properties that can be adjusted. To demonstrate this, right-click your PivotChart and select Properties. This opens the Properties dialog box shown in Figure 4-41. Go to the General tab.

The idea here is to select the object with which you want to work to expose the adjustable properties. Fore example, if you wanted to add labels to your series, you would select Series from the Select drop-down as shown in Figure 4-42.

With the Series properties exposed, you can tailor its properties to suit your needs. In Figure 4-43, you are adding data labels to your PivotChart.

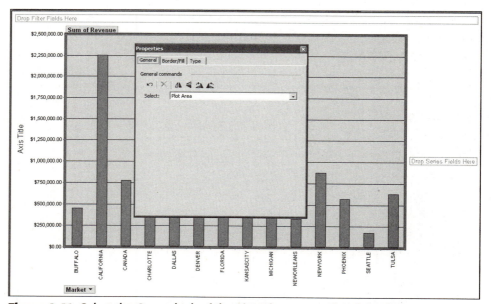

Figure 4-41: Select the General tab of the PivotChart properties dialog box.

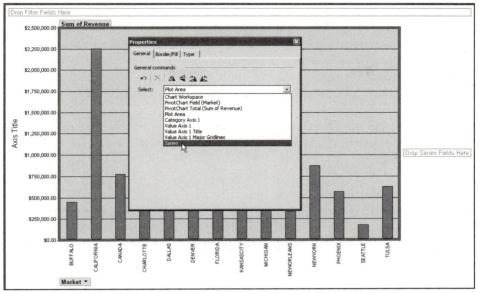

Figure 4-42: Selecting the Series object exposes its modifiable properties.

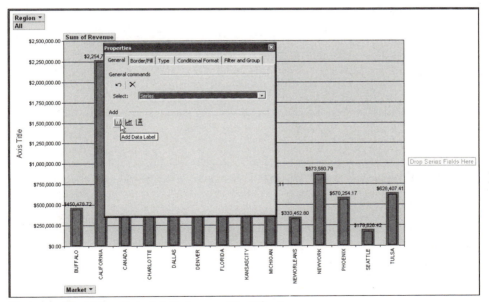

Figure 4-43: Adding Data Labels to your PivotChart.

Of course, data labels have properties that can be modified as well. Go back to the General tab of the Properties dialog box and select the series data labels you just added. As you can see in Figure 4-44, the Select drop-down list box has been updated to include Series Data Labels 1.

Twenty minutes of experimenting with each object's properties will give you a solid level of proficiency at formatting PivotCharts in Access.

> **NOTE** As of this writing, you cannot export PivotCharts from Access to Excel. Again, this is due to the fact that Access and Excel use entirely different charting engines.

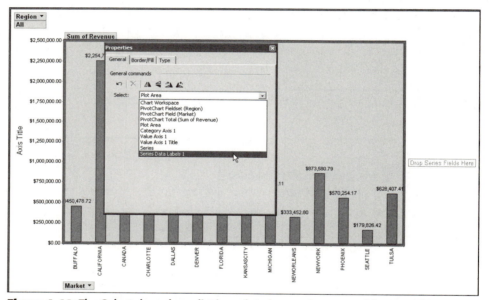

Figure 4-44: The Select drop-down list is updated every time you add a new object to your chart.

Summary

From a data analysis point of view, PivotTables and PivotCharts are some of the most powerful data-crunching tools found in Access. With a PivotTable, you can group, summarize, and perform a wide variety of calculations in a fraction of the time it takes by hand. In addition, you can interactively change the content and shape of your analysis by dragging data fields from one area of the PivotTable to another. This enables you to dynamically change your perspective, recalculate totals to fit the current view, and interactively drill down to the detail records. Pivot charts enhance your analytical tools by allowing you to display your PivotTables graphically, in chart form. By applying your knowledge of Excel PivotTables to Access, you can completely change the way you analyze your Access data.

CHAPTER 5

Getting Access Data into Excel

Quite often in complex analysis, Access is used as an analytical back end to manipulate and process data. With its universal usage, Excel is often used on the front end for presenting and reporting the results. If you plan to integrate Access and Excel in this way, you must find an efficient means to move your data between applications. In Chapter 1, we covered ways to get Excel data into Access. This chapter explores the most efficient ways to get Access data into your Excel workbook.

There are numerous ways to get data from Access to Excel. We will cover each of these, with a specific emphasis on the circumstances that would suggest one method over another. The bulk of the chapter discusses the use of Microsoft Query in Excel, a powerful means of consistently and interactively moving data into Excel.

Different Options for Importing Access Data

As mentioned in the introduction, there are numerous ways to get your Access data into Excel. More troublesome than learning these individual methods, however, is knowing when a particular method is more efficient than another! In this section, we introduce several ways to get data into Excel and examine what circumstances make one method better suited than another.

The Drag-and-Drop Method

For simplicity and ease, you just can't beat the drag-and-drop method. Try this — simultaneously open Excel and the Access database from which you want to import. For this exercise, use the `Zalexcorp.accdb` sample database. Now resize each application's window such that they are both fully visible on your screen (see Figure 5-1).

Select the Access object you want to import in the Navigation pane. For this exercise, let's use the PriceMaster table. Click the PriceMaster table icon and hold down the mouse button. Now drag the mouse cursor over to a blank worksheet in Excel. Release the mouse button when you are hovering over the worksheet in which you want your data (this exercise is called *dragging and dropping* for the one reader not yet familiar with Windows). Let's have a look at the result (see Figure 5-2).

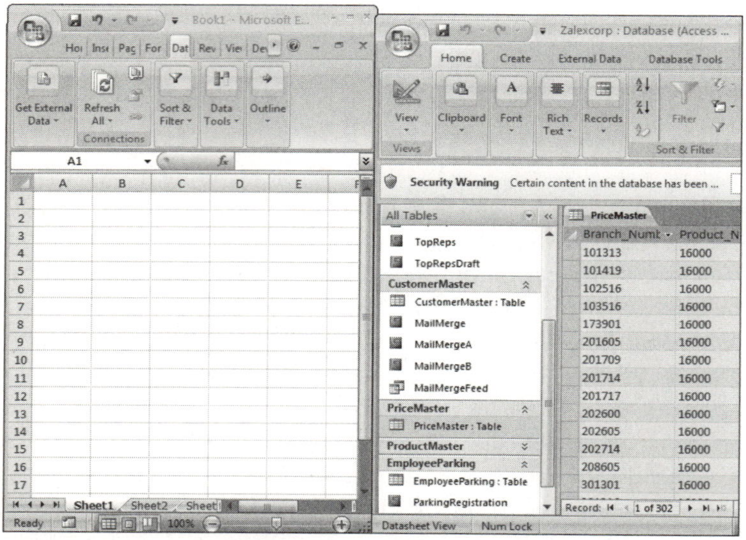

Figure 5-1: Illustrating the drag-and-drop method: Step 1

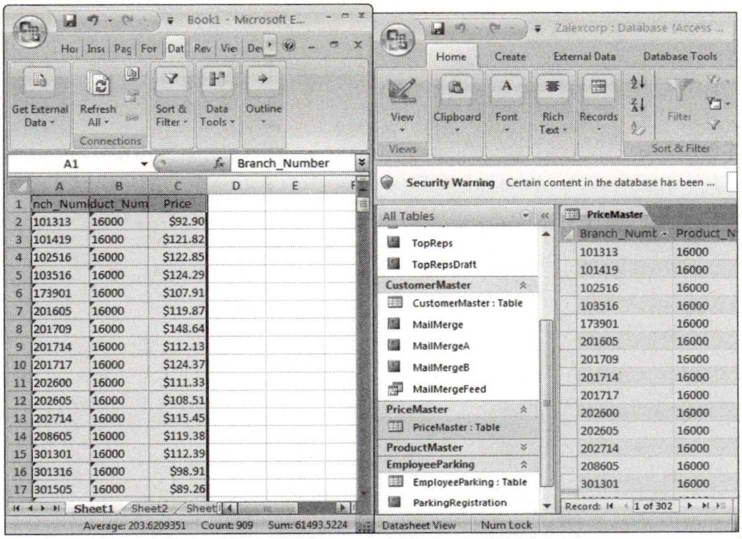

Figure 5-2: Illustrating the drag-and-drop method: Step 2

Well, this concludes this section on importing Access into Excel. Seriously though, the drag-and-drop method is very useful when you are doing a quick, one-time analysis where you need a specific set of data in Excel. It is not so useful if:

- You expect this step to occur routinely, as a part of a repeated analysis or report.

- You expect the users of your Excel report to get or refresh the report data via this method.

- It's not possible or convenient for you to simply open up Access at the time you need the data.

For these scenarios, it is much better to use the techniques outlined in the following sections.

Exporting the Data from Access

You may recall from Chapter 1 that Access has an Export data feature similar to its Import data feature. Exporting Access data to Excel is yet another technique to get your data into a worksheet.

With the `Zalexcorp.accdb` database open, click the PriceMaster table again in Navigation view. When this table is selected, browse to the External Data ribbon icon and select the Excel icon from the Export tab. The menu should look like Figure 5-3.

When you select the Excel icon, the Export wizard will fire up and ask you where you would like to send your data. The default option is to export the data into a new Excel file (see Figure 5-4).

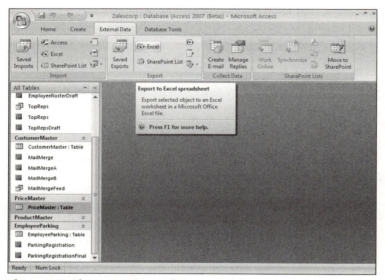

Figure 5-3: The export External Data menu in Access

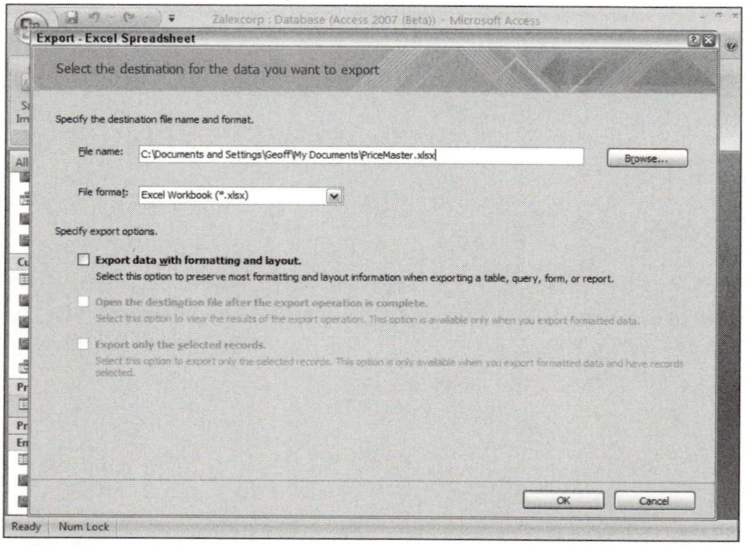

Figure 5-4: The Export wizard in Access

You have a few discretionary options you can specify in the Excel Export wizard. We already discussed the file location option. You can also specify the file type, which may come in handy if you need to export to an earlier version of Excel. In addition, you will notice the "preserve formatting" option. This has little impact on exporting tables and is more relevant if you want to preserve formatting you've worked hard to develop in a report.

CAUTION You may export your Access object to an existing Excel file instead of creating a new file. There are several things you must be aware of though. First, if you export to an existing Excel file, Access will export the object as a named range and as a new sheet in Excel. By default, the name of the exported object is the name of the table or query in Access. Be cautious if you have an object with the same name in your Excel workbook as it may be overwritten. For example, if you export the PriceMaster table to an Excel worksheet that already has a worksheet named PriceMaster, you will get a dialog box asking if you want to overwrite the existing PriceMaster object. If you click Yes, the existing worksheet will be overwritten. Second, if you want to export your data to a new range, make sure the workbook to which you are exporting is closed. If you try to export a new range to an open workbook, you will likely get the following cryptic error in Access: "Unexpected error from external database driver (1309)". If the workbook is open, you cannot export a new data range to an open workbook or change the range that the Access data will be exported to. You may overwrite an existing range in an open workbook, however.

For this exercise, select the Export data with formatting and layout check box in the Export wizard. Now notice that a second option is available that asks whether you want to open the file for viewing after export. Select that as well and then click OK. Excel opens to show your exported data and in Access, the last wizard page comes up asking whether you want to save your export steps. The former can be useful if you expect to perform numerous exports of a similar type and do not want to click through the export menu. Leave the box unselected and click OK to see your final exported data in Excel (see Figure 5-5).

Note that you have a new Excel file open that has the same name as the exported table. It's worth repeating here that you can export your Access object to an existing worksheet instead. Just remember that your exported Access object will show up as a named range in a new worksheet in Excel. That named range will have the same name as the Access object you exported. In this case, the file object, the worksheet object, and the named range object are all given the same name: PriceMaster.

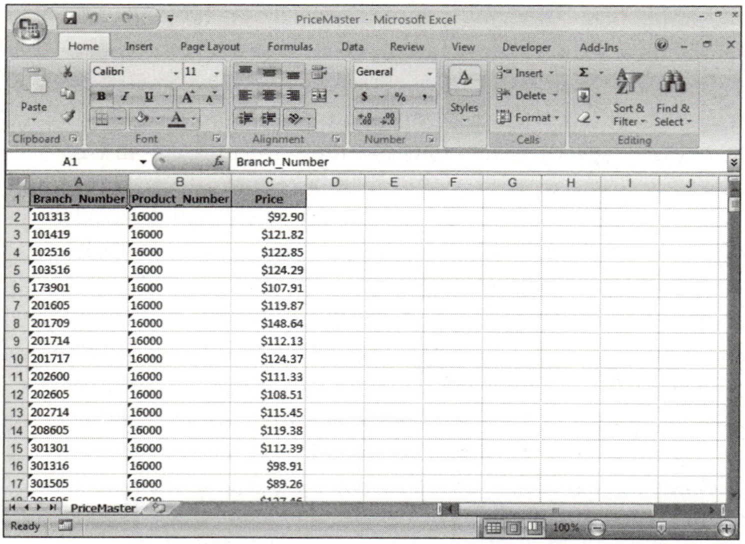

Figure 5-5: Exported data from Access viewed in Excel

As with dragging and dropping, this export from Access method is useful when you already have Access up and running. Unlike dragging and dropping, however, this method can be used effectively, if you expect to export a certain table or query repeatedly from Access into a specified worksheet. These export steps can easily be automated through macros — a topic for Chapter 6. The limitation of this export method is that it is done within Access. If you are creating an Excel report where data refresh must be under the Excel user's control, this method is not viable. In that case, importing data using Microsoft Query in Excel is the better option.

Using the Get External Data Menu

In Excel 2007, Microsoft made importing Access data from the Excel user interface very simple — it's right there on the ribbon. Technically, the option was available in earlier versions of Excel, just buried several layers deep in somewhat cryptic menu titles.

In truth, this method is very similar to using Microsoft Query. Both establish an ongoing, refreshable data connection between Excel and Access. The main differences are in user interactivity and the ability to use queries to select custom datasets from Access. If you want to establish an import connection to Excel from a pre-made Access table or query but you don't want the complexity of sorts, filters, and building custom queries, this is the method to use. Let's walk through an example.

In Excel, select the Data tab from the ribbon, click the Get External Data menu and select the From Access icon. An import dialog box pops up that will then walk you through the process. For this example, import a table from the `Zalexcorp.accdb` Access data from the Excel interface (see Figure 5-6).

The first step is to browse for the Access database. If the database from which you want to import is local, browse to the file location and open it. If you have an Access database on a network drive at your employer, you can select that database — provided you have the proper authorization and access.

Next, the Select Table dialog box opens, asking you which Access objects you want to import. Notice that all the queries and tables are available for us to grab (see Figure 5-7).

Next, choose the PriceMaster table and click OK to continue importing. This opens the final Import table dialog box, which asks how you want to view the table and where you want the data to reside. Choose to view the data as a table (simply a flat file — not as a PivotTable) and put it in Sheet1 (see Figure 5-8). Click OK; you now have Access data in your Excel worksheet.

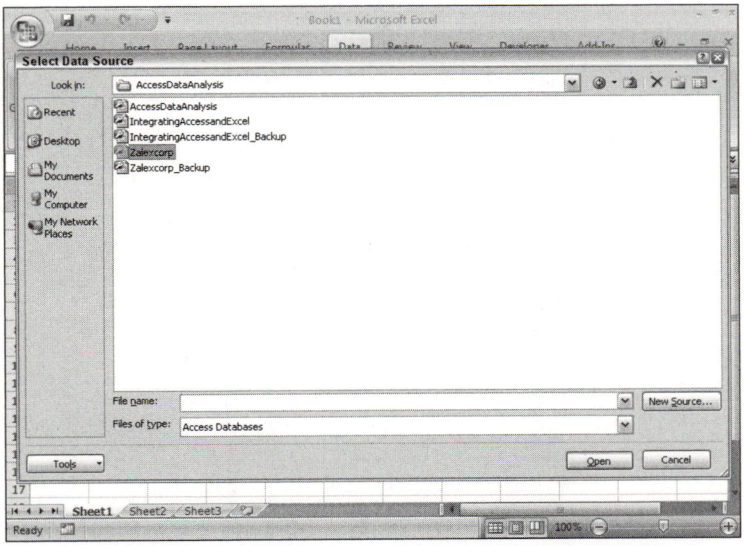

Figure 5-6: Choose a file from the Select Data Source dialog box.

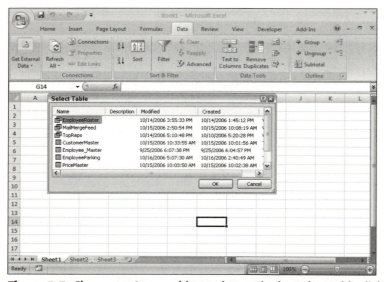

Figure 5-7: Choose an Access object to import in the Select Table dialog box.

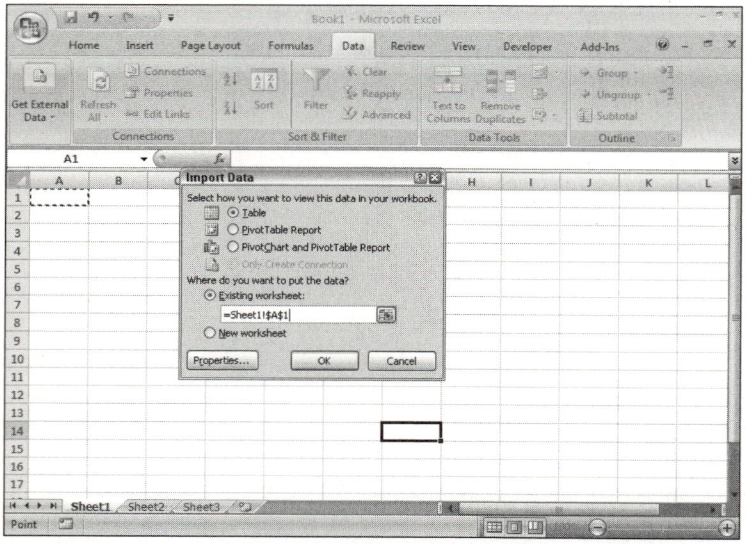

Figure 5-8: Choosing how and where to view our Access data

In a way, you can think of this method as a much-abbreviated version of using Microsoft Query. As with Microsoft Query, you have established a refreshable data connection between the two applications. What you give up, however, is the ability to use sorts, filters, and even multiple table joins to customize the data you bring into Excel. In the next section, we will expand on these and additional reasons for choosing Microsoft Query as an import tool.

Using Microsoft Query

Later sections will walk through the specifics of how to use Microsoft Query. In this section we will summarize many of the advantages of Microsoft Query and under which circumstances this tool is a better data import choice than the methods discussed previously.

■ Microsoft Query is not limited to importing data from Access. In fact, Excel, Access, and many other file types can easily be manipulated with Microsoft Query. This obviously comes in handy if you need to import non-Access–based data into your Excel worksheet.

■ With Microsoft Query, you can manipulate the data you want to import. When exporting data from Access or importing data using the Access icon, you can only import an existing object. If, however, you want to select only certain records from an existing table or even create a new query, you are out of luck. Not so with Microsoft Query! You can select records from Access objects subject to your own criteria or even user supplied criteria! In addition, Microsoft Query allows you to query more than one Access object through joins, essentially creating custom queries — all through the Excel user interface.

■ Like the Get External Data option, Microsoft Query establishes a refreshable data connection through the Excel user interface. You can specify (subject to some constraints) when data is refreshed. More importantly, you can ask the user for input that dictates what data is imported. Best of all, the user of your application doesn't have to know anything about Access or Microsoft Query for your application to work.

Now that we've summarized the strengths of using Microsoft Query to get data from Access into Excel, let's take a closer look at how you can use the tool.

Introduction to Microsoft Query

Now that we have introduced the various methods of getting Access data into Excel, it is time to explore the most powerful method more deeply. Specifically, we will cover the use of Microsoft Query. As an introduction, we will cover using Microsoft Query with the Microsoft Query Wizard. Then we will examine more advanced concepts using Microsoft Query without the wizard.

Using the Microsoft Query Wizard

Your first foray into Microsoft Query will be with the Microsoft Query Wizard. This wizard is a very user-friendly interface that runs as part of Microsoft Query. Functionality is largely limited to sorts and filters. However, the wizard serves as a useful and friendly introduction to the broad power of Microsoft Query.

Starting the Query Wizard

We will begin by firing up the Microsoft Query Wizard from the Get External Data menu under the Data tab of the Excel ribbon. After selecting the Get External Data menu, you will be presented with variety of options. To start Microsoft Query, you must choose the From Other Sources option and then select From Microsoft Query from the drop-down menu. Figure 5-9 shows what the menu will look like.

After Microsoft Query opens, you will see the Choose Data Source dialog box, which asks what kind of data source you want to open. The data sources are organized into three tabs (see Figure 5-10):

- The default tab selected in this dialog box is the Databases tab. You will notice that the last item in the Databases tab is an Access database. Since using non-Access data sources is really beyond the scope of this book, we won't discuss the details of importing other data sources here. Just be aware, however, that Microsoft Query has the capability to import from non-Access and even non-Excel sources.

- The second tab is the Queries tab. Your saved queries can be found here. Going through the Microsoft Query Wizard steps creates a query and allows you to save it. Choose the saved query as your Data Source, and Microsoft Query immediately has all the information about database connection, source tables, join relationships, and criteria.

- The third tab is the OLAP Cubes tab. Using OLAP cubes as a Microsoft Query data source is beyond our scope here.

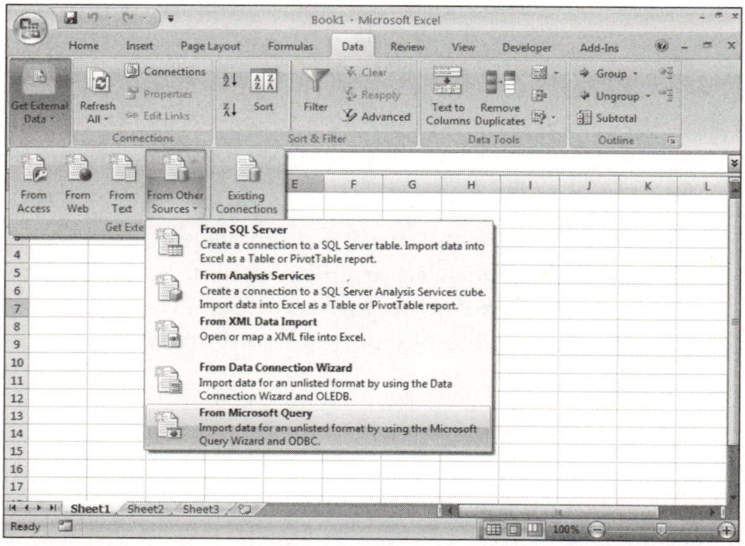

Figure 5-9: Start the Microsoft Query Wizard from the Get External Data menu.

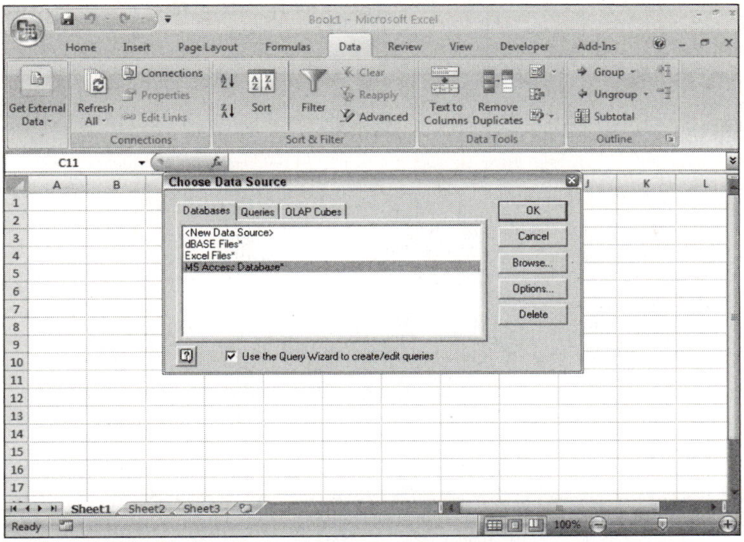

Figure 5-10: The Choose Data Source dialog box

Choosing and Modifying Your Data with the Query Wizard

For this exercise, source some data from `Zalexcorp.accdb`, a Microsoft 2007 Access database, through Microsoft Query. Take the following steps:

1. From the Choose Data Source dialog, choose <New data source> from the Databases tab. This opens the Create New Data Source dialog box.

2. Type a name for your data source at the top of the dialog box, for example, ZalexCorp (see Figure 5-11).

3. In the drop-down list box below, choose a type of driver for the database to which you want to connect. From this drop-down menu, make sure you select Microsoft Access Driver (`*.mdb`, `*.accdb`), as shown in Figure 5-12.

4. Click Connect. This opens the ODBC Microsoft Access Setup dialog box (see Figure 5-13).

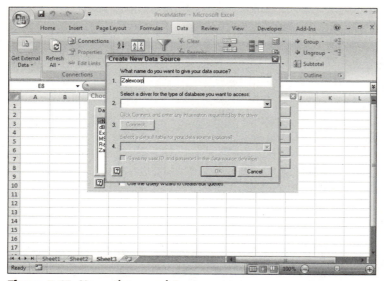

Figure 5-11: Name the new data source.

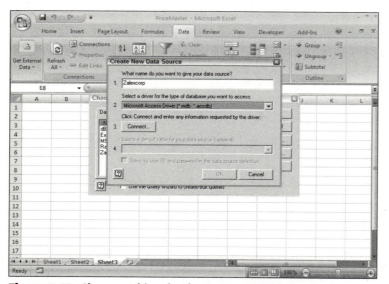

Figure 5-12: Choose a driver for the Access 2007 data source.

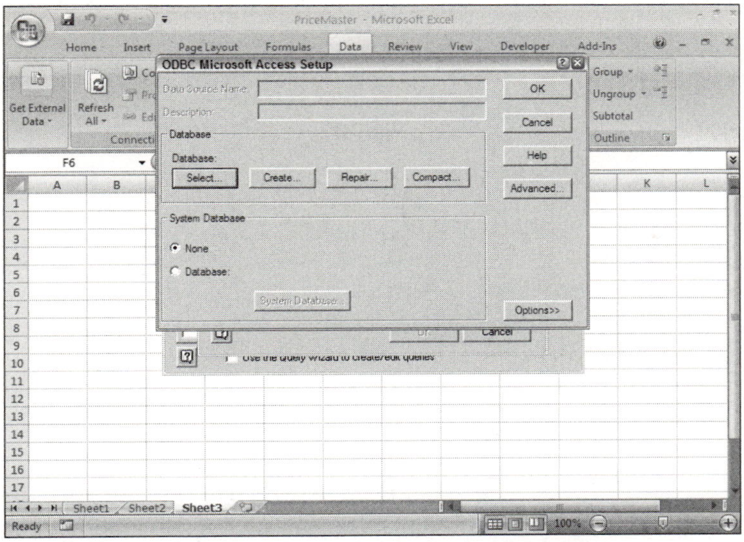

Figure 5-13: The ODBC Microsoft Access Setup dialog box

5. Click the Select button in the Database section to browse for your database in the Select Database dialog box (see Figure 5-14).

6. After you have selected your database, continue to click OK until you come back to the Choose Data Source dialog box. Zalexcorp now shows up in the list of Databases (see Figure 5-15).

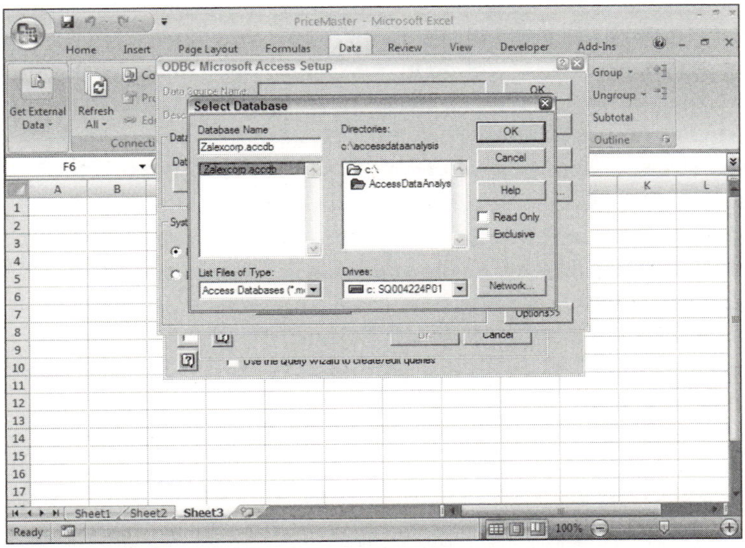

Figure 5-14: Select your Access 2007 database.

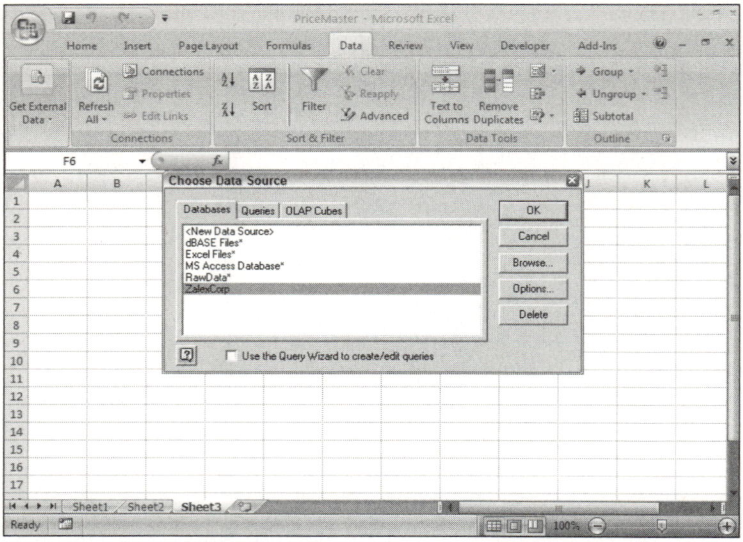

Figure 5-15: ZalexCorp is now in the list of databases.

7. After selecting ZalexCorp and clicking OK, you are presented with a dialog box that shows the objects within the Zalexcorp database. From this dialog box, you may import both tables and queries. For this basic example, continue to work with the PriceMaster table. Click the plus sign to the left of the table name and you see the available fields from that table.

CAUTION Why go through the steps to import an Access database when there is a Microsoft Access Database* option in the Choose Data Source dialog box? Wouldn't that route be easier? If you browse for an Access 2007 database after choosing Microsoft Access Database* from the Choose Data Source dialog box, something very strange happens — you won't find it. For some reason, the default extension given to an Access database when chosen from the Databases tab is `*.mdb`. Although this is the correct extension for Access 2003 and earlier databases, it is not the correct file extension for Access 2007. For Access 2007 the database file extension is `*.accdb`. This appears to be the result of an oversight from the folks at Microsoft. Fortunately, you may take the steps outlined previously to link to an Access 2007 database file.

TIP Microsoft Query works equally well for non-local databases (those that reside on a networked drive or even on the Web). In the Select Database dialog box, you'll find a drop-down menu with a list of computer drives available to you. Choosing a database file from a network drive already mapped to your computer, is as simple as choosing that drive from the drop-down menu, and browsing the file hierarchy until you find the database you are looking for. The Network button fires up a wizard to help you connect to a network drive or folder to which you are not currently mapped.

Choosing Data Fields in the Query Wizard

To pull these fields into your query, simply select each one and then click the right-facing arrow to move the field into the Columns in your query box. A quick way to choose all the fields in a table is to select the table (without expanding it) and then click the arrow to move the fields in this table over to the Columns in your query box.

CAUTION If the owner of the Access database you are importing from has established relationships among the Databases tables (see Chapter 2 for a description of relationships), you may be able to pull in fields from multiple tables with the wizard. If relationships have not been established within Access, you will be limited to querying a single table. This is another way of saying that the wizard does not support making joins between tables (again, see Chapter 2) when importing Access data.

By default, the Query Wizard sorts the fields in the order in which you choose them. For example, choosing Price first, then Branch_Number, and then Product_Number results in a Price, Branch_Number, and Product_Number ordering, even though the source table is not ordered this way.

Ordering of your fields becomes important when you want to apply sorts. If you want to change field ordering after you have selected your fields, you can use the up and down arrows to the right of the Columns in your query box.

Next, change the sort order from the default table order so that it is sorted by Product_Number, then by Branch_Number, and then by Price. Select the Product_Number field in the Columns in your query box and press the up arrow until Product_Number is on top. The dialog box should look like Figure 5-16.

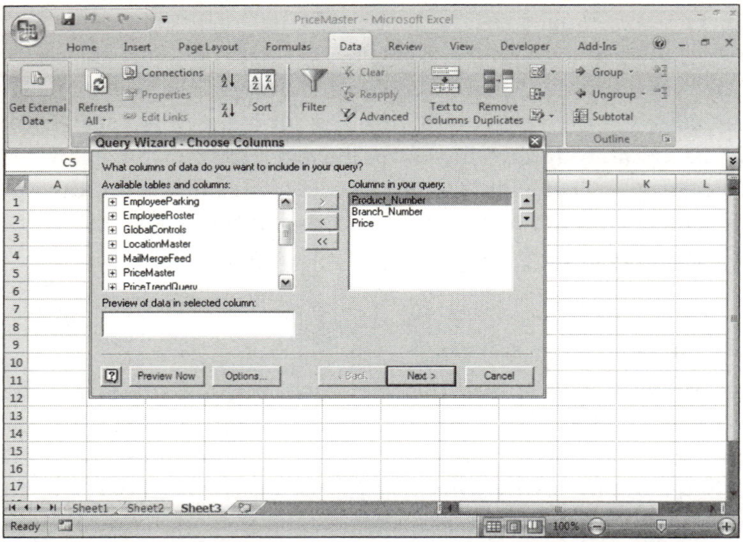

Figure 5-16: Reordering column fields in the Microsoft Query Wizard

Another useful tool in this dialog box is the Preview Now button in the bottom-left dialog box corner. Clicking this button enables you to view the data fields in a specified column without actually having to run the query. Figure 5-17 displays a sample of the Product_Number column fields in the lower-left corner of the Query Wizard.

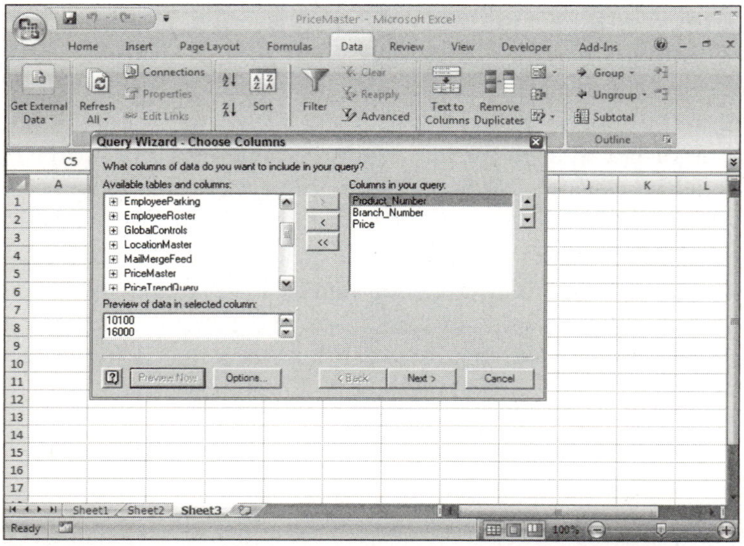

Figure 5-17: Previewing data fields in the Microsoft Query Wizard

Filtering Data in the Microsoft Query Wizard

The next pane of the Microsoft Query Wizard gives you options to filter your data. This pane is optional and clicking Next advances you to the next pane with no filtering. If you have ever used the AutoFilter function in Excel 2003 or earlier, this dialog box will no doubt look familiar.

To activate a filter, select the field you want to filter from the Column to filter box on the left. You will notice that the filter options on the right side of the wizard are now enabled. The first field enables you to select a condition from a drop-down menu (for example, equals, does not equal, or greater than or equal to). The second field enables you to specify criteria for this condition. You may also combine these filters with Boolean, or logical, operators. This section of the wizard allows you to combine up to three filters with AND/OR logical operators.

> **CAUTION** You should be aware of a special pitfall when using any filter criteria, especially when using intrinsically coded data such as the preceding branch number example. What happens if your company violates historic branch numbering protocol and opens a new Oregon branch with a branch number beginning with 2? In that case the report that has been working well for the past six months will stop working. Worse, you may not be told that branch numbering no longer follows a quasi-logical pattern! A much better option is to include a country field in your database and filter on that field. You can do this by using joins in Microsoft Query, a topic we will cover shortly.

Sorting Data in the Microsoft Query Wizard

The next Microsoft Query Wizard option allows you to provide a custom sort to your data. You access the Sort Order window of the wizard by clicking Next in the filtering window. As shown in Figure 5-19, you can apply only three consecutive sorts to your data. For this example, first sort ascending by Product_Number and then ascending by Branch_Number.

A REAL EXAMPLE USING THE WIZARD CRITERIA PANE

Suppose you want to bring list price data for ZalexCorp U.S. branches into a spreadsheet. Because you are a brilliant data analyst who is intimately familiar with my company's data structure, you know that all branch numbers greater than 899999 are outside of North America. You also happen to know that, for some reason beyond logic, your company has designated all branches beginning with 2 as Canadian branches.

To isolate U.S. branches, then, you can combine two filters with an AND Boolean operator. The first condition gives you all branches less than 900000. That takes care of non-North American branches. Your next condition, separated by the AND operator, gives you all branches not beginning with a 2 (see Figure 5-18). Those rascally Canadians are taken care of now.

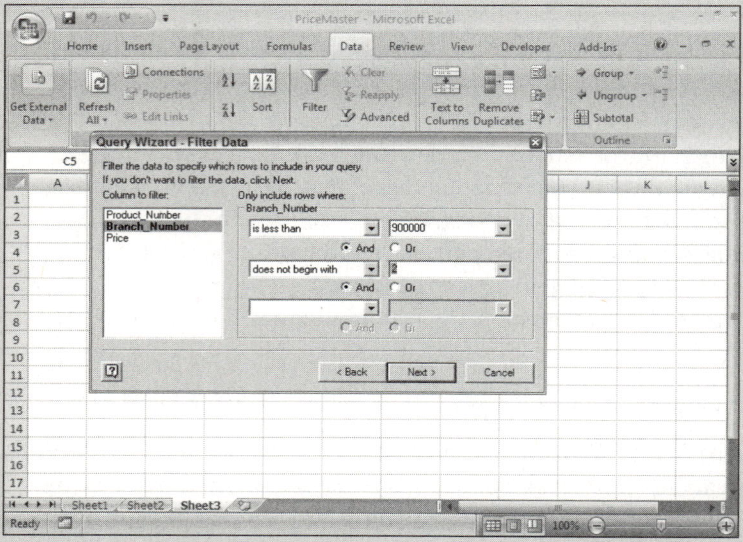

Figure 5-18: Using filter conditions in the Query Wizard

Note that the criteria used, 900000 and 2, do not explicitly exist anywhere as data fields. They were not chosen from the criteria drop-down list but instead typed in manually.

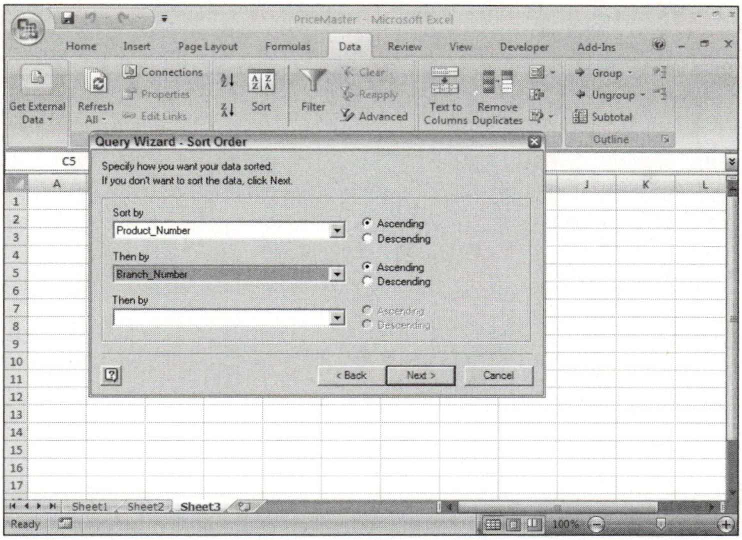

Figure 5-19: Sorting in the Microsoft Query Wizard

Importing the External Data

You are almost ready to bring your data into Excel. Selecting Next from the Sorting wizard opens a dialog box asking whether you want to return the data to Excel or further modify the query in Microsoft Query. Also note the Save query button. Clicking this button enables you to save your query so you can access it from the Queries tab of the Choose Data Source dialog box. At this point, forgo saving your query and instead choose to view our data in Excel.

Clicking Next opens the Import Data dialog box, where you decide where and how you want to import your data. As shown in Figure 5-20, you can import your data as a table, a PivotTable report, or a PivotChart and Pivot-Table report. For this example, choose to import the data as a table.

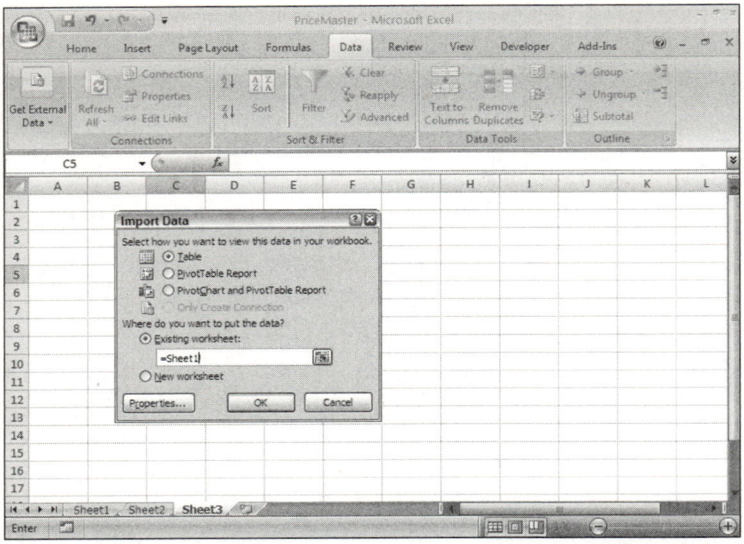

Figure 5-20: Choose the location and form of external data in the Microsoft Query Wizard.

Before you advance to the next step, examine the Properties button on this dialog box. Selecting the Connection Properties dialog box gives you some useful options for choosing how to refresh your newly created data connection (see Figure 5-21).

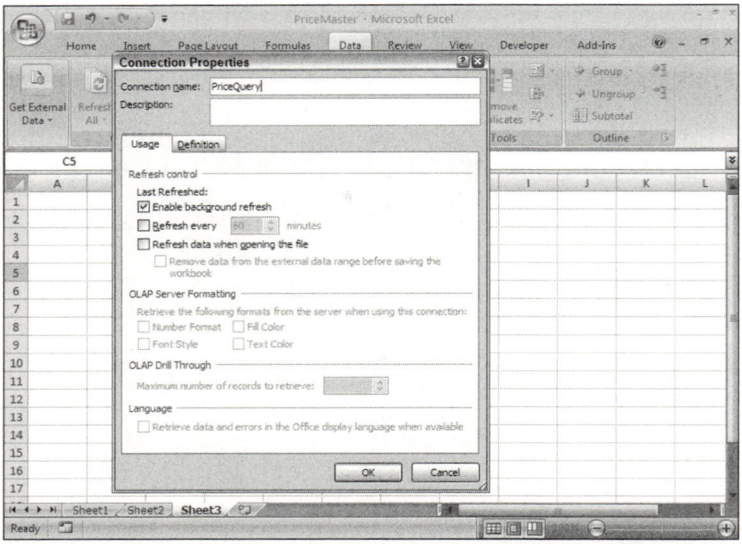

Figure 5-21: Data refresh options through the Properties button in the Microsoft Query Wizard

Note the three refresh options at the top of the properties dialog box:

- ▪ Option 1 asks whether you want to enable background refresh. This option enables you to continue to use Excel while the data connection is refreshing. It is quite useful for large data refreshes or slow connections.

- ▪ Option 2 enables you to specify a specific time interval in which to refresh your data — obviously crucial if you expect the source data to be updated often.

- ▪ Option 3 enables you to choose the data to be refreshed every time the user opens your Excel file.

In using Microsoft Query to bring in your data, you are not just copying and pasting for a one-time analysis. In fact, you are establishing a connection to an external data source that is refreshed according to your mandate — regardless of who uses your Excel file. After selecting the connection properties and clicking OK, you will be returned to the Import Data dialog box.

To finish importing your data, choose to import your modified Access table as a table in Excel located in cell B1. Select the OK button and your data will finally be imported.

Modifying External Data Range Properties

Microsoft Query gives you several ways to deal with data when the number of rows changes. Right-click the PriceMaster table you just imported, select Table, and then select External Data Properties. This opens the External Data Properties dialog box (see Figure 5-22).

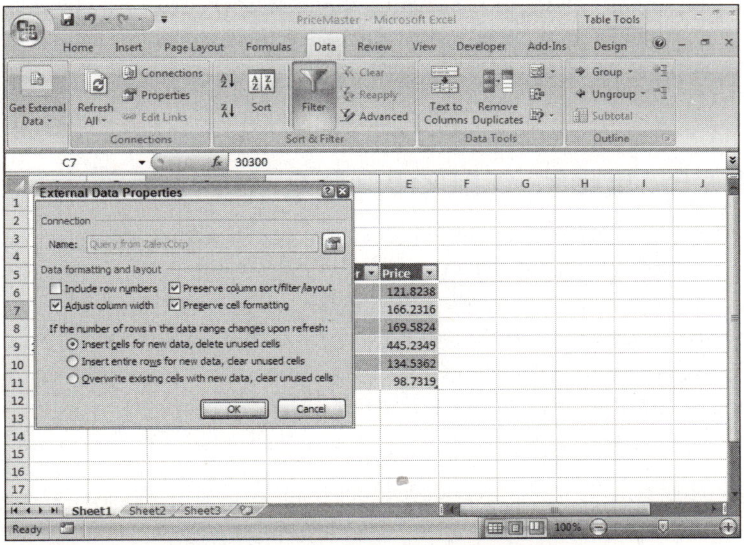

Figure 5-22: The External Data Properties dialog box

Three radio buttons at the bottom of the dialog box specify how Excel should handle increases or decreases in the number of rows upon refresh. How your formulas behave depends on which external data properties you choose.

▪ **Insert cells for new data, delete unused cells:** When data rows decrease, you may have errors in adjacent cells that reference your external range. The cells these formulas referenced are deleted, so you will get a #VALUE error in your formula cells.

▪ **Insert rows for new data, clear unused cells:** When the unused cells are cleared instead of deleted, the formula may no longer return an error. Instead, it continues to reference cells from the original range — even though some of them are blank now. This could still give you erroneous results.

▪ **Overwrite cells for new data, clear unused cells:** The third option should be the same as option two when rows decrease as unused cells are cleared.

TIP Have you ever had formulas referencing a range of data in a worksheet, only to have the number of rows change when you updated the data source? Depending on how you set up your analysis, you are either updating formulas with the new range or updating named ranges with new cell references. Either option is a serious pain in the neck and a time-waster! Use Microsoft Query and you'll never have to do that again! When Microsoft Query imports your data, the entire range and each column are named. If the rows change on refresh, Microsoft Query automatically changes the named range references to point to the right rows. Just make sure all your formulas reference the external data named ranges and, you are good to go!

Going Beyond the Wizard in Microsoft Query

Using the Microsoft Query Wizard is undoubtedly user-friendly. The cost of user-friendliness, however, is decreased functionality. Yes, the Microsoft Query Wizard can establish your connection, enables you to browse tables and fields, and even to apply some basic filters and sorts. If you want to import fields from more than one table and modify how two tables are joined in your query, you are simply out of luck with the wizard. Getting advanced functionality requires you to go beyond the wizard and start diving into Microsoft Query.

Introduction to the Microsoft Query Interface

Your introduction to Access queries in Chapter 2 gives you a strong foundation for working with Microsoft Query. You can think of Microsoft Query as a slightly softer (read user-friendly) version of the Access Query Design view — except you are building the query and controlling the interface all from Excel.

To start Microsoft Query, select Get External Data → From Other Sources → From Microsoft Query. Remember the Use the Query Wizard to create/edit queries check box we mentioned earlier? Now it's time to clear this check box.

Selecting the Database

Select ZalexCorp from the Data Source dialog box. Clicking Next opens the Add Tables dialog box, which asks you to add tables. Now you begin the departure from the wizard. Remember what you learned while working with Access queries in Chapter 2 and you will be fine. This dialog box is simply asking which tables you want to add for your custom query — just like in Access. You simply want to query the PriceMaster table, so select PriceMaster from the list, click Add, and then click Close on the Add Tables dialog box to move on (see Figure 5-23).

Now you see the Microsoft Query interface. Your panic meter ought to be low right now — this interface looks strikingly familiar to the query Design view that you learned in Chapter 2. There are enough subtle differences, however, that warrant our reviewing the interface a bit more closely.

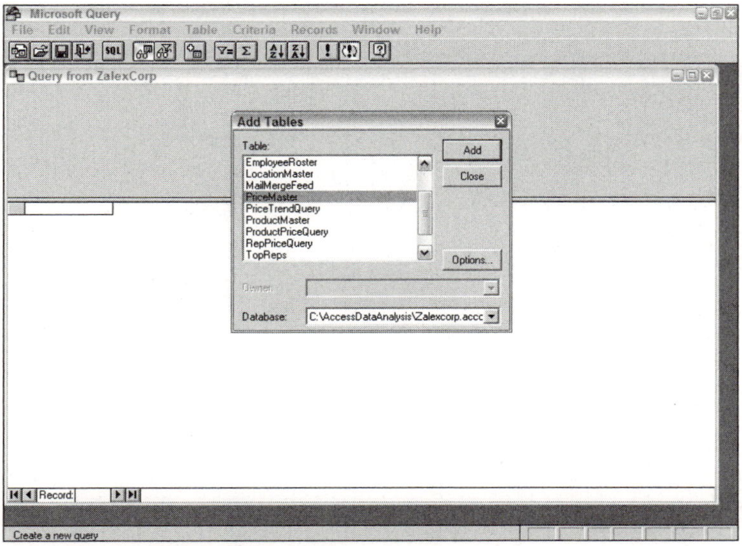

Figure 5-23: Add tables to Microsoft Query

The Microsoft Query Interface

First make sure that you can see all the panes in the Microsoft Query interface. Select View from the Microsoft Query window and verify that there are check marks next to both Tables and Criteria. When done, your interface should look like Figure 5-24.

The interface has three main sections. The top section where you see the PriceMaster table is the table view section. This is very similar to the Access Query Design view and is where you can see tables you've added and specify the join relationships between those tables.

The next section is the criteria section. In the Access Query Design view, the records you want to include in your query and any screening criteria are more or less integrated — not so in Microsoft Query. The middle section is solely for applying criteria to the query — you may have a field in the criteria section that you have not selected for your query. Select a field from the drop-down menu and enter screening criteria below it. This is where we will replicate the filtering we did through the soft and fuzzy interface of the Microsoft Query Wizard.

The bottom section is the data section. Here we differ even more from the Access interface. Microsoft Query enables you to select and see the data in your query. To see your data in Access you must either run the query or view a subset of the data in preview mode.

Enough of summaries and introductions. Time to get into some details. In the next section, you will import your PriceMaster data via Microsoft Query and introduce some added functionality through the wizard.

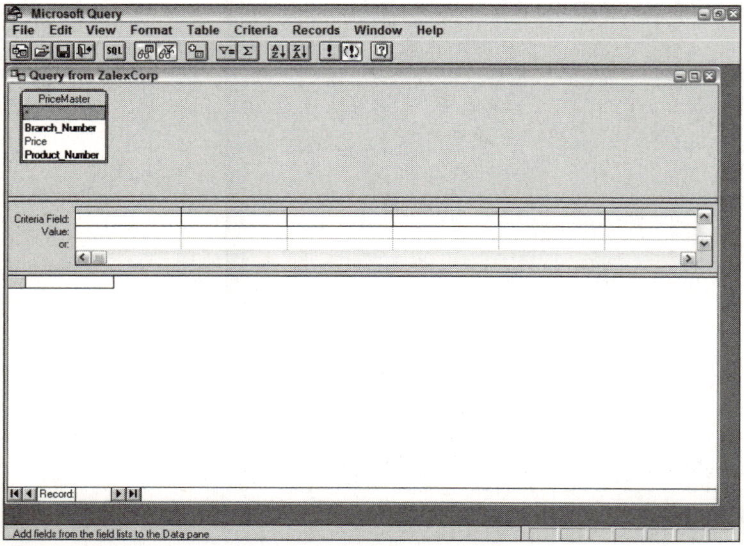

Figure 5-24: The main Microsoft Query interface

Using Microsoft Query to Import Data

First, you must add data to your query. This is as simple as double-clicking fields from the table view above. Alternatively, you could go down to the first row in the Data view and select fields from the drop-down list. Note that as soon as you add a field, the actual query data shows up in the data section. The Microsoft Query interface should look like Figure 5-25.

Adding Criteria in Microsoft Query

Now that you have your data, apply your criteria. Remember from the Query Wizard section that you need to pull all Branch_Numbers that are less than 900000 and that do not start with 2. Working with logical operators as criteria is not as simple as in the wizard, but it is quite similar to what you've learned in Access.

The first criterion is easy. You will just add Branch_Number to the Criteria section from the drop-down menu, and in the criteria field type **<'900000'** (see Figure 5-26). The great thing about having an immediate preview of your data is that you can instantly see whether our criterion worked. In this case, it looks like it did!

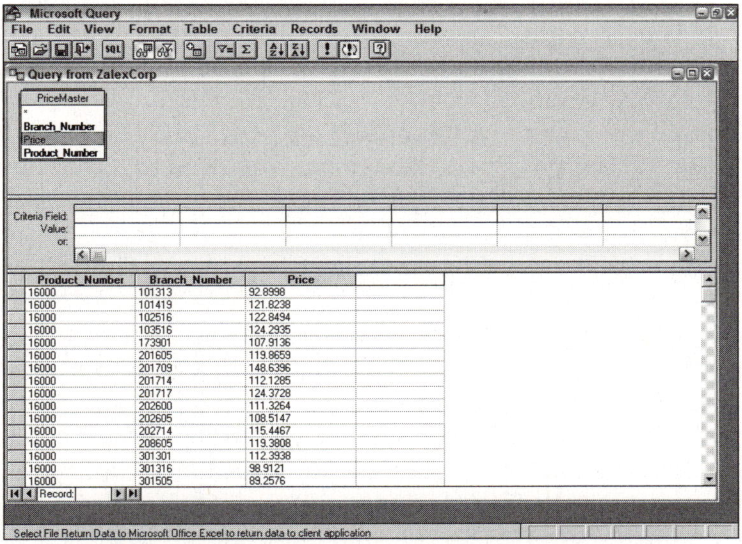

Figure 5-25: Data fields viewed in the Microsoft Query interface

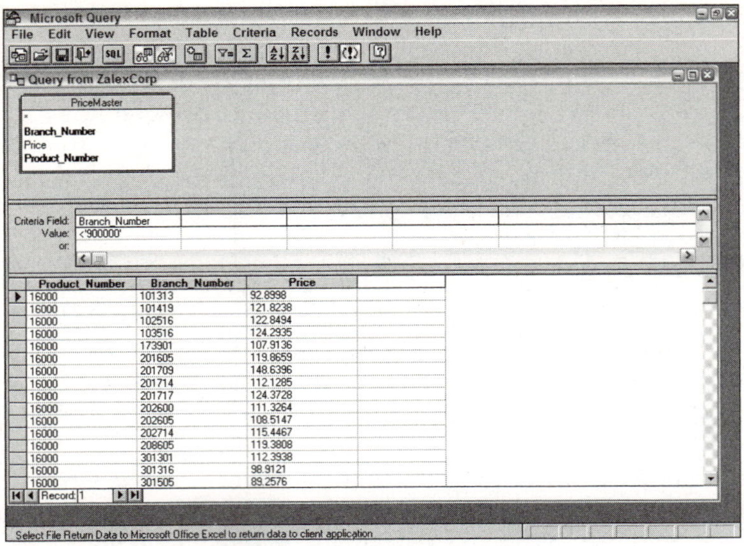

Figure 5-26: Add one criterion to Microsoft Query

Now it gets a bit trickier. You need to add another criterion with an AND operator. To produce the AND operator you add Branch_Number once more to the criteria section from the drop-down list. Alternatively, you could have modified your first criteria by adding the AND logical operator and then typing your second criterion expression.

This is simple enough, but how do you replicate the "does not begin with" operator that the Query Wizard gave you? Remember, you need to screen out all those crazy Canadian branches that begin with 2. Fortunately, Microsoft Query still retains some soft and fuzzy interfaces. Double-click in the Value row of the criteria section and the Edit Criteria dialog box shown in Figure 5-27 opens.

Now you just scroll down and find the "does not begin with" operator and then type **2** in the Value box. At this point, the Microsoft Query interface should resemble Figure 5-28.

Note that Microsoft Query inserted some text for you in the second value column. In essence, Microsoft Query translated your input to the dialog box into something it can actually understand — Structured Query Language (SQL). Although learning to write in SQL is beyond the scope of this book, it is helpful to understand there is a (more or less) common language behind all relational database queries.

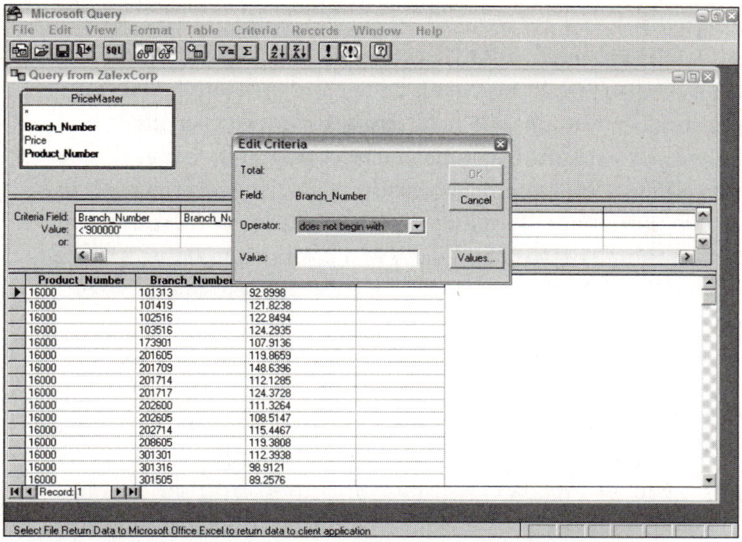

Figure 5-27: Use the Edit Criteria dialog box in Microsoft Query

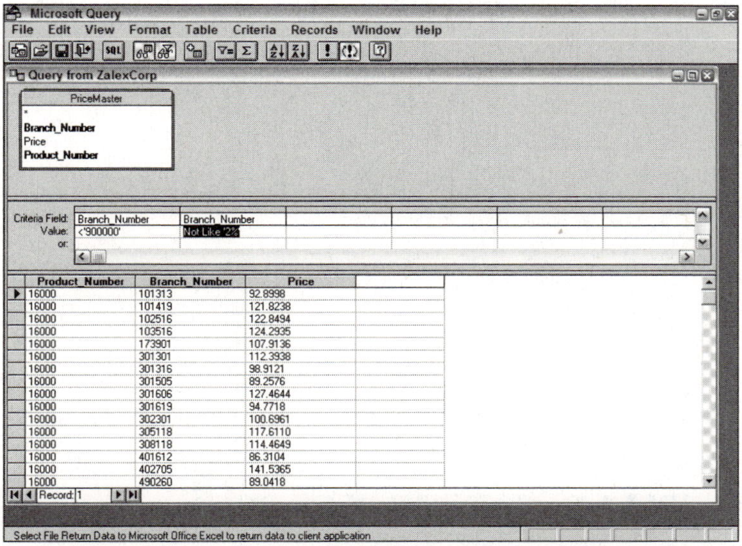

Figure 5-28: Criteria section results from using the Edit Criteria dialog box

CAUTION Although SQL has a common structure, the syntax can be different between relational database applications. Surprisingly, there is even a difference in syntax between SQL in Microsoft Query and SQL in Microsoft Access. An example shows up in the wild card character of your second Branch_Number criterion. Microsoft Query uses a % character as a placeholder for a character string of indefinite length. Microsoft Access, however, uses the * character. Subtle syntax differences like these can cause a lot of frustration when trying to do something in Microsoft Query you are used to doing another way in Access — or vice versa. Just know these differences exist and be wary when working between applications.

Adding Sorts in Microsoft Query

Now you need to add our sort to our query. Remember from the previous section that you want to first sort by Product_Number and then by Branch_Number, both in ascending order. Choose Records from the Microsoft Query dialog box and then select Sort. This opens the Sort dialog box shown in Figure 5-29.

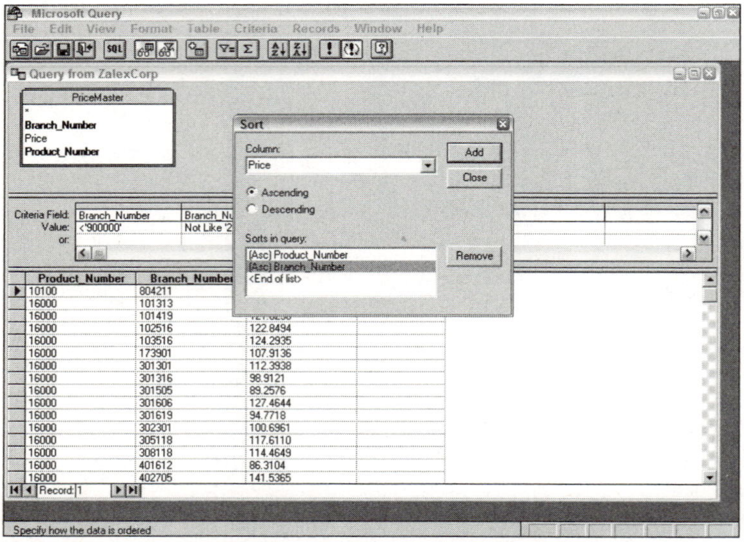

Figure 5-29: The Sort dialog box in Microsoft Query

Adding your sort is as simple as selecting Product_Number, choosing the Ascending radio button and then clicking Add. Now repeat the exercise for Branch_Number and you are done!

TIP For a quick sorting shortcut, select both the Product_Number and Branch_Number columns in the Data view. Now press the ascending sort icon on the Microsoft Query dialog box and you have your sort! Microsoft Query applies the ascending sort first to whichever column is left-most and then works to the right applying subsequent sorts. This shortcut only works, however, if you are applying the same kind of sort (such as ascending or descending) to all your selected columns.

Adding a Custom Field

In this section, we will expand a bit on the additional things you can do with Microsoft Query versus the wizard. Specifically, we will demonstrate how to add a custom/calculated field with a data field that concatenates Product_Number and Branch_Number.

Assume that your imported data will be used as a reference table to bring in a price given a user's choice of branch number and product number. You can do this easily with the Excel VLOOKUP function. You can match the concatenation of Branch_Number and Product_Number to your imported data's identical custom field. Then you can tell VLOOKUP to return the column associated with price. (If you are not familiar with the VLOOKUP function, refer to the Excel online Help.) When you add your concatenated field to your imported data within Microsoft Query, it becomes a part of your named external data range. When you refresh the data and more or fewer rows come in, the named range is automatically updated as well. Therefore, the VLOOKUP function can reference this named external range and you can be assured that it will capture your refreshed data — regardless of whether rows increase, decrease, or remain unchanged.

Adding this custom field is relatively simple. Go to a blank column to the far right in the data section. In that blank column, enter **[Product_Number]** and **[Branch_Number]** separated by the ampersand (**&**) concatenation operator. Technically, the brackets are not required in Microsoft Query, but it is best practice to include them.

Move the new column to the far left by dragging and dropping it. Double-click the field and give it a more meaningful name, like Index. Have a look before you import your data into Excel (see Figure 5-30).

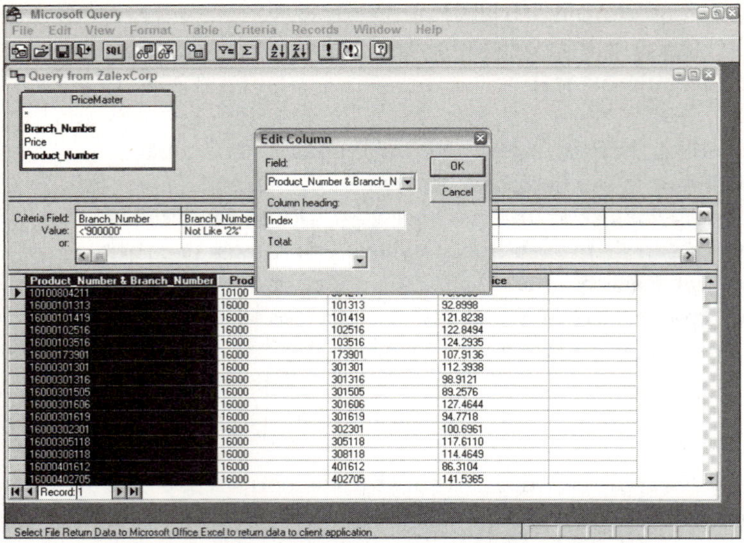

Figure 5-30: View of a concatenated field in Microsoft Query

To import your data, go to the File menu and select Return Data to Microsoft Excel. This is opens the dialog box shown in Figure 5-20 that asks how and where the data should be imported. Select Table, choose cell A1 and then press OK. Your data is now imported.

Advanced Use of Microsoft Query

Now that we have covered the basics of Microsoft Query, it is time to explore some more advanced functionality. Specifically, we will cover using joins to bring in data from more than one table, creating custom fields with SQL, and adding user-defined parameters to increase interactivity.

Using Joins

We covered joins and data relationships extensively in Chapter 2. All you need to do here is review any steps that are different and discuss the limitations of Microsoft Query in this area. In general, you will find using joins in Microsoft Query quite similar to using them in Access.

Let's flesh out a real-world scenario to illustrate the power of joins and parameters. Assume your Marketing VP wants to compare transaction price to list price by branch. She wants to get a feel for which locations are discounting price more heavily than others are.

In prior examples, you concatenated Branch_Number and Product_Number to create a third field that was your unique identifier for list price. You could have used this field with a VLOOKUP function to match list price to transaction price — provided that you imported yet another table for transactions and created yet another concatenated field for matching your tables.

You can skip this convoluted exercise, however, by joining your tables of interest in Microsoft Query. To compare transaction pricing and list pricing, two tables are of interest — TransactionMaster, which houses the detailed volume and revenue data, and PriceMaster, which houses the list prices for all branches and products. Add these tables in Microsoft Query.

To create your joins, select the field you want to join, and then drag and drop that field onto the same field (although it need not have the same name) in the second column. Do this once for Branch_Number and then repeat the process for Product_Number. The default join Microsoft Query creates for you is an inner join. Recall from Chapter 2 that an inner join selects records only where there is a match between the joined fields. You will want to keep this as an inner join. Having two inner joins is equivalent to joining your tables on one virtual field — the concatenation of Branch_Number and Product_Number (see Figure 5-31).

Now simply double-click the fields you want in your query. To keep it simple, pull in Branch_Number, Product_Number, Sales_Amount and Transaction_Quantity from TransactionMaster. Next, pull in Price from PriceMaster so you have list price.

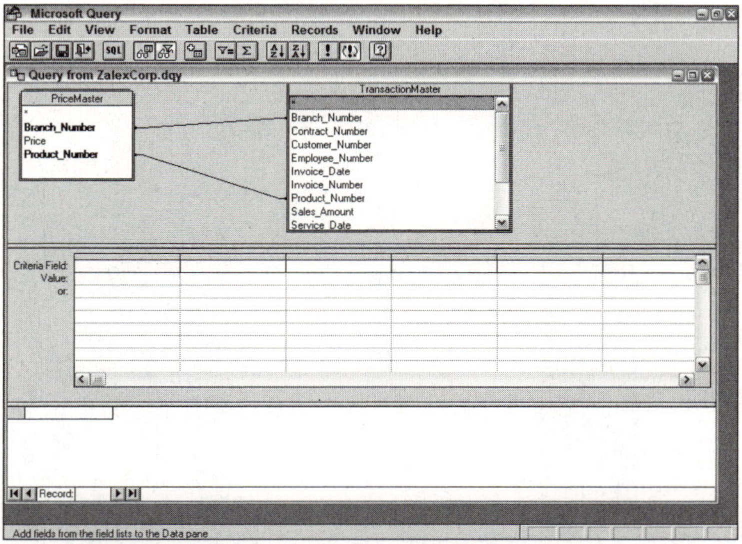

Figure 5-31: Using two inner joins in Microsoft Query

Because the underlying data is much more granular than the fields you have pulled in, you will need to change your query to a Group By query with Total fields. Add a Sum Total to Sales_Amount and Transaction_Quantity. To sum the Sales_Amount field, double-click the column heading to bring up the Edit Column dialog box. Choose Sum from the Total drop-down menu (see Figure 5-32). Do the same thing to the Transaction_Quantity field.

> **TIP** Microsoft Query allows more than just a sum operation for field totals in a Group By query. You can perform an average, perform a count, return the largest record or return the smallest record on the underlying data. To access these different operations, continue clicking the summation icon until you cycle to the operation you want. The data label will automatically change to reflect the operation you've chosen (for example, Avg of Sales_Amount to denote the average operation).

> **TIP** You may want to perform a Group By query without performing a Totals operation on a field. This becomes important when the dataset you are querying has duplicate records. An easy way to eliminate these duplicate records is by changing to a Group By query. To do this without a Totals operation, go to View → Query Properties and select the Group Records check box. If you do perform a Totals operation on a field (like Count, Sum or Average) you do not need to select Group Records from the Query Properties dialog box — Microsoft Query automatically assumes you are doing a Group By query.

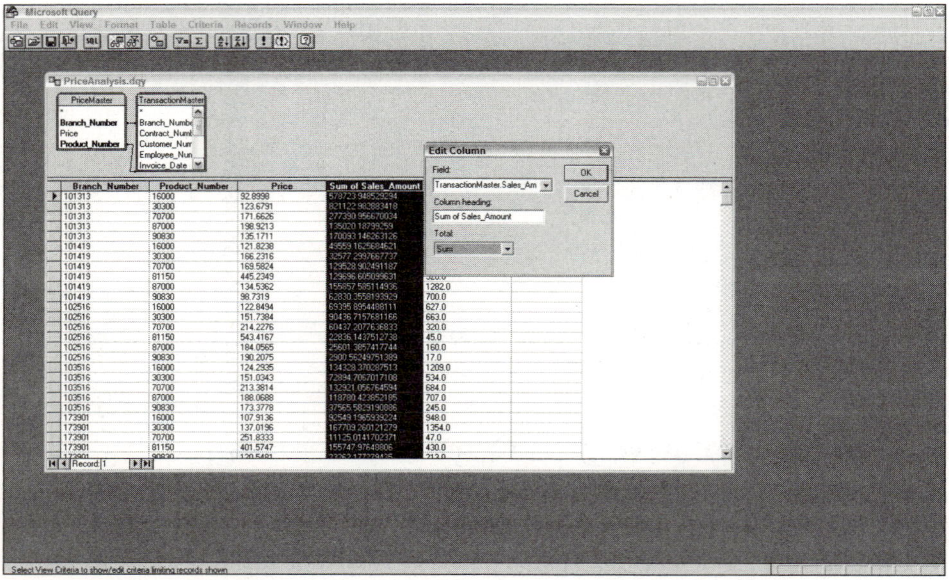

Figure 5-32: Add sum totals in Microsoft Query.

Modifying SQL to Create Custom Fields

So far, you have the basic raw materials for your pricing analysis. You have the list price, which you brought in from your PriceMaster table. What about the transaction price, though? To get that you must divide total sales by total quantity for each branch/product number combination. Of course you could perform this calculation once you get your data into Excel, but isn't there an easier way?

Unfortunately, it is at this stage where you stretch the boundaries of Microsoft Query. The tool does not provide a graphical user interface for making the custom expression we need to calculate our transaction price. You can do it, but it requires some tweaking of the underlying SQL code. Before you can tweak that code, you need a quick primer on SQL.

A Very Brief Primer on SQL

SQL (Structured Query Language) is the underlying code for querying basically all forms of relational databases. It may sound intimidating at first, but the underlying structure is quite simple.

Like any programming language, SQL is a set of instructions for your computer. It is a set of instructions specifically detailing where and how your computer should retrieve a set of data.

A simple SQL statement tells our computer to SELECT certain fields FROM a specified database object WHERE certain criteria that you specify are met. There are other modifiers you can add to your statement, such as ORDER BY to specify a sort and GROUP BY to specify that our query should be grouped. These are relatively straightforward, however. Let's look at a sample SQL statement underneath the PriceMaster query you used earlier.

```
SELECT Product_Number, Branch_Number, Price
FROM PriceMaster
WHERE (Branch_Number Not Like '2%') AND (Branch_Number<'900000')
```

This almost looks more straightforward than the Microsoft Query interface. And this is all the SQL you need to know to start modifying Microsoft Query.

Creating the Field

Before you start tweaking SQL code, think for a minute about the field expression you want to add. You want an expression for transaction price, which arithmetically is given by

```
Sales_Amount/Transaction_Quantity
```

Actually, the precise expression should be

```
Sum(Sales_Amount)/Sum(Transaction_Quantity)
```

Do you see why you must calculate the sum before you divide to get the correct transaction price? If you answer, "Because this is a Group By query," then you are spot on accurate. In a Group By query, each field must be either an expression or a grouping. You want only one transaction price for each Branch and Product. Therefore, your transaction price must be an expression.

Now that you know what you want, you must figure out how to modify the SQL. Take a look at the SQL code behind your current query by selecting the SQL icon from the Microsoft Query dialog box. You get a dialog box with the SQL code. Here is the code:

```
SELECT TransactionMaster.Product_Number, ⊃
TransactionMaster.Branch_Number, PriceMaster.Price, ⊃
Sum(TransactionMaster.Sales_Amount) AS 'Sum of Sales_Amount', ⊃
Sum(TransactionMaster.Transaction_Quantity) AS 'Sum of ⊃
Transaction_Quantity'
FROM `C:\ACCESSDATAANALYSIS\Zalexcorp.accdb`.PriceMaster ⊃
PriceMaster, `C:\ACCESSDATAANALYSIS\Zalexcorp.accdb`.⊃
TransactionMaster TransactionMaster
WHERE TransactionMaster.Branch_Number = PriceMaster.Branch_Number ⊃
AND TransactionMaster.Product_Number = PriceMaster.Product_Number
GROUP BY TransactionMaster.Employee_Number, ⊃
TransactionMaster.Product_Number, PriceMaster.Branch_Number, ⊃
PriceMaster.Price
```

Before you panic, take a minute to isolate the SELECT, FROM, WHERE structure we discussed before. Even though the syntax is messier, you still have the underlying structure.

Your first step is to figure out where you should add the transaction price expression. Rather than speculate, let's examine the SQL code for clues. After the SELECT statement, notice the following piece of code:

```
Sum(TransactionMaster.Sales_Amount) AS 'Sum of Sales_Amount'
```

If this SQL statement were translated into plain English, it might read:

```
Computer, select the field Sales_Amount and sum it—then name the ⊃
new field 'Sum of Sales_Amount'
```

If you use clues from the preceding lines of code to create your own custom expression, it might read:

```
Sum(TransactionMaster.Sales_Amount)/Sum(TransactionMaster. ⊃
Transaction_Quantity) AS 'TransactionPrice'
```

Type your new line of SQL into the SQL dialog box to see whether your guess actually works. Notice a comma separates each field statement in the SELECT section, so be sure to add a comma before adding the SQL code. Your code should look like Figure 5-33.

TIP You may have noticed that custom field names are by default enclosed in single quotation marks in Microsoft Query SQL view. Access SQL view uses square brackets to denote custom field names. The SQL views of both applications will recognize double quotation marks as well. Any of these three characters can be used interchangeably to denote a custom name. Alternatively, if a name has no spaces in it you may omit these demarcation characters all together.

Click OK to close the SQL dialog box. Now you can view your new expression in Data mode (see Figure 5-34).

Do a spot check on the math by manually calculating TransactionPrice from Sum of Sales_Amount and Sum of Transaction_Quantity. It checks out. Now save this query as PriceAnalysis and your Excel file as PriceMaster so you can move on.

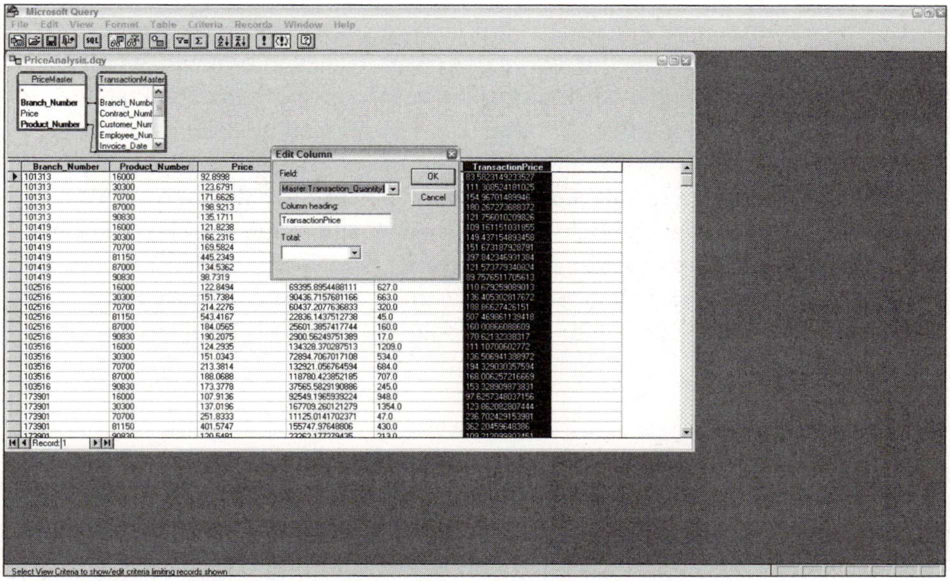

Figure 5-33: The TransactionPrice custom expression in SQL view

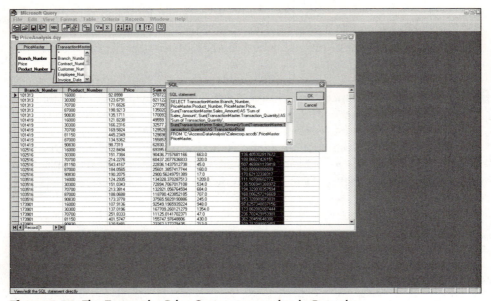

Figure 5-34: The TransactionPrice Custom expression in Data view

TIP The advanced user can use the SQL view to circumvent the inherent limitations in Microsoft Query. Later in this chapter you will summarize these limitations, one of which is constraining the user to no more than two tables when using an outer join. This limitation can be bypassed by writing the correct SQL code into the SQL view. You don't have to be an SQL guru to do this. Try this: Fire up Access, go to ZalexCorp and develop your 3+ table query with outer joins in Query Design. Right-click your query and select SQL view from the drop-down menu. Now copy the SQL statement, go to your SQL view in Microsoft Query and paste it in. You get a warning that the query cannot be displayed graphically. Click OK and you should see your 3+ table query in Data view.

Adding User Defined Parameters in Microsoft Query

In this section, we will explore the user interactivity available through Microsoft Query. Specifically, we will cover user-defined parameters.

Recall from Chapter 2 that a parameter is a criterion in a query that is supplied dynamically by the user every time the query is run. In the criteria section, you enclose some text in brackets. As long as that text does not match any field within your query design, Access treats the string enclosed in brackets as a parameter. Running the query prompts a message box to come up asking the user for the value of the parameter. Whatever the user enters is what Access treats as the query criterion. The same is true of Microsoft Query.

> **CAUTION** It is best practice not to use spaces when naming parameters. For example, it is better to name the parameter [Enter_Branch_Number] than to name it [Enter Branch Number]. Using spaces can cause errors when running the query.

A Simple User-Defined Parameter

Assume that your marketing VP wants to distribute your price analysis to branch managers. Branch managers are interested in pricing for their branch and do not want to wade through data for other branches. So create a Branch_Number user defined parameter by modifying our PriceAnalysis query.

From the Data ribbon tab, choose Get External Data → From Other Sources → From Microsoft Query. Since you saved your previous query as PriceAnalysis, you can find that query under the Queries tab in the Choose Data Source dialog box (see Figure 5-35).

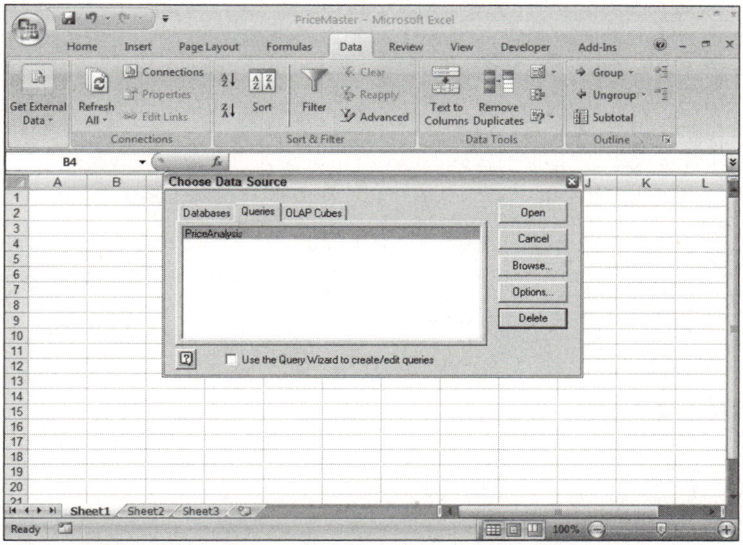

Figure 5-35: Choose a saved query as the data source.

Click Open to view your query. Verify that Criteria view is selected (View → Criteria). Next, you need to enter your parameter, enclosed in brackets, under the Branch_Number field. For this example, use [Enter_Branch_Number].

> **CAUTION** When you have a parameter on a joined field and that field exists in your query, Microsoft Query gets real picky. Specifically, if you added Branch_Number from TransactionMaster to your query, you must add Branch_Number from PriceMaster in the Criteria view for your parameter. We don't know why Microsoft Query gets so fussy about this, but you will get a "Too few parameters" error if you forget.

Return your data to Excel from the File menu of Microsoft Query. When prompted for the Branch_Number value, enter **101313**. When your data is in Excel, right-click the external data range and choose Refresh from the menu. Users will see the following dialog box for entering their branch numbers (see Figure 5-36).

Advanced Example of User-Defined Parameter

The previous example allows some user interactivity, but it is still very clunky. At a minimum, it would be nice to have the user choose from some sort of drop-down list of branch numbers. In addition, it would be nice to allow the user to choose a different branch and then have the data automatically refresh, rather than manually refresh when they want a branch number.

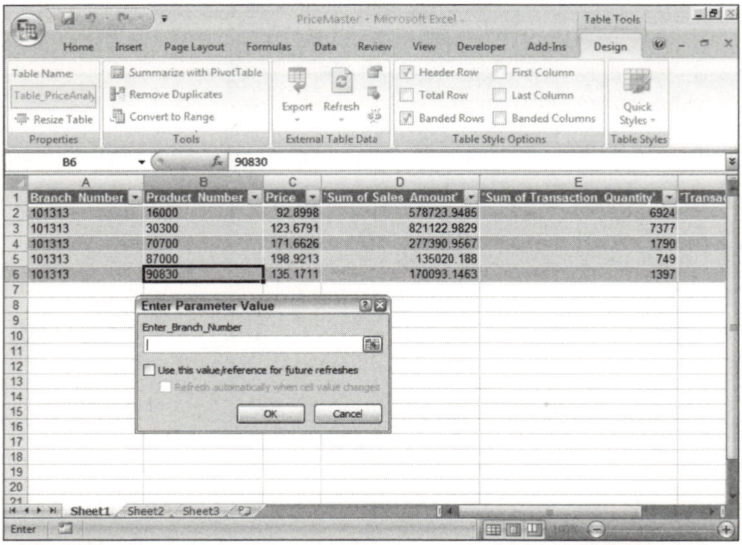

Figure 5-36: Users are prompted for a user parameter in Excel.

Look at Figure 5-36 again. Note that Excel gives you two check boxes. The first enables you to specify a cell where Excel will look for your parameter for future data refreshes. The second check box triggers your data to refresh each time the parameter value changes. To link your parameter query to a cell value so that the data changes every time the cell changes, you must enter a cell reference in the text box and select both check boxes. You will do this in subsequent steps.

If you insert a Form control so the user can choose from a list of branch numbers, you can use the output of that control as your data refresh parameter mentioned in the prior paragraph. Before starting, insert a few rows above your External range to make room for the control. In addition, insert a column to the far left of the External Range for some working space. Follow these steps:

1. To insert a control, you need to make sure the Developer tab is added to your Excel ribbon. The Excel ribbon enables you to record macros, view VBA code and insert controls. Go to the Microsoft Office icon and then select Excel Options from the menu. On the Popular tab, verify that Show Developer tab in the Ribbon is selected.

2. Select Developer tab → Controls → Insert → Form Control and choose a combo box control (see Figure 5-37).

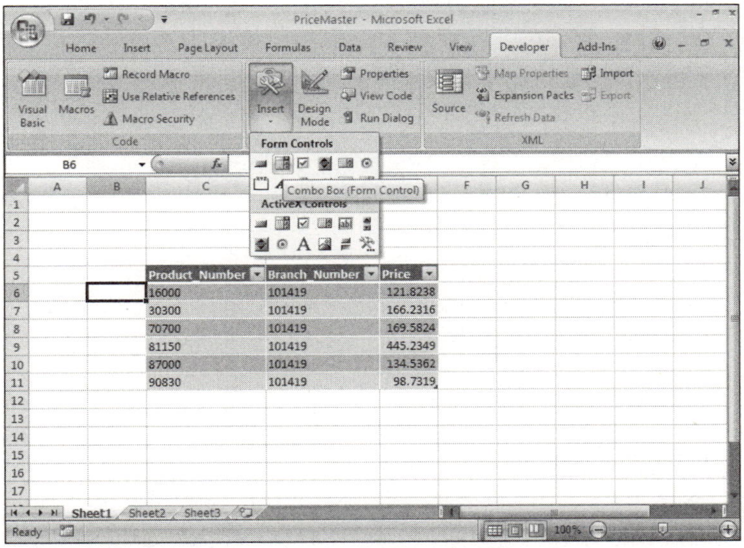

Figure 5-37: Choose a combo box Form control.

3. Draw the combo box control on the empty rows above the external data range. With the combo box selected, right-click and choose Format from the drop-down menu. This opens the Format Control dialog box (see Figure 5-38). You need to modify the Input range and Cell link fields on the Controls tab. The Input range field enables you to specify a range of cells housing data from which the user can choose. The Cell link field enables you to send the output of the control (the field the user chooses from the drop-down) to the cell of your choice. Type in cell **A8** for your Cell link field. Before you specify the Input range, you need to develop a list of branch numbers from which the user can choose.

4. Bring in a list of unique branch numbers to populate the control. Using Microsoft Query, bring a list of branch numbers from LocationMaster into Sheet2. Note that the list should occupy range A2:A46.

5. Return to the Input range field of the Form control. The fill list occupies range A2:A46 on Sheet2, so enter that range into the Input range field. At this point, the Control Format dialog box should look like Figure 5-39.

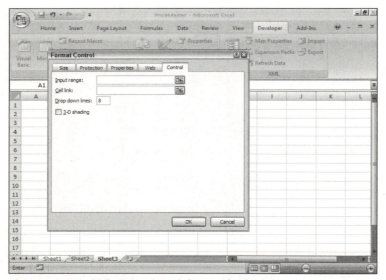

Figure 5-38: Initial properties of the combo box

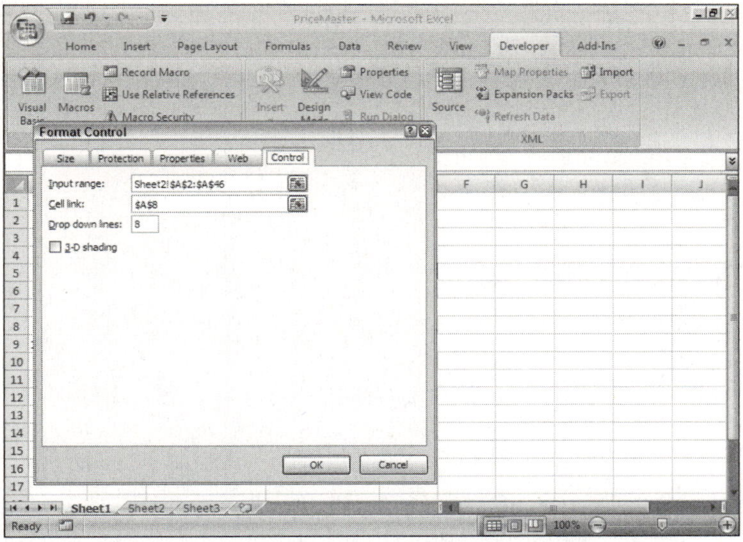

Figure 5-39: Final properties of the combo box

6. The Form control returns the position of the data element chosen, but not the data element itself. You must translate the position of the data element within the data range to the actual value of the data element chosen. The Excel INDEX function does the trick. The INDEX function returns the value of a data element in a range given the position of that data element. Look at the syntax in Figure 5-40. The control returns the number 2, indicating the branch number chosen is the second element in the data range. The INDEX function translates the data element's order into its value, 101419.

7. Ensure that your external data range references cell A9 to pick up the parameter value. You must also ensure that the data refreshes when the parameter value changes. Right-click the external data range and choose Table → Parameters. At this point, the Parameters dialog box looks like Figure 5-41. Don't forget to turn off Design mode by clearing Design Mode from the Developer tab.

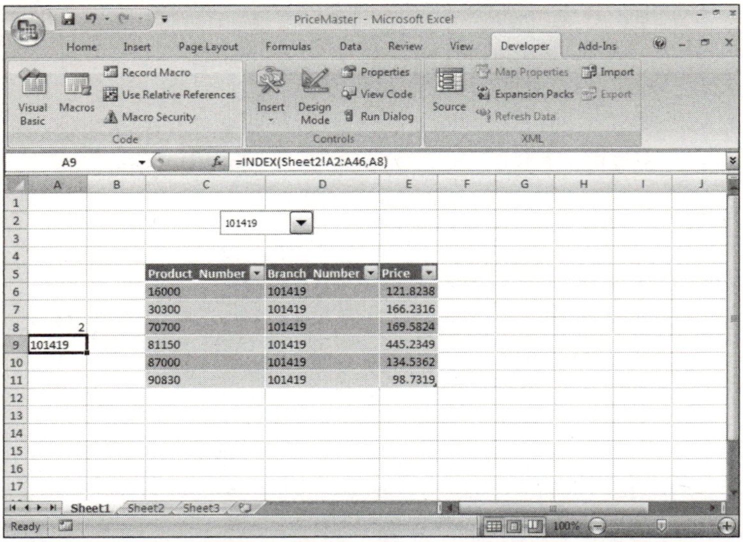

Figure 5-40: Use the INDEX function to return the value of a data element given the position of the data element in a range.

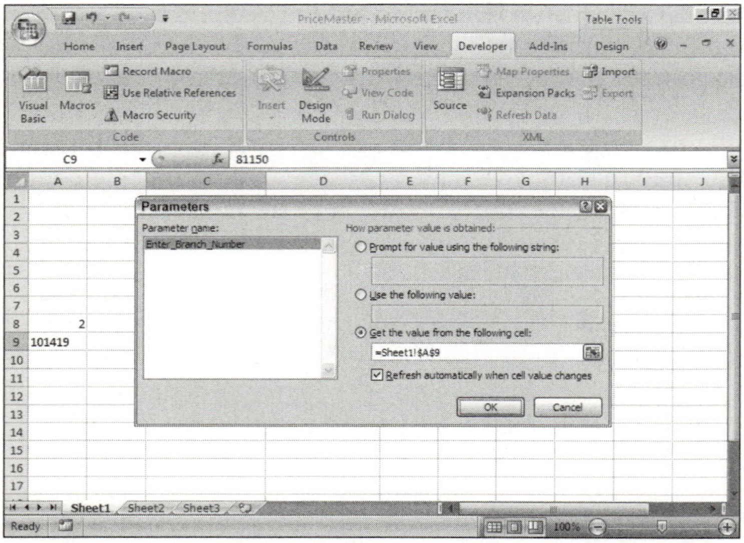

Figure 5-41: The Parameters dialog box in external range properties

All that's left is a little formatting to make the worksheet a bit more professional and user friendly. Do the following:

- Hide column A as you don't want your user to modify cells or be confused by the values in that column.

- Hide the Sum of Sales_Amount and Sum of Transaction_Quantity so you can easily compare List Price to Transaction Price.

- Add some text to the left of the combo box to let users know what they need to do.

- Format the column labels such that the text is wrapped and format Price and TransPrice as Currency.

- Add a column at the end of the External data that calculates percent discount from list.

The final result should resemble Figure 5-42.

You now have a nifty Excel pricing analysis that is exactly what your hypothetical boss wanted. If the source data changes — no worries — it is instantly refreshed when the user changes Branch_Numbers.

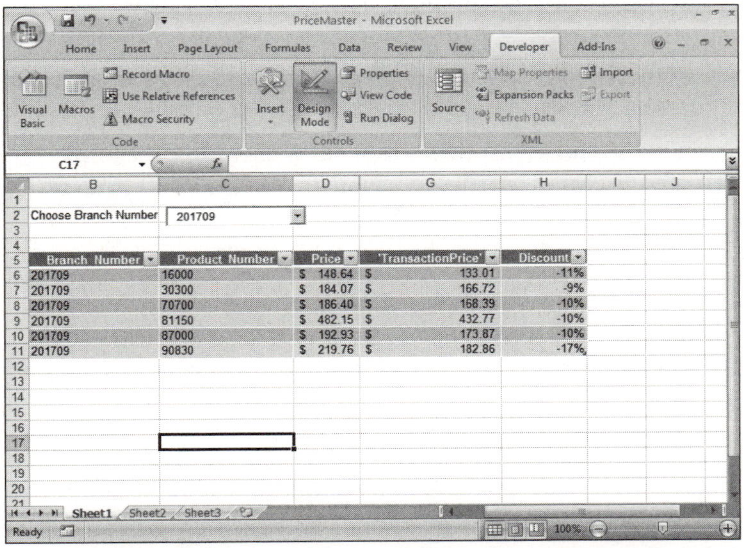

Figure 5-42: Final view of price analysis based on imported access data

Limitations of Microsoft Query

By now, you have probably realized both the strengths and weaknesses of Microsoft Query. On the plus side, you have a relatively powerful tool that enables you to use some of the benefits of querying relational databases. You can establish an automated data connection to a local or remote database. In addition, you can customize this data connection by specifying how and when the connection is refreshed. You can also specify sorts, filters, and even joins of two tables or queries to customize the data you bring in.

The limitations are summarized in the following sections. Often you can create workarounds to these limitations; sometimes you may have to use another tool altogether.

The Microsoft Query Wizard

The Microsoft Query Wizard provides an extremely user-friendly interface for importing external data. The user-friendliness, however, comes at a price. For example:

- Your data source is limited to one table or one query — joins among tables or queries are not allowed with this wizard. The only exception is when a table's relationships have been predefined by the database owner.
- Calculated or custom fields are not allowed.
- You are constrained to a fairly limited set of sorts and filters — only three consecutive sorts can be applied as well as three consecutive filters separated by AND/OR Boolean operators.

Microsoft Query

Microsoft Query provides additional functionality over the Microsoft Query Wizard but has limitations itself.

- Calculated fields are limited to a select few — namely, Sum, Count, Average, Max, and Min. Customized expressions are not available through the Microsoft Query user interface.
- Creating custom expressions or complex joins requires modifying the underlying SQL statement. Although this is certainly doable, it requires some knowledge of and comfort with SQL.
- The data source dialog box does not recognize extensions from Access 2007. This is probably an oversight and may be corrected soon. The workaround requires adding a new data source with a driver that recognizes the *.accmdb extension.

Summary

This chapter summarizes the various ways you can get your data from Access into Excel. We started with some simple methods appropriate for one time imports and ad hoc analyses. We closed the chapter with an extended discussion of Microsoft Query — a useful add-on that provides refreshable data connections, relational database querying functionality, and support of user-defined parameters.

Leveraging Macros in Excel and Access

This chapter introduces the tremendous productivity gains available from using Excel and Access macros. Specifically, you will cover macro creation and use in both applications (it is quite different). Additionally, you will use some concrete examples to demonstrate how macros can improve your productivity and better integrate Excel and Access. The chapter presupposes no prior knowledge of Visual Basic for Applications (VBA) coding. Those readers who wince at the thought of coding can breathe a collective sigh of relief — until Chapter 7, that is!

What Is a Macro?

Perhaps you have used macros before and have heard of VBA. If so, you are probably asking yourself, "Just what is a macro?" Moreover, what does it do, and how is it different from VBA, a procedure, or a function?

A General Definition

In the most general sense, a *macro* is a set of instructions, or code, that tells Excel or Access to execute any number of tasks. The underlying language of the macro is Visual Basic for Applications, or VBA. If you've already read

Chapter 7, you'll notice this definition is quite similar to that of VBA code. So what is the difference?

The difference is that macros do not presuppose any knowledge of the underlying code that makes up a macro. How is this possible? It is possible because both Excel and Access provide a friendly user interface to translate instructions that you can understand (for example, hide this sheet, execute this query, etc.) into a set of instructions that Excel and Access can understand (for example, VBA code).

So, to summarize, a macro is

■ A set of VBA instructions that executes a task or tasks in Excel or Access

■ Created or recorded through a user interface that requires little or no knowledge of the underlying code on the part of the user to function properly

This chapter covers both the Excel and Access macro interfaces in detail.

Why Use a Macro?

Most people can get their heads around the concept of a macro and even VBA. The barrier for beginners to use macros, however, is that it is often hard to figure out when and where they can be effectively used. The following sections summarize some of the most common and effective uses for macros in both Access and Excel.

Creating User Friendly Interfaces

Often you will be creating a spreadsheet for someone else's use. If the audience for your spreadsheet has limited knowledge of Excel or is managerial (often these groups overlap considerably), you may find it necessary to make your spreadsheets a bit more user friendly. Here are some examples:

■ Format and print a worksheet or range of worksheets at the touch of a button

■ Navigate a multi-sheet worksheet with one navigation page with a go-to button for each sheet in your workbook

■ Save the open document in a specified location and then close the application at the touch of a button

Obviously, each of the preceding examples can be performed in Excel without the aid of a macro. However, the neophyte user of your workbook will surely appreciate that these multi-step processes are available at the touch of one clearly labeled button!

Automating Repetitive Tasks

Although creating user-friendly interfaces is more relevant to Excel, practice of automating repetitive tasks suits both Excel and Access. Say you are running 10 action queries in Access and exporting the resulting table into Excel for reporting purposes. All these steps can be performed with one Access macro.

However, automating repetitive tasks is not just isolated to the realm of Access macros. Here is a simple example. Have you ever needed to refresh multiple PivotTables at any given time? Without a macro, you would need to right-click each individual PivotTable and select Refresh. Imagine what a pain it would be if you had to refresh six or seven PivotTables across multiple worksheets. However, a macro can take care of this with a button or shortcut key press. Automating repetitive tasks is a great application for macros in Excel.

Formatting Cell Ranges

Perhaps the most common use of Excel macros is repeatedly applying consistent formats to multiple cell ranges. Say that you've been given a workbook with 20 worksheets with similarly formatted tables on each sheet. The only problem is that the formatting is distracting or just hideous.

You could manually format each sheet. The more elegant solution, however, is to record your formatting changes in a macro and assign it to a shortcut key. Even better, you could save this macro in your `Personal.xls` workbook and have this formatting macro available to you every time you open Excel. You will learn more about the `Personal.xls` macro workbook later in this chapter, but for now you can no doubt see the benefits of using macros in a situation like this one.

Clearly, the preceding sections do not represent a comprehensive list of the uses of macros. However, these examples should hint at the ubiquitous scenarios where Excel and Access macros are powerful and relevant.

Comparing Macros in Excel and Access

Although your generalized macro definition holds for both Excel and Access, the differences are substantial enough that they are worth mentioning. Recall that our definition states that a macro is a set of VBA instructions that executes a task and is created or recorded through a user interface. The next sections explore how that definition breaks down concerning macros in each specific application.

Creating Macros in Microsoft Excel

The macro user interface in Excel is called the *Macro Recorder*. It is aptly named because that is exactly what it does — it records pretty much everything you do! Fire up the Macro Recorder, and every keystroke you enter, every sheet you delete, and every tab you select is converted to its VBA equivalent. In this sense, the Macro Recorder is more free form and flexible when compared to the interface in Access.

Because Excel converts every action to its VBA equivalent, using the Macro Recorder is an excellent way to learn VBA itself! If you want to find out how to insert a worksheet in VBA, simply fire up the Macro Recorder and insert a sheet. When you look at your macro in the Visual Basic Editor, you can see the essential piece of code for completing your action!

Creating Macros in Microsoft Access

The user interface for creating macros in Access is quite different. To create a macro in Access, you need to open a macro template in Design view. In the Design view you can create a list of predefined actions to be executed in order when you run your macro. Because the actions you can choose from are predefined, the Access macro interface is slightly less flexible and much more structured than the macro interface you find in Excel. However, this by no means makes Access macros less powerful than those created in Excel.

The differences between Excel and Access macros will become clearer as you explore each in greater detail and with examples. So, with preliminary introductions out of the way, the next section dispenses with generalities and dives into creating macros with Excel.

Introducing Excel Macros

In this section, you explore using macros in Excel. You will

- Learn the critical components of the macro user interface
- Cover critical security issues new to macros in Excel 2007
- Walk through specific examples of Excel macros in action

Using the Macro Recorder

Before you can record or view macros in Excel 2007, you must ensure the Developer tab is visible from the Excel ribbon. Not only does the Developer tab let you view and record macros, but it also enables the Controls menu, which enables you to insert buttons and other objects that you may tie your macros to. To enable the Developer tab, select the Windows icon and then select Excel options. In the Excel Options dialog box, make sure the Popular options are showing and ensure that the Show Developer tab in the Ribbon check box is selected (see Figure 6-1).

The Macro Recorder User Interface

Now that you have the Developer tab in the Excel ribbon, you can fire up the Macro Recorder and examine other critical macro options. Start up the Macro Recorder by selecting Record Macro from the Developer tab. You get the Record Macro dialog box (see Figure 6-2).

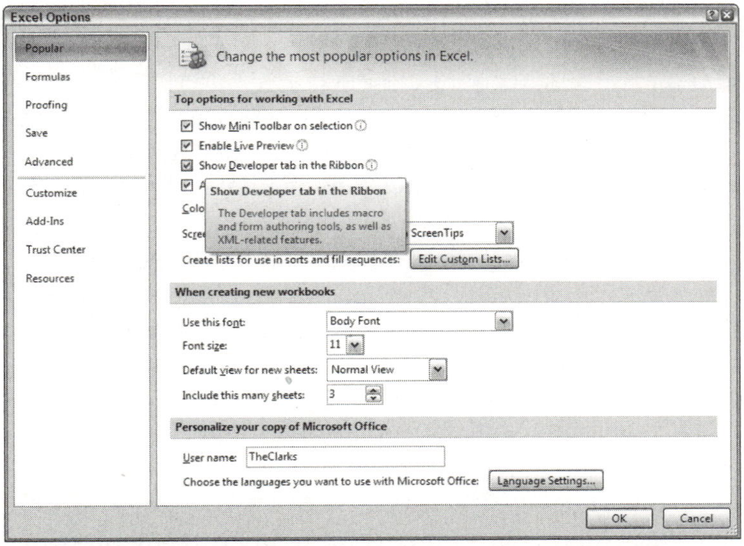

Figure 6-1: Making sure the Developer tab is in the Excel ribbon

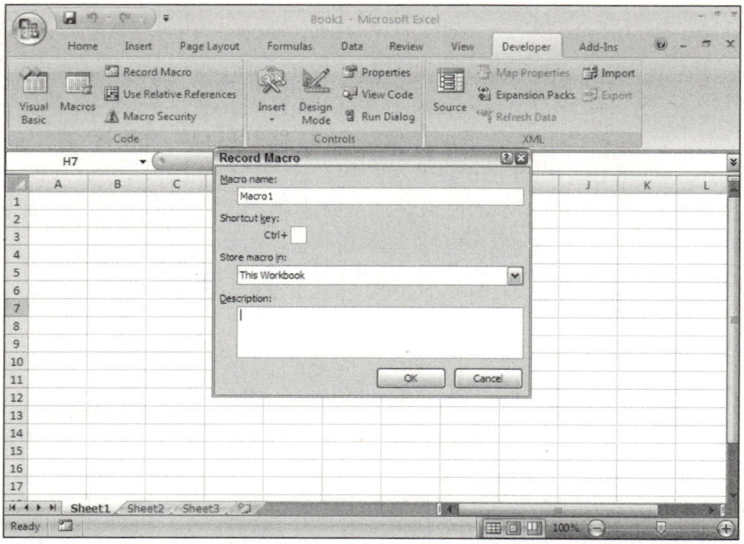

Figure 6-2: The Macro Recorder user interface

There are four parts of the Macro Recorder interface:

- **Macro name:** At the top is a space for your macro name. This should be self-explanatory. Excel gives a default name to your macro, for example, Macro1, but it is best practice to give your macro a name more descriptive of what it actually does. For example, you might name a macro that formats a generic table as FormatTable.

- **Shortcut key:** Below the macro name field is the Shortcut key field. Every macro or piece of code needs an event, or something to happen, for it to run. This event can be a button press, a workbook opening, or in this case, a key stroke combination. When you assign a shortcut key to your macro, entering that combination of keys will trigger your macro to run. This is an optional field. You need not enter a shortcut key to run your macro.

- **Location:** Next, you find the Store macro in: field. The default option Excel gives us is This Workbook. Storing your macro in This Workbook simply means that the macro is stored along with the active Excel file. The next time you open that particular workbook, the macro will be available to run. Similarly, if you send the workbook to another user, that user will be able to run the macro as well (provided the macro security is properly set by your user — but more on that later).

- **Description:** Last, you see an option to enter a description for your macro. This is an optional field, but can come in handy if you have numerous macros in a spreadsheet or if you need to give a user a more detailed description about what the macro does.

STORING A MACRO IN THE PERSONAL MACRO WORKBOOK

One of the options in the Store macro in: field is the Personal Macro Workbook. The Personal Macro Workbook is created automatically for you by Excel. The workbook is hidden (that is, it is not visible or accessible) until you record a macro and choose to store it in the Personal Macro Workbook.

What is so special about the Personal Macro Workbook and why would anyone want to store a macro there? When you store a macro in your Personal Macro Workbook, that macro is accessible to you regardless of what workbook you have available to you. In other words, the macro you recorded and stored is always accessible.

Macros that serve a generic utility are often good candidates to store in your Personal Macro Workbook. For example, suppose you are often asked to troubleshoot spreadsheets that have tons of hidden worksheets in them. You prefer to have those worksheets visible when trying to understand the spreadsheet model. Sure, you could step through them and manually make each sheet visible. Instead, you can have the following snippet code in your Personal Macro Workbook.

```
1  Sub MakeVisible()
2  Dim MySheet As Worksheet
3  For Each MySheet In ActiveWorkbook.Worksheets
4  MySheet.Visible = xlSheetVisible
5  Next MySheet
6  End Sub
```

The preceding code is not a macro by your strict definition. Why? Because this code cannot be generated with the Excel user interface. However, it is important to note that any piece of code can be stored in the Personal Macro Workbook — not just code recorded by the Macro Recorder.

The preceding code might look like Greek right now, but it is not that complicated. The lines of code work as follows:

1. This line tells Excel there is a set of VBA instructions that has the name `MakeVisible`. Incidentally, lines 1 and 6 are generated when you create a macro and give it a name.

2. Line 2 declares a specific type of variable, called an object variable, and tells Excel this variable represents a worksheet.

3. The next line starts a looping process. It says for each worksheet (designated by the object variable `MySheet`) in the active workbook, do the command(s) starting in the next line.

4. Line 4 sets the visible property of the worksheet in question so it is visible.

5. Line 5 concludes the loop, telling Excel to go to the next worksheet in the workbook.

6. The last line tells Excel your block of instructions is complete.

Do not worry if you do not completely follow all steps in this code. You will dive into VBA coding in more detail in Chapter 7.

Recording Macros with Absolute References

Now that you have learned the basics of the Macro Recorder interface, it is time to go deeper and begin recording macros. The first thing you need to understand before you begin is that Excel has two modes for recording — absolute reference and relative reference.

Excel's default recording mode is an absolute reference. As you may know, the term *absolute reference* is often used in the context of cell references found in formulas. When a cell reference in a formula is an absolute reference, it will not automatically adjust when the formula is pasted to a new location.

The best way to understand how this concept applies to macros is to try it out. Open the `Chapter6_SampleFile.xlsx` file and let's record a macro that counts the rows in the Branchlist worksheet (see Figure 6-3).

Before recording, make sure cell A1 is selected. Now fire up the Macro Recorder by selecting Record Macro from the Developer tab. Name the macro AddTotal, choose This Workbook for the save location, and press OK. Now Excel is recording your macro steps. While Excel is recording, perform the following steps:

1. Select cell A16 and type **Total** in the cell.

2. Select the first empty cell in Column D (D16) and type = **COUNTA(D2:D15)**. This gives a count of branch numbers at the bottom of column D. You need to use the COUNTA function because the branch numbers are stored as text.

3. Press Stop Recording from the Developer tab to end recording the macro.

The formatted worksheet should look similar to Figure 6-4.

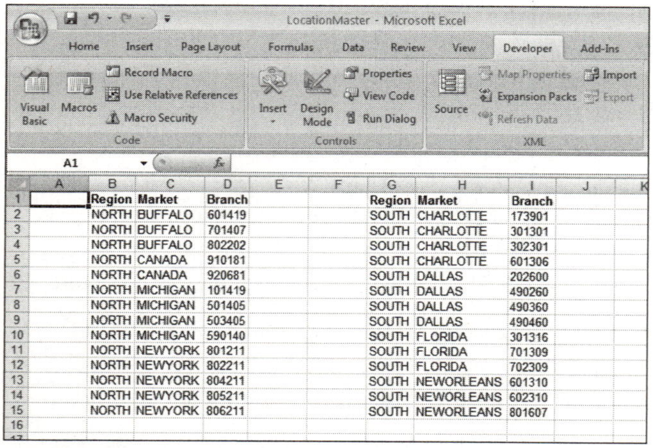

Figure 6-3: Pre-totaled worksheet

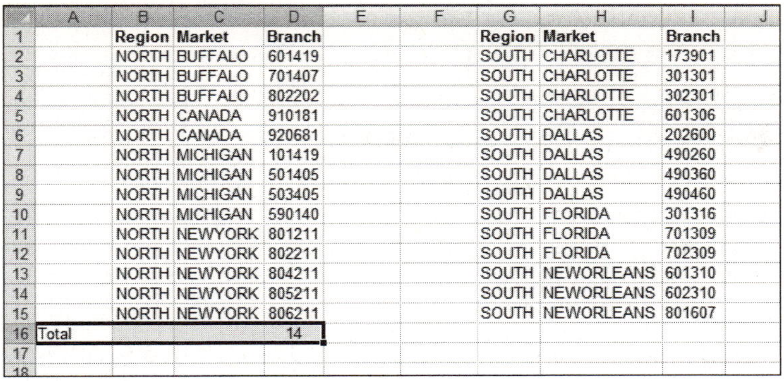

	A	B	C	D	E	F	G	H	I	J
1		Region	Market	Branch			Region	Market	Branch	
2		NORTH	BUFFALO	601419			SOUTH	CHARLOTTE	173901	
3		NORTH	BUFFALO	701407			SOUTH	CHARLOTTE	301301	
4		NORTH	BUFFALO	802202			SOUTH	CHARLOTTE	302301	
5		NORTH	CANADA	910181			SOUTH	CHARLOTTE	601306	
6		NORTH	CANADA	920681			SOUTH	DALLAS	202600	
7		NORTH	MICHIGAN	101419			SOUTH	DALLAS	490260	
8		NORTH	MICHIGAN	501405			SOUTH	DALLAS	490360	
9		NORTH	MICHIGAN	503405			SOUTH	DALLAS	490460	
10		NORTH	MICHIGAN	590140			SOUTH	FLORIDA	301316	
11		NORTH	NEWYORK	801211			SOUTH	FLORIDA	701309	
12		NORTH	NEWYORK	802211			SOUTH	FLORIDA	702309	
13		NORTH	NEWYORK	804211			SOUTH	NEWORLEANS	601310	
14		NORTH	NEWYORK	805211			SOUTH	NEWORLEANS	602310	
15		NORTH	NEWYORK	806211			SOUTH	NEWORLEANS	801607	
16	Total			14						
17										
18										

Figure 6-4: Post-totaled worksheet

Now you have recorded your first macro and seen the results. To understand the importance of absolute versus relative referencing, you need to examine the underlying code. To examine the code, select Macros from the Developer tab. You see the Macro dialog box (see Figure 6-5).

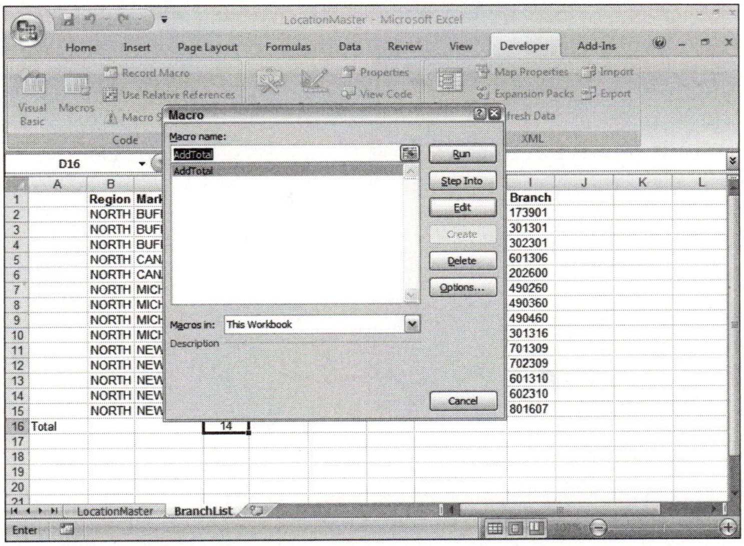

Figure 6-5: The Excel Macro dialog box

From the Excel Macro dialog box, select the AddTotal macro and click Edit to view the code behind the macro. Your code should look something like the following:

```
Sub AddTotal()
    Range("A16").Select
    ActiveCell.FormulaR1C1 = "Total"
    Range("D16").Select
    ActiveCell.FormulaR1C1 = "=COUNTA(R[-14]C:R[-1]C)"
End Sub
```

This is Excel's translation of your actions into VBA code. Pay particular attention to lines two and four of the macro code. When you asked Excel to select cell range A16 and then D16 that is exactly what it selected. Because the macro was recorded in absolute reference mode, Excel interpreted your range selection as absolute. In other words, if you select cell A1 that is what Excel gives you. So what, you ask? In the next section you take a look at what the same macro looks like when recorded in relative reference mode.

Recording Macros with Relative References

In the context of Excel macros, *relative* means relative to the currently active cell. So you should use caution with your active cell choice — both when you record the relative reference macro and when you run it.

To record the macro in relative reference mode, simply select the Use Relative References option from the Developer ribbon tab before you start recording (see Figure 6-6).

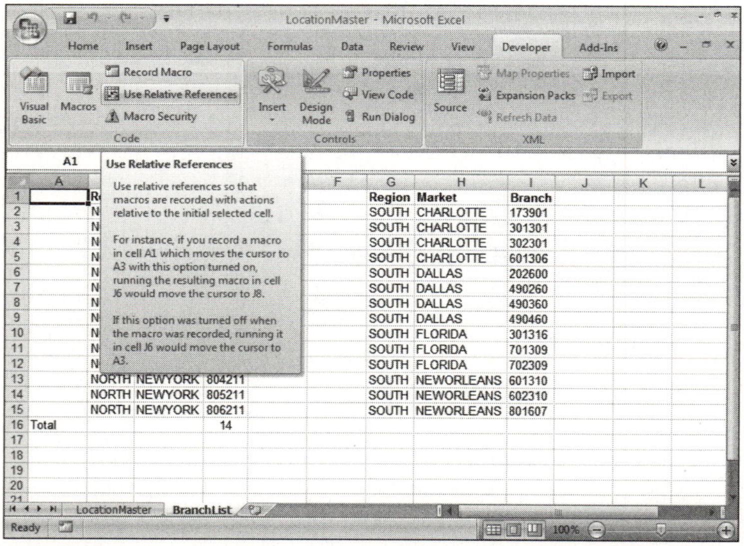

Figure 6-6: Selecting relative reference macro recording

Now you can record the macro using the same steps as in the prior section, but this time with Use Relative References selected. Make sure that you have selected cell A1 before you begin. Name the macro AddTotalRelative and store it in This Workbook. Open the Excel Macro dialog box again, select the Add TotalRelative macro, and click Edit to view the code behind the macro. Your code should look something like the following:

```
Sub AddTotalRelative()
    ActiveCell.Offset(15, 0).Range("A1").Select
    ActiveCell.FormulaR1C1 = "Total"
    ActiveCell.Offset(0, 3).Range("A1").Select
    ActiveCell.FormulaR1C1 = "=COUNTA(R[-14]C:R[-1]C)"
End Sub
```

Do you notice anything different about code lines two and four? There are no references to any specific cell ranges at all! Of course you see A1, but that's just the starting point. How does this code define where to *make* the changes? Take a quick look at what the relevant parts of this VBA code really mean:

- **Line 2:** Excel uses the `Offset` property of the active cell. Remember that before you recorded the macro, you selected cell A1. The VBA code tells Excel to move 15 rows down and 0 columns across from cell A1. The `Select` method then tells Excel to make this cell the active cell now.

- **Line 4:** Remember that the active cell is now A16, the cell 15 rows down and 0 columns across from A1. You now encounter the `Offset` property again, telling Excel to select the cell 0 rows down and 3 columns to the right of A16.

What is the value of using relative references in macros; what is the value of not having references to specific cell ranges as happens with absolute references? Consider the following example. If you wanted to automatically add totals to the second block of data in Figure 6-4, you would not be able to do it with the AddTotal macro. Why not? Because this macro would continually add totals to the first block of data — because it explicitly references cells A16 and D16.

However, you can add totals to the second block of data if you format the second block with the AddTotalRelative macro. You simply need to select cell F1 this time and then run the macro from the Excel Macro dialog box. Because the macro applies the totals *relative* to the currently active cell, the totals are applied correctly.

For this to work you simply need to ensure that you have selected the correct starting cell before running the macro *and* the block of data has the same number of rows and columns as the data on which you recorded the macro.

Figure 6-7 shows how you run this macro from the Macro dialog box.

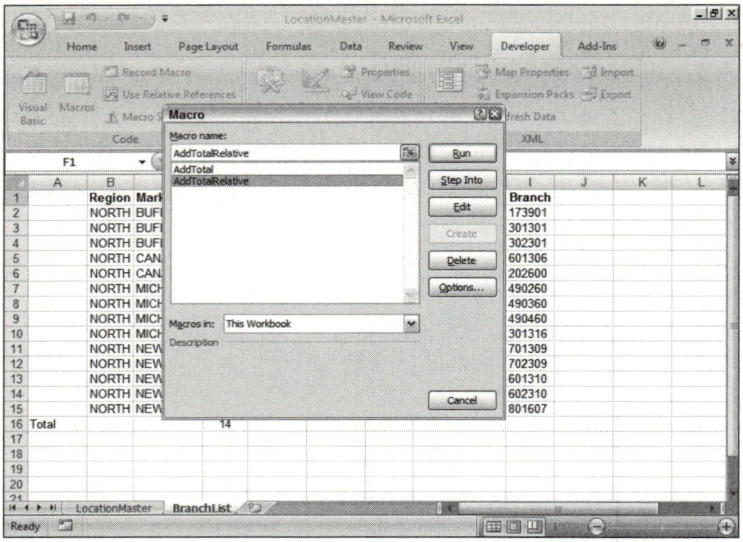

Figure 6-7: Running a macro from the macro dialog box

Figure 6-8 shows the results to ensure the macro worked as you wanted.

Whew, it did! This simple example should give you a firm conceptual grasp of macro recording with relative references. Having this conceptual grasp can save you time and frustration down the road. Later in this chapter you cover more sophisticated examples — clearly illustrating the impressive productivity available with Excel macros.

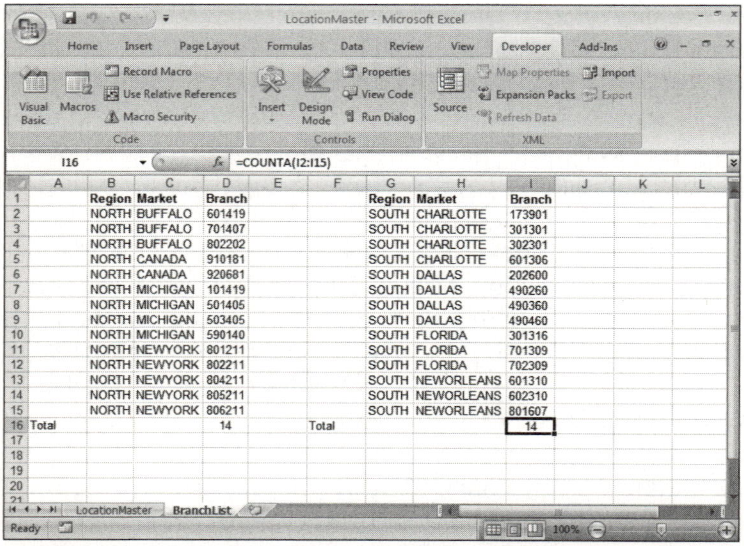

Figure 6-8: Adding totals with the relative reference macro

Macro Security in Excel 2007

Microsoft introduced some significant security changes for Office 2007. There are several pieces of this change that you must understand for you and your spreadsheet users to use macros effectively. Specifically, you need to know about:

- Default security settings
- The Office Trust Center
- Macro-disabled Excel file extensions

Default Excel Security Settings

One of the most significant changes for Excel 2007 is that macros are disabled by default under certain circumstances. For example, if you create the Excel macro file and use it on your computer, your macros work fine. However, when another user tries to use macros in a file you have created, the macros are disabled.

With earlier versions of Excel, you would often see a pop-up box informing you that the file contains macros. Depending on your Excel security settings, you would have the option to enable or disable macros in the file. This is no longer the case for 2007.

If users open one of your Excel 2007 files, they get a small message under the ribbon stating that macros have been disabled. The message looks like Figure 6-9.

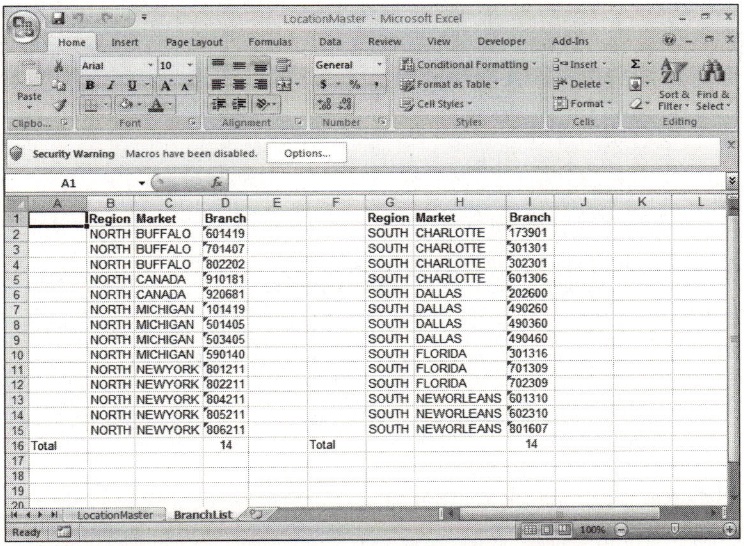

Figure 6-9: Message notifying that macros are disabled

The users must click the Options button beside the warning message and that button gives you a dialog box with the option to enable macros (see Figure 6-10).

The Office Trust Center

Central to security changes in Excel 2007 is the Office Trust Center. The Office Trust Center is the centralized location to manage security preferences for all Microsoft Office 2007 applications. To access the Trust Center, select the Windows icon and then Excel options. Then from the Excel Options dialog box select the Trust Center (see Figure 6-11).

Why introduce the Office Trust Center here? It is because you can bypass default Excel macro settings through adjusting the Trust Center settings. Specifically, you need to add a trusted location (see Figure 6-12).

A *trusted location* is a directory that is deemed a safe zone where only trusted workbooks are placed. A trusted location allows you and your clients to run a macro-enabled workbook with no security restrictions, as long as the workbook is in that location.

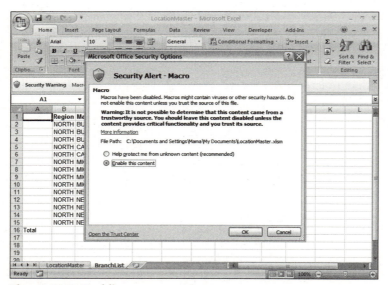

Figure 6-10: Enabling macros option

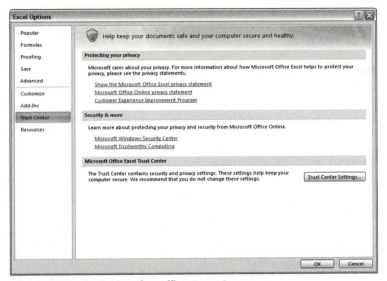

Figure 6-11: Accessing the Office Trust Center

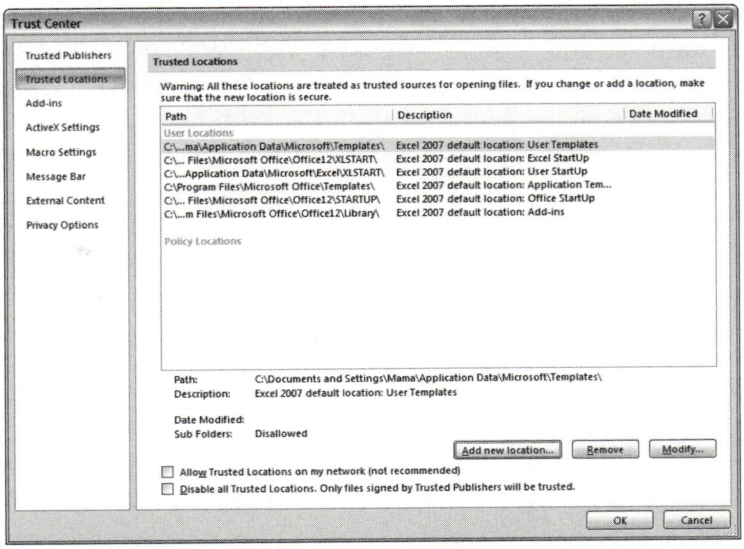

Figure 6-12: The Trusted Locations dialog box

To set up a trusted location, follow these steps:

1. Select the Macro Security button on the Developer tab. This activates the Trust Center dialog box.

2. Select the Trusted Locations button.

3. Select Add New Location.

4. Click Browse to specify the directory that will be considered a trusted location.

When you specify a trusted location, any Excel file that is opened from this location will have macros automatically enabled. The idea is to have your clients specify a trusted location and use your Excel files from there. For example, when you download the support files for this book, they will be stored in the folder `C:\Integration` by default. If you add this folder to your trusted locations list (as shown in Figure 6-13), you won't have a problem running the macros and other VBA code in the sample files.

Macro-Disabled Excel File Extensions

The last security issue you need to be aware of is that, by default, Excel 2007 workbooks with the file extension *.xlsx* cannot contain macros. So if you record a few macros in your workbook and then save the workbook as an XLSX file, your macros will automatically be removed from the workbook. Of course Excel warns you that VB content will be disabled when saving a workbook with macros as an XLSX file.

If you have a file with macros, you must save the file as an Excel Macro-Enabled Workbook. The extension for this file is *.xlsm*. You have the option to save your Excel file with macros enabled from the Save As menu (see Figure 6-14).

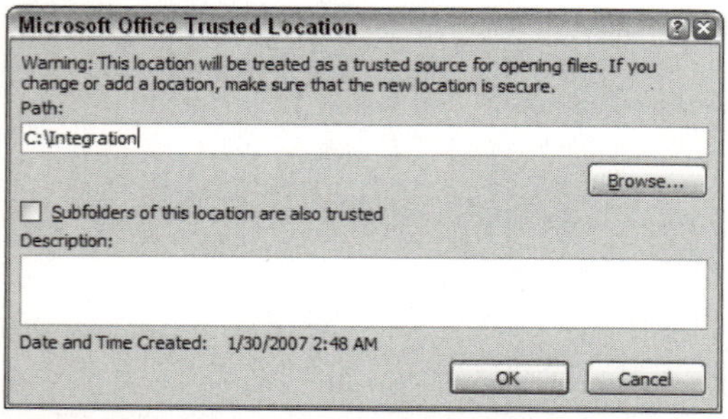

Figure 6-13: Adding a trusted location

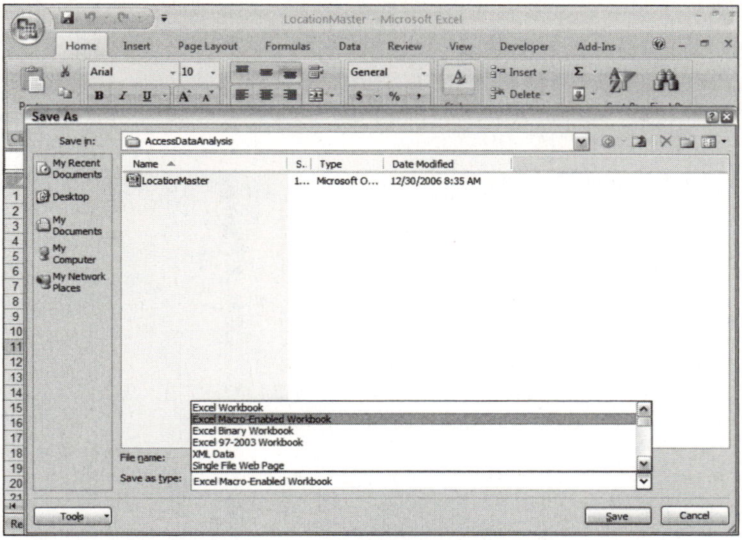

Figure 6-14: Saving a workbook as macro-enabled

Excel Macro Examples

In this next section, you explore specific macro examples in Excel. The goal is to illustrate general concepts of how and where macros can be applied by using concrete examples. Use these examples to spur your own creative thinking about using macros in your spreadsheets.

Macro for Navigating a Spreadsheet

Macros can spruce up multi-sheet workbooks by establishing a professional looking user interface and easing navigation for the spreadsheet user. In this example, you add a navigation sheet with macros to a four-worksheet price dashboard. Open the `Chapter6_SampleDashboard.xlsx` file and take a look at the workbook before adding navigation (see Figure 6-15).

As you can see, the dashboard has four worksheets outlining various aspects of product pricing. Four worksheets may not sound like much to navigate, but the same macro concepts can be applied to much larger workbooks.

The aim with the navigation sheet is to provide one sheet where the user can view all available report names. The user can then click a button to go to the desired sheet, without having to slog through all the worksheet tabs.

To get started, add a new sheet named Navigation and then hide the other four worksheets. Then, add a Form button for navigation. To add a Form button, go to the Developer tab and select the Insert controls icon (see Figure 6-16).

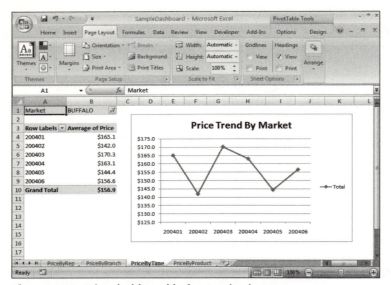

Figure 6-15: Price dashboard before navigation macros

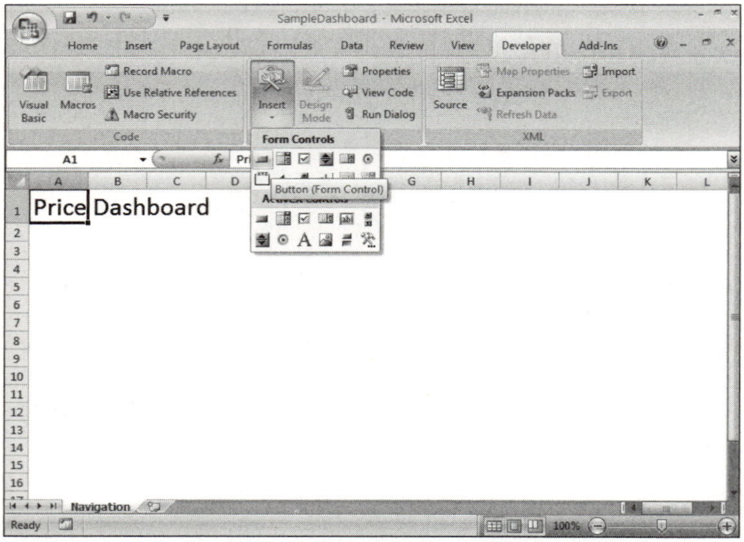

Figure 6-16: Adding form buttons to the navigation sheet

As soon as you add the form button, you get the Assign Macro dialog box (see Figure 6-17). This immediately gives you the opportunity to assign a macro that will be run at the click of the Form button. You do not have any macros to assign yet, but you know that you can when you are ready!

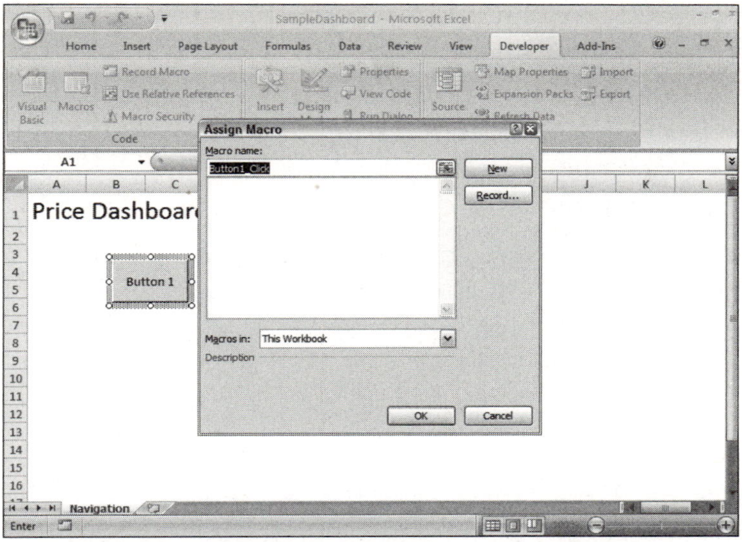

Figure 6-17: The Assign Macro dialog box

Click Cancel on the Assign Macro dialog box and continue adding three more buttons. Edit the text within each button so that each corresponds to a worksheet to which you will navigate. Your navigation worksheet should look something like Figure 6-18.

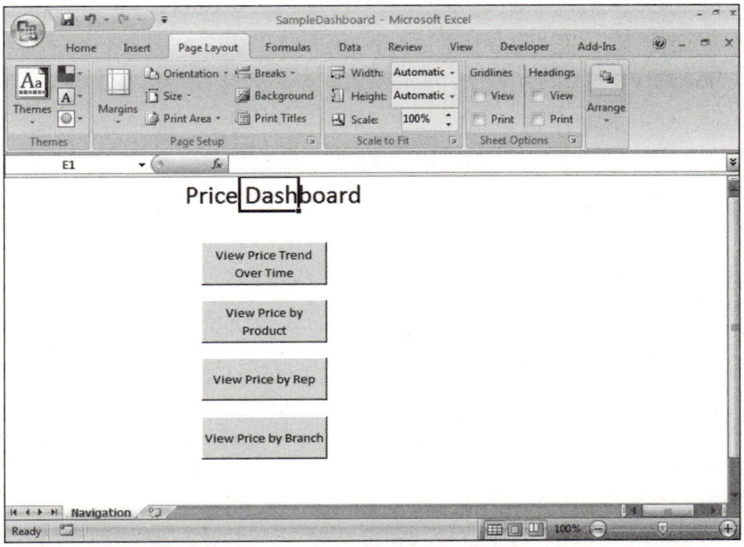

Figure 6-18: Navigation sheet with form buttons

When you have the navigation buttons, you can start recording the macros. Take the following steps to record a macro that will make the PriceByTime sheet visible.

1. From the Developer tab, select Record Macro. There is no need to select the Relative Reference icon.

2. Name the macro **ViewPriceByTime** and store it in This Workbook.

3. Hover your cursor over the Navigation worksheet name, right-click, and select Unhide from the drop-down menu.

4. You now see a menu of hidden worksheets. Select the PriceByTime sheet and click OK (see Figure 6-19).

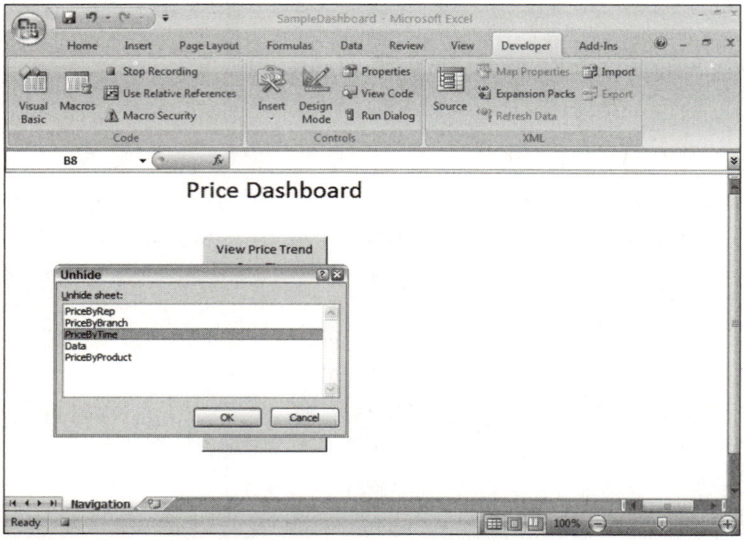

Figure 6-19: Unhide the PriceByTime worksheet

5. Now select the Navigation worksheet, right-click, and select Hide from the drop-down menu.

6. Select Stop Recording from the Developer tab.

Now you have your first macro that makes the PriceByTime sheet visible and then hides the Navigation sheet. You need to add one more button and macro to close the navigation loop. Add a form button to the PriceByTime worksheet that takes you back to the Navigation page (see Figure 6-20). Then record another macro that hides the PriceByTime sheet and unhides the Navigation sheet. Simply follow Steps 1 through 6, but hide and unhide the appropriate sheets.

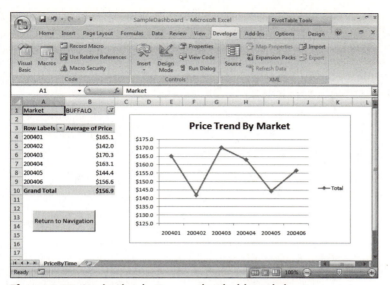

Figure 6-20: Navigation button on the dashboard sheet

Now, you need some event to fire the macro. When you added the form buttons, you saw the Assign Macro dialog box. A Form button click makes a great event to trigger the macro. Go back to the Navigation sheet and right-click the first form button. Select Assign Macro from the drop-down menu to bring up the Assign Macro dialog box (see Figure 6-21).

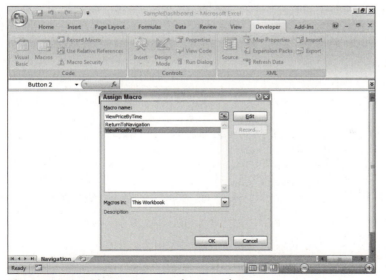

Figure 6-21: Assign a macro to the Form button

VBA CODE FROM THE MACRO RECORDER

Take a quick look at the underlying code of the **ViewPriceByTime** macro to make sure you understand what is going on. From the Developer tab, select Macros. From the Macro dialog box select the **ViewPriceByTime** macro and click Edit (see Figure 6-22).

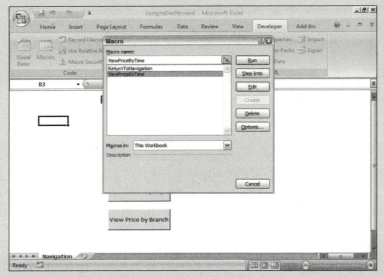

Figure 6-22: Viewing underlying macro code

The underlying code should look something like this:

```
Sub ViewPriceByTime()
    Sheets("Navigation").Select
    Sheets("PriceByTime").Visible = True
    Sheets("Navigation").Select
    ActiveWindow.SelectedSheets.Visible = False
End Sub
```

Excel generated a simple piece of code that unhides and hides the correct worksheets. As simple as the code seems at first, it does contain some redundant steps. Line 2 selects the Navigation sheet but performs no operation with it. Line 4 selects the Navigation sheet, and then Line 5 tells Excel to hide the selected sheet. In fact, the preceding code could be simplified as follows:

```
Sub ViewPriceByTime()
    Sheets("PriceByTime").Visible = True
    Sheets("Navigation"). Visible = True
End Sub
```

> The point of this exercise is twofold. First, the Macro Recorder logs your keystrokes and does not read your mind. As such, the code produced is often redundant and not terribly elegant. Second, the absolute best way to learn VBA is to examine and tweak the code that the Macro Recorder generates. You do not have to know VBA to do this. All that is required is initiative and some common sense. Since you bought this book, you obviously have an abundance of both.

Choose the appropriate macro, in this case ViewPriceByTime, and click OK. Now browse back to the PriceByTime tab and assign the ReturnToNavigation macro to that button.

Now you have a set of working navigation macros that enable the user to quickly flip back and forth between the main navigation page and the Price-ByTime page. Complete the exercise for the remaining navigation buttons and worksheets, and you have a user-friendly navigation structure for the price dashboard.

TIP Rather than use the Macro Recorder six more times to complete all the macros required in the last example, simply tweak the underlying code a bit in the Visual Basic (VB) Editor. Clicking the Edit button from the Macro menu opens the VB editor. Highlight the code, copy it, and then paste it six times. Now simply rename each macro with an appropriate name and change the sheet references so they are correct for each macro. Assign macros to your buttons, and you are done.

Macro for Formatting

Consistent, repeatable, and quick formatting is one of the easiest and most common uses for Excel macros. In this example, you write a macro that formats a table. The rub is that this macro formats a table with a variable number of rows and columns. Before starting, take a look at the generic table of data you want to format (see Figure 6-23).

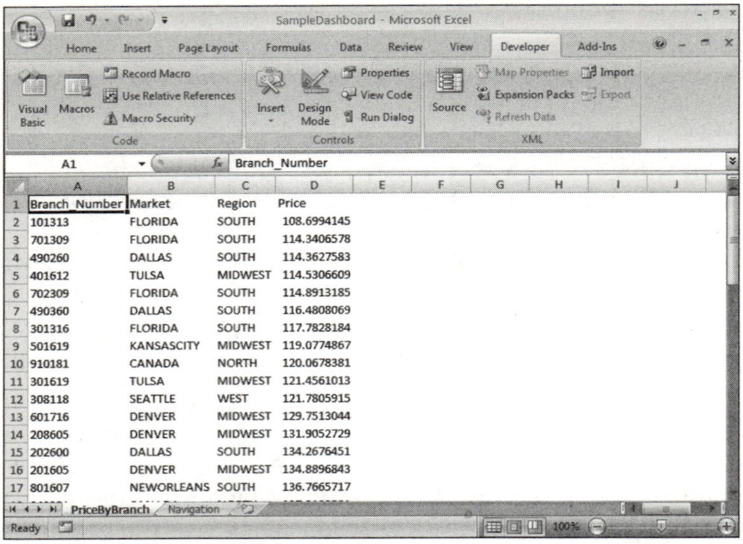

Figure 6-23: Unformatted Excel table

To ensure the macro is flexible enough to accommodate variable row and column numbers, make sure to click the Use Relative References button on the Developer tab. Take the following steps to record the macro:

1. Before recording, make sure cell A1 is selected. As long as the block of data starts in cell A1, the macro should work.

2. Press Record Macro, name the macro FormatTable, and save it in This Workbook. Also assign a shortcut key of Ctrl+t, which will trigger the macro to run.

3. Press Shift+Ctrl+Right Arrow key to select the entire first row. The great thing about this shortcut is that it highlights the entire first row, regardless of how many columns.

4. With the heading row highlighted, apply some formatting. Make the text bold, center justified, and with a gray background color.

5. Press the Down Arrow key once. You see cell A2 selected.

6. Next, format the rest of the table. Press Shift+Ctrl+Right Arrow followed by Shift+Ctrl+Down Arrow. The remainder of the table is selected.

7. Apply formatting here as well. Format the Number style to currency and center justify the cells.

8. Press Stop Recording.

That's it. You have a macro that will consistently format any contiguous table of data, regardless of the number of rows or columns (see Figure 6-24).

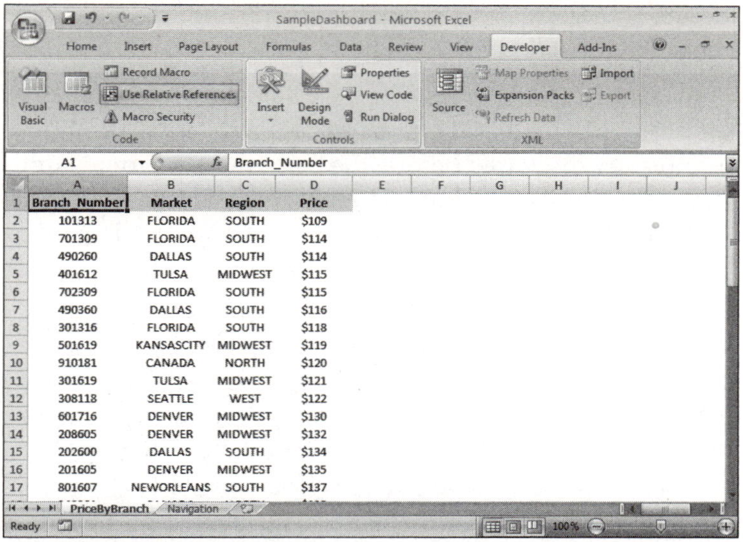

Figure 6-24: Formatted Excel table

Take a peek at the code to see what you can learn. Recall that to view the code you click Macro from the Developer tab, click FormatTable from the menu, and select Edit. The code should look something like this:

```
Sub FormatTable()
1.      ' FormatTable Macro
        ' Keyboard Shortcut: Ctrl+t
2.          Range(Selection, Selection.End(xlToRight)).Select
            Selection.Font.Bold = True
            With Selection.Interior
                .Pattern = xlSolid
                .PatternColorIndex = xlAutomatic
                .ThemeColor = xlThemeColorDark1
                .TintAndShade = -0.149998474074526
                .PatternTintAndShade = 0
            End With
            ActiveCell.Offset(1, 0).Range("A1").Select
3.          Range(Selection, Selection.End(xlToRight)).Select
            Range(Selection, Selection.End(xlDown)).Select
            With Selection
                .HorizontalAlignment = xlCenter
                .VerticalAlignment = xlBottom
                .WrapText = False
                .Orientation = 0
                .AddIndent = False
                .IndentLevel = 0
                .ShrinkToFit = False
                .ReadingOrder = xlContext
                .MergeCells = False
```

```
                End With
                Selection.NumberFormat = "$#,##0"
       End Sub
```

Looking at some of the highlighted and numbered snippets of the preceding code should be instructive. As discussed before, the best way to become familiar with VBA code is to use the Macro Recorder and then examine the resulting code. Because the next chapter introduces VBA, this exercise is a good preview.

1. The first block of code highlighted starts with an apostrophe. An apostrophe signals VBA that any text following is a comment and is not to be interpreted as code. Excel automatically inserts a few comment lines when you use the Macro Recorder. Comment lines become much more meaningful when you are doing longer pieces of coding — the kind you will learn about in the next chapter.

2. The code beside numeral 2 is interesting and useful. This is Excel's translation of your Shift+Ctrl+Right Arrow shortcut key. Take note of the xlToRight constant in this line.

3. Now look at the code beside numeral 3. This is Excel's interpretation of using shortcut keys to select the contiguous block of cells in your table not including the top row labels. Remember that you used a combination of Shift+Ctrl+Right Arrow followed by Shift+Ctrl+Down Arrow shortcut key. The first line is identical to the code beside numeral 2. The second line differs in that xlToRight is replaced by xlDown. Do you notice a theme? Now you know the VBA syntax for selecting an entire block of cells contiguous to whatever cell is currently active. This is how you can use the Macro Recorder to learn VBA!

Macros in Microsoft Access

Although the Access macro still fits the generalized definition of a macro, Access macros differ substantially from macros in Excel.

As indicated earlier in this chapter, the most substantial difference between Excel and Access macros is that the Access macro interface is much more structured and predefined. Whereas the Excel Macro Recorder records keystrokes and translates them into VBA, the Access macro interface is a template of steps or actions you can perform. Although these actions are broad in scope, there is a limited set of them.

Macro Security in Access 2007

The Security changes in Office 2007 dramatically affect Access as well as Excel. Specifically, macros and VBA content will be disabled by default in your Access databases. A small message below the Access ribbon will notify you that certain content (that is, VBA) is disabled (see Figure 6-25).

In addition to any VBA being disabled, certain macro actions are also disabled. What does that mean? Well, Access 2007 comes with over 65 macro actions that you can use in your processes. However, the new security features in Access 2007 prevent 26 of those macro actions from running unless the Access database you are working with is trusted. (*Trusted* means that you have explicitly told Access that the macros within the database are of no threat and can be run freely.) The following Macro Actions require a trusted database to run. Running any one of these 26 macro actions in an untrusted database causes an error.

CopyDatabaseFile	RunApp
CopyObject	RunSavedImportExport
DeleteObject	RunSQL
Echo	Save
OpenDataAccessPage	SendKeys
OpenDiagram	SetValue
OpenFunction	SetWarnings
OpenModule	ShowToolbar
OpenStoredProcedur	TransferDatabase
OpenView	TransferSharePointList
PrintOut	TransferSpreadsheet
Quit	TransferSQLDatabase
Rename	TransferText

NOTE Although the RunCommand macro action does not, in itself, require a trusted database to run, many of its arguments do. Therefore, you may find that when using the RunCommand macro action, it can require a trusted database depending on the action you are trying to take.

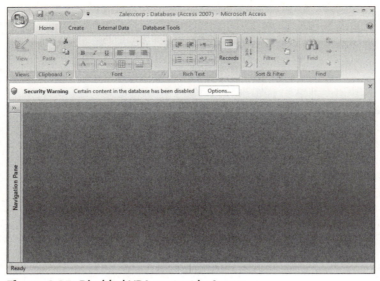

Figure 6-25: Disabled VBA content in Access

As in Excel, you can manually enable macro and VBA content by selecting the Options button next to the security warning message. This opens a dialog box where you can choose to enable macros for the database in which you are working (see Figure 6-26).

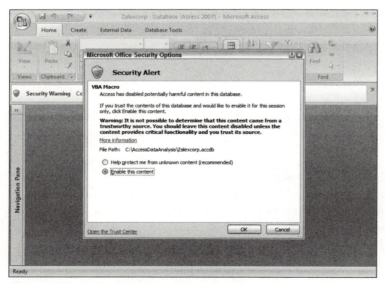

Figure 6-26: Dialog box to enable macros in Access

As with Excel, the best way to work around the security issues in Access 2007 on a long-term basis is to use the database in a Trusted Location. To set up a trusted location in Access, follow these steps:

1. Select the Office icon in the upper-left corner of the application window, and then select the Access Options button.

2. Click the Trust Center button, and then select Trust Center Settings.

3. Select the Trusted Locations button.

4. Select Add New Location.

5. Click Browse to specify the directory that will be considered a trusted location (see Figure 6-27).

After you have specified a trusted location, all databases opened from that location are, by default, opened with macros enabled.

Creating Your First Access Macro

Now that you know the key difference between Access and Excel macros is in the interface, you can examine the Access macro user interface in more detail.

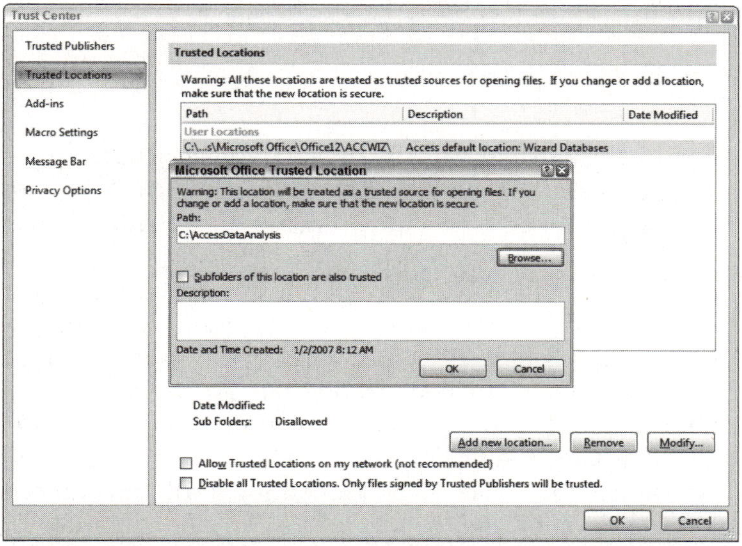

Figure 6-27: Adding a trusted location in the Access Trust Center

The Macro Design Template

To access the Macro Design Template, go to the Create tab on the ribbon. Select the Macro button on the far right. Choose Macro from the drop-down menu (see Figure 6-28).

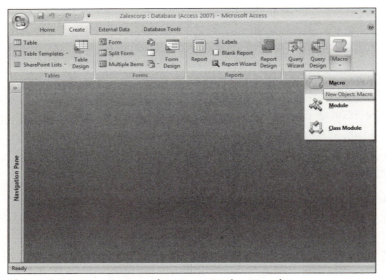

Figure 6-28: How to open the Macro Design Template

Now you see the Macro Design Template. By default, you should see three columns corresponding to Action, Arguments, and Comment. Select a cell in the Action column, and you will see a drop-down menu of available actions (see Figure 6-29).

Each row in the Macro Design Template corresponds to a specific task that you want Access to execute. Beside the Action column is the Argument column. If the Argument column is not visible, simply select the Argument icon from the Show/Hide menu from the Create ribbon tab. An *argument* is an additional piece of information provided so that the action is performed correctly. The last column is the Comment column. Here you can enter free-form text that describes what your action does. This is an optional column, but can be helpful for longer or more complex macros.

In the next section, you will dive deeper into the available actions and the corresponding arguments. When you see what actions are available, it will become clearer how and where Access macros can be useful.

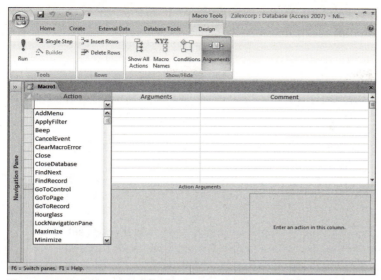

Figure 6-29: Action menu in the Macro Design Template

Common Actions in Access Macros

By default, Access shows only a subset of the available actions. To view all the actions in the drop-down menu, select Show All Actions from the Show/Hide menu of the Design tab (see Figure 6-30).

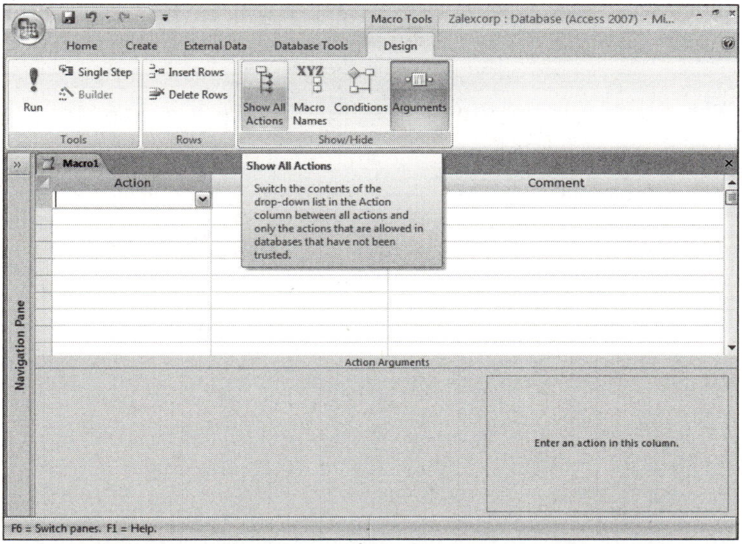

Figure 6-30: Show all available actions in the Macro Design Template

Now that all actions are available, let's discuss a handful of the most useful ones for data analysis and integration with Excel.

OpenQuery

This action is the workhorse for Access data analysis. Complex, multistep data analysis in Access often entails a series of action queries to process raw data — Make Table, Append, Update, and Delete queries. The OpenQuery action runs these action queries for you (see Figure 6-31).

The OpenQuery action takes three arguments. The most important is the query name. Clicking in the Query Name box produces a drop-down list of all queries in your Access database. Choose the appropriate action query, and you are set.

> **TIP** It helps to give your queries alpha or numeric prefixes if you want to run a set of ordered action queries with a macro. For example, a set of three ordered action queries might be named A_MakePriceMaster, B_AppendNewData, and C_UpdateDateField. This makes choosing the appropriate macro from the Query Name drop-down much easier.

The remaining arguments are the View argument and the Data Mode argument. The default value for View is Datasheet. Keep this default value to run any action query. The Data Mode argument sets whether the query can add or update any records. The default value is Edit, which allows adding and updating records with your queries. To run action queries, keep the default value at Edit.

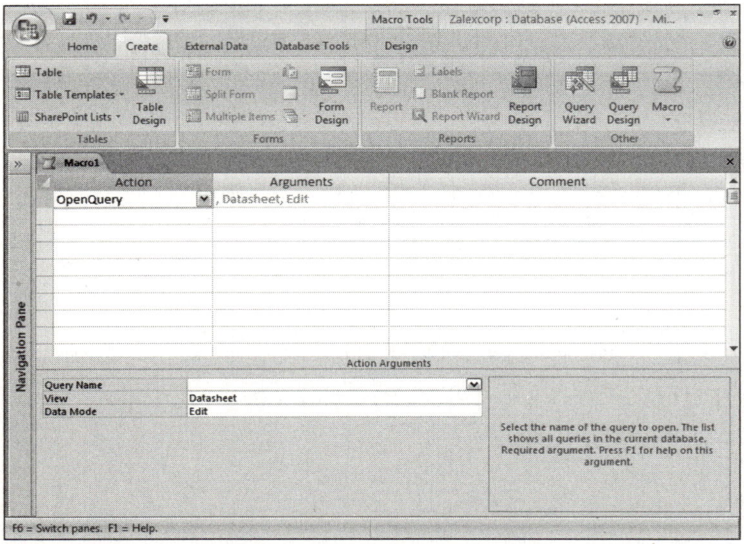

Figure 6-31: Arguments for the OpenQuery action

TransferSpreadsheet

This action is one of the most useful for integrating Excel and Access. The TransferSpreadsheet action can both import an Excel worksheet into Access and export an Access table or query into Excel. Whether you export or import depends on which arguments you choose (see Figure 6-32).

- **Transfer Type argument:** Here you specify whether to import a spreadsheet into Access or export an Access object (a query or table) into Excel. There is also a Link option in the drop-down menu. Linking an Excel worksheet is an alternative to importing it.

CROSS-REFERENCE Refer to Chapter 1 for reasons why one method might be more fitting than the other for your particular application.

- **Spreadsheet Type argument:** Access can accommodate different types of spreadsheets, including both Excel and Lotus 1-2-3 (see Figure 6-33). Perhaps the most important choice is that of Excel Workbook for Office 2007 or earlier versions of Excel. Access can import or export to several earlier versions of Excel.

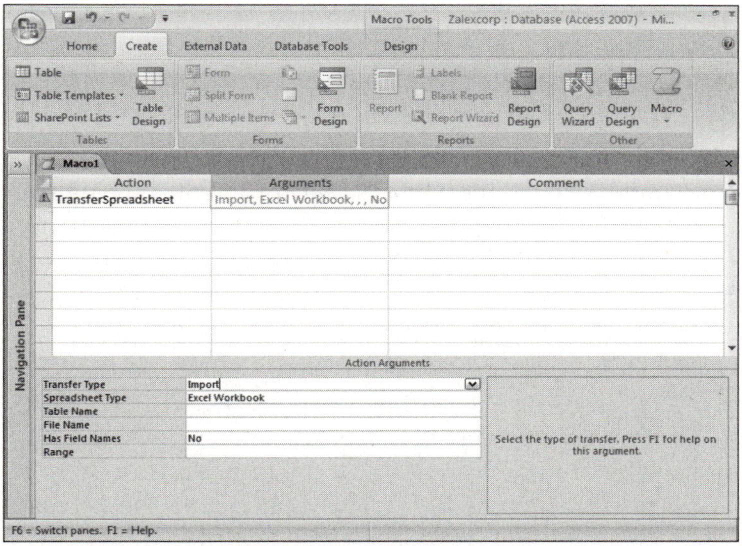

Figure 6-32: TransferSpreadsheet arguments

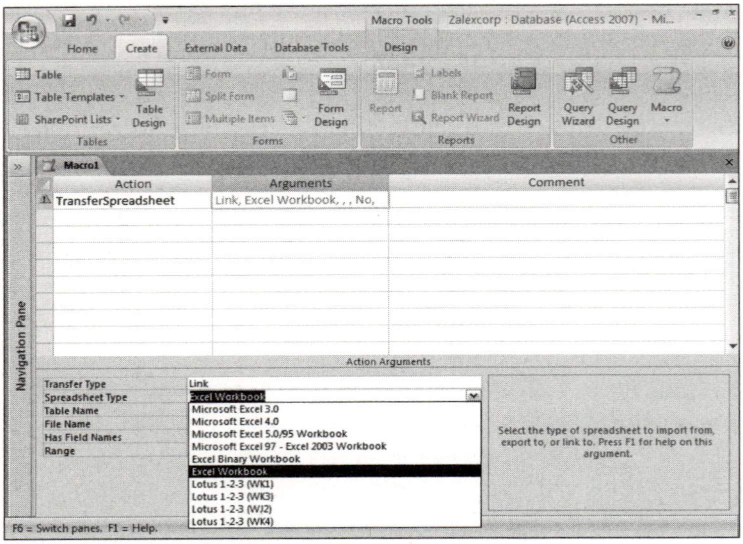

Figure 6-33: Spreadsheet Type argument choices

- **Table Name argument:** The Table Name argument takes on different types of values depending on whether you select Import or Export in the Transfer Type argument field. When you are exporting from Access to Excel, the Table Name argument will be the name of the Access object you want to export. You enter the name of a table or query in this field. You will not have a drop-down menu to choose from, so you must manually type in the table or query name.

  When importing a spreadsheet, the Table Name argument is the name of the Access table to which you will import. If the table name does not exist, Access will create a new table with that name. If the table name already exists, Access will append the imported spreadsheet to the existing Access table.

- **File Name argument:** This argument is both the file name and the full directory path of the file you are importing or exporting. When importing, you must specify an existing spreadsheet file. When exporting, you may specify an existing or non-existing file. If the Excel spreadsheet you export to does not exist, a new file will be created with the Access table or query name. If the Excel spreadsheet you export to does exist, a new worksheet will be created with the Access table or query name. The file name will not be changed.

  You do not have the option to browse when entering your file path name. Take note of the precise location of your file. You will have to manually enter it into this argument field.

TIP If you have trouble manually typing in the full directory path for the file you want to export or import, open Microsoft Explorer and browse to the location of the file. At the top of the Explorer menu, you will see the addres bar that contains the full path of your current location. Copy that address and paste it into the File Name argument.

■ **Has Field Names and Range arguments:** These last two are relatively simple and straightforward arguments. Putting Yes in the Has Field Names argument means the first row of data imported, exported, or linked will be treated as column headings. Selecting No means the first row will be treated like regular data.

CAUTION When importing or exporting data, the first few rows of data will be used to determine the default data type for each field. If your data has text column headings and you select No in the Has Field Names argument, you risk having your field data types misinterpreted. Specifically, you may have number fields treated as text.

The Range argument allows you to specify an Excel cell range or a named range to import or link. Use this option if you want to import a selection of cells rather than the entire worksheet.

SetWarnings Action

The SetWarnings action enables you to turn off system messages while your macro is running (see Figure 6-34). Assume you have 10 action queries in your macro. Without setting SetWarnings to No, Access stops the macro for each modal message generated by these action queries. For example, before an Update query executes the user gets a message stating Access is about to update *X* many records. The user must click OK to get the query to run. Set-Warnings turn these messages off.

CAUTION If you use the SetWarnings action in your macro, you should use it twice. Specifically, set the SetWarnings action to No in the very first step and set it to Yes in the very last step in your macro. If you forget to set the argument back to Yes, your action queries will run without the normal warning message boxes.

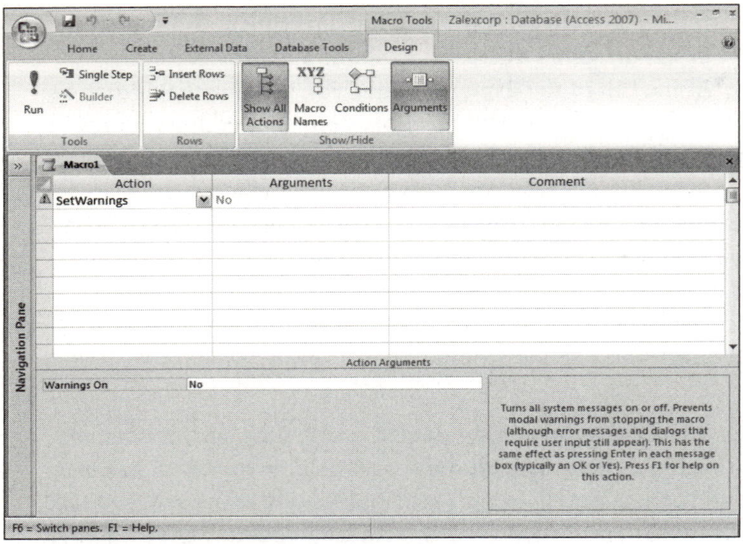

Figure 6-34: SetWarnings action and argument

MsgBox Action

The MsgBox action has multiple uses, but I use it most often at the end of my macro to let me know when it has completed running. When the MsgBox action runs, a user input box pops up on the screen. If you add the MsgBox item at the beginning or middle of your macro sequence, the macro will pause until the user clicks the OK button. Figure 6-35 gives you a look at the MsgBox arguments.

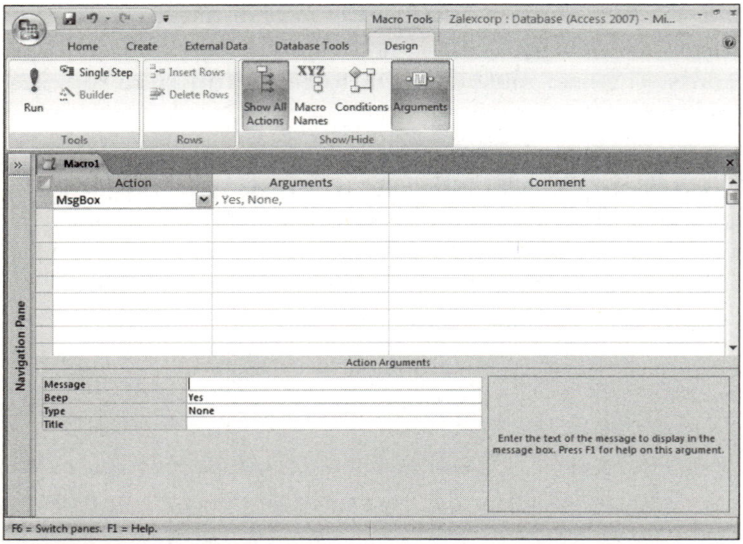

Figure 6-35: MsgBox arguments

The Message argument enables you to free-form type the text you want the user to see within the box. The Beep argument should be self-evident. Make the argument Yes if you want an audible warning when the message box opens. The Type argument gives you options for different icons in the message box, and the Title argument lets you customize the text in the message box title bar. Take a look at an example of a message box with an Information icon that notifies you the macro has completed running (see Figure 6-36).

Access Macro Example

This next section applies what you have learned about Access macro actions and arguments with a tangible example. You will create a report of the top 25 percent service reps by total revenue in each geographic region. This type of report is ideal for Access because you can use a Top Records query for each region.

You could make a similar report in Excel, but it would require significant manual processing. First, review the steps to create such a report in Excel.

1. Create an MS Query data link to the database that houses transaction level detail and employee information. Create a query that brings in service reps by total revenue by region.

2. In your Excel spreadsheet, create four separate tables of service reps, one table for each region. Rank them by revenue.

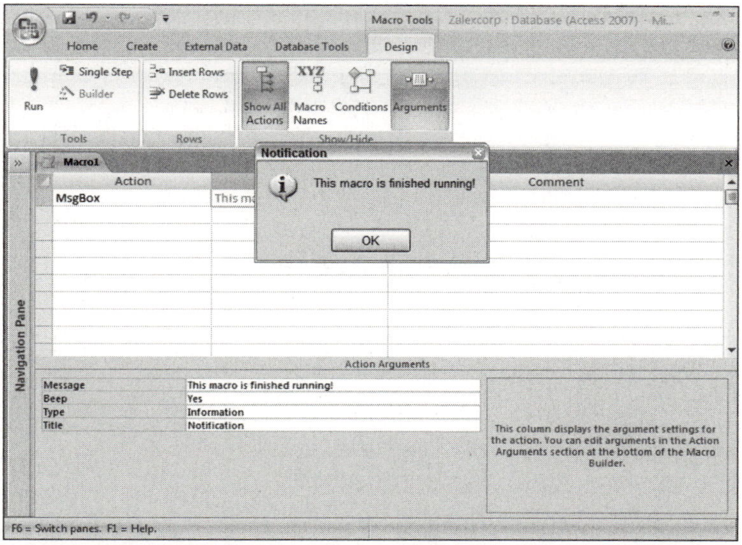

Figure 6-36: Sample message box signifying the macro is finished running

3. Then sort each table in descending order by revenue and identify the 75th percentile rep for each region using the Excel PERCENTILE function.

4. Apply some conditional formatting that highlights those reps in each region. For example, assume the 75th percentile rep in the North region had $50,000 in revenue. You apply some conditional formatting on all North service reps that highlighted those with revenues greater than $50,000.

5. Now repeat the same exercise for the remaining regions.

Now consider that every time you update this report you must repeat Steps 1 through 4. For different months, the revenue cutoff for the 75th percentile service rep will change. This may not seem like a lot of effort. Consider, however, if you had to replicate the report for 14 markets or for 59 branches. My head is starting to hurt already!

Now tackle the same report in Access. Assume that you have updated transaction revenue data in your Access database

1. First, you need to create a Make Table query for one region only (for this example, the West region) to establish your table of top 25 percent reps. You use the Top Records function set to 25 percent and make sure the query is in descending order by the sum of revenue. This query makes a table with the top 25 percent of West region service reps by revenue. Name the new table TopRepTable. Close and save this query as A_MakeWestTable. Figure 6-37 illustrates what the query should look like.

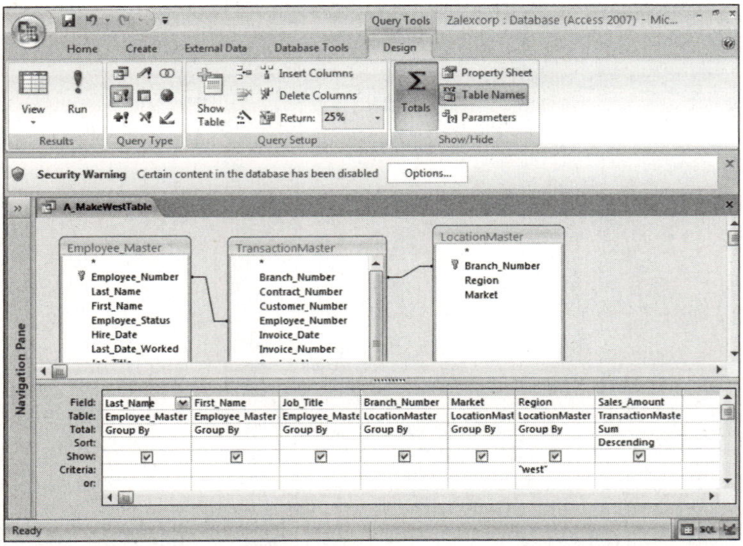

Figure 6-37: Make Table query design for top 25 percent of West reps

2. Run your newly created A_MakeWestTable query. This makes the TopRepTables table you need to build the rest of your queries.

3. Create the Append query you see in Figure 6-38. Note that you are appending the results to the TopRepTable table. Close and save your Append query as B_AppendNorthTable.

4. Repeat Step 2 for the remaining regions. Make sure you change the region criterion correctly in each query. Also, make sure you name each query with an alpha prefix to denote the query order.

The TopRepTable is now complete with the top 25 percent of service reps by region. Now that the underlying queries are set up, you can turn your attention to completing the macro steps. Open the Macro Design Template. Save the macro as RefreshTopReps. Now you can assign the steps to your macro.

1. Turn warnings off with the SetWarnings action set to No. This ensures the macro does not hang up waiting for erroneous user input.

2. In Steps 2 through 6, use the OpenQuery action to run one Make Table query and three Append queries. Make sure the correct query is specified in the argument section of each step (see Figure 6-39).

3. Export the TopRepTable to an Excel spreadsheet so report users can easily view and manipulate the information. Use the TransferSpreadsheet action. Set the path to `C:/AccessDataAnalysis/TopReps`. This creates a new spreadsheet titled TopReps (see Figure 6-40).

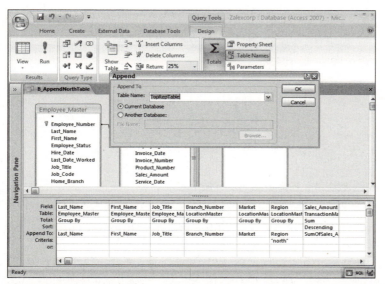

Figure 6-38: Append table query design for top 25 percent of North reps

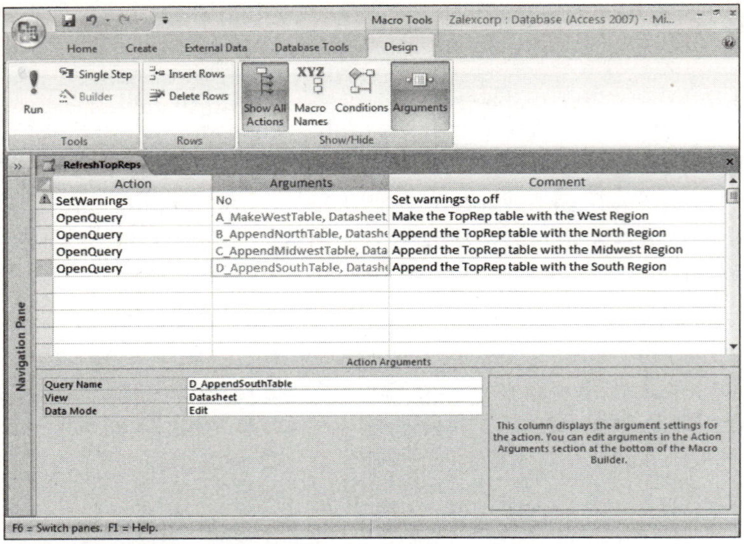

Figure 6-39: Macro design for running your newly created queries

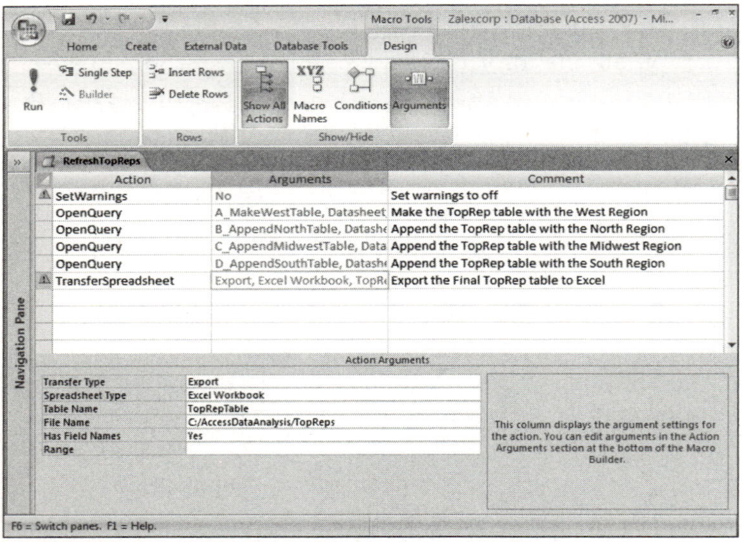

Figure 6-40: Macro design for TransferSpreadsheet action

4. Now add a message box that tells that the macro is finished running. Any descriptive text in the Message argument will do. As a last step, remember to turn warnings back on with the SetWarnings action and the argument set to Yes. The final macro should look like Figure 6-41.

All that is left is to see whether the macro works. To run the macro, double-click the RefreshTopReps icon from the navigation pane. If you are in Macro Design view, select the Run icon at the top left of the Design menu. You should see something like Figure 6-42 if the macro runs successfully.

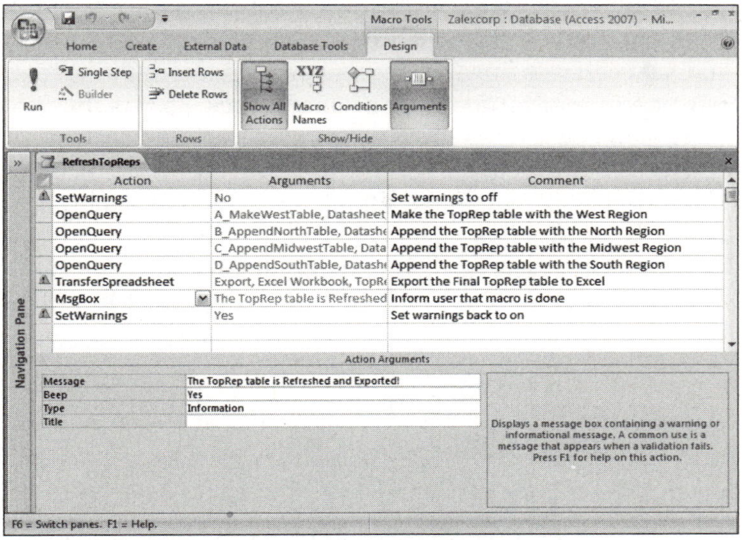

Figure 6-41: RefreshTopRep macro final design

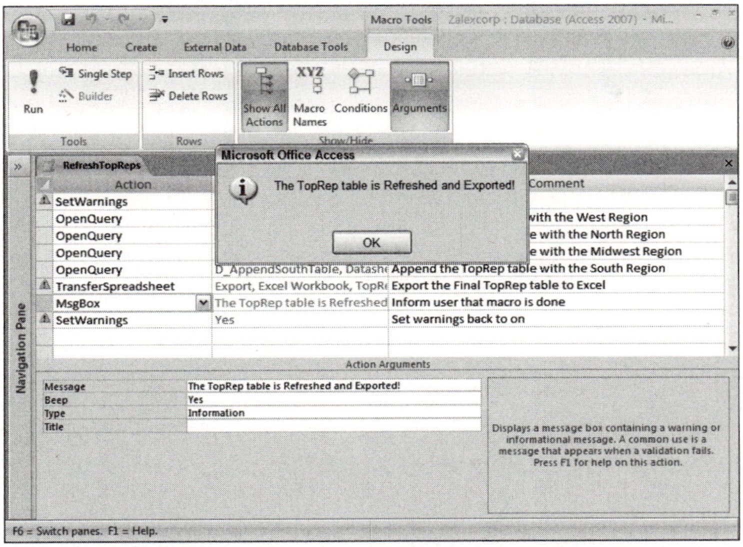

Figure 6-42: RefreshTopRep macro after successfully running

So far everything appears successful! Open the TopReps Excel spreadsheet to see how it looks. Scroll down to ensure that service reps from all regions are present and that they are rank ordered by revenue (see Figure 6-43).

Now compare the actions required to produce this report manually in Excel versus producing it with an Access macro. They both require comparable effort if producing a one-time report. Honestly, how many reports are really one-time efforts? Think about the incremental effort of producing this report on a monthly basis in Excel versus using the Access macro method. The Access macro produces a refreshed report at the click of one button. That is the productivity power of Access macros.

On your own, record a formatting macro that spruces up the TopReps Excel report. Use the macro you recorded in the Excel macros section as a template. You may want to put the Excel data into a PivotTable and experiment with different PivotTable report views. Make sure you try automating some of these steps with the Excel Macro Recorder. Through initiative and experimentation, you will be amazed at what you can automate with Excel and Access macros!

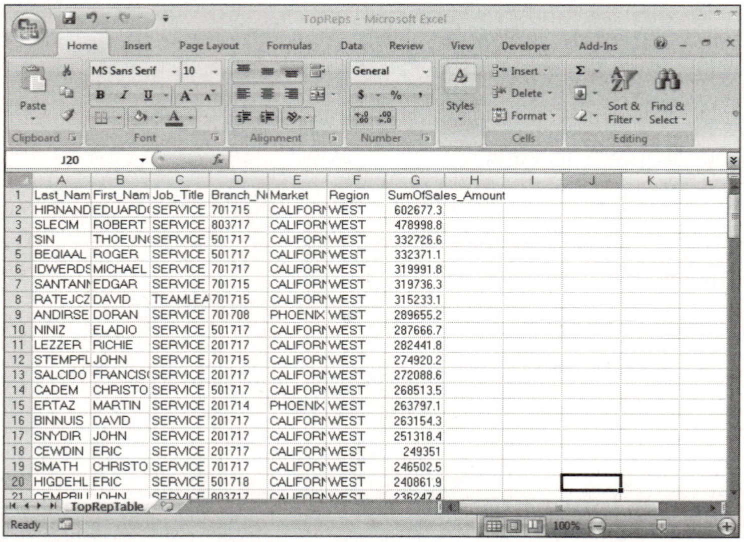

Figure 6-43: TopReps Excel spreadsheet

Summary

A macro is a set of instructions, or code, that tells Excel or Access to execute any number of tasks. Macros in Excel and Access are very different from one another. In Excel, macros are used as a way to record actions that can be played back when needed. Excel macros are analogous to programming a phone to dial a specific telephone number when you press a special key. In Access, however, macros are used to execute a set of pre-programmed functions, much like a list of menu options on your TV that can be fired when selected. These pre-programmed functions are called macro *actions*.

You can leverage macros to automate recurring analytical processes, ensure consistency in your analytical processes, and simplify your processes with user-friendly interfaces.

VBA is the engine for macros in Excel, Access, and all other Microsoft Office applications. Learning the basics of VBA will take your macros and your productivity to a completely different level. This is the subject of the next chapter.

Advanced Integration Techniques

VBA Fundamentals

Chapter 6 introduced you to the power of macros in automating processes in Excel and Access. In this chapter, we expand on Chapter 6 by pulling back the covers on macros and exploring what makes them work.

Like many people, your authors cut their teeth in VBA programming by creating Access and Excel macros and then tweaking the bits of code to see how it worked. Before long, there was enough familiarity with the language to greatly improve our Excel and Access applications. Fear or unfamiliarity with programming languages did not deter us, and it should not deter you.

If you are a programming neophyte, have no fear. The goal of this chapter is not to make you an expert VBA programmer. Indeed, you don't have to be a programming guru to harness the power of VBA in either Excel *or* Access. After reading this chapter, you will have enough familiarity with VBA to start coding to improve your analyses.

TIP The purpose of this chapter is to give you an understanding of the fundamental concepts used in the techniques demonstrated in the latter chapters of this book. Bear in mind that this chapter is written to provide you an introductory look at VBA. If you are interested in an in-depth look at programming Excel and Access VBA, consider picking up one of the following titles:

- *Excel 2007 VBA Programmer's Reference* (by John Green, Stephen Bullen, Rob Bovey, Michael Alexander, ISBN: 978-0-470-04643-2)

- *Beginning Access 2007 VBA* (by Denise Gosnell, ISBN: 978-0-470-04684-5)

- *Access 2007 VBA Programming For Dummies* (by Alan Simpson, ISBN: 978-0-470-04653-1)

- *Excel 2007 VBA Programming For Dummies* (by John Walkenbach, ISBN: 978-0-470-04674-6)

These books offer a solid introduction to VBA that is ideal for novice Access programmers.

What Is VBA?

Visual Basic for Applications (VBA) is a computer programming language. In the most simplistic terms, a programming language is a set of instructions that tell your computer what to do. Take this silly snippet of VBA code for example:

```
Sub SayHi()
    MsgBox "hi, you are in " & Application.Name
End Sub
```

The first line tells the computer, "computer, create a set of instructions and call this set of instructions SayHi." The next line is the actual set of tasks the computer must carry out. In this case, we are telling the computer, "computer, display a simple box on the screen that greets the user and tells her what Microsoft Application she is using." The last line simply tells our computer that this set of instructions is finished now. In VBA, this set of instructions is called a *procedure*. A procedure is a block of code that performs a set of instructions in VBA.

An important thing to remember is that VBA is a programming language for the Microsoft Office Suite of Applications. This means VBA code has the same structure, syntax and meaning regardless of whether you are in Excel, Access, Word, or Outlook. It also means that you can write a set of instructions in one Microsoft application (like Excel) that can tell another application what to do (like run a query in Access and export the results to a new sheet in my work-book)! Pretty cool stuff.

VBA as an Object-Oriented Programming Language

There is another crucial concept to understand before diving into coding, the Object-Oriented Programming model. Most modern programming languages are object-oriented. What does it mean to be object-oriented? I like to think of it this way: A programming language tells the computer what to do. *Objects* are the library of "things" that the programming language can manipulate. From using computers you are already familiar with many of these "things." For example, tables, dialog boxes, folders, and even programs are objects. Most identifiable "things" are considered to be objects in object-oriented programming.

Objects and Collections

Objects are arranged in a containerized hierarchy. In Excel, the top of this hier-archy is the Application object, called Excel. If you were working in Access, the Application object would be Access. Underneath the Application object in both Access and Excel, there are a series of other objects. In Access, some exam-ples of objects would be the Database Object, the Table object, the Query object and the Form Object. Examples of Excel objects underneath Application are Workbooks (a collection of all Workbook objects), ActiveWorkbook (the cur-rently open and selected workbook object), and ActiveWindow (the currently active window objects). You will notice from the examples that objects can be both collections of other objects (Workbooks) or individual objects (Active-Workbook). A *collection*, also an object, is a set of objects in the same class. Depending on your Excel settings, opening a new workbook will create a Col-lection of three worksheets named Sheet1, Sheet2, and Sheet3.

VBA has a specific syntax for denoting the relative hierarchy of objects. Con-sider the Excel workbook object. It contains worksheet objects, which in turn contain cell range objects. To reference a cell A1 in Sheet1, you must tell VBA which workbook and worksheet to look in. If you had multiple open work-books, each with multiple worksheets, there could be numerous cell A1s! How does VBA know which cell A1 you want? VBA enables you to reference your specific cell range by including each object in the hierarchy separated by a period (.). For example, setting a value of 3 to cell A1 in Sheet1 of an Excel workbook titled Book1 would look like this:

```
Workbooks("Book1").Worksheets("Sheet1").Range("a1").Value = 3
```

The astute reader may have noticed that this statement was not preceded by the Application object. Most times this reference is not needed, as it is assumed.

Properties, Methods, and Arguments

Objects have characteristics, or *properties*. For example, a query in Access is an object that has a Name, and a cell range has a Value. In the previous example we changed the Value property of the cell range to 3.

Objects also have actions that can be performed on them. These actions are called *methods*. For example, the currently active cell in a worksheet has a method called Clear, which clears the contents of the cell. Code that would delete the value 3 I just assigned to cell A1 would look like this:

```
Workbooks("Book1").Worksheets("Sheet1").Range("a1").Clear
```

Properties and methods sometimes require additional information to reference the correct property or perform the right action. These additional pieces of information are called *arguments*. There is an important syntax distinction between arguments for properties and arguments for methods. Arguments for methods are followed by the method statement and each argument is separated by a comma. Arguments for a property are enclosed in parentheses right after the property statement. Following are a couple of examples to make arguments more clear.

First look at code that provides the arguments for a method:

```
Workbooks("Book1").Protect "paco", True, True
```

Protect is a method that can be performed on a Workbook to help keep the file secure. It has three optional arguments: password, structure, and windows. In this piece of VBA code, we told Excel to protect Workbook1 with the password paco. We also told Excel not to allow the user to rearrange windows or even insert or delete sheets.

What does it mean that an argument is optional? It simply means that you, as the coder, can enter values for none, all, or any number of these arguments. If you choose to enter one or two optional arguments, but not all, you must insert a comma after the arguments you choose to omit. For example, to protect a workbook's structure and windows without making it password protected, the following syntax is required:

```
Workbooks("Book1").Protect , True, True
```

The following line of code illustrates supplying arguments to a property. Here we are using the Offset property of the range object. The offset property is the location of the 1 row lower and 2 columns to the right of cell A1. Here you will notice that the two arguments are enclosed in parentheses and separated by a comma. This snippet of code displays the value in the cell C2 of the active worksheet.

```
MsgBox Range("a1").Offset(1, 2).Value
```

Don't worry, you don't have to remember all the arguments for all methods you might want to use. Excel VBA provides several resources to help you here. Perhaps the most useful is to select List Properties/Methods from the Edit menu in VBA (you can also use the keyboard shortcut Ctrl+J). Selecting this option lets you view the optional and required arguments for a method and allow you to see all available properties and methods for a specific object. By default, VBA should show you the properties/methods list when you enter an object, property, or method in the Visual Basic Editor. If it does not, simply select the Auto List members check box from the Tools → Options menu item in the Visual Basic Editor. Alternatively, you can use the VBA help feature, which has a great deal of information on objects, properties, and methods.

Object-oriented programming works so well because the things you want to manipulate are prepackaged with properties, actions you can take on them, and a logical, structured hierarchy. Because of this, programming is actually made much more simple and powerful. If you doubt it, contemplate how easy it would be to insert a new worksheet by giving your computer a series of 0s and 1s! Typing Worksheets.Add in your Visual Basic Editor seems a lot simpler!

Extended Analogy of the Object Model

Let us illustrate the Object Model in a more tangible, although slightly silly, example.

Suppose your family has two cars, each of which can be considered an object. In fact, your collection of cars is also an object. Your favorite car is a highly modified 2006 Ford Mustang GT. All car nuts name their pride and joy, and you are no exception. Naturally, you name your favorite car Paco.

In VBA, naming your car might look something like this: `MyCars(1).Name = "Paco"`. MyCars is an object, the collection of all the cars you own. This object has an argument, 1, that specifies which member of your collection you are referencing. Of course, this member is also an object. This member of your collection has a property called Name, which you changed with the code above.

Like most objects, Paco is a container for other objects. Paco has a power train and an electrical system, among other things. Even Paco's PowerTrain object is a container for still more objects. PowerTrain contains the objects like engine, transmission, axle, and so on.

Paco has methods, which are actions performed on specified objects. For instance, Paco's engine object has a ChangeOil method. Here's what changing Paco's oil might look like if you could manipulate it in VBA. If Paco really understood VBA, your car maintenance duties would become a lot easier.

```
Sub ChangeOil()
    MyCars("Paco").PowerTrain.Engine.ChangeOil
End Sub
```

Sometimes Paco needs certain pieces of information to refer to the right hierarchical object or execute the right method. In VBA, these pieces of information are called arguments. One of your favorite Paco methods is called `BigSmokeyBurnout`. Paco's `BigSmokeyBurnout` method requires two pieces of information to be properly executed. Here's how you would execute a `BigSmokeyBurnout` in VBA:

```
Sub BigSmokeyBurnout ()
    Rpm = 6000
    PopClutch = True
    MyCars("Paco").BigSmokeyBurnout Rpm, PopClutch
End Sub
```

Here you created two variables, one for engine revolutions per minute and the other a true/false flag for popping the clutch. Can you almost smell the billowy, acrid cloud of tire smoke?

The Visual Basic Editor or VBE

Now that you have learned about object-oriented programming and looked at a few code examples, it is time to explore where our VBA code is written and stored. In both Excel and Access, VBA code is written in the Visual Basic Editor (VBE). In both Excel and Access, the VBE can be accessed with the shortcut Alt+F11. Alternatively, the VBE can be accessed in Excel by selecting the Developer tab from the ribbon and then selecting the Visual Basic icon. Depending on how Excel 2007 is setup, the Developer tab may not show up in your ribbon by default. If it is not there, simply click the Office icon in the top left corner and select Excel options at the bottom of the menu. If you select the Personalize screen, you will see a check box entitled Show Developer tab in the ribbon (see Figure 7-1). Make sure this check box is selected.

As the versions of VBE in Access and Excel are very similar, we'll demonstrate the parts with Excel only. We'll call out significant differences where they exist. In Figure 7-2 you see the VBE opened with three windows, the Project Explorer window, properties window, and the code window. We'll explore the two most important, the Project Explorer and code windows, in the following sections.

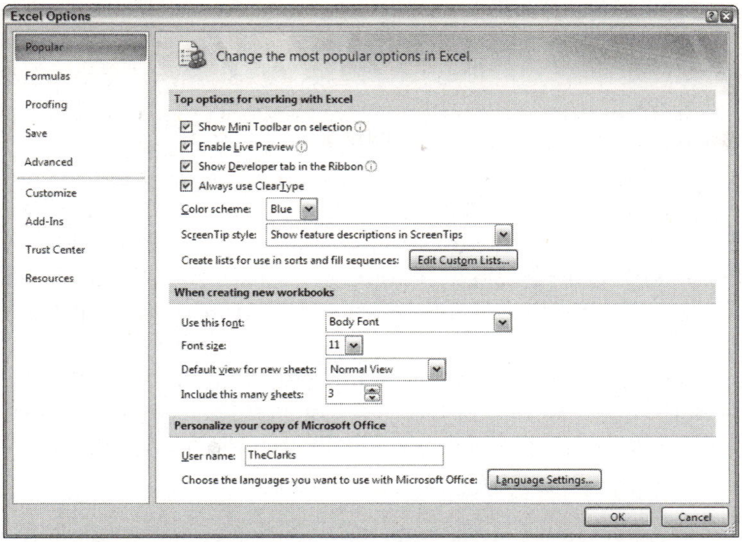

Figure 7-1: Ensuring the Developer tab shows up in the ribbon

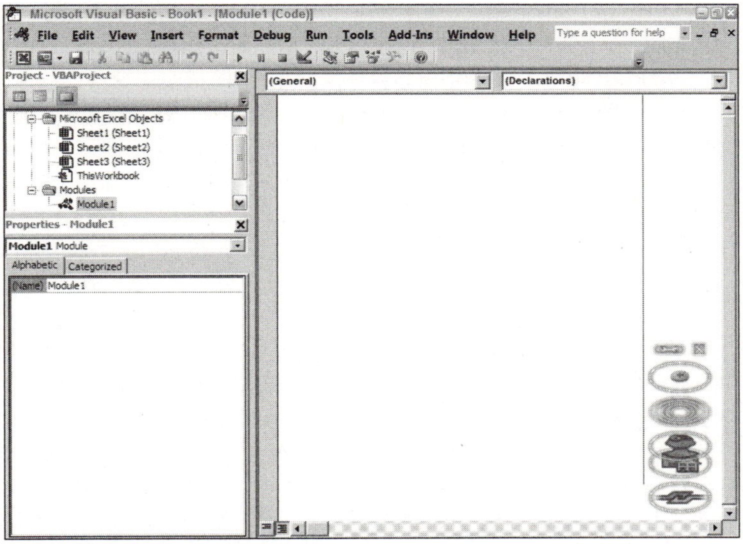

Figure 7-2: The VBE windows

Project Explorer Window

In the upper-left side of the VBE, you'll see the Project Explorer window and its workbooks/projects. In Figure 7-2, you'll notice one project corresponding to the one open workbook. In general, you will see a project for each open workbook you have — even those hidden or protected. You can think of the Project Explorer window as the organizational structure of your application. Within each workbook, you'll see all the objects associated with the workbook. In this example you Sheet1, Sheet2, Sheet3, an object for the workbook itself titled ThisWorkbook and an object called Module1 that houses code for the workbook. Unless you have recorded a macro in your workbook, you will not see a module object in the Project Explorer window by default. However, when you recorded macros in Chapter 6, Excel automatically inserted a module to contain the code of each macro you recorded. To insert a module on your own, simply select Insert → Module from the VBE menu.

Code Window

Not surprisingly, your VBA coding goes in the code window. In Figure 7-2, the code window is for the object Module1. As we discussed before, a module houses code for the whole workbook and the code can be accessed and run anywhere within the workbook.

Code doesn't have to be stored only in a module. You can access a code window for any object in the project. Keep in mind, however, that code residing in an object like a worksheet can only be run in that particular worksheet. Later examples will make this concept clearer.

Code and Events

Now that we know where to put the code, what do we do with it? After you recorded a macro in Chapter 6, you had to tie it to some user action to get it to run. The macro recorder gives you the option to assign a shortcut key to the macro. You may also have had experience tying a macro to a graphical figure that, when pressed, will run your code. Typing a shortcut or clicking a graphic are actions called *events*. Invariably your code will be triggered by some action or event.

Let's walk through a short example of some event-triggered coding. By double-clicking the ThisWorkbook object in the Project Explorer window, you'll get a code window. This code window is specific to the open workbook, Book1 (see Figure 7-3).

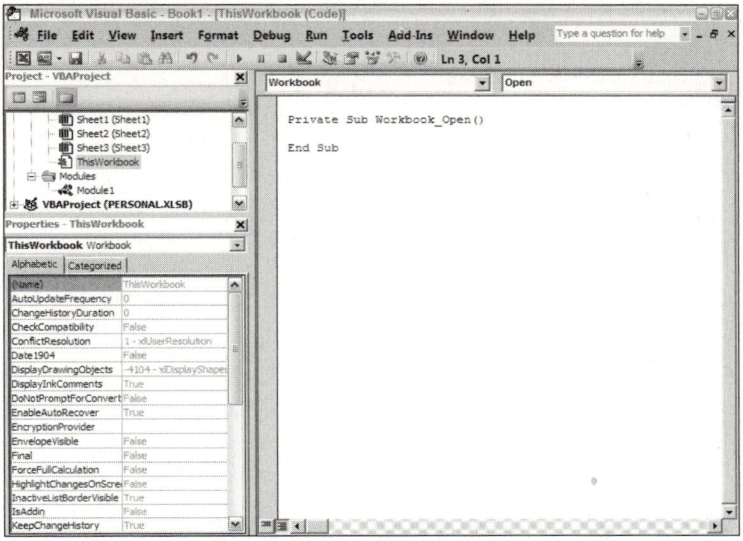

Figure 7-3: VBA code window for ThisWorkbook

At the top of the code open code window, you will see two drop-down menu boxes. Click the left side drop-down menu and select Workbook. This means any coding here will be specific to the workbook selected in the Project Explorer window to the left. After you select Workbook from the drop-down menu, note that Excel automatically inserts the following structure for a VBE procedure.

```
Private Sub Workbook_Open()

End Sub
```

Now notice the top-right menu that says Open. Click the arrow next to Open to see the drop-down menu (see Figure 7-4). You can think of this as an event menu for the open workbook. Any of the events in this drop-down menu will trigger the code in the ThisWorkbook code window. Select Before-Close from this menu and you see another structure for a VBA procedure entitled `Workbook_BeforeClose`.

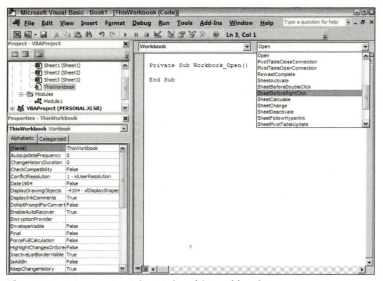

Figure 7-4: Event menu items for ThisWorkbook

Variables

Variables in VBA are exactly like the variables in basic Algebra. A *variable* is a placeholder for a value in an equation. Variables are critical to all VBA programming. Let's look at the following line of VBA code. How many variables can you identify?

```
Torque = a1 * Rpm ^ 4 + b1 * Rpm ^ 3 + c1 * Rpm ^ 2 + d1 * Rpm + e1
```

There are seven variables to be exact. Variables can take on a nearly infinite number of values. In this example, the value of the variable Torque will change contingent of the value of variables Rpm, a1, b1, c1, d1, and e1.

Object Variables

Variable need not only represent numbers or text. One of the most powerful aspects of VBA is that variables can represent objects. Look at the following code example that uses object variables:

```
Public Sub VisibleSheets()
    Dim MySheet As Worksheet
    For Each MySheet In ActiveWorkbook.Worksheets
        If MySheet.Visible = False Then MySheet.Visible = True
    Next MySheet
End Sub
```

In this example, the variable MySheet represents a worksheet object. The remaining code performs an operation on all the worksheets in the open workbook. This operation would not be possible without the use of an object variable.

Array Variables

In addition to being numbers, text, and objects, variables can also be arrays. An array is a list of data stored as one entity. Arrays can have multiple dimensions, but we will only cover one- and two-dimensional arrays. A simple list is an example of data that can be stored in a one-dimensional array. Let's say the following list is an array titled MyFavoriteCars.

Mustang GT

Corvette Z06

Porsche 911

VW Bus

We can reference a particular data element in the array by including the data element's position in the list. For example, `MyFavoriteCars(2)` contains the text string Porsche 911. VBA's default way of indexing an array makes the first data element `MyFavoriteCars(0)`. Although there are four items in this array, VBA references their positions as 0, 1, 2, and 3.

Constants

Constants are a specific subtype of variables. A *constant* is a variable that, once assigned a value, doesn't change. Let's say that in the preceding example, a1, b1, c1, d1, and e1 were all constants and we set the value of those constants at the beginning of our code block. How is this useful? The answer is that using constants can be a real effort-saver. If you hard-coded a value several places in your application but later needed to change the value, you'd have to find and replace every instance of that hard-coded number. By using a constant, you would only have to change the value once.

Declaring Variables

VBA coding best practice is to declare your variables at the beginning of your procedures or functions. By declaring your variables, you are telling VBA you are going to be using a variable with a specific name, which will contain a value of a specific data type. Declaring variables in VBA entails using the `Dim` statement. The following lines of code declare variables used in prior examples.

```
Dim Torque as Double
Dim Rpm As Integer
```

```
Dim a1 As Double
Dim b1 as Double
Dim c1 as Double
Dim d1 as Double
Dim e1 as Double
Dim MyFavoriteCars(0 to 3) as String
```

You'll notice that the data types in VBA share a striking similarity to the Access data types we discussed in Chapter 1. This is not by accident. You should be aware that VBA does not require you to declare your variables and specify a data type. As we mentioned before, however, it is wise to declare your variables. It is particularly important to declare variables that will represent objects.

Variable Scope

Variables in VBA also have scope, which indicates where these variables exist and retain their value. Local variables are declared within a procedure and exist only within that procedure. In essence, this means that when VBA is not executing that procedure, it forgets all about that variable and frees up memory space associated with storing it. Other procedures, even in the same module, can use the same variable name without any confusion. Any variable declared within a procedure is local and specific only to that procedure.

To make a variable available to all procedures in a specific module, you simply must declare the variable before the first procedure in the module. If you want to make the variable available to all procedures in all modules, you must use some slightly different syntax in your declaration statement. Specifically you would use the Public statement instead of the Dim statement and once again make the declaration line come before the first procedure in any module.

Procedures and Functions

Before delving too deep into actual coding, it's important that we draw a distinction between two different types of code blocks: procedures and functions. Let's go back to the opening and closing lines Excel automatically inserts when we record a macro.

```
Public Sub Macro1()
    'code goes here
End Sub
```

The public statement simply tells Excel that the set of instructions that follows should be made available to any part of the open workbook. The Sub statement tells Excel that the lines of code are a procedure. As we discussed earlier, a procedure is a set of instructions that perform certain tasks involving Excel objects. How is a function different then? A function can be thought of as a specific subset of a procedure. A function is a procedure that performs tasks and returns a single value. Here is an example of function syntax:

```
Public Function MyFunction()
    'code goes here
End Function
```

The easiest way to conceptualize a function is to think about the large number of built-in Excel functions. The Excel SUM function returns one value, the summation of all selected cells. Likewise VLOOKUP and HLOOKUP are also examples of functions in Excel.

Procedures

Recall that a procedure is a block of code that executes a set of instructions. So how do we get a procedure to run? One way we talked about earlier is to use the built-in VBA event procedure structures that activate a code segment on some action or event associated with the object in question. Still another way is to use the Call method. The general structure for calling a procedure is as follows:

```
Call LocationofProcedure.ProcedureName(Arguments)
```

The LocationofProcedure statement is simply the object in which the code resides. If all your code resides in the same module, then you do not have to include the LocationofProcedure in your Call statement. Likewise, if your procedure takes no arguments or arguments that are optional, you don't have to include those either.

Let's look at a real example of calling procedures in VBA. The worksheet in Figure 7-5 is a navigation page for an Excel application. The worksheet contains several buttons (which are objects) that call procedures to help the user quickly navigate around the spreadsheet application.

A quick glance at the worksheet tells us that each button presumably navigates the user to a different worksheet that requires some form of user input. Now let's look at the code behind those navigation buttons (see Figure 7-6).

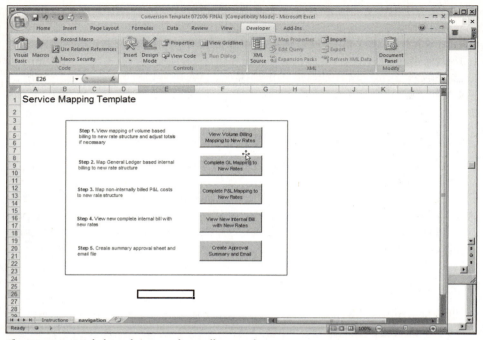

Figure 7-5: Worksheet buttons that call procedures

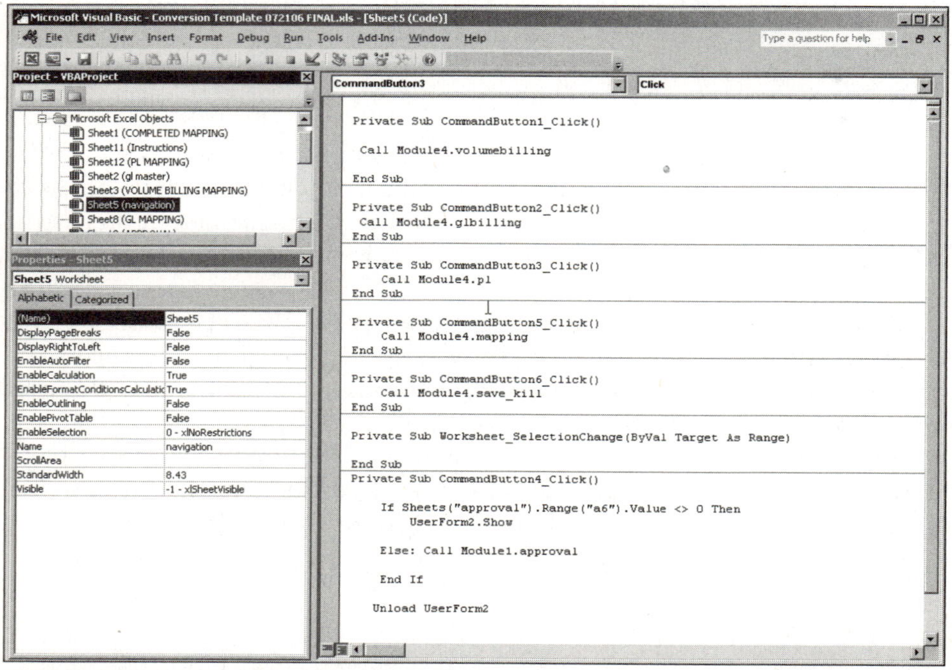

Figure 7-6: VBA code that calls procedures

There are important things to note in this figure. First, Sheet5(navigation) is highlighted in the Project Explorer window and at the very top of the VBE editor you can see that the code window contains the code for Sheet5 and all objects in Sheet5. Here is the code associated with CommandButton1, an object within Sheet5:

```
Private Sub CommandButton1_Click()
    Call Module4.volumebilling
End Sub
```

The declaration statement contains the word `Private`. A procedure declared as Private simply means that the code can only be accessed or executed within the object the code resides in. In other words, you would not be able to write code residing in another worksheet that could call or run this particular procedure. The `Public` statement, conversely, simply means the procedure can be called from anywhere in the workbook.

Note also that we have used the built-in Excel event procedure manager with this code segment. We created a button labeled CommandButton1 and then selected Click from the event menu in the top-right corner of the code window. So, what happens when this button is clicked by a user? The following line of code is executed:

```
Call Module4.volumebilling
```

The statement tells VBA to call a procedure named `volumebilling` that resides in the code repository object entitled Module4. Let's have a look at the statements in the `volumebilling` procedure (see Figure 7-7).

Note that we are in the code window of Module4. The first procedure in this module is our code of interest, `volumebilling`. When the `call` statement is executed, VBA immediately locates the `volumebilling` procedure in Module4 and executes the statements therein. The first statement un-protects the workbook, while the remaining statements make the worksheet in question visible and then select cell A1 of that worksheet. Before ending, the procedure re-protects the workbook. When the procedure is finished executing, VBA goes back to the code within CommandButton1 to execute any remaining statements. Of course, there are none, so VBA is finished for the time being.

You should usually place all your code used by your spreadsheet in a module. Code in a module is accessible from anywhere in the spreadsheet. In addition, it helps organize your application to have the majority of your code in a centralized location. You can rename your modules to something more meaningful than Module4, and you can certainly use more than one module to store your code. These decisions are dictated by programmer preference and the goal of your application.

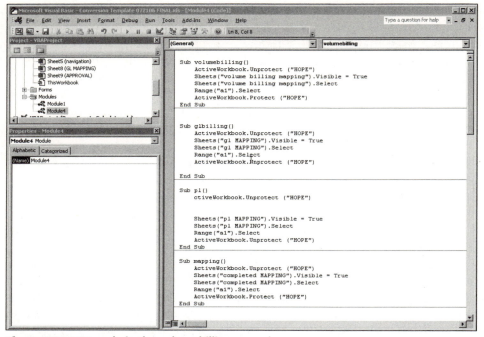

Figure 7-7: VBA code in the volumebilling procedures

Functions

Recall that a function is a type of procedure that returns only one value. In VBA you can use (some) of the built-in Excel or Access functions, or you can create your own custom function depending on the needs of your application. Be aware, however, that you cannot use a built-in Excel function that has a VBA equivalent. VBA gives you an error. For example, you may be familiar with the Excel function SQRT() that returns the square root of a specified number. VBA has its own syntax for this operation called Sqr(). Attempting to use the Excel built function in VBA results in an error. Let's have a look at how you would properly use the Excel SUMIF() function, a function not found in VBA, with VBA code:

```
Sub SumIf()
    Dim a As Double
    a = Application.WorksheetFunction.SumIf(Range("i3:i5"), ">2000")
    MsgBox a
End Sub
```

To access the built-in Excel function you must reference the `Worksheet-Function` property of the Application object. Reference the appropriate Excel function, pass on the correct arguments, and you are in business!

As you code more, you'll come across scenarios where creating a custom function will help your analysis a lot. When you find that your code is repeatedly performing a calculation that returns one value, even if that value represents an array, then your code is a prime candidate for a custom function. Let's look at a simple example of custom function syntax:

```
Function EngineModel(Year)
    Select Case Year
        Case Is >= 2005: EngineModel = "4.6L, 3V"
        Case 1996 To 2004: EngineModel = "4.6L, 2V"
        Case 1982 To 1995: EngineModel = "5.0L"
        Case Is < 1982: EngineModel = "Uncertain"
    End Select
End Function
```

This simple function is called `EngineModel`, and it returns a text string associated with the stock engine in V8 trim for the late model Ford Mustang. This function takes only one argument, Year, which is enclosed in parentheses in the first line of code declaring the function name. The function returns one value depending on value of the integer, Year.

Functions are not called in the same fashion as procedures. Look at the following string of code employing the custom function created previously:

```
Sub EnterYear()
    a = InputBox("Enter the year of your Mustang")
    MsgBox "Your engine model is " & EngineModel(a)
End Sub
```

Line two asks the user for input and assigns the value of that input to the variable a. In the next line, VBA displays a message box with the value of the `EngineModel` function. As soon as VBA sees the function has an argument, it immediately executes the function code and then displays the function value in the message box.

VBA Coding Fundamentals

So far, we have discussed VBA, object-oriented programming, where your code is stored, and how to get your code to run. In this section, we will explore some VBA coding concepts illustrated by simple but meaningful examples. Specifically we will cover coding that manipulates objects and coding that controls execution.

Code that Manipulates Objects

Our first category of code covers the manipulation of objects. Although all code can be described (at some level) as manipulating objects, this type of code is used exclusively for that aim. The `With...End With` construct is a useful shortcut when performing several operations on a single object. The `For Each...Next` construct deals specifically with performing operations on Collections, which are a specific type of object.

With...End With Construct

The `With...End With` construct is used when you want to perform several actions on one selected object. Very often, you'll see the `With...End With` construct when performing several formatting methods on a selected range. In Chapter 6 you saw this when you recorded macros to execute formatting code. However, this construct can be used when performing several actions on any object, not just a range of cells. Let's say that I wrote some code to perform several operations on a PivotTable in the selected worksheet. Specifically, I want to set the page field, column, row, and data to specific values and then refresh the PivotTable. The following code does just that for the PivotTable object named PivotTable1.

```
Sub Pivot()
    ActiveSheet.PivotTables("PivotTable1").PivotFields("Date"). _
    Orientation = xlColumnField
    ActiveSheet.PivotTables("PivotTable1").PivotFields("Customer_Name"). _
    Orientation = xlPageField
    ActiveSheet.PivotTables("PivotTable1").PivotFields("ProductName"). _
    Orientation = xlRowField
    ActiveSheet.PivotTables("PivotTable1").PivotFields("SumOfRevenue"). _
    Orientation = xlDataField
End Sub
```

This code manipulates an existing PivotTable and creates a crosstab report of revenue by product name and date. The following code produces the exact same result using the `With...End With` structure. Notice how much cleaner the code is and how much space it saves.

```
Sub Pivot()
    With ActiveSheet.PivotTables("PivotTable1")
        .PivotFields("Date").Orientation = xlColumnField
        .PivotFields("CustomerName").Orientation = xlPageField
        .PivotFields("ProductName").Orientation = xlRowField
        .PivotFields("SumOfRevenue").Orientation = xlDataField
    End With
End Sub
```

For Each-Next Construct

This construct is very useful when you need to perform an operation on every member in a collection (for example, every worksheet in the active workbook or every cell range in a selection). The following example of code cycles through each worksheet in the active workbook, checks to see whether it is hidden, and changes the worksheet to be visible if it is hidden. The code also contains an If-Then structure, which we will cover a little later in this chapter.

```
Public Sub VisibleSheets()
    Dim MySheet As Worksheet
    For Each MySheet In ActiveWorkbook.Worksheets
        If MySheet.Visible = False Then MySheet.Visible = True
    Next MySheet
End Sub
```

In the second line of code we declare a variable, `MySheet`, as an object. This object variable represents a Worksheet. The variable `MySheet` could take any name, but it's common coding practice to name an object variable in the format `MyObject`. For example, `MyCell`, `MyRange`, `MyForm`, would be common names for the object variables in question. The third line of code starts the `For Each...Next` construct. It says, "For every sheet in the active workbook, I want you to perform an operation." Line four of the code is that operation. Line five simply tells Excel to move on to the next sheet in the collection. Pretty nifty!

Code that Controls Execution

The next set of code constructs controls the execution of code. If you've had any programming experience in any computer language, these concepts will be familiar. If you haven't had any programming experience, the concepts are still relatively simple. They can be categorized into looping code and logic code. Looping code performs the same set of instructions in a repeated loop subject to specified criteria. These criteria can be a number of iterations or an evaluation of a logical expression (do something until or while a certain condition is met). Logical code enables you to execute instructions once specified conditions are met.

For...Next Construct

You will notice some similarities between the `For...Next` loop and the `For Each...Next` code structure we just covered. Both constructs repeat or loop a set of operations. The following code loops through cells in a contiguous range of data and deletes rows if the value in the specified cell is null. This piece of code also demonstrates other useful properties that are worth exploring in a bit more detail.

```
Sub DeleteRows()
    Dim NumRows As Integer
    Dim Count as Integer
    NumRows = Range("A1").CurrentRegion.Rows.Count
    For Count = NumRows - 1 To 0 Step -1
        If Range("a1").Offset(Count,0).Value = "" Then _
Range("a1").Offset(Count, 0).EntireRow.delete
    Next Count
End Sub
```

The Range object in code line four has a very useful property called Current Region. The CurrentRegion property returns a range of cells contiguous to cell A1 and bounded by empty rows and columns. In essence, this property returns an object that is a solid block of data around the selected cell. It may seem weird that a property can indeed return an object, but this is an important concept in object-oriented programming that will become more familiar with more programming experience. This solid block of data in turn has a property called Rows, which is the selection of rows within this block of data. Rows also has a Count property, which is simply the count of the number of rows in the selection. Therefore, with one line we have referenced the number of rows with a solid, contiguous block of information surrounding cell A1.

The fifth line of code starts the For...Next loop. If there are 100 rows in the block of data surrounding cell A1, code line five says, "counting backward from 99 to 0, perform the following operation." "Step -1" is the syntax that tells our loop to count backward. This argument is optional. The default step value in For-Next loops is positive one.

The operation to be performed 100 times is an If...Then construct we will explore later in this chapter. The code translates to the following: Look at the value of the cell Count rows down and 0 rows across from cell A1. If that cell's value is null, then delete the entire row associated with this cell. The Next statement simply says to continue the loop.

Why do we count backward instead of forward? It's not exactly intuitive, so let's look at the following example. Say our selection has two consecutive blank rows, rows 5 and 6. If we were counting forward, then our code would work fine up until deleting row 5. When row 5 is deleted, the rows beneath row 5 all get moved up by one row. Now the old row 6 is the new row 5! When our counter loops, VBA now evaluates row 6. Our code just skipped over the consecutive blank row.

Do Until...Loop Construct

The Do Until...Loop construct is another valuable coding technique that is particularly useful when you wish to continue a loop until a particular condition is met. Whereas For...Next loops only a specified number of times, the Do Until...Loop loop continues until the logical condition is met, regardless of the number of times the loop executes! Let's look at an example.

```
Sub WriteTorqueData()
    Dim Rpm, RedLine, Torque, a1, b1, c1, d1, e1 As Double
    Dim Count as Integer
    Sheets("Output").Range("A1").Select
    Do Until Rpm > RedLine
        Torque = a1 * Rpm ^ 4 + b1 * Rpm ^ 3 + c1 * _
Rpm ^ 2 + d1 *  Rpm + e1
        ActiveCell.Offset(Count, 0).Value = Rpm
        ActiveCell.Offset(Count, 1).Value = Torque
        Count = Count + 1
        Rpm = Rpm + 100
    Loop
End Sub
```

This specific piece of code is from an Excel-based racing simulator that a partner and I developed. The procedure writes data for a torque versus rpm curve to a worksheet entitled Output. The variables in the procedure allow this code segment to be used multiple times depending on the specifics of the car chosen by the user.

The code line before the `Do Until...Loop` loop selects cell A1 in the sheet where the code output is to be written. The `Do Until` statement informs VBA to execute the subsequent lines of code until the value of the variable Rpm exceeds that of the variable `RedLine`. The code within the Do Until loop updates the value of the variable Torque given the Rpm value, writes the value of the Rpm and Torque values to the selected worksheet and then increments a counter variable (Count) by one and the Rpm variable by 100. The loop continues to run until the value of the variable Rpm exceeds that of the variable Redline.

Looping Code: Do...While Loop Construct

The Do While-Loop construct is virtually the mirror image of the Do Until-Loop code. Rather than continuing the code loop until a logical expression is met, Do While-Loop continues the code loop until the logical expression is violated. Let's convert the prior Do Until-Loop construct into a Do While-Loop construct.

```
Sub WriteTorqueData()
    Dim Rpm, RedLine, Torque, a1, b1, c1, d1, e1 As Double
    Dim Count as Integer    Sheets("Output").Range("A1").Select
    Do While  Rpm <=  RedLine
        Torque = a1 * Rpm ^ 4 + b1 * Rpm ^ 3 + c1 * Rpm ^ 2 + _
d1 *  Rpm + e1
        ActiveCell.Offset(Count, 0).Value = Rpm
        ActiveCell.Offset(Count, 1).Value = Torque
        Count = Count + 1
        Rpm = Rpm + 100
    Loop
End Sub
```

Note that the only change to this block of code is to line five, the start of the loop. Rather than continuing the loop until Rpm exceeds Redline, the loop continues while Rpm is less than or equal to Redline. Logically, the code blocks are identical. Only the syntax separates them. Depending on the code you want to execute in the loop, one structure may be more manageable than the other.

Logical Code: If...Then and If...Then...Else...End If Constructs

You have seen a couple of examples of `If...Then` coding earlier in the chapter. Let's explore `If...Then` in a bit more detail. The `If` portion of this construct evaluates a logical expression. If the logical expression is true, the code after the `Then` statement is executed. If the logical expression is not true, then VBA moves on to the next line of code. Here is a closer look at a prior example of If-Then.

```
If Range("a1").Offset(Count, 0).Value = "" Then
    Range"a33").Offset(Count, 0).EntireRow.delete
End If
```

The logical expression in this `If...Then` block is whether a specific cell value, the one Count rows down and 0 rows across from cell A1, is null. If this expression is true, then the row associated with this cell is deleted. What happens if the logical expression is false? Nothing. The code after the `Then` statement is ignored and VBA moves on to the next line.

Sometimes you may want to execute more than one line of code if the logical expression in your `If...Then` statement is true. There is a slightly different syntax under this scenario.

```
Private Sub Workbook_BeforeClose (Cancel As Boolean)
        a = MsgBox("are you sure  you want to close?", vbYesNo)
    If a = vbYes Then
        Cancel = False
        ActiveWorkbook.SaveAs "C:/Temp/Backup"
    Else
        Cancel = True
    End If
End Sub
```

When there is more than one line of code you want to execute when the logical expression is true, you must use an `If...Then...Else...End If` construct. In the preceding code, the second line assigns the value of user input coming from a message box to a variable named a. There are two arguments we've passed to the `MsgBox` object. One is the text to display in the box. The second is the argument `vbYesNo`, which makes the `MsgBox` display a Yes and a No button instead of just one OK button. (The default is for `MsgBox` to just display OK.)

This message box returns a value, which depends on which button the user pressed. Now we come to the `If...Then...End If` construct. If the user selects Yes from the message box, the two lines of code immediately after the `Then` statement will be executed. First, the variable Cancel will be set to `False`, which means that the Close operation will continue on exiting from this procedure. Second, the active worksheet is saved with a specific path and file name. If, however, the logical expression is false, the code after the `Else` statement is executed and the Close operation will be canceled on exit of the procedure.

Logical Code: Select Case Construct

If-Then statements work well when evaluating a logical expression that has only two potential values, namely `True` or `False`. What happens, however, when you want to execute different code contingent on more than two results? It is possible to accomplish this using multiple `If...Then` statements. However, `Select Case` coding is a much easier and more elegant coding solution. `Select Case` works in a similar fashion to `If...Then`, but you can specify code instructions for more than two alternatives. Here is an example:

```
Select Case Rpm
    Case Is < 1000
        Msgbox "You stalled the car"
    Case 1000 to 3250
        Msgbox "You launched the car successfully"
    Case 3250 to 4500
        Msgbox "Your gonna need new tires"
    Case Is > 4500
        Msgbox "Your gonna need new tires and a new clutch"
End Select
```

The preceding code evaluates a variable named Rpm. The variable represents the engine revolutions per minute when accelerating a manual transmission car from a dead stop (remember Paco's `BigSmokeyBurnout` method earlier in the chapter?). Depending on the value of that variable, one of four different code segments is executed. Let's reproduce this result with nested `If...Then` statements to demonstrate the power of `Select Case...End Select` coding:

```
If Rpm < 1000 Then
    MsgBox "You stalled the car"
Else
    If Rpm < 3250 Then
        MsgBox "You launched the car successfully"
    Else
        If Rpm < 4500 Then
            MsgBox "Your gonna need new tires"
```

```
            Else
                MsgBox "Your gonna need new tires and a new clutch"
            End If
        End If
    End If
```

First, the preceding code requires 13 lines instead of only 10 with the `Select Case...End Select` code. More importantly, the code logic is easier to follow, as the logic is sequential rather than nested.

Getting Help with VBA

Fortunately, VBA has several useful built-in help functions that come in quite handy when you are stuck. One of the most useful is VBA's auto list option. When in the VBE, select the Tools menu and then select Options. On the Editor tab of the Options dialog box, make sure the Auto List Members check box is selected (see Figure 7-8). When this box is selected, you will notice that as soon as you enter the period separator in your line of code, you will get a pop-up menu.

This menu contains a list of all properties and methods associated with the object you just referenced (see Figure 7-9). Objects contained within your referenced object are also in the list. If you are not sure what the correct syntax of a method or property is, the Auto List menu will prompt you with a list and even give you the correct format for any arguments required.

Figure 7-8: Selecting the Auto List Members box

Another useful help tool is the Object browser (see Figure 7-10). The Object browser gives you access to the object hierarchy within VBA. Select an object and immediately see all the container objects, methods, properties, and events. The Object browser can be accessed by selecting the View tab and then selecting the Object browser menu item, or by pressing F2.

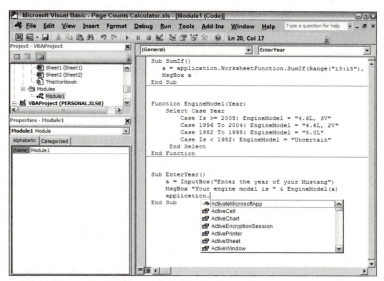

Figure 7-9: The Auto List Members menu

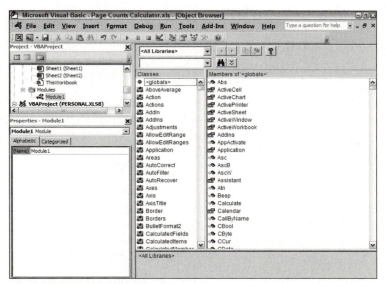

Figure 7-10: The Object browser

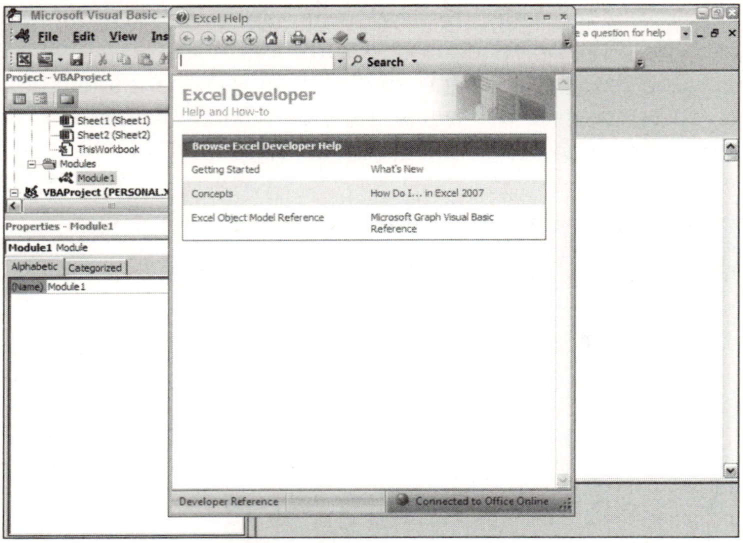

Figure 7-11: The Visual Basic Help window

The last source of help is simply selecting Microsoft Visual Basic Help from the VBE help menu or pressing F1. Visual Basic Help is very well organized with a graphical object model reference, a "How do I" section, and a getting started section for beginners. Each of these sections makes for some interesting browsing, but if you have a more specific question, you can simply enter some descriptive text in the search window.

Summary

By now, you have developed grounding in the basics of VBA and can see the potential productivity and quality gains in your Access and Excel analyses. In later chapters, we will build on these fundamentals. Remembering the following key points will help as you progress in using VBA to integrate Access and Excel.

- VBA is a programming language for Microsoft Office applications. It provides a set of instructions you can use to manipulate objects within Access and Excel.

- Like most modern programming languages, VBA is an object-oriented programming language. VBA contains a structured hierarchy of "things" that can be manipulated with commands. For example, at the top of the VBA hierarchy is the Microsoft application. Within the Excel Application object, you have the Workbook, Worksheet, and Range objects, among others.

■ VBA objects have properties, or characteristics. These properties can be modified with simple VBA code. For example, an Excel worksheet has a Visible property that indicates whether the worksheet can be seen by the workbook user. Objects can also have methods, or operations that can be performed to or with them. Methods take arguments, additional pieces of information to clarify the action being performed.

■ VBA code is contained within a procedure or a function. Both denote a discrete set of instructions, or code. A function differs from a procedure in that a function is a set of instructions that returns a value. Procedures have no such constraints.

■ Variables and constants can be used within VBA to simplify coding and to make it more robust. A variable is a placeholder that can take on any number of values. A variable can be a number, text string, or even an object. A constant is type of variable that takes on only one value within a block of code.

■ You can manipulate objects and control execution within VBA. Object manipulation is done with constructs like With...End With and For Each...Next. Controlling execution with VBA code can be through looping or logical coding blocks. Looping code (Do Until...Loop, for example) repeatedly performs a set of instructions. You may specify when the loop ends through giving it a specific number of iterations or having the loop continue until certain conditions are met. Logical code (Select Case...End Select, If Then...End If) will let you perform different blocks of instruction based on the evaluation of certain conditions.

■ There are multiple sources of help if you get stuck in VBA. First, be sure the Auto List Members option is selected in the Tools → Options menu from the VBE. Auto List Members will tell you the objects, methods and arguments available *as* you enter your code. If you need more detailed help, be sure to use the VBA Help feature and the Object browser from the View menu.

CHAPTER 8

Using VBA to Move Data Between Excel and Access

Throughout the first few chapters of this book, you have discovered several ways to move data between Access and Excel. Although many of those techniques will suit your needs just fine, each one retains an aspect of manual involvement. That is to say, each one involves manual setup, management, and maintenance. In this chapter, you will explore how to leverage VBA (along with some data connection technologies) to make your life even easier by making your data transfer processes virtually hands free.

Note the phrase, "along with some data connection technologies". In reality VBA, in and of itself, does not have the capability to connect and manipulate external data. You need to combine VBA with a helper technology to work with external data sources. Although there are many technologies that enable you to automate your data processes, you will focus on using ADO (ActiveX Data Objects) and SQL (Structured Query Language).

Why bother using VBA when the manual processes work just fine? First, VBA enables you to process data without the need to create and maintain multiple queries and macros. Also with VBA, you can perform complex, multi-layered procedures that involve looping, record-level testing, and `If...Then...Else` checks without the need to inundate your processes with many queries and temporary tables. Finally, the one-two-three combination of VBA, ADO, and SQL is extremely powerful and relatively easy to understand and implement. In fact, as you go through this chapter, you will immediately start to think about the ways the techniques found here will help you optimize your Excel and Access integration projects.

> **NOTE** True to its purpose, all the techniques in this chapter involve writing some basic code. To stay focused on the data analysis aspect of these techniques, this chapter does not explain in detail the VBA behind them. If you are new to VBA, you may want to read Chapter 7 first if you haven't done so already. Chapter 7 gives you a firm understanding of the basic concepts used in this chapter.

Understanding ADO Fundamentals

When trying to grasp the basics of ADO, it helps to think of ADO as a tool that will help you accomplish two tasks: connect to a data source and specify the dataset with which to work. In the following section, you will explore the fundamental syntax you will need to know in order to do just that.

The Connection String

First you must connect to a data source. To do this, you must give VBA some information. This information is passed to VBA in the form of a *connection string*. A connection string is fundamentally nothing more than a text string that holds a series of variables (also called *arguments*), which VBA uses to identify and open a connection to a data source. Although connection strings can get pretty fancy with a myriad of arguments and options, there are a handful of arguments that are commonly used when connecting to either Access or Excel. If you're new to ADO, it helps to focus on these commonly used arguments:

- `Provider`: This argument tells VBA the type of data source with which you are working. When using Access or Excel 2007 as the data source, the `Provider` syntax reads:

  `Provider=Microsoft.ACE.OLEDB.12.0`

  If your data process has to run on a machine that does not have Office 2007 on it, you will need to use the `Provider` for earlier versions of Access and Excel:

  `Provider=Microsoft.Jet.OLEDB.4.0`

- `Data Source`: This argument tells VBA where to find the database or workbook that contains the data needed. With the `Data Source` argument, you will pass the full path of the database or workbook.

For example:

```
Data Source=C:\Mydirectory\Northwind 2007.accdb
```

- ▪ `Extended Properties`: This argument is typically used when connecting to an Excel workbook. This argument tells VBA that the data
  source is something other than a database. When working with an
  Excel 2007 workbook, this argument would read:

```
Extended Properties=Excel 12.0
```

  If your data process will need to run on a machine that does not have
  Office 2007 on it, you will need to use the `Extended Properties` for
  the earlier versions of Excel:

```
Extended Properties=Excel 8.0
```

- ▪ `User ID`: This argument is optional and only used if a user id is
  required to connect to the data source:

```
User Id=MyUserId
```

- ▪ `Password`: This argument is optional and only used if a password is
  required to connect to the data source:

```
Password=MyPassword
```

Take a moment now to see a few examples of how these arguments are put
together to build a connection string.

TIP Notice that each argument is surrounded by quotes and use the
ampersand (&) along with an underscore (_) character. This is a simple
technique used to break up the text string into readable parts. The preceding
code is the same as writing:

```
"Provider=Microsoft.ACE.OLEDB.12.0;Data Source= C: MyDatabase.accdb"
```

The purpose of breaking up the text string into parts is to make the code easy
to read and manage within the Visual Basic Editor. The first line starts the
string, and each subsequent line is concatenated to the previous line with the
ampersand (&) character. The underscore (_) character is used as a continuation
marker, indicating that the code on the next line is part of the code on the
current line. This is similar to the way a hyphen is used in writing to continue a
word that is broken into two lines.

Connecting to an Access database:

```
"Provider=Microsoft.ACE.OLEDB.12.0;" & _
"Data Source= C:\MyDatabase.accdb"
```

Connecting to an Access database with password and user ID:

```
"Provider=Microsoft.ACE.OLEDB.12.0;" & _
"Data Source= C:\MyDatabase.accdb;" & _
"User ID=Administrator;" & _
"Password=AdminPassword"
```

Connecting to an Excel workbook:

```
"Provider=Microsoft.ACE.OLEDB.12.0;" & _
"Data Source=C:\MyExcelWorkbook.xlsx;" & _
"Extended Properties=Excel 12.0"
```

Access connection string that will run on systems without Office 2007 installed:

```
"Provider=Microsoft.Jet.OLEDB.4.0;" & _
"Data Source= C:\MyDatabase.mdb"
```

Excel connection string that will run on systems without Office 2007 installed:

```
"Provider=Microsoft.Jet.OLEDB.4.0;" & _
"Data Source=C:\MyExcelWorkbook.xls;" & _
"Extended Properties=Excel 8.0"
```

Declaring a Recordset

In addition to building a connection to your data source, you will need to define the data set with which you need to work. In ADO, this dataset is referred to as the *recordset*. A `Recordset` object is essentially a container for the records and fields returned from the data source. The most common way to define a `Recordset` is to open an existing table or query using the following arguments:

```
Recordset.Open Source, ConnectString, CursorType, LockType
```

The `Source` argument represents the data that is to be extracted. This is typically a table, query, or an SQL statement that retrieves records. Initially, you will use tables and queries to select records from a data source, Later in this chapter, you will learn how to build SQL statements to fine tune data extracts on–the-fly.

The `ConnectString` argument represents the connection string used to connect to your chosen data source.

The `CursorType` argument represents how a `Recordset` allows you to move through the data to be extracted. The `CursorType` arguments commonly used are

- `adOpenForwardOnly`: This is the default setting; if you don't specify a `CursorType`, the `Recordset` will automatically be `adOpenForward-Only`. This `CursorType` is the most efficient type because it only allows you to move through the `Recordset` one way; from beginning to end. This is ideal for reporting processes where data only needs to be retrieved and not traversed. Keep in mind that you cannot make changes to data by when using this `CursorType`.

- `adOpenDynamic`: This is typically used in processes where there is a need for looping, moving up and down through the dataset, or the ability to dynamically see any edits made to the dataset. This is typically memory and resource intensive and should be used only when needed.

- `adOpenStatic`: This is ideal for returning results quickly because it essentially returns a snapshot of your data. However, this is different from `adOpenForwardOnly` , because it allows you to navigate the returned records. In addition, when using this `adOpenStatic`, the data returned can be made updateable by setting its `LockType` to something other than `adLockReadOnly`.

The LockType argument is used to specify whether the data returned by the `Recordset` can be changed. The `CursorTypes` commonly used are

- `adLockReadOnly`: This is the default setting; if you don't specify a `LockType`, the `Recordset` will automatically be set to `adLockRead-Only`. This is typically used when there is no need to change the data that is returned..

- `adLockOptimistic`: This `LockType` allows you to freely edit the data of the records that are returned.

The following sections provide a few examples of how to declare a `Recordset` using the arguments you just covered.

Return Read Only Data from a Table or Query

Any of these `Recordset` declarations would return a `Recordset` that is read-only. Note that you can use a table name or an SQL statement in each one of these examples:

```
MyRecordset.Open "MyTable", ConnectString

MyRecordset.Open "SQL", ConnectString, adOpenForwardOnly,adLockReadOnly
```

Return Updateable Data from a Table or Query

Any of these `Recordset` declarations would return updateable data. Note that you can use a table name or an SQL statement in each one of these examples:

```
MyRecordset.Open "SQL", ConnectString, adOpenStatic, adLockOptimistic

MyRecordset.Open "SQL", ConnectString, adOpenDynamic, adLockOptimistic
```

Writing Your First ADO Procedure

Now it's time to put together the ADO fundamentals you have explored thus far to create your first ADO procedure. In this section, you will build a procedure that transfers an Access table into an Excel spreadsheet.

Referencing the ADO Object Library

Before you do anything with ADO, you must first set a reference to the ADO object library. Just as each Microsoft Office application has its own set of objects, properties, and methods, so does ADO. Since Excel does not inherently know the ADO object model, you will need to point Excel to the ADO reference library.

Start by opening a new Excel workbook and the Visual Basic Editor.

TIP Remember that in both Excel and Access, the VBE can be accessed with the shortcut Alt + F11.

Alternatively, the VBE can be accessed in Excel by selecting the Developer tab from the ribbon, and then selecting the Visual Basic icon.

Depending on how Excel 2007 is set up, the Developer tab may not show up in your ribbon by default. If it is not there, simply click the Office icon in the top left corner and select Excel Options at the bottom of the menu. In the Personalize menu, you will see the check box Show Developer tab in ribbon. Make sure this check box is checked.

When you are in the Visual Basic Editor, go to the application menu and select Tools → References. This opens the References dialog box shown in Figure 8-1. Scroll down until you locate the latest version of the Microsoft ActiveX Data Objects Library, click the check box next to it, and then click OK.

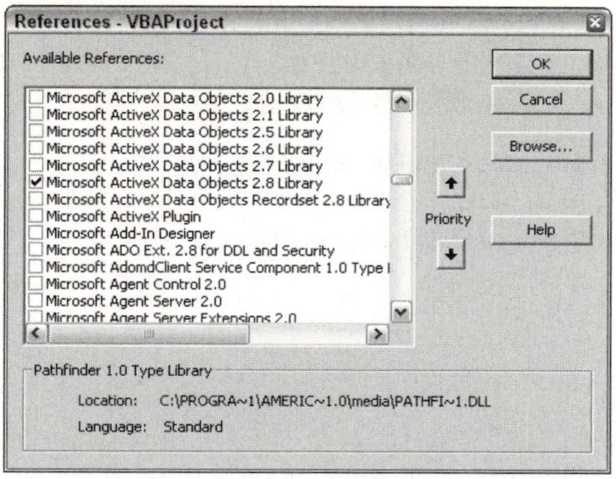

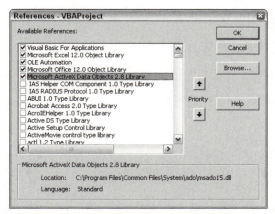

Figure 8-1: Select the latest version of the Microsoft ActiveX Data Objects Library.

NOTE It is normal to have several versions of the same library displayed in the References dialog box. It's generally best to select the latest version available. You will notice that in Figure 8-1, the latest version of the Microsoft ActiveX Data Objects Library is 2.8. Don't be too concerned if you only have earlier versions available; the examples in this chapter will run fine with those earlier version.

After you click the OK button, you can open the Reference dialog box again to ensure that your reference is set. You will know that your selection took effect when the Microsoft ActiveX Data Objects Library is selected in the Reference dialog box (see Figure 8-2).

Figure 8-2: Open the References dialog box again to ensure that a reference to Microsoft ActiveX Data Objects Library has indeed been set.

> **NOTE** You have just walked through setting a reference to the Microsoft ActiveX Data Objects Library using Excel. Keep in mind that these are the same steps you would take when performing the same task in Access.
>
> Also, keep in mind that the references you set in any given workbook or database are not applied at the application level. This means that you need to repeat these steps with each new workbook or database you create.

Writing the Code

When you have a reference set to the ADO Object Library, open a new module in the Visual Basic Editor by selecting Insert → Module. Start a new Sub procedure called `GetAccessData`. In that procedure, enter the following code:

> **TIP** Installing the sample files for this book will ensure that you have the Access database referenced in the following code. You will also find a workbook called `Chapter8_SampleFiles.xls` containing this procedure along with the others found in this chapter.
>
> When writing your own procedures, you will alter the connection string to reference the path for your data source.

```
Sub GetAccessData()

'Step 1: Declare your Variables
    Dim MyConnect As String
    Dim MyRecordset As ADODB.Recordset

'Step 2: Declare your Connection String
    MyConnect = "Provider=Microsoft.ACE.OLEDB.12.0;" & _
                "Data Source= ⤵
C:\Integration\IntegrationDatabase.accdb"

'Step 3: Instantiate and Specify your Recordset
    Set MyRecordset = New ADODB.Recordset
    MyRecordset.Open "Products", MyConnect, adOpenStatic, ⤵
adLockReadOnly

'Step 4: Copy the Recordset to Excel
    Sheets("Your First ADO Procedure").Select
    ActiveSheet.Range("A2").CopyFromRecordset MyRecordset

'Step 5: Add Column Labels
    With ActiveSheet.Range("A1:C1")
        .Value = Array("Product", "Description", "Segment")
```

```
        .EntireColumn.AutoFit
    End With

End Sub
```

Let's take a moment to talk about what you are doing in each step.

Step 1: Declaring the Necessary Variables

In Step 1, you first declare two variables: a string variable to hold the connection string, and a `Recordset` object to hold the results of the data pull. In this example, the variable called `MyConnect` holds the connection string identifying the data source. Meanwhile, the variable called `MyRecordset` holds the data that is returned by the procedure.

Step 2: Declaring the Connection String

In Step 2, you define the connection string for the ADO procedure. In this scenario, you are connecting to the `InegrationDatabase.accdb` found on the C drive.

Step 3: Assigning Data to Your Recordset

Once you have defined your data source, you can fill your `Recordset` with some data. In Step 3, you specify your `Recordset` will be read-only and filled with data from the Products table found in the `IntegrationDatabase.accdb` Access database. When writing your own procedures, you can replace the Products table name with that of your own tables.

Also notice in Step 3 that you set the `MyRecordset` variable to a new `ADODB.Recordset` (Set MyRecordset = New ADODB.Recordset). VBA requires that you instantiate the `Recordset` object before it can be used.

Step 4: Copying the Recordset into Excel

By the time you reach Step 4, the `MyRecordset` object is filled with data from the Products table. In Step 4, you use the Excel `CopyFromRecordset` method to get it out and into your spreadsheet. This method requires two pieces of information: the location of the data output and the `Recordset` object that holds the data you need. In this example, you are copying the data in the `MyRecordset` object onto the sheet called Your First ADO Procedure starting at cell A2.

Step 5: Adding Column Labels

Interestingly enough, the `CopyFromRecordset` method does not return column headers or field names. This is the reason for Step 5 where you add the column headers yourself. In Step 5, you are telling Excel to fill cells A1 through C1 with the respective values in the array. Then you tell Excel to AutoFit those columns so that all the data can be seen.

Using the Code

Be sure to save your changes, and then close the Visual Basic Editor. At this point, you can run your procedure simply by running the GetAccessData macro.

Better still, you can get fancy and assign the macro to a button. This gives you and your clients an easy way to call the ADO procedure whenever you need to refresh the data extract from Access.

Start by selecting the Insert icon from the Developer tab on the Excel ribbon. Click the Form button as demonstrated in Figure 8-3, then click anywhere on your spreadsheet to drop the button on the sheet.

You see the Assign Macro dialog box shown in Figure 8-4. Simply click the macro name to assign the macro to the button and click the OK button.

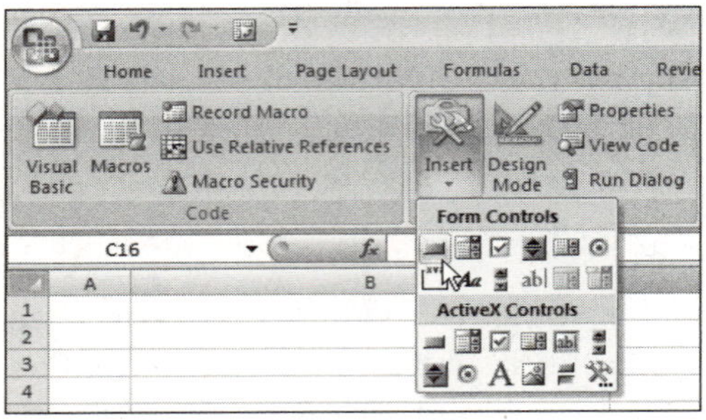

Figure 8-3: Insert a Form button

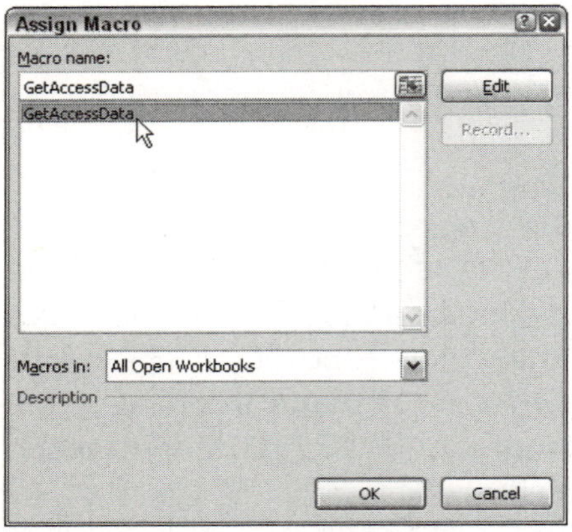

Figure 8-4: Assign a macro to the button

The reward for all your efforts is a worksheet that pulls data directly from Access at the click of a button! Remember, this is all without the use of third-party applications (MS Query) or manual manipulation. With ADO and VBA, you can build all the necessary components one time in a nicely packaged macro, and then simply forget about it. As long as the defined variables in your code (that is the data source path, the `Recordset`, the output path) do not change, then your ADO-based procedures will require virtually zero maintenance.

Understanding SQL Fundamentals

SQL (commonly pronounced "sequel") stands for *Structured Query Language*. It is the language used to perform various tasks in database management systems such as Access. In fact, it is the cornerstone of any automated data manipulation processes.

Although the combination of ADO and VBA enable you to take some broad stroke swipes at data, bringing SQL into the mix enables you to customize your data processes, giving you flexibility that ADO alone cannot provide. For example, incorporating SQL into you procedures can enable you to apply filters to your data extracts, aggregate your datasets on-the-fly, and perform actions on your datasets such as add, delete and update data.

In this next section, you will learn the fundamental concepts of SQL, and how to implement SQL statements in your ADO procedures.

Basic SQL Syntax to Select Data

Selecting or extracting data from a dataset is the most basic function that can be accomplished with SQL. However, the SQL language offers many arguments and clauses that enable you to enhance your data extracts beyond selecting an entire table. Let's start your introduction to SQL by exploring some of the syntactic constructs that allow you to select data.

The SELECT Statement

The SELECT statement is the cornerstone of SQL. The SELECT statement enables you to retrieve records from a dataset. The basic syntax of a SELECT statement is

```
SELECT column_name(s)
FROM table_name
```

You can retrieve specific columns from your dataset by explicitly defining the columns in your SELECT statement:

```
SELECT Employee_Number, Last_Name, First_Name
FROM Employee_Master
```

NOTE Any column in a dataset that has a name that includes spaces or a non-alphanumeric character must be enclosed within brackets ([ ]) in your SQL statement. For example, the SQL statement selecting data from a column called **Last Name** would look like this: SELECT [Last Name] FROM EmployeeTable.

Also, any column name that uses a SQL-reserved word needs to be enclosed in brackets. For example, you can imagine that a column named Select causes problems unless it is enclosed in brackets as such: SELECT [Select] FROM EmployeeQuery. A SQL-reserved word is a word that has a predefined meaning in SQL. Refer to the Access help to get a list of reserved words.

Selecting All Columns

Using the wildcard (*) enables you to select all columns from a dataset without having to define every column explicitly.

```
SELECT *
FROM Employee_Master
```

The WHERE Clause

The WHERE clause is used in a SELECT statement to filter your dataset and conditionally select specific records.

The WHERE clause is used to pass criteria to your SQL statements, enabling you to evaluate each record in your dataset and selectively filter only the ones you need.

This affords you a tremendous amount of flexibility that can only be achieved through SQL. Take a moment to look at a few example SQL statements that use criteria to filter records.

This SQL statement retrieves only those employees whose last name is Jehnsen:

```
SELECT Employee_Number, Last_Name, First_Name
FROM Employee_Master
WHERE Last_Name = "JEHNSEN"
```

This SQL statement retrieves only those employees whose hire data is later than May 16, 2004:

```
SELECT Employee_Number, Last_Name, First_Name
FROM Employee_Master
WHERE Hire_Date > #5/16/2004#
```

> **NOTE** In the two examples here, the word JEHNSEN is wrapped in quotes ("JEHNSEN") and the date 5/16/2004 is wrapped in the pound signs (#5/16/2004#). When referring to a text value in your SQL statement, you must place quotes around the value. When referring to a date, you need to use number symbol.

Expanding Your Search with the Like Operator

By itself the Like operator is no different than the equal (=) operator. For example, the following two SQL statements return the same number of records:

```
SELECT Employee_Number, Job_Title
FROM Employee_Master
WHERE Job_Title="TEAMLEAD 1"

SELECT Employee_Number, Job_Title
FROM Employee_Master
WHERE Job_Title Like"TEAMLEAD 1"
```

The benefit of the Like operator becomes apparent when used with wildcard characters. This enables you to expand the scope of your search to include any record that matches a pattern. The primary wildcard character used in Access is the asterisk (*). The asterisk represents any number and type characters.

For example, the following SQL statement selects all records where Field1 starts with the letter "A".

```
SELECT Field1
FROM Table1
WHERE Field1 Like "A*"
```

This SQL statement selects all records where Field1 includes the letter "A".

```
SELECT Field1
FROM Table1
WHERE Field1 Like "*A*"
```

NOTE When using SQL with ADO, the asterisk wildcard character will not return any records; even if you are querying an Access database. Instead of the asterisk, you will need to use is the percent sign (%) wildcard character.

Grouping and Aggregating with the GROUP BY Clause

The GROUP BY clause makes it possible to aggregate records in your dataset by column values. When you create an aggregate query in Design view, you are essentially using the GROUP BY clause. The following SQL statements demonstrate how to apply GROUP BY to apply various types of aggregation.

Get the count of employees in every branch:

```
SELECT Home_Branch, Count(Employee_Number)
FROM Employee_Master
GROUP BY Home_Branch
```

Get the sum of revenue for each Region and Market combination:

```
SELECT Region, Market, Sum(Revenue)
FROM PvTblFeed
GROUP BY Region, Market
```

Get the average revenue for each Region and Market combination.

```
SELECT Region, Market, Avg(Revenue)
FROM PvTblFeed
GROUP BY Region, Market
```

The HAVING Clause

When you are using the GROUP BY clause, you cannot specify criteria using the WHERE clause. Instead, you will need to use the HAVING clause. The following SQL statement groups the Home_Branch field and only gives you the count of employees in branch 601306:

```
SELECT Home_Branch, Count(Employee_Number)
FROM Employee_Master
GROUP BY Home_Branch
HAVING Home_Branch = "601306"
```

Creating Aliases with the AS Clause

The AS clause enables you to assign aliases to your columns and tables. There are generally two reasons you would want to use aliases: either you want to make column or table names shorter and easier to read, or you are working with multiple instances of the same table and you need a way to refer to one instance or the other.

Creating a Column Alias

The following SQL statement groups the Home_Branch field and gives you the count of employees in every branch. In addition, the alias MyCount has been given to the column containing the count of employee number by including the AS clause.

```
SELECT Home_Branch, Count(Employee_Number)AS MyCount
FROM Employee_Master
GROUP BY Home_Branch
```

Creating a Table Alias

This SQL statement gives the Employee_Master the alias MyTable.

```
SELECT Home_Branch, Count(Employee_Number)
FROM Employee_Master AS MyTable
GROUP BY Home_Branch
```

Setting Sort Order with the ORDER BY Clause

The ORDER BY clause enables you to sort data by a specified field. The default sort order is ascending; therefore, sorting your fields in ascending order requires no explicit instruction. The following SQL statement sorts the resulting records in by Last_Name ascending, then First_Name ascending:

```
SELECT Employee_Number, Last_Name, First_Name
FROM Employee_Master
ORDER BY Last_Name, First_Name
```

To sort in descending order, you must use the DESC reserved word after each column you want sorted in descending order. The following SQL statement sorts the resulting records in by Last_Name descending, then First_Name ascending:

```
SELECT Employee_Number, Last_Name, First_Name
FROM Employee_Master
ORDER BY Last_Name DESC, First_Name
```

SELECT TOP and *SELECT TOP PERCENT*

When you run a `Select` query, you are retrieving all records that meet your definitions and criteria. When you run the `SELECT TOP` statement, or a top values query, you are filtering your returned dataset to show only a specific number of records.

```
SELECT TOP 25 Branch_Number, Sum(Sales_Amount) AS Sales
FROM TransactionMaster
GROUP BY Branch_Number
ORDER BY Sum(Sales_Amount) DESC
```

Bear in mind that you don't have to be working with totals or currency to use a top values query. In the following SQL statement, you are returning the 25 employees that have the earliest hire date in the company, effectively producing a seniority report:

```
SELECT TOP 25 Employee_Number, Last_Name, First_Name, Hire_Date
FROM Employee_Master
ORDER BY Hire_Date ASC
```

Writing Your First ADO/SQL Data Extract

Writing a data extract procedure with ADO and SQL is very similar to writing an ADO procedure to extract data directly from an Access table. The difference is that instead of specifying a table name as the data source, you pass an SQL statement that defines the data you need. Start a new module and enter the following code.

TIP Be sure that you have set a reference to the ADO object library as outlined in the section "Referencing the ADO Object Library" earlier in this chapter.

```
Sub GetAccessData_With_SQL()

'Step 1: Declare your variables
    Dim MyConnect As String
    Dim MyRecordset As ADODB.Recordset
    Dim MySQL As String

'Step 2: Declare your connection string
    MyConnect = "Provider=Microsoft.ACE.OLEDB.12.0;" & _
                "Data Source= ⊃
C:\Integration\IntegrationDatabase.accdb"

'Step 3: Build your SQL statement
    MySQL ="SELECT Region, Market, Product_Description," & _
```

```
            " Sum(Revenue) AS Rev, Sum(TransactionCount) AS Units" & _
            " FROM PvTblFeed" & _
            " GROUP BY Region, Market, Product_Description"

    'Step 4: Instantiate and specify your recordset
        Set MyRecordset = New ADODB.Recordset
        MyRecordset.Open MySQL, MyConnect, adOpenStatic, adLockReadOnly

    'Step 5: Copy the recordset to Excel
          Sheets("ADO and SQL").Select
          ActiveSheet.Range("A2").CopyFromRecordset MyRecordset

    'Step 6: Add column labels
        With ActiveSheet.Range("A1:E1")
            .Value = Array("Region", "Market", "Product_Description", _
            "Revenue", "Transactions")
            .EntireColumn.AutoFit
        End With

End Sub
```

Running this code queries the Access database and aggregates records on-the-fly to return data to an Excel sheet. Let's take a moment to talk about what you are doing in each step.

Step 1: Declaring the Necessary Variables

In Step 1, you declare three variables: a string variable to hold the connection string, a `Recordset` object to hold the results of the data pull, and a second string variable to hold your SQL statement. In this example, the variable called `MyConnect` holds the connection string identifying the data source. Meanwhile, the variable called `MyRecordset` holds the data returned by the procedure and the variable called `MySQL` holds the SQL statement.

Step 2: Declaring the Connection String

In Step 2, you define the connection string for the ADO procedure. In this scenario, you are connecting to the `IntegrationDatabase.accdb` found on the C drive.

Step 3: Building the SQL Statement

In Step 3, you assign a SQL statement in the form of a text string to the `MySQL` variable. Notice that the SQL statement is broken up into separate strings, each string followed by the ampersand (&) character along with an underscore (_) character. This technique is used to break up the complete SQL string into readable parts, making the code easier to read and manage. The first line starts the string, and each subsequent line is concatenated to the previous line with the ampersand (&). The underscore (_) is used as a continuation marker, indicating that the code on the next line is part of the code on the current line.

Step 4: Assigning Data to Your RecordSet

In Step 4, you specify that your Recordset will be read-only and filled with data returned from your SQL statement.

Step 5: Copying the Recordset into Excel

In Step 5, you use the Excel CopyFromRecordset method to get the returned dataset into your spreadsheet. In this example, you are copying the data in the MyRecordset object onto the sheet called ADO and SQL starting at cell A2.

Step 6: Adding Column Labels

In Step 6, you add header columns by telling Excel to fill cells A1 through E1 with the respective values in the array. Then you tell Excel to AutoFit those columns so that all the data can be seen.

Using Criteria in Your SQL Statements

Passing criteria through your SQL statements enables you to evaluate each record in your dataset and selectively filter only the ones you need. This affords you a tremendous amount of flexibility that can only be achieved through SQL. Take a moment to review a few example SQL statements that use criteria to filter records.

TIP To get a sense of the impact of using criteria, try replacing the SQL statement in the example you just walked through with any one of the statements listed here.

Set Numeric Criteria

Setting numeric criteria is quite simple; just select the operator you want and you're done. In this example, you are selecting only those records that show revenues greater than $2,000.

```
" SELECT * FROM PvTblFeed" & _
" WHERE Revenue > 2000"
```

Set Textual Criteria

When setting a criterion that is textual or text type, you will need to wrap your text in single quotes. In this example, you are selecting only those records that belong to the Denver market.

```
" SELECT * FROM PvTblFeed" & _
" WHERE Market = 'Denver'"
```

Set Date Criteria

When setting criteria for a date type field, you will need to wrap your criteria in pound (#) signs. The pound signs tag the criteria string as a date. In this example, you are selecting only those records that have an effective date after June 30, 2004.

```
" SELECT * FROM PvTblFeed" & _
" WHERE Effective_Date > #30/Jun/2004#"
```

Set Multiple Criteria

It's important to mention that you are not limited to one criterion. You can evaluate multiple criteria with your SQL statements by simply using the AND operator. In the following example, you are selecting only those records that have an effective date after June 30, 2004 *and* belong to the Denver market:

```
" SELECT * FROM PvTblFeed" & _
" WHERE (Effective_Date > #6/30/2004#) AND (Market = 'Denver')"
```

You can evaluate multiple criteria using the OR operator as demonstrated in the next example. In the following sample, you are selecting only those records belong to either the Denver market or the Charlotte market:

```
" SELECT * FROM PvTblFeed" & _
" WHERE (Market = 'Denver') OR (Market = 'Charlotte'")
```

TIP Note that in the multiple criteria examples each criterion is wrapped in parentheses. The parentheses are not actually necessary; the SQL statement is valid without the parentheses. However, the parentheses are useful in visually separating the criteria, allowing for easy reading.

Using the LIKE Operator

The LIKE operator is useful when you need to evaluate records against a pattern instead of hard-coded criteria. For example, the following sample selects all records belonging to any market that starts with a C (that is, Canada, Charlotte, California).

Access users will note that the wildcard character used in the WHERE clause is not the asterisk (*)typically used in Access. Instead, the percent sign (%) is used. This is because the SQL statement will be passed through ADO, which only validates the percent sign as a wildcard character.

```
" SELECT * FROM PvTblFeed" & _
" WHERE (Market Like 'C%')"
```

TROUBLESHOOTING ERRORS IN YOUR SQL STATMENTS

Troubleshooting a SQL statement in VBA can be one of the most frustrating exercises you will undertake, primarily for two reasons. First, you are working in an environment where the SQL statement is broken up into pieces. Although this makes it easier to determine what the SQL statement is doing, it makes debugging problematic since you cannot readily see the statement as a whole. Second, the error messages you get when SQL statements fails are often times vague, leaving you to guess what the problem may be.

Here's a handy little trick you can implement to make troubleshooting a SQL statement a bit easier. Pass your SQL statement to a message box. The message box enables you to see your SQL statement as a whole and more easily point out where the discrepancy lies. Take for example the following SQL statement:

```
MySQL ="SELECT Region, Market, Product_Description," & _
       " Sum(Revenue) AS Rev, Sum(TransactionCount) AS Units" & _
       "FROM PvTblFeed" & _
       "GROUP BY Region, Market, Product_Description"
```

This particular statement fails and throws the error shown here in Figure 8-5.

Figure 8-5: This error message is vague and practically useless.

The trick is to pass the MySQL1 string variable to a message box as demonstrated here:

```
MySQL ="SELECT Region, Market, Product_Description," & _
       " Sum(Revenue) AS Rev, Sum(TransactionCount) AS Units" & _
       "FROM PvTblFeed" & _
       "GROUP BY Region, Market, Product_Description"
MsgBox (MySQL)
```

This activates a message box that contains your SQL statement in its entirety (see Figure 8.6). Here, you can review the SQL and determine that the culprits for the error are two missing spaces, one before the FROM clause and one before the GROUP BY clause.

Missing spaces

Microsoft Excel

SELECT Region, Market, Product_Description, Sum(Revenue) AS Rev, Sum(TransactionCount) AS UnitsFROM PvTblFeedGROUP BY Region, Market, Product_Description

OK

Figure 8-6: Using a message box enables you to more easily pinpoint errors in your SQL statements.

That's right; two measly spaces cause the entire SQL statement to fail. Remember, these lines of code are not separate SQL statements, they are actually pieces of on SQL statement that have been broken down into parts. They will be pieced back together when the function is executed. In that light, you have to consider, and include, all syntax that is necessary to create a valid SQL statement; including spaces. In this example, the fix for the error is simply to add a space before the FROM and GROUP BY clauses.

```
MySQL ="SELECT Region, Market, Product_Description," & _
       " Sum(Revenue) AS Rev, Sum(TransactionCount) AS Units" & _
       " FROM PvTblFeed" & _
       " GROUP BY Region, Market, Product_Description"
```

Common Scenarios Where VBA Can Help

There are numerous ways you can use the fundamentals you have learned in this chapter. Of course, it would be impossible to go through each example here. However, there are some common scenarios where VBA can greatly enhance integration between Excel and Access.

Query Data from an Excel Workbook

Up until now, you have used Access as the data source for your data pulls. However, use can also use an Excel workbook as a data source. To do so, you would simply build an SQL statement that references the data within the Excel workbook. The idea is to pinpoint the dataset in Excel to query by passing either a sheet name, a range of cells, or a named range to the SQL statement.

- **Query the entire worksheet:** To query all the data on a specific worksheet, you would pass the name of that worksheet followed by the dollar sign ($) as the table name in your SQL statement. Be sure to encapsulate the worksheet name with square brackets. For example:

  ```
  "SELECT * FROM [MySheet$]"
  ```

> **NOTE** If the worksheet name contains spaces or characters that are not alphanumeric you will need to wrap the worksheet name in single quotes. For example, `Select * from ['January; Forecast vs. Budget$']`

- **Query a range of cells:** To query a range of cells within a given worksheet, you would first identify the sheet as described previously, and then add the target range. For example:

  ```
  "SELECT * FROM [MySheet$A1:G17]"
  ```

- **Query a Named Range:** To query a named range, simply use the name of the range as the table name in your SQL statement. For example:

  ```
  "SELECT * FROM MyNamedRange"
  ```

The following code demonstrates how to query data from an Excel worksheet. In this example, the entire used range in the SampleData worksheet is queried to return only those records that belong to the North Region.

```
Sub GetData_From_Excel_Sheet()

'Step 1: Declare your variables
    Dim MyConnect As String
    Dim MyRecordset As ADODB.Recordset
    Dim MySQL As String

'Step 2: Declare your connection string
    MyConnect ="Provider=Microsoft.ACE.OLEDB.12.0;" & _
               "Data Source=C:\Integration\↷
Chapter8_SampleFile.xls;" & _
               "Extended Properties=Excel 12.0"

'Step 3: Build your SQL Statement
    MySQL = " SELECT * FROM [SampleData$]" & _
            " WHERE Region ='NORTH'"

'Step 4: Instantiate and specify your recordset
    Set MyRecordset = New ADODB.Recordset
    MyRecordset.Open MySQL, MyConnect, adOpenStatic, adLockReadOnly

'Step 5: Clear previous contents
    Sheets("Excel Data Pull").Select
```

```
        ActiveSheet.Cells.Clear

'Step 6: Copy the recordset to Excel
        ActiveSheet.Range("A2").CopyFromRecordset MyRecordset

'Step 7: Add column labels
        With ActiveSheet.Range("A1:F1")
            .Value = Array("Region", "Market", "Product_Description", _
            "Revenue", "Transactions", "Dollar per Transaction")
            .EntireColumn.AutoFit
        End With

End Sub
```

Step 1: Declaring the Necessary Variables

In Step 1, you declare three variables: a string variable to hold the connection string, a `Recordset` object to hold the results of the data pull, and a second string variable to hold your SQL statement. In this example, the variable called `MyConnect` holds the connection string identifying the data source. Meanwhile, the variable called `MyRecordset` holds the data returned by the procedure and the variable called `MySQL` holds the SQL statement.

Step 2: Declaring the Connection String

In Step 2, you define the connection string for the ADO procedure. In this scenario, you connect to an Excel workbook, thus the reason for the `Extended Properties` argument.

Step 3: Building the SQL Statement

In Step 3, you assign a SQL statement in the form of a text string to the `MySQL` variable. Here, you build the SQL statement just as though you were working with a database, only you pass the worksheet name as the table. You will note that NORTH is encased in single quotes. In SQL statements, you can use single and double quotes interchangeably.

Step 4: Assigning Data to Your RecordSet

In Step 4, you specify that your `Recordset` be read-only and will be filled with data returned from your SQL statement.

Step 5: Clearing Cell Contents

In Step 5, you are clearing the "Excel Data Pull" worksheet before copying the `Recordset`. This ensures that all data from the previous pull has been removed before bringing in fresh data.

Step 6: Copying the Recordset into Excel

In Step 6, you use the Excel `CopyFromRecordset` method to get the returned dataset into your spreadsheet. In this example, you are copying the data in the `MyRecordset` object onto the sheet called Excel Data Pull starting at cell A2.

Step 7: Adding Column Labels

In Step 7, you add header columns by telling Excel to fill cells A1 through F1 with the respective values in the array. Then you tell Excel to AutoFit those columns so that all the data can be seen.

Append Records to an Existing Excel Table

Often you don't necessarily want to overwrite the data in your Excel worksheet when you bring in fresh data. Instead, you may want to simply add or append data to the existing table.

In a typical scenario, you would hard-code the location or range where you want a given recordset to be copied. In these situations, this location must dynamically change to reflect the first empty cell in your worksheet. The following code demonstrates this technique:

```
Sub Append_Results()

'Step 1: Declare your variables
    Dim MyConnect As String
    Dim MyRecordset As ADODB.Recordset
    Dim MyRange As String

'Step 2: Declare your connection string
    MyConnect = "Provider=Microsoft.ACE.OLEDB.12.0;" & _
                "Data Source= ⤶
C:\Integration\IntegrationDatabase.accdb"

'Step 3: Instantiate and specify your recordset
    Set MyRecordset = New ADODB.Recordset
    MyRecordset.Open "Products", MyConnect, adOpenStatic, ⤶
adLockReadOnly

'Step 4: Find first empty row and use that to build a dynamic range
    Sheets("AppendData").Select
    MyRange = "A" & _
    ActiveSheet.Cells.SpecialCells(xlCellTypeLastCell).Row + 1

'Step 5: Copy the Recordset to First Empty Row
    ActiveSheet.Range(MyRange).CopyFromRecordset MyRecordset

End Sub
```

Step 1: Declaring the Necessary Variables

In Step 1, you declare three variables: a string variable to hold the connection string, a `Recordset` object to hold the results of the data pull, and a second string variable to hold text that will represent a cell reference. In this example, the variable called `MyConnect` holds the connection string identifying the data source. Meanwhile, the variable called `MyRecordset` holds the data that is returned by the procedure and the variable called `MyRange` holds a text string that represent a cell reference.

Step 2: Declaring the Connection String

In Step 2, you define the connection string for the ADO procedure. In this scenario, you connect to the `IntegrationDatabase.accdb` found on the C drive.

Step 3: Assigning Data to Your RecordSet

In Step 3, you specify that your `Recordset` is read-only and will be filled with data from the Products table found in the `IntegrationDatabase.accdb` Access database.

Step 4: Finding the First Empty Cell

The goal in Step 4 is to dynamically determine the first available empty cell that can be used as the output location for the data pull. The first step in accomplishing this goal is to the find the first empty row. This is relatively easy to do thanks to the Excel `SpecialCells` method.

Using the `SpecialCells` method, you can find the last used cell in the worksheet, and then extract the row number of that cell. This gives you the last used row. To get the row number of the first empty row you simply add 1; the next row down from the last used row will inherently be empty.

The idea is to concatenate the `SpecialCells` routine with a column letter (in this case "A") to create a string that represents a range. For example, if the first empty row turns out to be 10, then the code shown here would return "A10".

```
"A" & ActiveSheet.Cells.SpecialCells(xlCellTypeLastCell).Row + 1
```

Trapping this answer in the `MyRange` string variable allows you to pass the answer to the `CopyFromRecordset` method in Step 5.

Step 5: Copying the Recordset into Excel

In Step 5, you use the Excel `CopyFromRecordset` method to get the returned dataset into your spreadsheet. In this example, you are copying the data in the `MyRecordset` object onto the sheet called AppendData starting at the cell that has been dynamically defined by the `MyRange` string.

Append Excel Records to an Existing Access Table

You will undoubtedly find a time when you will need to pull data from an Excel file into an Access table. Again, there are several ways to get Excel data in Access, but using the one-two-three combination of VBA, ADO, and SQL can provide some flexibility not easily attained using other methods.

The following code demonstrates how to query data from an Excel worksheet and append the results to an existing Access table. In this example, the SampleData worksheet is queried to return only those records that belong to the North Region.

```
Sub GetData_From_Excel_Sheet()

'Step 1: Declare your variables
    Dim MyConnect As String
    Dim MyRecordset As ADODB.Recordset
    Dim MyTable As ADODB.Recordset
    Dim MySQL As String

'Step 2: Declare your connection string
    MyConnect = "Provider=Microsoft.ACE.OLEDB.12.0;" & _
                "Data ⤵
Source=C:\Integration\Chapter8_SampleFile.xls;"& _
                "Extended Properties=Excel 12.0"

'Step 3: Build your SQL statement
    MySQL = " SELECT * FROM [SampleData$]" & _
            " WHERE Region ='NORTH'"

'Step 4: Instantiate and specify your recordset
    Set MyRecordset = New ADODB.Recordset
    MyRecordset.Open MySQL, MyConnect, adOpenStatic, adLockReadOnly

'Step 5: Instantiate and specify your Access table
    Set MyTable = New ADODB.Recordset
    MyTable.Open "ExcelFeed", CurrentProject.Connection, ⤵
adOpenDynamic, adLockOptimistic

'Step 6: Loop through each record and add to the table
    Do Until MyRecordset.EOF
    MyTable.AddNew
        MyTable!ActiveRegion = MyRecordset!Region
        MyTable!ActiveMarket = MyRecordset!Market
        MyTable!Product = MyRecordset!Product_Description
        MyTable!Revenue = MyRecordset!Revenue
        MyTable!Units = MyRecordset!Transactions
        MyTable![Dollar Per Unit] = MyRecordset![Dollar ⤵
Per Transaction]
    MyTable.Update
```

```
        MyRecordset.MoveNext
        Loop

End Sub
```

Step 1: Declaring the Necessary Variables

In Step 1, you declare four variables:

- MyConnect is a String variable that holds the connection string identifying the data source.
- MyRecordset is a Recordset object that holds the results of the data pull.
- MyTable is a Recordset object that provides the structure of the existing table.
- MySQL is a String variable that holds your SQL statement.

Step 2: Declaring the Connection String

In Step 2, you define the connection string for the ADO procedure. In this scenario, you are connecting to an Excel workbook, thus the reason for the Extended Properties argument.

Step 3: Building the SQL Statement

In Step 3, you assign a SQL statement in the form of a text string to the MySQL variable. Here, you build the SQL statement just as though you were working with a database, only you pass the worksheet name as the table.

Step 4: Assigning Data to Your RecordSet

In Step 4, you specify that your Recordset is read-only and will be filled with data returned from your SQL statement.

Step 5: Open the Target Access Table into a Recordset

In Step 5, open the pre-existing local ExcelFeed table into a Recordset. There are a few things to note about the Recordset declaration in Step 5.

First, note that the connection argument is referencing the internal connection CurrentProject.Connection. This standard connection is used when assigning a local table to a Recordset.

Second, note that the CursorType and LockType arguments are adOpen-Dynamic and adLockOptimistic, respectively. This ensures that the local table can be updated to append the new records.

Step 6: Loop Through the Query Results, Adding Each Record to the Table

In Step 6, you loop through the records in the results `Recordset` and add each record to the local ExcelFeed table.

First, you start the loop by declaring that the procedure will `Do Until MyRecordset.EOF`. This tells VBA to keep looping through the `MyRecordset` Recordset until it hits the EOF (end of file). Next, you use the `AddNew` method of the `Recordset` to add a new empty record to the local ExcelFeed table represented by the `MyTable` Recordset.

From here, you simply fill the fields in the empty record you just created with the values that were returned from your SQL statement. Note that each field in the ExcelFeed table (represented by the `MyTable` Recordset) has its counterpart in the `MyRecordset` Recordset.

After each record, you must call the `Update` method, as in `MyTable .Update`. This ensures that your changes are saved. Finally, calling the `MoveNext` method ensures that the cursor moves to the next record before looping back.

Querying Text Files

Text files are not only a source of data, but also very much part of daily data operations. Given this fact, it's worth looking into how to pull data from text files using ADO and SQL. The connection string that is used to source a text file is as follows:

```
MyConnect = "Provider=Microsoft.ACE.OLEDB.12.0;" & _
            "Data Source= C:\Integration\;" & _
            "Extended Properties=Text"
```

A closer look at the `Data Source` argument reveals that only the file's directory is specified as the source for the data; not the actual file itself. The `Extended Properties` argument is set to `Text`.

Besides the difference in the construct of the connection string, querying a text file is very much similar to querying an Excel workbook.

```
Sub GetData_From_Text_File()
'Step 1: Declare your variables
    Dim MyConnect As String
    Dim MyRecordset As ADODB.Recordset
    Dim MySQL As String

'Step 2: Declare your connection string
    MyConnect = "Provider=Microsoft.ACE.OLEDB.12.0;" & _
                "Data Source=C:\Integration\;" & _
                "Extended Properties=Text"

'Step 3: Build your SQL statement
```

```
        MySQL = " SELECT * FROM SalesData.csv"

    'Step 4: Instantiate and specify your recordset
        Set MyRecordset = New ADODB.Recordset
        MyRecordset.Open MySQL, MyConnect, adOpenStatic, adLockReadOnly

    'Step 5: Clear previous contents
          Sheets("Query Text").Select
          ActiveSheet.Cells.Clear

    'Step 6: Copy the recordset to Excel
          ActiveSheet.Range("A2").CopyFromRecordset MyRecordset

    'Step 7: Add column labels
        With ActiveSheet.Range("A1:F1")
            .Value = Array("Region", "Market", "Product_Description", _
            "Revenue", "Transactions", "Dollar per Transaction")
            .EntireColumn.AutoFit
        End With

    End Sub
```

Summary

Although there are many methods to move data between Access and Excel using their interfaces, many of these methods retain an aspect of manual involvement. VBA can help make your data transfer processes virtually hands-free.

VBA, in and of itself, does not have the capability to connect and manipulate external data. You need to combine VBA with helper technologies such as ADO (ActiveX Data Objects) and SQL (Structured Query Language). ADO is a tool that helps you accomplish two tasks: connect to a data source and specify the dataset with which to work. SQL allows you to customize your data processes, giving you the flexibility to filter, group, and sort your results.

The combination of VBA, ADO, and SQL is extremely powerful and relatively easy to understand and implement. Using these three tools together, you can process data without the need to create and maintain multiple queries and macros. You can also perform complex, multi-layered procedures that involve looping, record level testing, and If...Then...Else checks without the need to inundate your processes with many queries and temporary tables.

CHAPTER 9

Exploring Excel and Access Automation

In the last few chapters, you have learned about several ways to automate your analytical processes to achieve higher productivity, controlled analysis, and reproducibility. In this chapter, automation takes on a different meaning. Here *automation* defines the means of manipulating or controlling one application with another. Why would you even want to control one application with another? Think about all the times you have crunched data in Access only to bring the results into Excel for presentation and distribution. Think about all the times you have sent Excel data to Access only to open Access and run a set of queries or output a report.

The reality is that each of these applications has its strengths that you routinely leverage through manual processes. So why not automate these processes? The goal of this chapter is to give you a solid understanding of how to use automation to control Excel from Access and vice versa.

Understanding the Concept of Binding

Each program in the Microsoft Office suite comes with its own Object Library. As you know, the *Object Library* is a kind of encyclopedia of all the objects, methods, and properties available in each Office application. Excel has its own object library, just as Access has its own object library, just as all the other

Office applications have their own object library. For Excel to speak to another Office program such as Access, you have to bind it to that program.

Binding is the process of exposing the Object Library for a server application to a client application. There are two types of binding: early binding and late binding.

> **NOTE** In the context of this discussion, a *client application* is the application that is doing the controlling, whereas the *server application* is the application being controlled.

Early Binding

With *early binding,* you explicitly point a client application to the server application's Object Library to expose its object model during design-time, or while programming. Then you use the exposed objects in your code to call a new instance of the application as such:

```
Dim XL As Excel.Application
Set XL = New Excel.Application
```

Early binding has several advantages:

- Because the objects are exposed at design time, the client application can compile your code before execution. This allows your code to run considerably faster than with late binding.

- Because the Object Library is exposed during design time, you have full access to the server application's object model in the Object Browser.

- You have the benefit of using IntelliSense. *IntelliSense* is the functionality you experience when you type a keyword and a dot (.) or an equal sign (=) and you see a pop-up list of the methods and properties available to you.

- You automatically have access to the server application's built-in constants.

Late Binding

Late binding is different in that you don't point a client application to a specific Object Library. Instead, you purposely keep things ambiguous, only using the CreateObject function to bind to the needed library at runtime, or during program execution.

```
Dim XL As Object
Set XL = CreateObject("Excel.Application")
```

BINDING CONVENTIONS IN THIS BOOK

For the purposes of this book, early binding is used for a couple of reasons. First, the design time benefits of early binding, such as IntelliSense, is ideal for discovering and experimenting with the methods and properties that come with Excel and Access. Secondly, this chapter is written in the context of building procedures that will help you increase productivity, not building an application that will be used by many users. In this light, version issues don't come into play, negating the need for late binding.

Late binding has one main advantage: it allows your automation procedures to be version-independent. That is, your automation procedure will not fail due to compatibility issues between multiple versions of a component. For example, suppose you decide to use early binding and set a reference to the Excel Object Library on your system. The version of the available library on your system will be equal to your version of Excel. The problem is that if your users have an earlier version of Excel on their machine, your automation procedure will fail. You do not have this problem with late binding.

Automating Excel from Access

Processes where Access data is moved to Excel lend themselves quite nicely to automation. This is primarily due to the nature of these two programs. Access typically serves as the data layer in most analytical processes, while Excel serves as the presentation. Because of this dynamic, you may find that you often send Access data to Excel to build charts, PivotTables, or some other presentation mechanism displaying the data. Excel Automation can literally take you out of the report building process, creating and saving Excel reports without any human interaction.

Creating Your First Excel Automation Procedure

For your first Excel automation trick, you will build a procedure in Access that automatically opens a new Excel workbook and adds a worksheet.

To start, open the `IntegrationDatabase.accdb` sample database that came with this book and start a new module by clicking on the Create tab in the ribbon and selecting Macro → Module.

Before you do anything, you must set a reference to the Excel Object Library. To do this, go up to the application menu and select Tools → References. The Reference dialog box shown in Figure 9-1 activates. Scroll down until you find the entry Microsoft Excel *XX* Object Library, where *XX* is your version of Excel. Select the check box next to the entry (see in Figure 9-1), and then click the OK button.

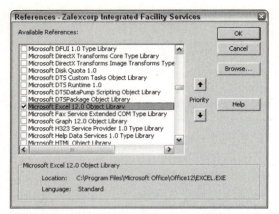

Figure 9-1: Select the Excel Object Library and click the OK button.

> **NOTE** If you don't set a reference to the Excel Object Library, Access will give you a compile error, giving you this message:
>
> ```
> Compile error: User-defined type not defined.
> ```
>
> The good news is that once you set a reference to the Excel Object Library in a particular database, it is set for good in that database.

Now that you have referenced the Excel Object Library, you can start writing code. Enter the following code into your newly created module:

```
Function MyFirstAutomationCode()

'Step 1:  Declare the variables you will work with.
    Dim xl As Excel.Application
    Dim xlwkbk As Excel.Workbook
    Dim xlsheet As Excel.Worksheet

'Step 2:  Start Excel, then add a workbook and a worksheet.
    Set xl = New Excel.Application
    Set xlwkbk = xl.Workbooks.Add
    Set xlsheet = xlwkbk.Worksheets.Add

'Step 3:  Make Excel visible
    xl.Visible = True

'Step 4:  Memory Clean up.
    Set xl = Nothing
    Set xlwkbk = Nothing
    Set xlsheet = Nothing


End Function
```

Step 1: Declaring the Necessary Variables

In Step 1, you first declare three variables:

- `xl` is an object variable that exposes the Excel `Application` object.
- `xlwkbk` is an object variable that exposes the Excel `Workbook` object.
- `xlsheet` is an object variable that exposes the Excel `Worksheet` object.

Step 2: Starting a New Instance of Excel with New Workbook and Worksheet

In Step 2, you first create a new instance of Excel and assign that instance to your `xl` object variable. From here, the `xl` object variable is your tie into the Excel application, exposing all objects, properties, and variables that you would normally have if you were working directly in Excel.

Next, you open a new workbook by using the `Workbooks.Add` method of the xl object variable. Note that you are assigning the new workbook to your `xlwkbk` variable. At this point, your `xlwkbk` variable actually represents a real workbook, exposing all objects, properties, and variables that you would normally have if you were working with a workbook directly in Excel.

Finally, you add a new worksheet by using the `Worksheets.Add` method of the `xlwkbk` object variable. Note that you are assigning the new worksheet to your `xlsheet` variable. At this point, your `xlsheet` variable actually represents a real worksheet, exposing all objects, properties, and variables that you would normally have if you were working with a worksheet directly in Excel.

Step 3: Making Excel Visible

By default, an instance of Excel that is created via automation is not visible. Although this is not necessary, it's generally a good practice to make the instance of Excel visible for a couple of reasons. First, should anything go wrong during the procedure, debugging will be easier if you can see the Excel spreadsheet. Secondly, you can easily close the instance of Excel in debug mode by closing out the Excel window. If the instance is not visible, you will have to kill it by going into the Windows Task Manager and ending the process there.

Step 4: Cleaning Up Memory by Closing the Open Objects

It is generally good practice to release the objects assigned to your variables. This reduces the chance of any problems caused by rogue objects that may remain open in memory. As you can see in the code, you simply set the variable to `Nothing`.

Congratulations! You have just created your first automation procedure.

Automating Data Export to Excel

Now that you have successfully created your first automation procedure, it's time to try something more meaningful; sending Access data to Excel, the first step in creating an Excel report from your Access analysis.

Sending One Recordset to Excel

The process of sending your Access data to Excel can generally be broken down into three main actions:

1. First, you identify the dataset you want to send to Excel and assign it to a `Recordset` object.

2. Next, you open Excel and copy the recordset to a spreadsheet using the Excel `CopyFromRecordset` method.

3. Finally, since the `CopyFromRecordset` method does not transfer column headings, you must add your dataset's column headings and add them to the spreadsheet.

Let's go through the following example procedure, where you will send the PvTblFeed table to a tab called Pivot Table Feed.

```
Function SendRecordset()

'Step 1: Declare the objects and variables you will work with
    Dim MyRecordset As ADODB.Recordset
    Dim xl As Excel.Application
    Dim xlwkbk As Excel.Workbook
    Dim xlsheet As Excel.Worksheet
    Dim i As Integer

'Step 2: Start Excel, then add a workbook and a worksheet
    Set xl = New Excel.Application
    Set xlwkbk = xl.Workbooks.Add
    Set xlsheet = xlwkbk.Worksheets.Add
    xlsheet.Name = "Pivot Table Feed"

'Step 3: Make the instance of Excel visible
    xl.Visible = True

'Step 4: Assign a dataset to the recordset object
    Set MyRecordset = New ADODB.Recordset
    MyRecordset.Open "PvTblFeed", CurrentProject.Connection

'Step 5: Copy the records to the active Excel sheet
    With xlsheet
    xl.Range("A2").CopyFromRecordset MyRecordset
```

```
        End With

 'Step 6: Add column heading names to the spreadsheet
        For i = 1 To MyRecordset.Fields.Count
        xl.ActiveSheet.Cells(1, i).Value = MyRecordset.Fields(i - 1).Name
        Next i

 'Step 7: Memory Clean up
        Set MyRecordset = Nothing
        Set xl = Nothing
        Set xlwkbk = Nothing
        Set xlsheet = Nothing

 End Function
```

Step 1: Declaring the Necessary Objects and Variables

In Step 1, you first declare five variables:

- `MyRecordset` is a Recordset object that will hold the results of the data pull.

- `xl` is an object variable that exposes the Excel `Application` object.

- `xlwkbk` is an object variable that exposes the Excel `Workbooks` object.

- `xlsheet` is an object variable that exposes the Excel `Worksheet` object.

- `i` in an integer variable that will be used to add column headings.

Step 2: Starting a New Instance of Excel with New Workbook and Worksheet

In Step 2, you create a new instance of Excel, open a new workbook and add a new worksheet. Note that you give the new worksheet a name, Pivot Table Feed.

Step 3: Making Excel Visible

In Step 3, you make the instance of Excel visible.

Step 4: Assigning Data to Your Recordset

In Step 4, you specify that your recordset will be read-only and will be filled with data from the PvTblFeed table found in the `IntegrationDatabase.accdb` Access database.

Step 5: Copying the Recordset into Excel

By the time you reach Step 5, the `MyRecordset` object is filled with data from the PvTblFeed table. In Step 5, you use Excel's `CopyFromRecordset` method to get it out and into your spreadsheet. In this example, you are copying the data onto your newly created sheet starting at cell A2.

Step 6: Adding Column Headers

As you know the `CopyFromRecordset` method does not return column headers or field names. There are several ways to fill in the column headers for a dataset. In Chapter 8, you used an array to fill in the column headers. This example demonstrates how you can enumerate through each field in the recordset to automatically get the name of each header and enter it into Excel.

Step 7: Cleaning Up the Open Objects

In Step 7, you release the objects assigned to your variables, reducing the chance of any problems caused by rogue objects that may remain open in memory.

Sending Two Datasets to Two Different Tabs in the Same Workbook

You sometimes come across a scenario where you have to send two or more datasets to Excel into different tabs. This is as easy as repeating parts of the automation procedure for a different recordset. The following code sends the PvTblFeed table to a tab called Pivot Table Feed, and then sends the Main-Summary table to another tab in the same the workbook.

```
Function SendMoreThanOneRecordset()

'Step 1: Declare the objects and variables you will work with
    Dim MyRecordset As ADODB.Recordset
    Dim xl As Excel.Application
    Dim xlwkbk As Excel.Workbook
    Dim xlsheet As Excel.Worksheet
    Dim i As Integer

'Step 2: Start Excel, then add a workbook and a worksheet
    Set xl = New Excel.Application
    Set xlwkbk = xl.Workbooks.Add
    Set xlsheet = xlwkbk.Worksheets.Add
    xlsheet.Name = "Pivot Table Feed"

'Step 3: Make the instance of Excel visible
    xl.Visible = True

'Step 4: Assign a dataset to the recordset object
    Set MyRecordset = New ADODB.Recordset
    MyRecordset.Open "PvTblFeed", CurrentProject.Connection

'Step 5: Copy the records to the active Excel sheet
    With xlsheet
    xl.Range("A2").CopyFromRecordset MyRecordset
    End With

'Step 6: Add column heading names to the spreadsheet
```

```
      For i = 1 To MyRecordset.Fields.Count
      xl.ActiveSheet.Cells(1, i).Value = MyRecordset.Fields(i - 1).Name
      Next i

'Step 7: Close active recordset: Repeat steps 4-6 for new a recordset
      MyRecordset.Close
      MyRecordset.Open "ForecastSummary", CurrentProject.Connection

      Set xlsheet = xlwkbk.Worksheets.Add
      xlsheet.Name = "Forecast Summary"

      With xlsheet
      xl.Range("A2").CopyFromRecordset MyRecordset
      End With

      For i = 1 To MyRecordset.Fields.Count
      xl.ActiveSheet.Cells(1, i).Value = MyRecordset.Fields(i - 1).Name
      Next i

'Step 8: Memory Clean up
      Set MyRecordset = Nothing
      Set xl = Nothing
      Set xlwkbk = Nothing
      Set xlsheet = Nothing

End Function
```

Automating Excel Reports: Without Programming Excel

Excel automation goes beyond getting your data to Excel. With Excel automation, you can have Access dynamically add formatting, set print options, add an AutoFilter, create PivotTables, build charts, and the list goes on.

However, the rub is there are countless actions you can take after your Access data reaches Excel. Where do you begin to learn how to create a Pivot-Table using VBA, create and format a chart with VBA, or even add an Auto-Filter? Although it's true there are many resources that can help you learn VBA, the reality is that this kind of a learning process takes trial and error as well as time to build experience working with the Excel object model. Even if programming Excel PivotTables and charts were within the scope of this book, there are enough nuances to Excel programming that any instruction that could fit into one chapter would fall short.

So what is an aspiring analyst to do? After all, the reason you are reading this book is that you need to implement automation now. The answer is to simply let Excel program for you!

CHECKING FOR RECORD COUNT BEFORE AUTOMATING EXCEL

Often times, the recordset you are sending to your spreadsheet will be a query that may or may not return records. Interestingly enough, you will not receive an error when you use the `CopyFromRecordset` method on an empty recordset. That means that it is completely possible to automate Excel, create a workbook, and copy no records to it. This can cause problems later, especially if you further your automation of Excel to include building a PivotTable, creating a chart, and so on.

The quick-and-easy workaround to this potential problem is to check your recordset for a record count before doing anything. As you can see in Step 3 of the example shown here, a simple `IF` statement evaluates the count of records in the recordset. If the record count is less than 1 (meaning the recordset is holding 0 records), the procedure will terminate. Otherwise, the procedure will continue.

```
'Step 1: Declare the objects and variables you will work with
     Dim MyRecordset As ADODB.Recordset


'Step 2: Start a new recordset
     Set MyRecordset = New ADODB.Recordset
     MyRecordset.Open "Employee_Master", & _
     "CurrentProject.Connection"


'Step 3:  Check RecordCount
  If MyRecordset.RecordCount < 1 Then
     MsgBox ("There are no records to output")
     Set MyRecordset = Nothing
     Exit Function
Else


'Continue with your automation code...
End If


End Function
```

In Excel, *macros* are used as a way to record actions that can be played back when needed. When you start recording a macro, Excel automatically generates one or more lines of code for every action you take. After you stop recording, you can open the macro to review, edit, or even copy the code that was generated. The idea here is after you send Access data to Excel, you can perform some actions on your data while recording a macro, and then copy the macro generated-code into the Access module where you have the automation procedure. The next time you run the automation procedure, the recorded macro actions will run right from Access.

To illustrate this concept, take some time to walk through the following demonstration.

1. In the sample database, execute the `SendRecordset` function in the module titled Excel_Automation_2. When the function finishes running, you should have an Excel spreadsheet that looks similar to the one shown in Figure 9-2.
2. In Excel, start a new macro, name it MyMacro and click the OK button. At this point, your macro starts recording your actions.
3. Make the following formatting changes:
   a. Click cell A1.
   b. Go to the Data tab and click the Filter icon.
   c. Select cells A1 through I1 and change the font style to bold.
   d. Select columns A through I, then click on the Home tab and select Format → AutoFit Column Width.
   e. Click cell A1.
   f. Select the Insert tab and click the PivotTable icon. This activates the Create PivotTable dialog box shown in Figure 9-3. Click the OK button to create the PivotTable.

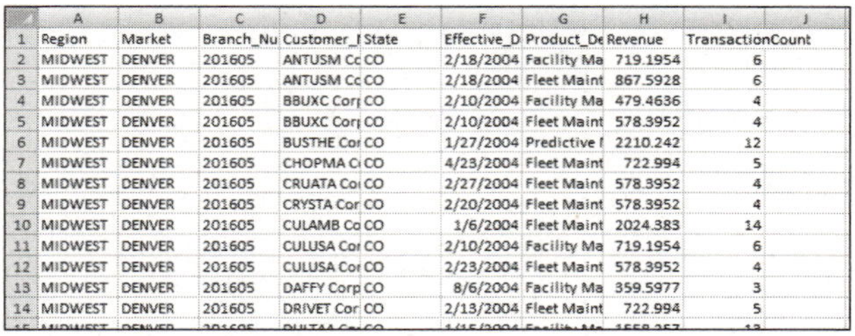

	A	B	C	D	E	F	G	H	I	J
1	Region	Market	Branch_Nu	Customer_I	State	Effective_D	Product_De	Revenue	TransactionCount	
2	MIDWEST	DENVER	201605	ANTUSM Cc	CO	2/18/2004	Facility Ma	719.1954	6	
3	MIDWEST	DENVER	201605	ANTUSM Cc	CO	2/18/2004	Fleet Maint	867.5928	6	
4	MIDWEST	DENVER	201605	BBUXC Corp	CO	2/10/2004	Facility Ma	479.4636	4	
5	MIDWEST	DENVER	201605	BBUXC Corp	CO	2/10/2004	Fleet Maint	578.3952	4	
6	MIDWEST	DENVER	201605	BUSTHE Cor	CO	1/27/2004	Predictive I	2210.242	12	
7	MIDWEST	DENVER	201605	CHOPMA C	CO	4/23/2004	Fleet Maint	722.994	5	
8	MIDWEST	DENVER	201605	CRUATA Co	CO	2/27/2004	Fleet Maint	578.3952	4	
9	MIDWEST	DENVER	201605	CRYSTA Cor	CO	2/20/2004	Fleet Maint	578.3952	4	
10	MIDWEST	DENVER	201605	CULAMB Co	CO	1/6/2004	Fleet Maint	2024.383	14	
11	MIDWEST	DENVER	201605	CULUSA Cor	CO	2/10/2004	Facility Ma	719.1954	6	
12	MIDWEST	DENVER	201605	CULUSA Cor	CO	2/23/2004	Fleet Maint	578.3952	4	
13	MIDWEST	DENVER	201605	DAFFY Corp	CO	8/6/2004	Facility Ma	359.5977	3	
14	MIDWEST	DENVER	201605	DRIVET Cor	CO	2/13/2004	Fleet Maint	722.994	5	

Figure 9-2: This is the spreadsheet you start with when you run the SendRecordset function.

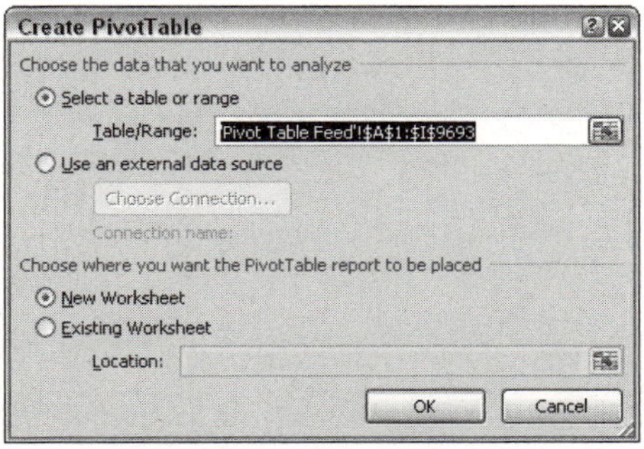

Figure 9-3: Create a new PivotTable.

g. A new PivotTable and a PivotTable Field List are displayed. In the PivotTable Field List, select the check boxes next to the following fields: `Region`, `Market`, `Revenue`, and `TransactionCount` (see Figure 9-4).

4. Click cell A1.
5. Stop the macro recording.
6. Now that you have finished recording the necessary actions, you can copy the macro-generated code out of Excel and into Access. To do this, click the Developer tab and select Macros. This opens the Macro dialog box shown in Figure 9-5. Select MyMacro then select Edit.

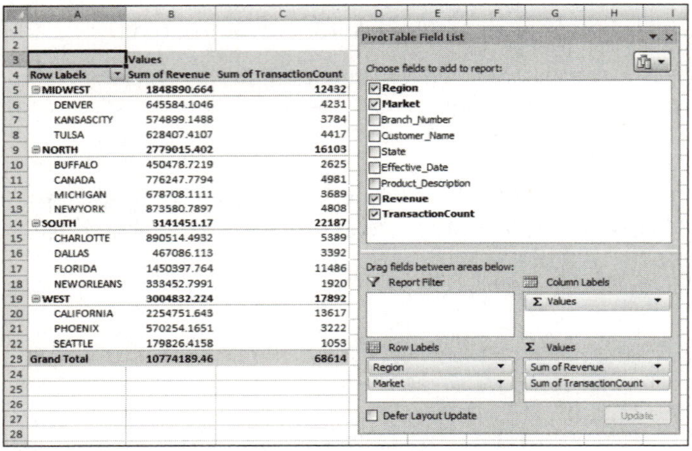

Row Labels	Sum of Revenue	Sum of TransactionCount
MIDWEST	1848890.664	12432
DENVER	645584.1046	4231
KANSASCITY	574899.1488	3784
TULSA	628407.4107	4417
NORTH	2779015.402	16103
BUFFALO	450478.7219	2625
CANADA	776247.7794	4981
MICHIGAN	678708.1111	3689
NEWYORK	873580.7897	4808
SOUTH	3141451.17	22187
CHARLOTTE	890514.4932	5389
DALLAS	467086.113	3392
FLORIDA	1450397.764	11486
NEWORLEANS	333452.7991	1920
WEST	3004832.224	17892
CALIFORNIA	2254751.643	13617
PHOENIX	570254.1651	3222
SEATTLE	179826.4158	1053
Grand Total	10774189.46	68614

Figure 9-4: Select the PivotTable fields.

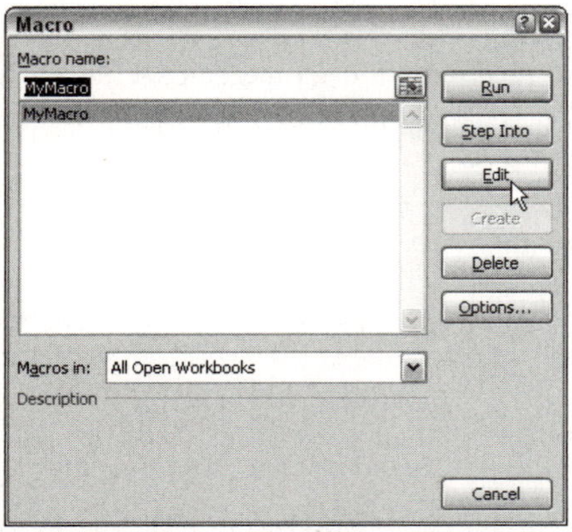

Figure 9-5: Open your newly created macro in Edit mode to copy to the macro-generated code.

7. The code in your macro should look similar to the code shown in Figure 9-6. At this point, all you have to do is select and copy all the code within the Sub procedure (don't include the comments or End Sub).

8. Open the Excel_Automation_2 module in Access and paste the code after the step where you enumerate through the column headings (Step 6) as shown in Figure 9-7.

```
(General)                                          MyMacro

  Option Explicit

  Sub MyMacro()
  '
  ' MyMacro Macro
  '
      Range("A1").Select
      Selection.AutoFilter
      Range("A1:I1").Select
      Selection.Font.Bold = True
      Columns("A:I").Select
      Selection.Columns.AutoFit
      Range("A1").Select
      Sheets.Add
      ActiveWorkbook.PivotCaches.Create(SourceType:=xlDatabase, SourceData:= _
          "Pivot Table Feed!R1C1:R9693C9", Version:=xlPivotTableVersion12). _
          CreatePivotTable TableDestination:="Sheet5!R3C1", TableName:="PivotTable1" _
          , DefaultVersion:=xlPivotTableVersion12
      Sheets("Sheet5").Select
      Cells(3, 1).Select
      With ActiveSheet.PivotTables("PivotTable1").PivotFields("Region")
          .Orientation = xlRowField
          .Position = 1
      End With
      With ActiveSheet.PivotTables("PivotTable1").PivotFields("Market")
          .Orientation = xlRowField
          .Position = 2
      End With
      ActiveSheet.PivotTables("PivotTable1").AddDataField ActiveSheet.PivotTables( _
          "PivotTable1").PivotFields("Revenue"), "Sum of Revenue", xlSum
      ActiveSheet.PivotTables("PivotTable1").AddDataField ActiveSheet.PivotTables( _
          "PivotTable1").PivotFields("TransactionCount"), "Sum of TransactionCount", _
          xlSum
      Range("A1").Select
  End Sub
```

Figure 9-6: Copy the macro-generated code out of Excel.

```
(General)

      End With

  'Step 6: Add column heading names to the spreadsheet
      For i = 1 To MyRecordset.Fields.Count
      xl.ActiveSheet.Cells(1, i).Value = MyRecordset.Fields(i - 1).Name
      Next i

  '***************Start Excel Formatting***************

      Range("A1").Select
      Selection.AutoFilter
      Range("A1:I1").Select
      Selection.Font.Bold = True
      Columns("A:I").Select
      Selection.Columns.AutoFit
      Range("A1").Select
      Sheets.Add
      ActiveWorkbook.PivotCaches.Create(SourceType:=xlDatabase, SourceData:= _
          "Pivot Table Feed!R1C1:R9693C9", Version:=xlPivotTableVersion12). _
          CreatePivotTable TableDestination:="Sheet5!R3C1", TableName:="PivotTable1" _
          , DefaultVersion:=xlPivotTableVersion12
      Sheets("Sheet5").Select
      Cells(3, 1).Select
      With ActiveSheet.PivotTables("PivotTable1").PivotFields("Region")
          .Orientation = xlRowField
          .Position = 1
      End With
      With ActiveSheet.PivotTables("PivotTable1").PivotFields("Market")
          .Orientation = xlRowField
          .Position = 2
      End With
      ActiveSheet.PivotTables("PivotTable1").AddDataField ActiveSheet.PivotTables( _
          "PivotTable1").PivotFields("Revenue"), "Sum of Revenue", xlSum
      ActiveSheet.PivotTables("PivotTable1").AddDataField ActiveSheet.PivotTables( _
          "PivotTable1").PivotFields("TransactionCount"), "Sum of TransactionCount", _
          xlSum
      Range("A1").Select
```

Figure 9-7: Copy the macro-generated code out of Excel.

TIP Be sure to paste your macro-generated code in a place within your procedure that makes sense. For example, you don't want to the procedure to encounter this code before the data has been sent to Excel. Generally, code generated in Excel can logically be added directly after the section of code that applies column headings.

Also, notice that in Figure 9-7, there is a clear marker that indicates where the Excel generated code starts. It's good practice to clearly define the point where you are working with code generated in Excel. This ensures that you can easily find the section of code in the event you need to replace it, or remove it altogether.

9. You're almost done. Now add the appropriate application variable name to each foreign object that is a direct property of that application object. In other words, since the objects and properties in the macro-generated code come from the Excel Object Library, you need to let Access know by prefacing each of these with the name you assigned to the Excel application. For example: `Range("A1").Select` would be edited to `xl.Range("A1").Select` because `xl` is the variable name you assigned to the Excel application object and `Range` is being used as a direct property of the Excel application. In this example, you prefix each one of the following objects with `xl.`: `Range`, `Selection`, `Columns`, `Cells`, `Sheets`, `ActiveWorkbook` and `ActiveSheet`. Figure 9-8 demonstrates what your code should look like after you have made this change.

```
(General)                                        ▼ |
'***************Start Excel Formatting***************
    xl.Range("A1").Select
    xl.Selection.AutoFilter
    xl.Range("A1:I1").Select
    xl.Selection.Font.Bold = True
    xl.Columns("A:I").Select
    xl.Selection.Columns.AutoFit
    xl.Range("A1").Select
    xl.Sheets.Add
    xl.ActiveWorkbook.PivotCaches.Create(SourceType:=xlDatabase, SourceData:= _
        "Pivot Table Feed!R1C1:R9693C9", Version:=xlPivotTableVersion12). _
        CreatePivotTable TableDestination:="Sheet5!R3C1", TableName:="PivotTable1" _
        , DefaultVersion:=xlPivotTableVersion12
    xl.Sheets("Sheet5").Select
    xl.Cells(3, 1).Select
    With xl.ActiveSheet.PivotTables("PivotTable1").PivotFields("Region")
        .Orientation = xlRowField
        .Position = 1
    End With
    With xl.ActiveSheet.PivotTables("PivotTable1").PivotFields("Market")
        .Orientation = xlRowField
        .Position = 2
    End With
    xl.ActiveSheet.PivotTables("PivotTable1").AddDataField xl.ActiveSheet.PivotTables( _
        "PivotTable1").PivotFields("Revenue"), "Sum of Revenue", xlSum
    xl.ActiveSheet.PivotTables("PivotTable1").AddDataField xl.ActiveSheet.PivotTables( _
        "PivotTable1").PivotFields("TransactionCount"), "Sum of TransactionCount", _
        xlSum
    xl.Range("A1").Select
```

Figure 9-8: Add the `xl.` variable tags you see here in bold font.

NOTE You only have to add the application variable name to objects and properties that are not being used as an object or property of a higher object. Take these two lines of code for example.

```
xl.Columns("A:I").Select
xl.Selection.Columns.AutoFit
```

Notice that when `Columns` is used as a property of the `Selection` object it is not prefaced with the variable name <u>xl.</u>

WARNING Be warned that skipping Step 9 causes you to get these seemingly unpredictable run-time errors:

- **Run-time error '1004': Method 'Range' of object '_Global' failed**
- **Run-time error '91': Object variable or With block variable not set**

10. Save your module and test it.

You have just built your first, fully automated, Excel report. Keep in mind that this is a simple example. The possibilities are as expansive as Excel itself. For example, you could create a chart, create a PivotTable, or apply subtotals. Using this method, you can literally create a report purely in VBA, and then run it whenever you want.

SUPPRESSING WARNING AND INFORMATIONAL MESSAGES IN EXCEL

When building your automation procedures, you may invoke some actions that require your input. For example, choosing to save a worksheet may invoke a message from Excel asking if you want to overwrite the previously saved file.

The problem with these types of messages is that they interrupt your automated procedures while Excel waits for an answer from you. Given that the purpose of automation is to remove the element of human interaction, this just won't do.

If you want to suppress Excel's warning and informational messages that pop up occasionally, use the Excel `DisplayAlerts` property. The `DisplayAlerts` property is analogous to Access' `SetWarnings` method; used to suppress application messages by automatically selecting Yes or OK for the user.

To suppress the Excel alerts insert the following code before your macro-generated code.

```
xl.Application. DisplayAlerts = False
```

To turn alerts back on, insert the following code after your macro-generated code.

```
xl.Application. DisplayAlerts =  True
```

Using Find and Replace to Adjust Macro-Generated Code

In the previous section, you learned there is a set of Excel objects and properties that need to be pointed back to the Excel `Application` object by prefacing them with the name you assigned to the Excel application. For example: `Range("A1").Select` would be edited to `xl.Range("A1").Select` because `xl` is the name you assigned to the Excel `Application` object.

The problem is that this can be quite an ordeal if you have recorded a macro that generated a substantial block of code. It would take a long time to search through the macro-generated code and preface each appropriate object or property. However, there are a set of Excel objects and properties used repeatedly in your macro-generated code. These are `Range`, `ActiveSheet`, `ActiveWorkbook`, `ActiveCell`, `Application`, and `Selection`. The good news is that you can leverage this fact by filtering these objects and properties into four most commonly used keywords.

The four most common keywords are

- `Range`
- `Selection`
- `Active`
- `Application`

This is where the Find and Replace functionality can come in handy. With Find and Replace, you can find these keywords and preface them all in one fell swoop. To do this, first select all the macro-generated code in the Visual Basic Editor, then select Edit → Replace. This activates the Replace dialog box shown in Figure 9-9.

As you can see, all you have to do is enter each keyword into the Find What drop-down list, and enter the prefaced keyword in the Replace With drop-down list. Keep in mind that depending on your macro-generated code, some of these keywords may not produce any hits, which is okay.

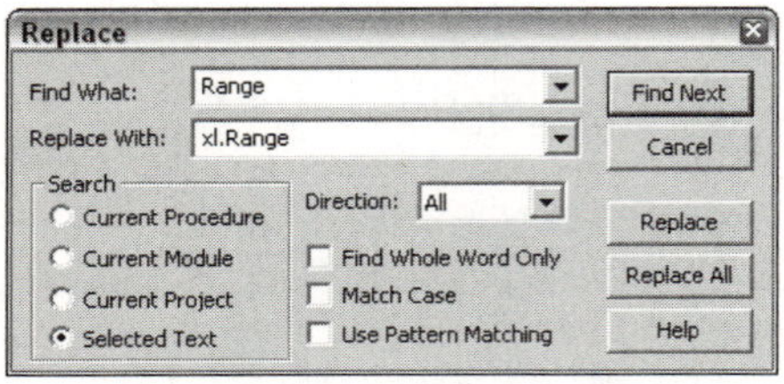

Figure 9-9: Use the Find and Replace functionality to preface the four most common key words.

WARNING In Figure 9-9, there is a search option called Selected Text. This means that any of the Find and Replace functionality that is applied is limited to the selected text. It is extremely important that you select the macro-generated code and ensure that the Selected Text option is active before you start any find and replace procedures. Otherwise, you could inadvertently change code in other parts of your module.

Bear in mind that these keywords only make up the bulk of the objects and properties that may need to be prefaced in your macro-generated code. There are others that you'll need to preface by hand, the most common of which are

- `Columns`
- `Cells`
- `Rows`

Why can't you preface these using Find and Replace? It's a question of object hierarchy. Often times, these are used as properties of higher objects, which means you would not need to preface them because the higher object is prefaced. Here's an example:

```
xl.Columns("A:I").Select
xl.Selection.Columns.AutoFit
```

Notice that when `Columns` is used as a property of the `Selection` object it is not prefaced. Prefacing the `Columns`, `Cells`, and `Rows`, properties manually, will ensure you don't unintentionally cause an error.

Running an Excel Macro from Access

Admittedly, bringing your Excel macro-generated code into Access and manipulating the code to run in an Access module can be a daunting prospect for some of you. Fortunately, there is an easier alternative for you.

The alternative is to keep the macro-generated code in Excel and simply fire the macro from Access. That is to say, Access will do nothing more than just call the macro and run it. The following code demonstrates how to fire a macro from Access:

```
Function RunExcelMacro()

'Step 1:  Declare the objects you will work with.
    Dim xl As Excel.Application
    Dim xlwkbk As Excel.Workbook

'Step 2:  Start Excel, then open the target workbook.
    Set xl = New Excel.Application
```

```
    Set xlwkbk = xl.Workbooks.Open("C:\Book1.xlsm")

'Step 3:  Make Excel visible
    xl.Visible = True

'Step 4:  Run the target macro
    xl.Run "Macro1"

'Step 5:  Close and save the workbook, then close Excel
    xlwkbk.Close (True)
    xl.Quit

'Step 6:  Memory Clean up.
    Set xl = Nothing
    Set xlwkbk = Nothing


End Function
```

Step 1: Declaring the Necessary Objects

In Step 1, you first declare two objects:

- xl is an object variable that exposes the Excel Application object.

- xlwkbk is an object variable that exposes the Excel Workbook object.

Step 2: Starting a New Instance of Excel with New Workbook and Worksheet

In Step 2, you create a new instance of Excel, open the target workbook; the workbook that contains the macro you need to run.

Step 3: Making Excel Visible

In Step 3, you make the instance of Excel visible.

Step 4: Running the Target Macro

In Step 4, you run the target macro.

Step 5: Closing and Saving the Target Workbook

In Step 5, you close and save the target workbook. The True argument in xlwkbk.Close(True) indicates that you want the workbook saved after the macro has run. If you do not want to save the target workbook, change this argument to False. Also in Step 5, you quit the Excel application, effectively closing the instance of Excel.

Step 6: Cleaning Up Open Objects

In Step 6, you release the objects assigned to your variables, reducing the chance of any problems caused by rogue objects that may remain open in memory.

Optimizing Macro-Generated Code

There is no arguing that the Excel Macro Recorder can prove to be an invaluable tool when building an automation procedure. The macro-generated code it provides can not only get you up and running quickly, but it can help you learn some of the programming fundamentals in Excel. The one drawback to using macro-generated code however is that the code itself is rather inefficient. This is because the macro recorder not only records the functional actions that give your macro its utility, but it also records mouse moves, mouse clicks, mistakes, redundant actions, and so on. This leaves you with lots of useless code that has nothing to do with macro's original purpose. Although the impact of this superfluous code is typically negligible, larger automation procedures can take speed and performance hits due to these inefficiencies. In that light, it's generally a good practice to take some time to clean up and optimize your macro-generated code.

Removing Navigation Actions

If you want to enter a formula in a cell within Excel, you have to select that cell first, and then enter the formula. Indeed, this is true with most actions; you have to select the cell first, and then perform the action. So as you are recording a macro, you are moving around and clicking each cell on which you need to perform an action. Meanwhile the macro recorder is generating code for all that navigation you are doing. However, the fact is that in VBA, you rarely have to explicitly select a cell before performing an action on it. Therefore, all that code is superfluous and is not needed. Consider the following macro-generated code.

```
Range("A1:I1").Select
Selection.Font.Bold = True
```

In this example, the macro is selecting a range of cells first, and then changing the font style to bold. It's not necessary to select the range first. This code can be changed to read:

```
Range("A1:I1").Font.Bold = True
```

Another version of this type of behavior is shown in the following code.

```
Range("A20").Activate
ActiveCell.FormulaR1C1 = "=4+4"
```

In this example, a cell is activated, then a formula is entered into the cell. Again, it is not necessary to select the cell before entering the formula. This code can be changed to read:

```
Range("A20").FormulaR1C1 = "=4+4"
```

Navigation code typically makes up a majority of the superfluous entries in your macro-generated code. These are easy to spot and change. Remember these general rules:

- If one line contains the word `Select` and the following line contains `Selection`, you can adjust the code.

- If one line contains the word `Activate` and the following line contains `ActiveCell`, you can adjust the code.

Deleting Code That Specifies Default Settings

Certain actions you take in Excel while recording a macro generate a predefined collection of default settings. To demonstrate what this means, open Excel and start recording macro. Click any cell and simply change the Font to 12-point font. Stop the recording. The code that is generated will look similar to this:

```
Range("A2").Select
With Selection.Font
    .Name = "Calibri"
    .Size = 12
    .Strikethrough = False
    .Superscript = False
    .Subscript = False
    .OutlineFont = False
    .Shadow = False
    .Underline = xlUnderlineStyleNone
    .ThemeColor = xlThemeColorLight1
    .TintAndShade = 0
    .ThemeFont = xlThemeFontNone
End With
```

Remember all you did was change the font of one cell, but here you have a litany of properties that reiterate default settings. These default settings are unnecessary and can be removed. This macro can and should be adjusted to read:

```
Range("A2").Font.Size = 12
```

TIP You can easily spot the lines of code that represent default settings because they are usually encapsulated within a `With` statement.

Cleaning Up Double Takes and Mistakes

Although you are recording a macro, you will inevitably make missteps and, as a result, redo actions once or twice. As you can imagine, the macro recorder will steadily record these actions, not knowing they are mistakes. To illustrate this, look at the following code:

```
Range("D5").Select
Selection.NumberFormat = "$#,##0.00"
Selection.NumberFormat = "$#,##0"
Range("D4").Select
Range("D5").Select
Range("A2").Select
With Selection.Font
    .Name = "Calibri"
    .Size = 12
    .Strikethrough = False
    .Superscript = False
    .Subscript = False
    .OutlineFont = False
    .Shadow = False
    .Underline = xlUnderlineStyleNone
    .ThemeColor = xlThemeColorLight1
    .TintAndShade = 0
    .ThemeFont = xlThemeFontNone
End With
Range("A2").Select
With Selection.Font
    .Name = "Calibri"
    .Size = 10
    .Strikethrough = False
    .Superscript = False
    .Subscript = False
    .OutlineFont = False
    .Shadow = False
    .Underline = xlUnderlineStyleNone
    .ThemeColor = xlThemeColorLight1
    .TintAndShade = 0
    .ThemeFont = xlThemeFontNone
End With
Range("D5").Select
```

Believe it or not, there is only one real action being performed here: Change the number format of cell D5. So, why are there so many lines of code? If you look closely, you will see that number formatting has been applied twice, first with two decimal places then with no decimal places. In addition, the font in Cell A2 was changed to 12 point font, then changed back to 10 point font. If you remove these missteps, you get a more efficient set of code.

```
Range("D5").NumberFormat = "$#,##0"
```

TIP When you hit the Undo command while recording a macro, the macro recorder actually erases the lines of code that represent the actions that you are undoing. In that light, make sure you utilize the Undo command before going back to correct your missteps. This ensures that you don't record mistakes along with good actions.

Temporarily Disabling Screen Updating

You will notice that while you are running an Excel macro, your screen flickers and changes as each action is performed. This is because the Excel default behavior is to carry out a screen update with every new action. Unfortunately, screen updating has a negative impact on macros. Because the macro has to wait for the screen to update after every action, macro execution is slowed down. Depending on your system memory, this can have a huge impact on performance.

To resolve this issue, you can temporarily disable screen updating by inserting the following code before your macro-generated code.

```
xl.Application.ScreenUpdating = False
```

To turn screen updating back on, insert the following code after your macro-generated code:

```
xl.Application.ScreenUpdating = True
```

NOTE In the preceding code example `xl` is the variable name assigned to the Excel Application object. This can be different depending on the variable name you give to the Excel Application object.

Automating Access from Excel

It typically doesn't occur to most Excel users to automate Access using Excel. Indeed, it's difficult for most to think of situations where this would even be necessary. Although there are admittedly few mind-blowing reasons to automate Access from Excel, you may find some of the automation tricks found in this section strangely appealing. Who knows? You may even implement a few of them.

Setting the Required References

You should be familiar with the fact that if you want to work with another object's object library, you must set references. To work with Access, you must set a reference to the Microsoft Access Object Library as illustrated in Figure 9-10. In addition to the Access Object Library, you will note that there is also a reference set to the Microsoft DAO Object Library. The *DAO* (Data Access Objects) *library* enables you to easily create and manipulate the database objects within Access.

NOTE It's generally best to select the latest version of the Microsoft DAO library available. You will notice that in Figure 9-10, the latest version of the Microsoft DAO Object Library is 3.6. Don't be too concerned if you only have earlier versions available; the examples in this chapter will run fine with those earlier versions.

At this point, open the Excel workbook called `Chapter9_Sample-Files.xls` installed with the sample files for this book. There you will find the code for the examples in this section. Take some time to review and test each example.

Running an Access Query from Excel

Here's a nifty technique for those of you who often copy and paste the results of your Access queries to Excel. In this technique, you use DAO to run an Access query in the background and output the results to Excel via a Recordset object.

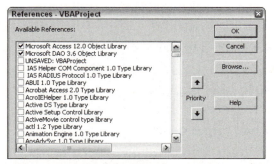

Figure 9-10: When automating Access, you should set a reference to both the Access Object Libraryand the DAO Object Library.

```
Sub RunAccessQuery()

'Step 1:  Declare your variables
    Dim MyDatabase As DAO.Database
    Dim MyQueryDef As DAO.QueryDef
    Dim MyRecordset As DAO.Recordset
    Dim i As Integer

'Step 2:  Identify the database and query
    Set MyDatabase = DBEngine.OpenDatabase _
    ("C:\Integration\IntegrationDatabase.accdb")
    Set MyQueryDef = MyDatabase.QueryDefs("Revenue by Period")

'Step 3:  Open the query
    Set MyRecordset = MyQueryDef.OpenRecordset

'Step 4:  Clear previous contents
    Sheets("Main").Select
    ActiveSheet.Range("A6:K10000").ClearContents

'Step 5:  Copy the recordset to Excel
    ActiveSheet.Range("A7").CopyFromRecordset MyRecordset

'Step 6: Add column heading names to the spreadsheet
    For i = 1 To MyRecordset.Fields.Count
    ActiveSheet.Cells(6, i).Value = MyRecordset.Fields(i - 1).Name
    Next i

End Sub
```

Step 1: Declaring the Necessary Variables

In Step 1, you first declare four variables:

- MyDatabase exposes your application via DAO.
- MyQueryDef is a query definition object that exposes the target query.
- MyRecordset is a Recordset object that holds the results of the data pull.
- i is an integer variable that will be used to add column headings.

Step 2: Setting the Target Database and Target Query

In Step 2, you specify the database that holds your target query as well as which query will be run. Assigning the query to a QueryDef object allows you to essentially open the query in memory.

Step 3: Opening the Query into a Recordset

In Step 3, you literally run the query in memory and output the results to a recordset. When the results are in a recordset, you can use it just as you would any other recordset.

Step 4: Clearing Contents in the Spreadsheet

In Step 4, you are clearing the Main worksheet before copying the recordset. This ensures that all data from the previous pull has been removed before bringing in fresh data.

Step 5: Copying the Recordset into Excel

In Step 5, you use the Excel `CopyFromRecordset` method to get the returned dataset into your spreadsheet. In this example, you are copying the data in the `MyRecordset` object onto the sheet called Main starting at cell A7.

Step 6: Adding Column Headers

In Step 6, you enumerate through each field in the recordset to automatically get the name of each header and enter it into Excel.

Running Access Parameter Queries from Excel

An *Access parameter query* is a kind of interactive query that prompts you for criteria before the query is run. Parameter queries are useful when you need to ask the query different questions using different criteria each time you run it. To get a firm understanding of how a parameter query works, look at the query illustrated in Figure 9-11. With this query, you will get the total revenue for each branch during the 200405 system period.

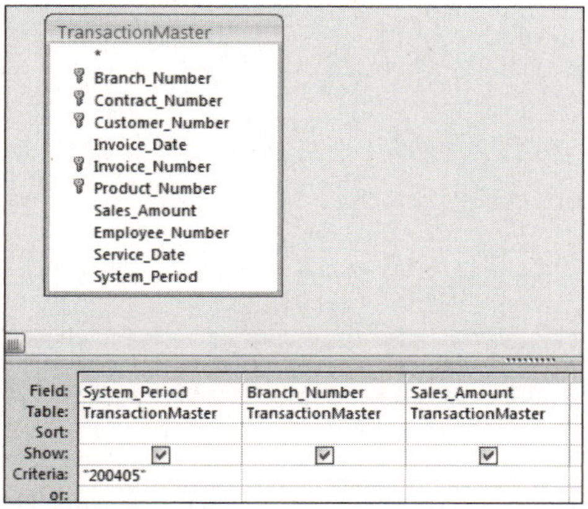

Figure 9-11: This query has a hard-coded criterion for system period.

Although this query gives you what you need, the problem is the criterion for system period is hard-coded as 200405. That means if you want to analyze revenue for a different period, you essentially have to rebuild the query. Using a parameter query allows you to create a *conditional analysis*; that is, an analysis based on variables you specify each time you run the query. Simply replace the hard-coded criteria with text you have enclosed in square brackets ([ ]), as shown in Figure 9-12.

Running a parameter query forces the Enter Parameter Value dialog box to open and ask for a variable (see Figure 9-13). Note that the text typed inside the brackets of the parameter appears in the dialog box. At this point, you would simply enter your parameter.

By the way, you are not in any way limited in the number of parameters you can use in your query. Figure 9-14 demonstrates how you can utilize more than one parameter in a query. When this query is run, you will be prompted for both a system period and a branch number, allowing you to dynamically filter on two data points without ever having to rewrite your query.

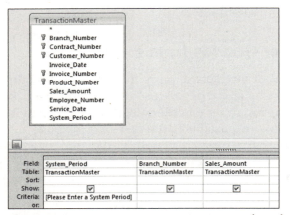

Figure 9-12: To create a parameter query, replace the hard-coded criteria with text enclosed in square brackets ([ ]).

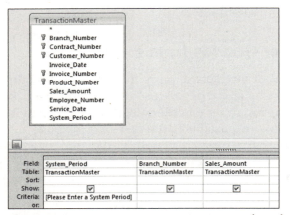

Figure 9-13: Enter your criteria in the Enter Parameter Value dialog box and click OK.

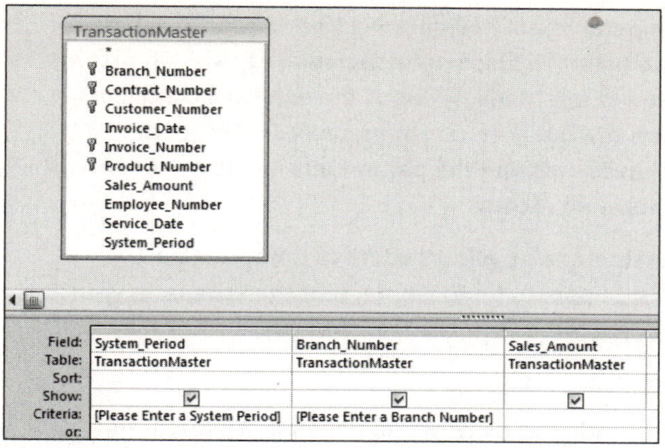

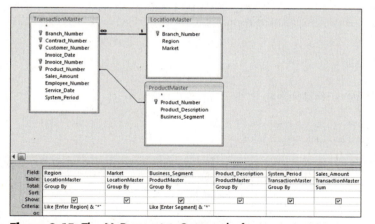

Figure 9-14: You can require multiple parameters in your parameter queries.

The idea behind running an Access parameter query with Excel is simple. Have the user input the parameters on your spreadsheet, then use automation to run the parameter query in memory and output the results to Excel.

In the sample database, you will find a query called `MyParameterQuery`. A quick look at this query in Design view reveals that this query checks for two parameters: region and business segment (see Figure 9-15).

Figure 9-15: The MyParametersQuery asks for two parameters.

TIP You will notice that the parameters in Figure 9-15 have been combined with the asterisk wildcard character (*). This useful technique forces all records to be returned if the parameter is left blank. Without the wildcard characters, blank parameters would cause the query to return no records. This trick essentially gives you the option of entering the parameters to filter the records, or ignore the parameter to return all records.

Using the wildcard with a parameter also allows users to enter in a partial parameter and still get results. Suppose, for example, that the criteria in your parameter query is

```
Like [Enter Lastname] & "*"
```

Entering A as the parameter would return all last names that start with the letter *A*.

Or, suppose the criteria in your parameter query is

```
Like "*" & [Enter Lastname] & "*"
```

Entering A would return all last names that contain the letter *A*.

Figure 9-16 illustrates that the "Chapter9_SampleFiles.xls" workbook has two cells designated as input fields: one for region and one for business segment.

Take a moment to review the code that brings it all together. This technique enables you to build some interesting reporting solutions with relatively little effort.

```
Sub RunAccessQuery()

'Step 1:  Declare your variables
    Dim MyDatabase As DAO.Database
    Dim MyQueryDef As DAO.QueryDef
    Dim MyRecordset As DAO.Recordset
    Dim i As Integer

'Step 2:  Identify the database and query
    Set MyDatabase = DBEngine.OpenDatabase _
    ("C:\Integration\IntegrationDatabase.accdb")
    Set MyQueryDef = MyDatabase.QueryDefs("MyParameterQuery")

'Step 3:  Define the Parameters
    With MyQueryDef
        .Parameters("[Enter Segment]") = Range("D3").Value
        .Parameters("[Enter Region]") = Range("D4").Value
    End With

'Step 4:  Open the query
```

```
          Set MyRecordset = MyQueryDef.OpenRecordset

   'Step 5:  Clear previous contents
          Sheets("Main").Select
          ActiveSheet.Range("A6:K10000").ClearContents

   'Step 6:  Copy the recordset to Excel
          ActiveSheet.Range("A7").CopyFromRecordset MyRecordset

   'Step 7: Add column heading names to the spreadsheet
          For i = 1 To MyRecordset.Fields.Count
          ActiveSheet.Cells(6, i).Value = MyRecordset.Fields(i - 1).Name
          Next i

   End Sub
```

Step 1: Declaring the Necessary Variables

In Step 1, you first declare four variables:

- MyDatabase exposes your application via DAO.
- MyQueryDef is a query definition object that exposes the target query.
- MyRecordset is a Recordset object that holds the results of the data pull.
- i is an integer variable that will be used to add column headings.

Step 2: Setting the Target Database and Target Query

In Step 2, you specify the database that holds your target query as well as which query will be run.

Step 3: Defining Parameters

In Step 3, you expose the query parameters to assign values to each one. As you can see, the name of each parameter matches the parameter name as entered in the Query Design view (see Figure 9-15 earlier). The values assigned to each parameter come from the corresponding input boxes on the Excel spreadsheet (see Figure 9-16 earlier).

Figure 9-16: The input fields correspond with the parameters in the query called MyParameterQuery.

Step 4: Opening the Query into a Recordset

Step 4 runs the query in memory and outputs the results to a recordset.

Step 5: Clearing Contents in the Spreadsheet

Step 5 clears the Main worksheet before copying the recordset, ensuring that all data from the previous pull has been removed before bringing in fresh data.

Step 6: Copying the Recordset into Excel

In Step 6, you use the Excel `CopyFromRecordset` method to get the returned dataset into your spreadsheet.

Step 7: Adding Column Headers

In Step 7, you enumerate through each field in the recordset to automatically get the name of each header and enter it into Excel.

Running an Access Macro from Excel

You can run Access macros from Excel, using automation to fire the macro without opening Access. This technique can not only be useful for running those epic macros that involve a multi-step series of 20 queries, but can also come in handy for everyday tasks like outputting Access data to an Excel file. For example, the code shown here will fire an Access macro that exports a table to an Excel file, and then opens the file with Excel.

NOTE Keep in mind that Access 2007 has new security features that may prevent your macros from running. Feel free to review Chapter 6 to learn how to manage macro security.

```
Sub OpenAccessMacro()

'Step 1:  Declare your variables
    Dim AC As Access.Application

'Step 2:  Start Access and open the target database
    Set AC = New Access.Application
    AC.OpenCurrentDatabase ("C:\Integration\IntegrationDatabase.accdb")

'Step 3:  Open the target report and send to Word
    With AC
        .DoCmd.RunMacro "MyMacro"
        .Quit
    End With

  Workbooks.Open "C:\MyExcel_Output.XLSX"

End Sub
```

Opening an Access Report from Excel

As discussed in Chapter 3, Access reports enable you to build professional looking reports that have a clean PDF-style look and feel. This example demonstrates how you can open your Access reports right from Excel. The appealing thing about this technique is that you don't see Access at all; the report goes straight to a Word rich text file!

> **NOTE** It takes a few seconds for Access to output the target report to rich text format. The larger the report, the longer the conversion takes. With very large reports, you may see the hourglass for a few minutes. Ultimately, you can weigh the options and decide what is your patience threshold.

```
Sub OpenAccessReport()

'Step 1:  Declare your variables
    Dim AC As Access.Application

'Step 2:  Start Access and open the target database
    Set AC = New Access.Application
    AC.OpenCurrentDatabase ("C:\Integration\IntegrationDatabase.accdb")

'Step 3:  Open the target report as a Word rich text file
    With AC
        .DoCmd.OpenReport "Revenue Report", acViewPreview
        .DoCmd.RunCommand acCmdOutputToRTF
        .Quit
    End With

End Sub
```

Opening an Access Form from Excel

There may be instances when you or your clients need to switch focus to an Access form. This example demonstrates how you can open an Access form from Excel.

```
Sub OpenAccessForm()

'Step 1:  Declare your variables
    Dim AC As Access.Application

'Step 2:  Start Access and open the target database
    Set AC = New Access.Application
    AC.OpenCurrentDatabase ("C:\Integration\IntegrationDatabase.accdb")

'Step 3:  Open the target form and make Access visible
```

```
With AC
    .DoCmd.OpenForm "MainForm", acNormal
    .Visible = True
End With

End Sub
```

NOTE You will notice that the last few examples you walked through make use of the Access `DoCmd` object. This object exposes methods that are essentially macro actions. That is to say, if you go to Access and start a new macro, the available actions you will see listed there are the same ones exposed via `DoCmd` methods. What's the point? The point is, you can perform virtually any action that a macro allows you to perform, simply by using the `DoCmd` object. This means that you can build a virtual Access macro strictly with VBA.

Compacting an Access Database from Excel

During your integrated processes, you may routinely increase or decrease the number of records and tables in your database. As time goes on, you will notice that your Access database will grow in file size. This is because Access does not release file space. All the space needed for the data you move in and out of your database will be held by your Access file, regardless whether the data is still there. In that light, it's critical that you run Compact and Repair on your Access database regularly. Among other things, running Compact and Repair database defragments your database, releasing any unused space and ensuring your database does not grow to an unmanageable size. There are several ways to run Compact and Repair on your database.

First, you can Compact and Repair your database manually. To do this, follow these steps:

1. Open your database and click on the Office icon.

2. Choose the Manage button and then select Compact and Repair Database as shown in Figure 9-17.

Figure 9-17: Selecting Compact and Repair Database

Another option is to set your database to automatically compact and repair each time you close it:

1. Click the Office icon in the upper -eft corner of the ribbon, then click the Access Options button. This opens the Access Options dialog box.

2. In the Access Options dialog, select Current Database to display the configuration settings for the current database. It is here that you will see the Compact on Close setting.

3. Select the Compact on Close check box and click the OK button to confirm the change.

Finally, you can compact and repair your database right from code. The following example demonstrates how to run Compact and Repair on an Access database directly from Excel.

```
Sub CompactRepairFromExcel()

'Step 1:  Declare your variables
    Dim OriginalFile As String
    Dim BackupFile As String
    Dim TempFile As String
```

```
'Step 2:   Identify the target database assign file paths
    OriginalFile = "C:\MyDatabase.accdb"
    BackupFile = "C:\MyDatabaseBackup.accdb"
    TempFile = "C:\MyDatabaseTemporary.accdb"

'Step 3:   Make a backup copy of database
    FileCopy OriginalFile, BackupFile

'Step 4:   Perform the compact and repair
    DBEngine.CompactDatabase OriginalFile, TempFile

'Step 5:   Delete the old database
    Kill OriginalFile

'Step 6:   Rename the temporary database to the old database name
    Name TempFile As OriginalFile

End Sub
```

Step 1: Declaring the Necessary Variables

In Step 1, you first declare three string variables that will hold file names.

Step 2: Assigning File Names

In Step 2, you are assigning each of the string variables a file name.

- The `OriginalFile` string variable is assigned the file path and name of the target database. This variable represents your database during the procedure.

- The `BackupFile` string variable is assigned the file path and name of a backup file you create during this procedure.

- The `TempFile` string variable is assigned the file path and name of a temporary file you create during this procedure.

Step 3: Making a Backup Copy of the Target Database

In Step 3, you use the `FileCopy` function to make a backup of the `Original-File` (the target database). Although this step is not necessary for the Compact and Repair procedure, it's generally a good practice to make a backup of your database before running this level of VBA on it.

Step 4: Executing the Compact and Repair

To understand what is going on from this point on, you must understand how Access actually performs the Compact and Repair task. When you compact and repair a database manually, it seems as though Access simply compresses your original database; this is not the case. Access actually creates a second file and essentially copies your original database minus the empty file space. Access then deletes the old file. You need to take the same action with your code.

In that light, Step 4 executes the Compact and Repair, specifying the original database and specifying the file path of the temporary database.

Step 5: Deleting the Old File

At this point, you have two copies of your database: the original database, and a second database, which is a copy of your original without the empty file space. Step 5 deletes the original database, leaving you with the copy.

Step 6: Renaming the Temporary File

In Step 6, you simply rename the temporary file, giving it the name of your original database. This leaves you with a database that is compacted and optimized.

Summary

Both Excel and Access applications have their strengths that you routinely leverage through manual processes. For example, you may routinely crunch data in Access only to bring the results into Excel for presentation. Or you may send Excel data to Access only to open Access and run a set of queries or output a report. The objective of automation is to take all manual intervention out of these processes by controlling one application with another.

Access data processing lends itself quite nicely to automation. The typical automation scenario is one where you send Access data to Excel and then use Excel automation to build charts, PivotTables, or some other presentation mechanism displaying the data. From Excel, you can use Access automation to fire an Access macro, run Access queries or even open Access reports.

Automation can literally take you out of the processes you have set up, allowing them to run without any human interaction.

CHAPTER 10

Integrating Excel and Access with XML

As intimidating as XML may seem, XML is really nothing more than a text file that contains data wrapped in Markup (tags that denote structure and meaning). These tags essentially make a text file machine-readable. The term *machine-readable* essentially means that any application or web-based solution designed to read XML files can discern the structure and content of your file.

Because XML is text-based, XML is not dependent on a specific application for construction, reading, or editing. This versatility makes XML an excellent integration mechanism.

In this chapter, you will gain a solid understanding of the fundamentals of XML. You will also get some context for XML functionality in Excel and Access by exploring some of the ways both Excel and Access allow you to work with XML data through the user interface.

Why XML?

Up to this point, you have explored several integration techniques that use well-established technologies that you are sure to feel comfortable with. So the question is: Why XML? Why should you explore a relatively new technology that, frankly, few in the Excel and Access community are using? There are three major benefits to using XML as an integration mechanism.

With XML, you can bypass those technologies that you may not feel comfortable with such as MS Query, SQL statements, or ADO. Imagine incorporating external data into your Excel or Access processes without the need to manage database connectivity or use complex SQL statements. And because XML files are nothing more than text files, the process of moving and refreshing data, in most cases, is faster and more streamlined.

Second, XML gives you more flexibility than standard text files. With XML, you can import and use only the columns of data that are required as opposed to importing the entire text file. You can also import different parts of the XML file to different locations instead of importing the entire block of text into one table.

The third and possibly most attractive reason to use XML is that you can simply refresh your XML maps to get new data. With text files, you would need to walk through the import process again. Of course, you could write some code to automate the import process, but again, XML enables you to bypass the need for that.

Can you survive without using XML? Sure, you can. However, there are enough attractive possibilities with XML to warrant a closer look.

Understanding XML

Before working with XML functionality, it's important to understand the makeup of an XML document and how each of its syntactic constructs work. Let's take a moment to explore the fundamental components of a standard XML document.

The XML Declaration

The first line of an XML document is called the XML declaration. Look at an example of a typical XML declaration:

```
<?xml version="1.0"? encoding="UTF-8" standalone="Yes"?>
```

The XML declaration typically contains three parts: a version attribute, an optional encoding attribute, and a standalone attribute.

- **Version attribute:** The version attribute tells the processing application that this text file is an XML document.

- **Encoding attribute:** The encoding attribute is primarily used to work around character encoding issues that may be raised when dealing with international characters and those outside of the Unicode/ASCII standard. Because XML documents are inherently Unicode, the encoding attribute is optional if the character encoding used to create the document is UTF-8, UTF16, or ASCII. Indeed, you will find that the character encoding is omitted from many of the XML documents you may encounter.

- **Standalone attribute:** The standalone attribute tells the processing application whether the document references an external data source. If the document contains no reference to external data sources, it is deemed to be stand-alone; thus having the Yes value. Because every XML document is inherently standalone, this attribute is optional for documents that do not reference an external source.

Processing Instructions

As their name implies, processing instructions provide explicit instructions to the processing application. These can be identified by distinctive tags comprised of left and right angle brackets coupled with question marks (<?, ?>). These instructions are typically found directly under the XML declaration and can provide any number of directives. For example, the following processing instruction would direct the use of Excel to open the given XML document.

```
<?mso-application progid="Excel.Sheet"?>
```

Comments

Comments allow XML developers to enter plain-language explanation or remarks about the contents of the document. Just as in VBA where the single quote signifies a comment, XML has its own syntax to denote a comment. Comments in XML begin with the < ! -- characters and end with the --> characters, as in the following example:

```
<!--Document created by Mike Alexander-->
```

Elements

An element is defined by a start tag and an end tag (for example, <MyData> </MyData>). Any data you enter in between the start and end tags makes up the contents of that element. As you can see in the following example, the document begins with <MyTable> and ends with </MyTable>; all the syntax you see in between these tags makes up the content for the MyTable element.

```
<?xml version="1.0"?>
<MyTable>
    <Customer>
        <Quarter>Q1</Quarter>
```

```
        <Region>North</Region>
        <Revenue>25000</Revenue>
    </Customer>
</MyTable>
```

The concept of tags will be a familiar one if you have worked with HTML. However, unlike HTML, tags in XML are not predefined. That is to say, the text "MyTable" has no predefined utility or meaning. You can change that text to anything and it would be all the same to the XML document. And herein, you stumble on the beauty of XML. XML allows you to create custom tags, tags to which you give definition and purpose. As long as you adhere to a few basic rules, you can create and describe any number of elements by creating your own custom tags. Here are the basic syntactic rules that must be followed when creating elements:

- Every element must have a start tag, represented by left and right angle brackets (<>), as well as a corresponding end tag represented by a left angle bracket, backslash and right angle bracket (</>). Naturally, to avoid errors, you need to use the same syntactical name within the start and end tags.

- Names in XML are case sensitive, so the start and end tags of an element must match in case as well as in syntax. For example, an element defined by the tags <Data> </data> would cause a parsing error. XML would be looking for the end tag for <Data> as well as the start tag for </data>.

- You must begin all Element names with a letter or an underscore, never a digit or other character. In addition, names that begin with any permutation of *xml* are reserved and cannot be used.

Elements can contain numbers, text, and even other elements. Elements are normally framed in a parent/child hierarchy. For example, in the MyTable example, the Customer element is a child of the MyTable root element. Likewise, the MyTable element is the parent of the Customer element. Following that logic, the Quarter, Region, and Revenue elements are the children of the Customer element. This parent/child hierarchy allows the XML document to describe the arrangement of the data as well as the content. Later in this chapter, you will discover how this parent/child hierarchy is leveraged to programmatically move around in XML documents.

The Root Element

The root element (which is always the top-most element in an XML document) serves as the container for all the contents within the document. Every XML document must have one (and only one) root element. The MyTable element shown in the following example is the *root element* for this particular XML document:

```
<?xml version="1.0"?>
<MyTable>
     <Customer>
            <Quarter>Q1</Quarter>
            <Region>North</Region>
            <Revenue>25000</Revenue>
     </Customer>
</MyTable>
```

In this example, the root element contains four elements, each one containing its own content.

Attributes

Attributes in XML documents come in two flavors: data attributes and metadata attributes. Data attributes are used to provide the actual data for an element. For example, the following attributes (name and age) provide the data for the Pet element.

```
<Pet name='Spot' age="4">Dog</Pet>
```

Notice that the age attribute is wrapped in quotes although the value itself is a number. This is because unlike elements, attributes are textual. This means that attributes must be wrapped in either single or double quotes.

Metadata attributes typically provide descriptive information about the contents of elements. For instance, in the following example, the Customer element has an attribute called id that provides that customer with a unique identifier.

```
<?xml version="1.0"?>


<MyTable>


        <Customer id="1"/>
        <Quarter>Q1</Quarter>
        <Region>North</Region>
        <Revenue>25000</Revenue>


</MyTable>
```

Many new users of XML find the concept of attributes versus elements a bit confusing. After all, most elements can be easily converted to attributes (or vice versa) and the XML document would parse just fine. For example, the

Customer id attribute could just as easily be presented in an element as such: `<id>1</ id >`. However, there are general rules of thumb that most XML documents seem to adhere to when it comes to elements versus attributes:

- If the content is not an actual data item but is instead a descriptor of the data (record number, index number, unique identifier, and so on), then an attribute is typically used.
- Elements are used for any content that consists of multiple values.
- If there is a chance that the content will expand in structure to include children, elements are typically used.

Namespaces

The idea behind namespaces is simple. Because XML lets developers create and name their own elements and attributes, there is a possibility that a particular name could be used in different contexts. For example, an XML document may use the name ID to describe both a customer id and an invoice id. Namespaces associate overlapping identifiers with Uniform Resource Identifiers (URI), allowing applications that process XML documents to make a distinction between similar names.

A URI is typically made up of a URL and a relative descriptor. For example, the following line defines a namespace. As you can image, xmlns stands for XML namespace.

```
Xmlns="http://www.datapigtechnologies.com/customers"
```

The fact that URLs are used to define namespaces leads many to believe that namespaces point to some sort of online source. The fact is that URLs are only used to provide some semblance of ownership to anyone reading the XML file. The goal of a namespace is merely to create a unique string. So you could technically use something like, `Xmlns="arbitrary_namespace"`, although it wouldn't be very useful in identifying ownership or utility.

As you can imagine, using a URL can lead to some fairly long namespace strings. Most XML developers get around this problem by creating namespace prefixes. A prefix is nothing more than an alias for the namespace. For example, the following namespace uses the prefix dpc. Then the dpc prefix is applied to an attribute.

```
Xmlns:dpc=http://www.datapigtechnologies.com/customers
<Invoice dpc:id="201">
```

You will notice that in the following example the namespace is placed directly into the root element. Any namespace declared within an element is automatically applied to all child elements.

```
<?xml version="1.0"?>
<MyTable xmlns="http://www.datapigtechnologies.com/customers">
    <Customer>
            <Quarter>Q1</Quarter>
            <Region>North</Region>
            <Revenue>25000</Revenue>
    </Customer>
</MyTable>
```

You might be wondering why a namespace would be used in a document where there are no duplicate names. This is primarily to avoid overlapping names with other XML documents that may be used in the same process or application.

Creating a Simple Reporting Solution with XML

In a reporting solution, you would typically have a data layer and a presentation layer. In this section, you will discover how XML can help you easily create a simple reporting solution where Access provides the data and Excel uses the data in some sort of a presentation layer.

Exporting XML Data from Access

Despite the anxiety that some people feel about XML, it's interesting to observe that most of the XML functionality built into Excel and Access requires no programming and little knowledge of databases. That is to say, all the steps you need to create an XML-based reporting solution can be performed using only the user interfaces that come with Excel and Access.

To start the export from Access, right-click on the SalesByRegion table found in the sample database and select Export → XML File. This opens the Export – XML File dialog box in which you specify the location where you would like your XML file to be saved. As shown in Figure 10-1, you want to specify a directory dedicated to your XML files.

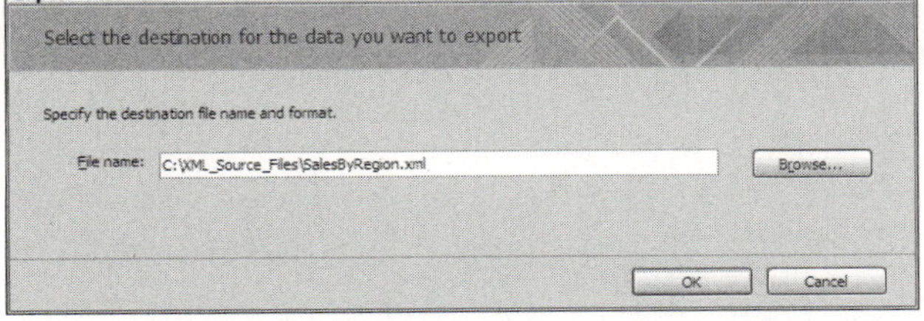

Figure 10-1: Activate the Export – XML File dialog box and specify a location to save your XML File.

TIP You can also start the export process by highlighting a table in your database, selecting the External Data tab in the ribbon, and then selecting More → XML File.

Clicking the OK button activates the Export XML dialog box illustrated in Figure 10-2. Here, you are given the option of exporting the schema definition and presentation specifications as well as the data. In this example, you only want the XML data exported; therefore you will uncheck all but that option in the dialog box.

NOTE The schema defintion exports as an *XSD* (Extensible Schema Definition) document, while the presentation specifications export as an *XSL* (Extensible Stylesheet Language) document. XSD files dictate the layout and sequencing for the data in an XML document, as well as the data types and default values for each element and attribute. An XSL file dictates the formatting rules for the document, controlling the way the XML data is presented. The topics of XSD and XSL are focused on areas outside the scope of this chapter, so we will not cover them in detail here. If you want to learn more about XSD and XSL, feel free to visit www.w3schools.com where you can get free tutorials on these topics.

When you click the OK button, your data will be saved to an XML file located in the location you specified.

Access then gives you the option to save your export process (see Figure 10-3). Here you can save the steps of the export process so you can perform the export at the touch of a button. Simply select that you want to save your export and give your export process a name. As shown in Figure 10-3, you can even create a task reminder in Outlook!

When your export process is saved, you can call it by clicking the Saved Exports button found on the External Data tab in the ribbon. This opens the Manage Data Tasks dialog box shown in Figure 10-4 where you can run your export process as often as you need.

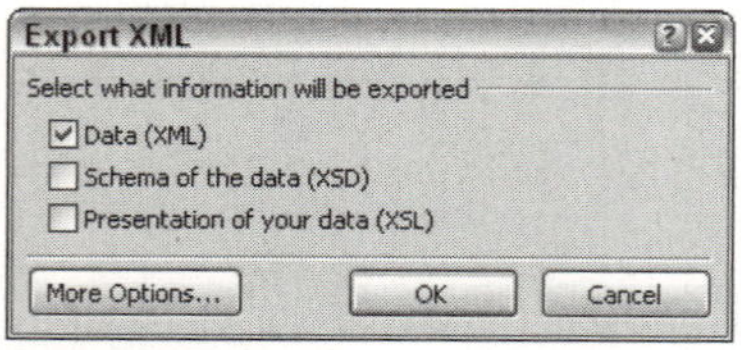

Figure 10-2: Choose to export only the XML file.

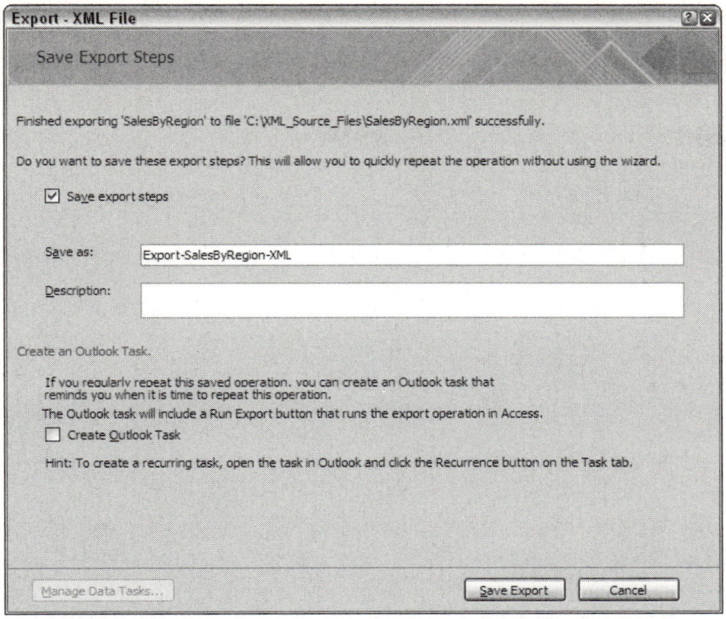

Figure 10-3: You can choose to save your export process so that it may be performed routinely with the touch of a button.

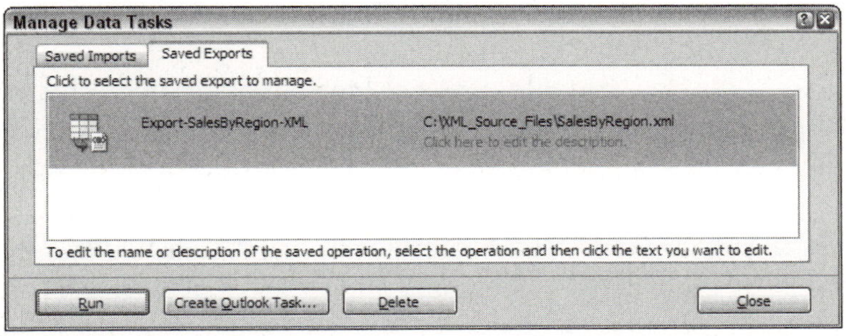

Figure 10-4: You can rerun your saved export process via the Manage Data Tasks dialog box.

As Figure 10-5 illustrates, you can even get fancy and automate your export by calling the saved export via a macro.

> **TIP** Want to export only specific records to XML? Write a query. You can export the results of a query to XML just as you would a table.

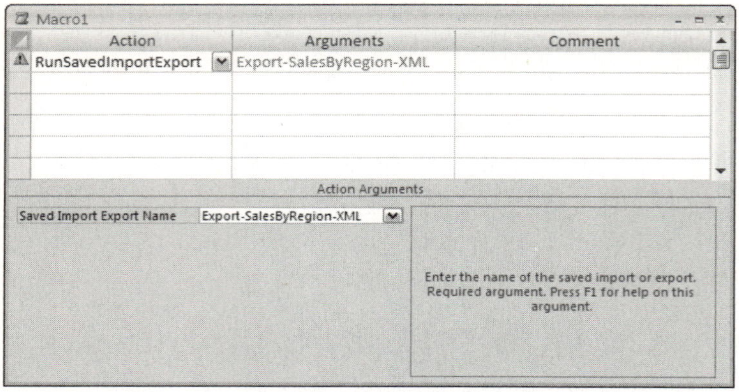

Figure 10-5: You can use the RunSavedImportExport macro action to automate the exporting of your XML data.

Utilizing XML Data in Excel

One of the simplest ways to utilize an XML document in Excel is to open it directly. To help demonstrate this, start Excel and open the `SalesByRegion.xml` file you just saved.

Excel immediately recognizes the file you are opening as an XML document, so it activates the Open XML dialog box shown in Figure 10-6.

Select As an XML table and click OK.

Because the `EmployeeSales.xml` file does not have an associated schema file (XSD), Excel will infer a schema from your XML document. This means Excel essentially creates an internal schema that dictates the rules for the document.

> **TIP** Again, an *XSD* or schema file dictates the layout and sequencing for the data in an XML document, as well as the data types and default values for each element and attribute.

From here, Excel automatically creates an XML list, mapping a range of cells to the elements in the source XML document (see Figure 10-7).

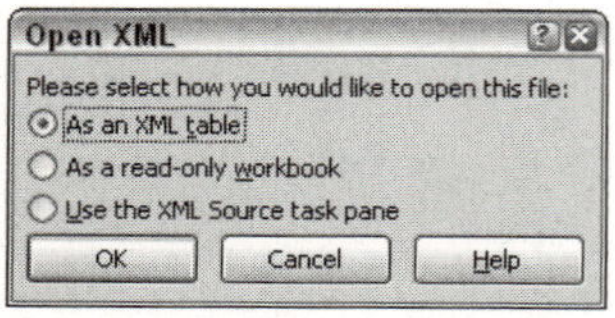

Figure 10-6: Choose to open your XML document as an XML table.

	A	B	C	D	E
1	generated ▾	Market ▾	SalesPeriod ▾	Revenue ▾	UnitsSold ▾
2	12/10/2006 17:03	Asia	P01	301051.0857	893
3	12/10/2006 17:03	Australia	P01	311228.1714	875
4	12/10/2006 17:03	Northern Europe	P01	744090.6286	1921
5	12/10/2006 17:03	South America	P01	346466.0571	1001
6	12/10/2006 17:03	Southern Europe	P01	461854.8571	1253
7	12/10/2006 17:03	United Kingdom	P01	845890.5143	2182
8	12/10/2006 17:03	United States	P01	519995.7143	1420
9	12/10/2006 17:03	Asia	P02	540548.0571	1508
10	12/10/2006 17:03	Australia	P02	500139.5429	1442
11	12/10/2006 17:03	Northern Europe	P02	1439830.914	3661
12	12/10/2006 17:03	South America	P02	474503.6571	1329
13	12/10/2006 17:03	Southern Europe	P02	904641.7714	2490
14	12/10/2006 17:03	United Kingdom	P02	1331700.629	3388
15	12/10/2006 17:03	United States	P02	918489.7714	2495

Figure 10-7: Your XML data is automatically mapped to your workbook.

NOTE You will note in Figure 10-7 that Access has included a field called *generated* specifying the date and time the XML extract was created. You can safely delete this column if it does not suit your needs.

So now what? Well, you can use this data as if it were a normal range. You can create a PivotTable report, build charts, apply some fancy conditional formatting, and so on. The nifty thing about this setup however, is that these cells are linked back to the XML document and can be refreshed with the latest data by right-clicking inside the XML list and selecting XML → Refresh XML Data!

To test out the refresh function, save your Excel file and close it. Now go back to Access and add a few records to the SalesByRegion table as demonstrated in Figure 10-8.

Next, re-export the SalesByRegion XML file. If you saved your export process, you can simply call it by clicking the Saved Exports button found on the External Data tab in the ribbon. If you did not save your export process, you will have to go through the steps of exporting your XML file. Either way, the idea is to replace the previously exported SalesByRegion.XML file. Therefore, you will need to save your export in the exact same file path you used previously.

After you have updated your XML document, you can return to your Excel file and refresh the XML list. As you can see in Figure 10-9, the newly added records will be included in the mapped range.

SalesPeriod ▾	Market ▾	Revenue ▾	UnitsSold ▾
P07	Asia	$100,000	100
P07	Australia	$100,000	100
P07	Northern Europe	$100,000	100
P07	South America	$100,000	100
P07	Southern Europe	$100,000	100
P07	United Kingdom	$100,000	100
P07	United States	$100,000	100
*			

Figure 10-8: Add another period's worth of records to the SalesByRegion table.

	A	B	C	D	E
1	generated	Market	SalesPeriod	Revenue	UnitsSold
44	12/10/2006 17:36	Asia	P07	100000	100
45	12/10/2006 17:36	Australia	P07	100000	100
46	12/10/2006 17:36	Northern Europe	P07	100000	100
47	12/10/2006 17:36	South America	P07	100000	100
48	12/10/2006 17:36	Southern Europe	P07	100000	100
49	12/10/2006 17:36	United Kingdom	P07	100000	100
50	12/10/2006 17:36	United States	P07	100000	100

Figure 10-9: Refreshing the XML list will include update your Excel file with fresh data.

Take a moment now to think about what XML enables you to do. Imagine building an Excel-based reporting system where all data that feeds your PivotTables and charts is linked back to XML files on a network server. You can imagine that those XML files could be updated on a nightly basis using an automated Access process. In addition, your client's workbooks could be designed to automatically refresh on open. Moreover, remember that you are essentially working with a text file, so your clients do not have to worry about server drivers, passwords, and the like.

TIP **If you are interested in programming XML in Excel, feel free to check out *Excel 2007 VBA Programmer's Reference*, published by Wiley, ISBN: 978-0-470-04643-2.**

Creating a Data Entry Process Using XML

In many data entry processes, Excel is used as the interface to enter the data and then the data is sent to an Access database to be stored and analyzed. In this section you will discover how XML can help simplify these sorts of processes as well.

The general idea in this exercise is to create a data entry template in Access and convert that template to an XML file. Then you will use that XML file to create a data entry form in Excel that can be completed and exported back out to XML. The final step is to pick up the XML with Access and import it into source table.

Creating the Data Entry Schema in Access

Start the process by building an Access table that will be used to generate the base XML and the schema file. This table will also be used to capture the results of your data entry exercise. Figure 10-10 illustrates the table that will be used in this example. Save this table as DataEntry.

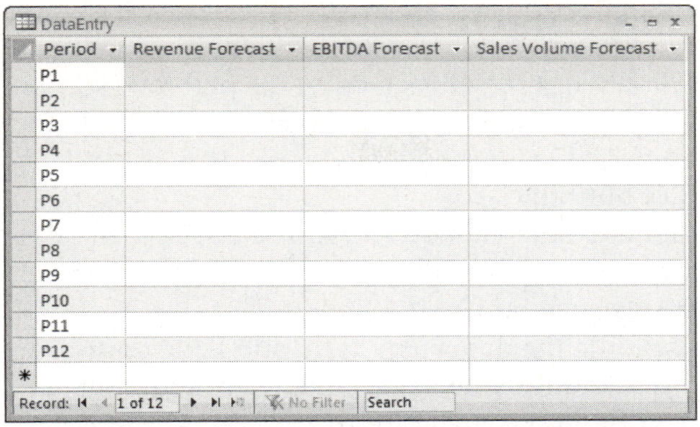

Figure 10-10: Build the Access table shown here and save as DataEntry.

NOTE What's all this talk about a schema file? Well, way back in Figure 10-2, you will remember that you chose to only export only the XML data; not the schema or presentation specifications. In this example, you will tell Access to create the schema file. Why? Doing so, will ensure that Access provides Excel with the information it needs to map the empty fields to your worksheet.

When you have created the source table, you can export an XML file from the source table using the same process outlined in Figures 10-1 through 10-3 earlier in this chapter, with one exception. In the step highlighted in Figure 10-2, you will need to tell Access to create the XSD file. Figure 10-11 illustrates what the Export XML dialog box should look like when both XML and XSD are selected.

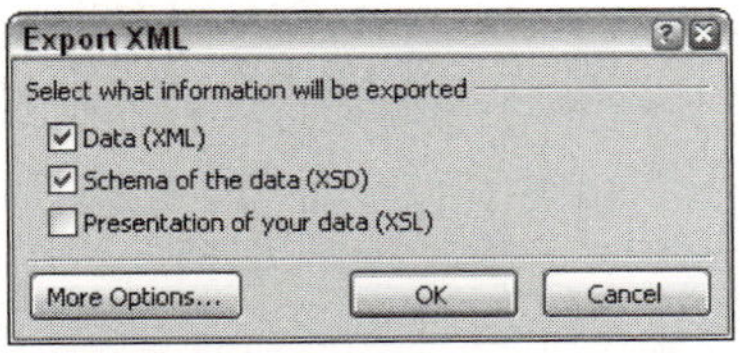

Figure 10-11: Tell Access to create both the XML and XSD files.

Setting Up the Data Entry Form in Excel

Start Excel and open the DataEntry.xml file you saved in the previous section. Excel will immediately recognize that the file you are opening is an XML document, activating the Open XML dialog box shown in Figure 10-12. Select "As an XML table" and click the OK button.

Note that Access has included a field called *generated* specifying the date and time the XML extract was created (see Figure 10-13). You need to delete this column to export your results back into XML.

Obviously, the idea is to distribute the data entry form and have your users complete it. So at this point, you should take some time to format your data entry form, making it easy to work with (see Figure 10-14).

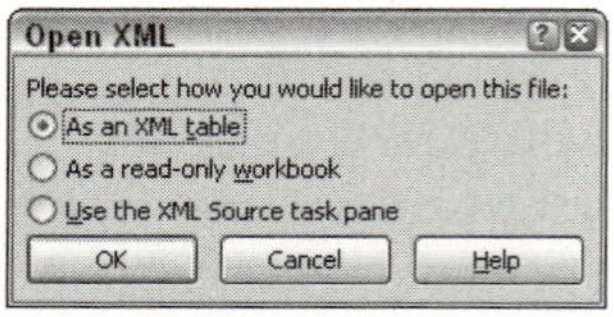

Figure 10-12: Choose to open your XML document as an XML table.

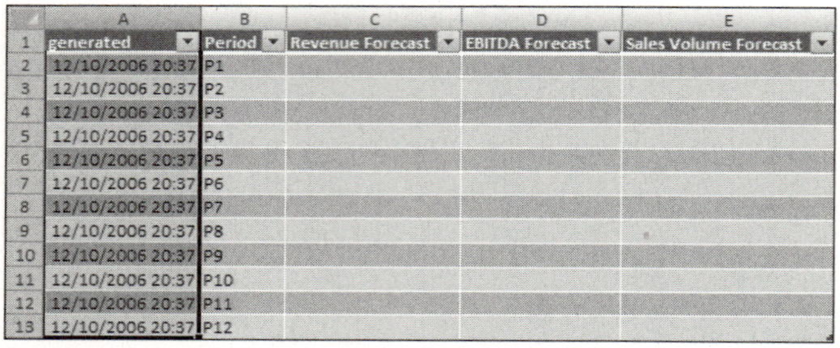

Figure 10-13: Delete the *generated* field.

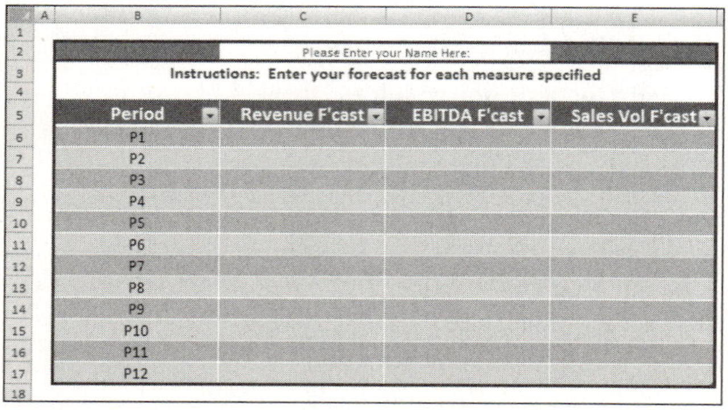

Figure 10-14: Take a moment to format your data entry form.

Exporting Results from Excel to XML

So, how do you get the data back into Access? When the data entry form is completed, Excel can export the data back into an XML file and save that file to a specified location. To test this, fill out your data entry form and right-click anywhere inside the list. This brings up a context menu where you will select XML → Export as shown in Figure 10-15.

Excel asks you to specify the file path of the exported XML. In this example, you replace the DataEntry.xml file you have saved (see Figure 10-16).

TIP Record a macro to capture the process of exporting the data in your XML list to an XML file path. When recorded, you can assign the macro to a button, allowing your users to export their results at the click of a button.

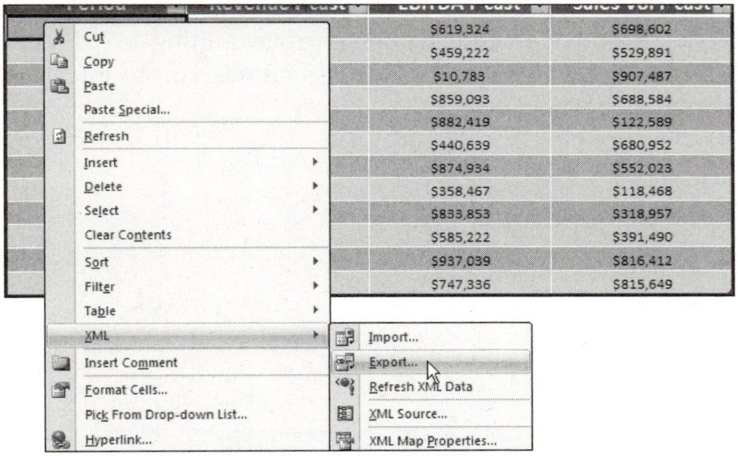

Figure 10-15: Export the data in your list back into an XML file.

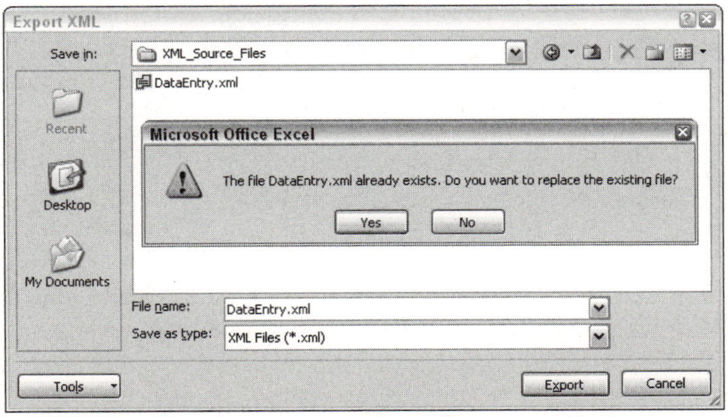

Figure 10-16: Replace the DataEntry.xml file you previously saved.

Getting the Results Back into Access

When you have an XML file with the results, all Access has to do is find the file and import it. Start by selecting the External Data tab in the ribbon. From there, select XML File under the Import group as illustrated in Figure 10-17.

This activates the Get External Data – XML File dialog box (see Figure 10-18) where you will be asked to specify the file path of the XML file you want to import.

When you click OK, the Import XML dialog box allows you to determine how the XML data is imported. As you can see here in Figure 10-19, you can choose to import only the XML structure, both the structure and the data, or you can choose to append only the data to an existing table. Since you have already created a table to capture the data, you will select the last option (Append Data to Existing Table).

After a few clicks, your DataEntry table is updated with the data from the XML file (see Figure 10-19).

Again, no data connections, no MS Query, and no programming are needed. Simply passing XML files between Excel and Access allows you to integrate data between the two programs.

Figure 10-17: Select XML File from the Import group

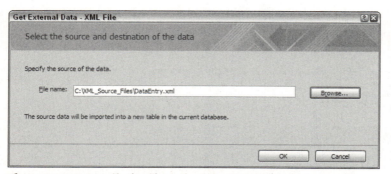

Figure 10-18: Specify the file path of the XML file to be imported.

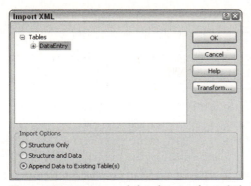

Figure 10-19: Append the data to the existing table DataEntry.

WHERE TO GO FROM HERE

The goal of this chapter is obviously not to make you an expert XML developer. Rather, the goal of this chapter is to give you a solid understanding of the aspects of XML you will need to be familiar with when working with XML in Excel and Access.

There are plenty of resources that expand on the techniques found here. So if the topic of using XML in your Excel and Access processes has captured your imagination, feel free to search these out:

- ◆ www.w3schools.com: This site provides some free tutorials on XML and other technologies such as XSD, Xpath, and so on.

- ◆ *Powering Office 2003 with XML* (ISBN: 978-0-7645-4122-3): Don't let the fact that this book covers Office 2003 deter you. Although Excel and Access 2007 come with new interfaces, the XML functionality in both of these programs remains virtually unchanged. Many of the techniques and exercises found in here work nicely with Office 2007.

- ◆ *Office 2003 XML* (ISBN: 978-0-7645-4122-3): Again, although this book covers Office 2003, many of the techniques and exercises found in here apply to Office 2007.

Summary

An XML document is little more than a text file containing data wrapped in tags denoting structure and meaning. These tags essentially make a text file machine-readable, which means that any application designed to read XML files can discern the structure and content of the XML document. Because XML is text-based, XML is not dependent on a specific application for construction, reading, or editing. This versatility makes XML an excellent integration mechanism.

With XML, you can bypass those technologies that you may not feel comfortable with such as MS Query, SQL statements, or ADO. You can incorporate external data into your Excel or Access processes without the need to manage database connectivity or use complex SQL statements.

Despite the anxiety that some people feel about XML, most of the XML functionality built in to Excel and Access requires no programming and little knowledge of databases. That is to say, all the steps you need to create an XML-based reporting solution can be performed using only the user interfaces that come with Excel and Access. For example, you can open an XML file directly with Excel. Excel immediately recognizes that the file you are opening is an XML document, so it opens the user-friendly Open XML dialog box.

The exercises in this chapter are very basic examples that use only a small fraction of the power of XML. Incorporating a little creative thinking and a handful of code via macros or VBA will allow you to create fairly robust XML-based processes that integrate Excel and Access quite nicely.

CHAPTER 11

Integrating Excel and Other Office Applications

Every data-oriented process has an application flow; a succession of applications that take the data from creation to the user. Sometimes a dataset is touched by only one application, such as when you're creating a report and presenting it in Excel. In many cases, however, data is moved from a database such as Access, is analyzed and aggregated in Excel, then is distributed through a Word document, PowerPoint presentation, or even e-mail.

As you know, the focus of this book has been on the integration of Excel and Access. However, it is worth looking at how Excel integrates with some other Office applications. In this chapter, you will do just that, learning how Excel can be integrated with some of the other applications in the Microsoft Office Suite.

Integrating Excel with Microsoft Word

It's not unusual to see a Word document that contains a table that originated in Excel. In most cases, that table was simply copied and pasted directly into Word. While copying and pasting data from Excel into Word is indeed a valid form of integration, there are countless ways to integrate Excel and Word that go beyond copying and pasting data. This section offers up a few examples, demonstrating different techniques that you can leverage to integrate Excel and Word.

Creating a Dynamic Link to an Excel Table

How many times have you copied and pasted the same Excel table into Word, only because the data changed? There is a better way. You can create a *dynamic link* to your Excel data, allowing your Word document to pick up changes to the table automatically.

When you copy and paste a range, you are simply creating a picture of the range. However, when you create a link to a range, Word stores the location information to your source field and then displays a representation of the linked data. The net effect is that when the data in your source file changes, Word updates its representation of the data to reflect the changes. To test this concept of linking to an Excel range, step through the following example:

1. Open the `Chapter11_SampleFile.xlsm` file and go to the Revenue Table tab. Select and copy the range of cells shown in Figure 11-1.

2. Open a Word document and place your cursor at the location you want the linked table to be displayed. Go to the Home tab in Word and select Paste → Paste Special as demonstrated in Figure 11-2.

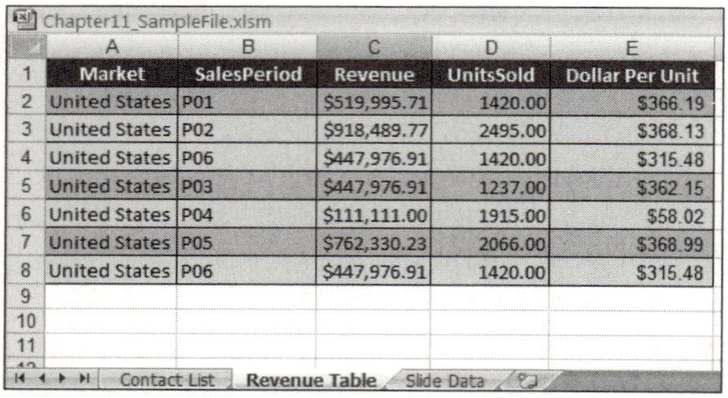

Figure 11-1: Copy your range of cells.

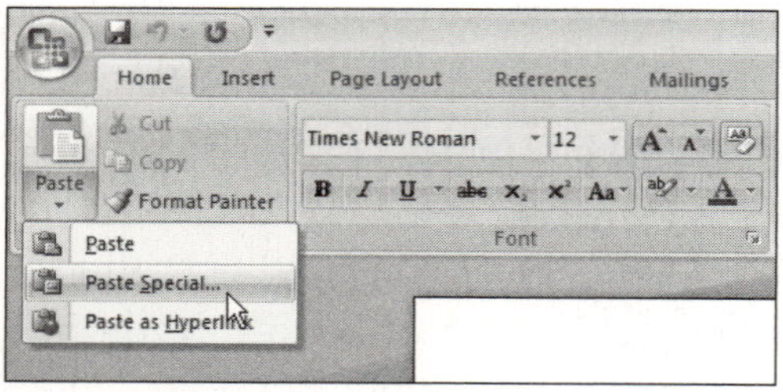

Figure 11-2: Select Paste Special from the Home tab in Word.

3. In the Paste Special dialog box, shown in Figure 11-3, select Paste Link and choose Microsoft Excel Worksheet from the list of document types.

4. Click OK to apply the link. At this point, you will have table that is linked to your Excel file (see Figure 11-4).

5. Open your Excel file and change some data as demonstrated in Figure 11-5.

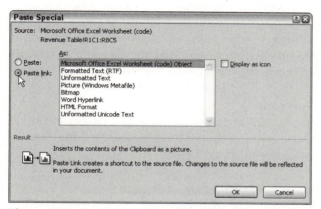

Figure 11-3: Be sure to select Paste Link and set the link as an Excel Workbook.

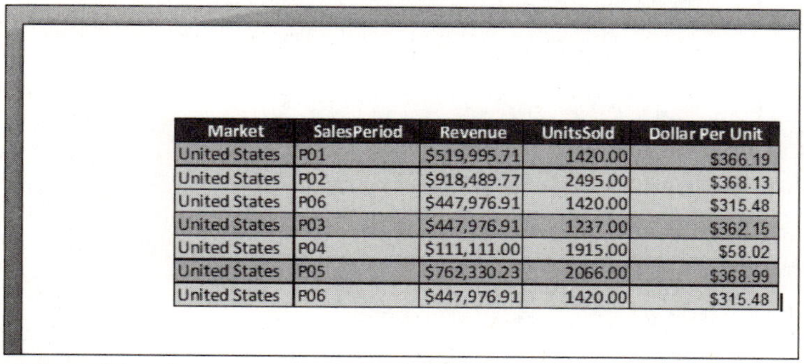

Market	SalesPeriod	Revenue	UnitsSold	Dollar Per Unit
United States	P01	$519,995.71	1420.00	$366.19
United States	P02	$918,489.77	2495.00	$368.13
United States	P06	$447,976.91	1420.00	$315.48
United States	P03	$447,976.91	1237.00	$362.15
United States	P04	$111,111.00	1915.00	$58.02
United States	P05	$762,330.23	2066.00	$368.99
United States	P06	$447,976.91	1420.00	$315.48

Figure 11-4: Your linked table is ready.

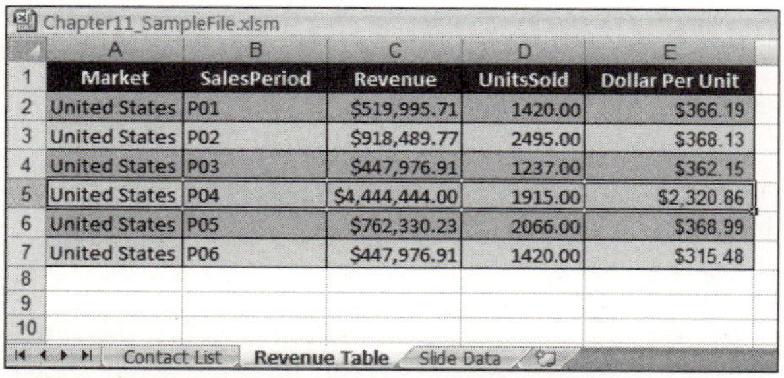

Chapter11_SampleFile.xlsm

	A	B	C	D	E
1	**Market**	**SalesPeriod**	**Revenue**	**UnitsSold**	**Dollar Per Unit**
2	United States	P01	$519,995.71	1420.00	$366.19
3	United States	P02	$918,489.77	2495.00	$368.13
4	United States	P03	$447,976.91	1237.00	$362.15
5	United States	P04	$4,444,444.00	1915.00	$2,320.86
6	United States	P05	$762,330.23	2066.00	$368.99
7	United States	P06	$447,976.91	1420.00	$315.48
8					
9					
10					

Contact List / Revenue Table / Slide Data

Figure 11-5: Make changes to the source Excel range.

6. Upon returning to Word, you will see that your linked table automatically captured the changes (see Figure 11-6)!

Word automatically captured the changes here because both the Word file and the source Excel file were open. Close and save both files and then open Word again. This time you see the message shown in Figure 11-7. Clicking the Yes button refreshes the link.

There may be situations where getting the message you see in Figure 11-7 is not ideal. For example, if you are distributing this document you may not want your clients to see this message. Also, you may have a linked table that contains data that doesn't change that often; no need for Word to automatically refresh on every open. In these situations, you may want to specify that you will always refresh the link manually. That is to say, you don't want Word to automatically try to refresh the link.

Right-click the linked table and select Linked Worksheet Object → Links. This opens the Links dialog box shown in Figure 11-8. Choose the target source file from the Source File list and select Manual Update.

Market	SalesPeriod	Revenue	UnitsSold	Dollar Per Unit
United States	P01	$519,995.71	1420.00	$366.19
United States	P02	$918,489.77	2495.00	$368.13
United States	P03	$447,976.91	1237.00	$362.15
United States	P04	$4,444,444.00	1915.00	$2,320.86
United States	P05	$762,330.23	2066.00	$368.99
United States	P06	$447,976.91	1420.00	$315.48

Figure 11-6: Word automatically captured the changes.

Microsoft Office Word

This document contains links that may refer to other files. Do you want to update this document with the data from the linked files?

Show Help >>

Yes   No

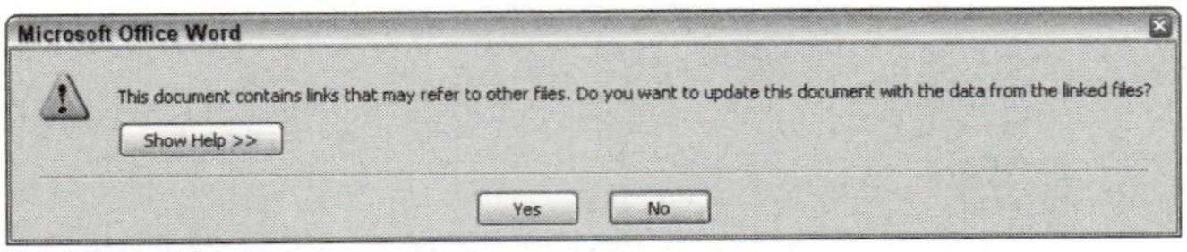

Figure 11-7: Click Yes to refresh the link.

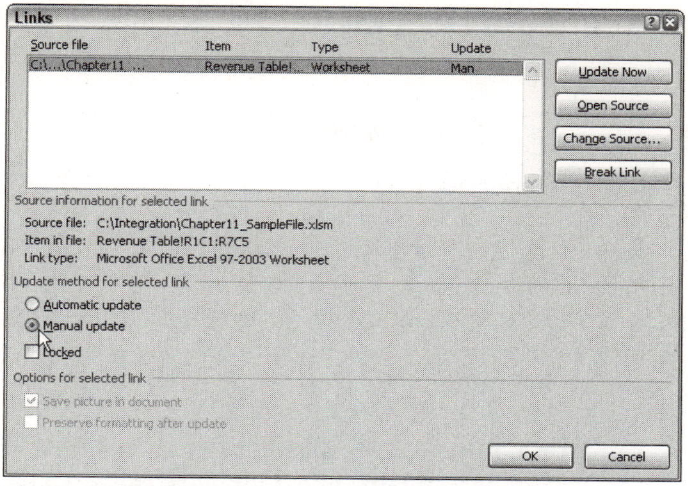

Figure 11-8: Tell Word you will always refresh manually.

To manually refresh the link at any time, simply right-click the linked table and select Update Link as shown in Figure 11-9.

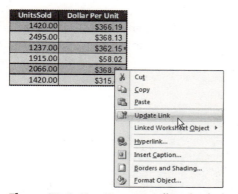

Figure 11-9: You can manually refresh the link at any time.

Getting Excel Data to a Word Document Using Automation

If you're more of the automation type, here is an example of how you can copy an Excel range into a Word document. The idea here is that instead of linking a table, you can create your document on-the-fly.

To set up for a process like this, you must have a template Word document already created. In that document, create a bookmark tagging the location where you want your Excel data to be copied.

To create a bookmark in a Word document, place your cursor where you want the bookmark, select the Insert tab, and select Bookmark. This activates the Bookmark dialog box shown in Figure 11-10. Here, you assign a name for your bookmark and click the Add button.

In the sample files, you will find a document called `PasteTable.docx`. This document is a simple template that contains one bookmark called Data-TableHere. In this example code, you copy a range to that `PasteTable.docx` template, using the DataTableHere bookmark to specify where to paste the copied range.

> **NOTE** This code is designed to run from Excel. Therefore, you will need to set a reference to the Microsoft Word Object Library. To do so, open the Visual Basic Editor in Excel and select **Tools → References**. This opens the Reference dialog box. Scroll down to the entry Microsoft Word *XX* Object Library, where the *XX* is your version of Word, and select it.

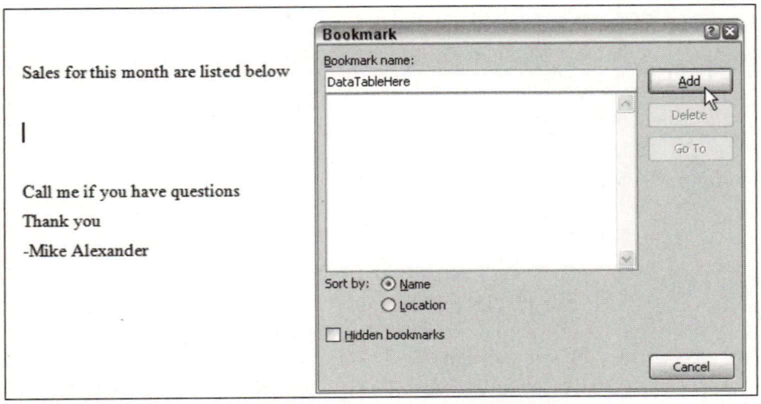

Figure 11-10: Name your bookmark and click Add.

```
Sub PasteExcelTableIntoWord()

'Step 1:  Declare your variables
    Dim MyRange As Excel.Range
    Dim wd As Word.Application
    Dim wdDoc As Word.Document
    Dim WdRange As Word.Range

'Step 2:  Copy the defined range
    Sheets("Revenue Table").Range("A1:E7").Copy

'Step 3:  Open the target Word document
    Set wd = New Word.Application
    Set wdDoc = wd.Documents.Open("C:\Integration\PasteTable.docx")
    wd.Visible = True

'Step 4:  Set focus on the target bookmark
    Set WdRange = wdDoc.Bookmarks("DataTableHere").Range

'Step 5:  Delete the old table and paste new
    On Error Resume Next
    WdRange.Tables(1).Delete
    WdRange.Paste 'paste in the table

'Step 6:  Adjust column widths
    WdRange.Tables(1).Columns.SetWidth _
    (MyRange.Width / MyRange.Columns.Count), wdAdjustSameWidth

'Step 7:  Reinsert the bookmark
    wdDoc.Bookmarks.Add " DataTableHere", WdRange

'Step 8:  Memory cleanup
    Set wd = Nothing
    Set wdDoc = Nothing
    Set WdRange = Nothing

End Sub
```

Step 1: Declaring the Necessary Variables

In Step 1, you first declare four variables:

- MyRange contains the target Excel range you want copied.
- wd is an object variable that exposes the Word Application object.
- wdDoc is an object variable that exposes the Word Document object.
- wdRange is an object variable that exposes the Word Range object.

Step 2: Copying the Excel Range

Step 2 copies a range from the Revenue Table worksheet. In this example, the range is hard-coded, but you can always make this range into something more variable.

Step 3: Opening the Target Word Document

In Step 3, you are opening an existing target Word document that will serve as your template. Note that your are setting the `Visible` property of the Word application to `True`. This ensures that you can see the action in Word as the code runs.

Step 4: Selecting the Target Bookmark

In Step 4, you use the Word `Range` object to set focus on the target bookmark. This essentially selects the bookmark as a range, allowing you to take actions in that range.

Step 5: Deleting the Old Table and Pasting the New Table

In Step 5, you delete any table that may exist within the bookmark, then you paste the copied Excel range. If you don't delete any existing tables first, the copied range will be appended to the existing data.

Step 6: Adjusting Column Widths

When pasting an Excel range in to a Word document, the column widths don't always come out clean. Step 6 fixes this issue by adjusting the column widths. Here, each column's width is set to a number that equals the total width of the table divided by the number of columns in the table.

Step 7: Reinserting the Bookmarks

When you paste your Excel range to the target bookmark, you essentially overwrite the bookmark. In Step 7, you re-create the bookmark to ensure that the next time you run this code, the bookmark is there.

Step 8: Cleaning Up the Open Objects

In Step 8, you release the objects assigned to your variables, reducing the chance of any problems caused by rogue objects that may remain open in memory.

Creating a Word Mail Merge Document

One of the most requested forms of integration with Word is the mail merge. In most cases, *mail merge* refers to the process of creating one letter or document for each customer in a list of customers. For example, suppose you had a list of customers and you wanted to compose a letter to each customer, With mail merge, you can write the body of the letter one time, then run the Mail Merge feature in Word to automatically create a letter for each customer; affixing the appropriate, address, name and other information to each letter.

To create your first mail merge process, walk through this next example:

1. Although it's not necessary, it's typically a good idea to create a template for your mail merge document. Creating a template before-hand allows you to take some time in constructing and formatting your letter or document. Figure 11-11 shows the `MyTemplate.docx` file found in the sample files for this book. Open this file.

2. Click the Mailings tab in Word and click Select Recipients → Use Existing List (see Figure 11-12). This opens a dialog box asking you to select your data source. Find and open `C:\Integration\MyContacts.xlsx`.

Allow me to personally thank you for expressing interest in our services. In response to your inquiry, we have provided a list of our product offerings along with an initial quote. I'm confident you will find our pricing to be extremely competitive.

Product Number	Product Description	Quote
16000	Facility Maintenance and Repair	$132.58
30300	Fleet Maintenance	$169.92
70700	Predictive Maintenance/Preventative Maintenance	$220.20
81150	Cleaning & Housekeeping Services	$581.62
87000	Landscaping/Grounds Care	$232.52
90830	Green Plants and Foliage Care	$189.52

Feel free to contact me with any questions you may have. I am very much looking forward to working with you, and hope to hear from you soon.

Kind Regards,

Mike Alexander
Managing Director
Zalexcorp Integrated Facility Services

Figure 11-11: Open your document template.

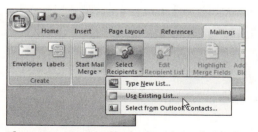

Figure 11-12: Specify the location of your list of recipients.

3. When you open an existing list of resources, you will see the dialog box shown in Figure 11-13. The most notable aspect of this step is that you can specify whether the file you are using as your list of recipients has a header row. If it does, the first row of the dataset is dedicated to column headers.

4. Return to the Mailings tab in Word and select the Address Block command button. This opens the Insert Address Block dialog box shown in Figure 11-14. Here, you specify how you want your address block to be compiled. Word takes all the components that make up an address and compiles them into a standard address format. Word typically does a good job at getting this right the first time, however you can configure the address block if needed.

5. At this point, you will see a marker in your document called Address Block (see Figure 11-15). You can move this tag to the most appropriate location.

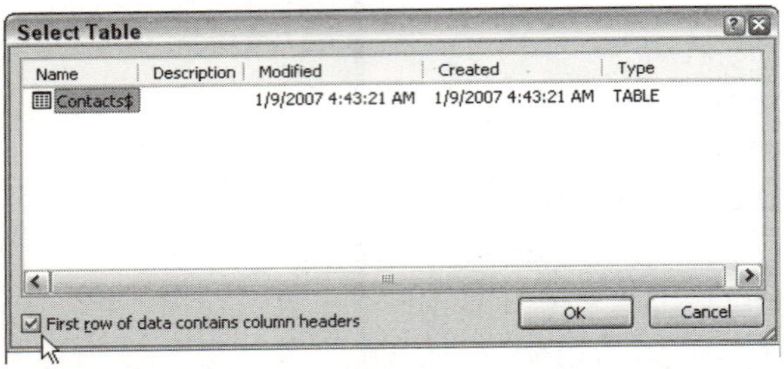

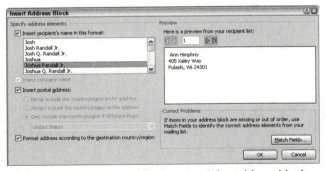

Figure 11-13: Specify whether your list of recipients has a header row.

Figure 11-14: Configure the format of the address block.

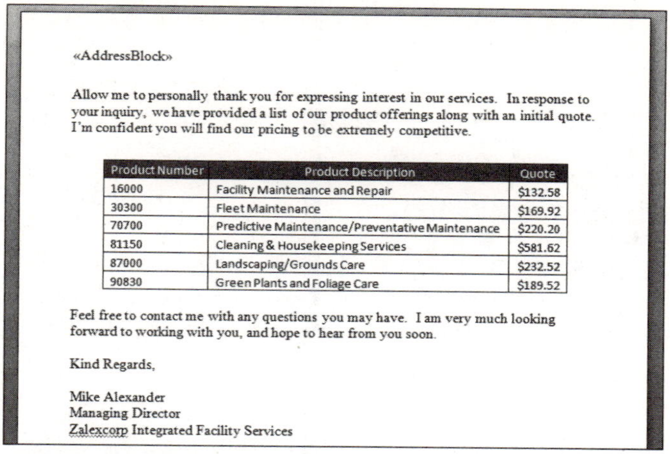

«AddressBlock»

Allow me to personally thank you for expressing interest in our services. In response to your inquiry, we have provided a list of our product offerings along with an initial quote. I'm confident you will find our pricing to be extremely competitive.

Product Number	Product Description	Quote
16000	Facility Maintenance and Repair	$132.58
30300	Fleet Maintenance	$169.92
70700	Predictive Maintenance/Preventative Maintenance	$220.20
81150	Cleaning & Housekeeping Services	$581.62
87000	Landscaping/Grounds Care	$232.52
90830	Green Plants and Foliage Care	$189.52

Feel free to contact me with any questions you may have. I am very much looking forward to working with you, and hope to hear from you soon.

Kind Regards,

Mike Alexander
Managing Director
Zalexcorp Integrated Facility Services

Figure 11-15: An address block marker is used to define where the address block will be placed.

6. Go back to the Mailings tab in Word and select the Greeting Line command button. This opens the dialog box shown in Figure 11-16. Here, you specify how you want your greetings to be configured.

7. At this point, you see an additional marker in your document called Greeting Line (see Figure 11-17). Again, you can move this tag to the location that is most appropriate.

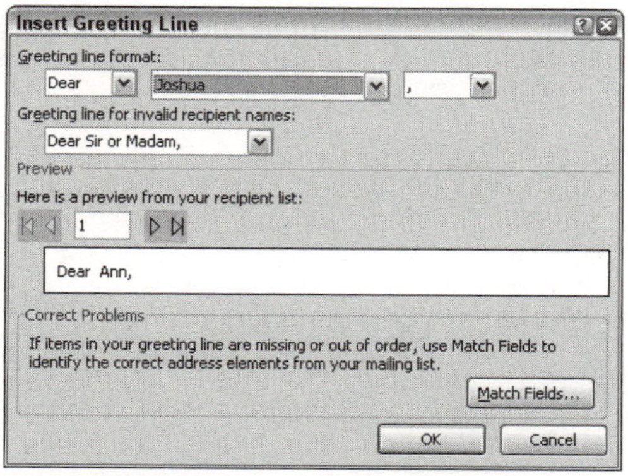

Figure 11-16: Configure the format of the greeting line.

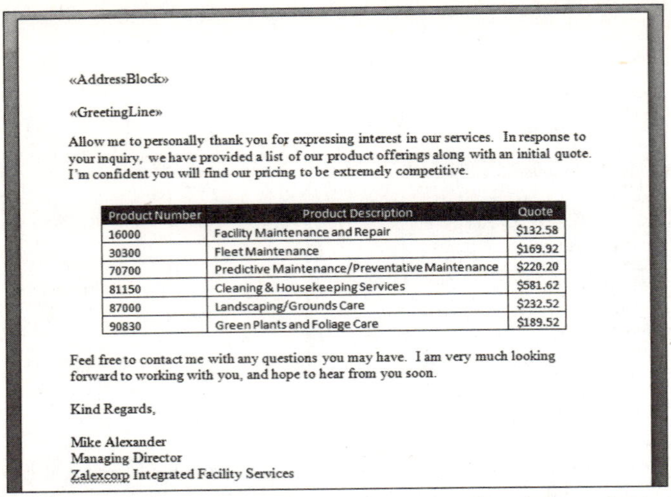

«AddressBlock»

«GreetingLine»

Allow me to personally thank you for expressing interest in our services. In response to your inquiry, we have provided a list of our product offerings along with an initial quote. I'm confident you will find our pricing to be extremely competitive.

Product Number	Product Description	Quote
16000	Facility Maintenance and Repair	$132.58
30300	Fleet Maintenance	$169.92
70700	Predictive Maintenance/Preventative Maintenance	$220.20
81150	Cleaning & Housekeeping Services	$581.62
87000	Landscaping/Grounds Care	$232.52
90830	Green Plants and Foliage Care	$189.52

Feel free to contact me with any questions you may have. I am very much looking forward to working with you, and hope to hear from you soon.

Kind Regards,

Mike Alexander
Managing Director
Zalexcorp Integrated Facility Services

Figure 11-17: A greeting line marker is used to define where the greeting will be placed.

8. Return to the Mailings tab and select the Finish and Merge command button. As shown in Figure 11-18, you can choose to edit the documents, print the documents, or send each document via e-mail. In this case, select Edit Individual Documents.

   As shown in Figure 11-19, the final product is a set of Word documents that contain your original template with personalized contact information for each person in your Excel contacts list.

Figure 11-18: Activate the mail merge and choose to edit the documents.

Ann Himphriy
405 Xaley Way
Pulaski, VA 24301

Dear Ann,

Allow me to personally thank you for expressing interest in our services. In response to
your inquiry, we have provided a list of our product offerings along with an initial quote.
I'm confident you will find our pricing to be extremely competitive.

Product Number	Product Description	Quote
16000	Facility Maintenance and Repair	$132.58
30300	Fleet Maintenance	$169.92
70700	Predictive Maintenance/Preventative Maintenance	$220.20
81150	Cleaning & Housekeeping Services	$581.62
87000	Landscaping/Grounds Care	$232.52
90830	Green Plants and Foliage Care	$189.52

Feel free to contact me with any questions you may have. I am very much looking
forward to working with you, and hope to hear from you soon.

Kind Regards,

Mike Alexander
Managing Director
Zalexcorp Integrated Facility Services

Figure 11-19: You have successfully performed your first mail merge!

Simulating the Word Mail Merge Function from Excel

If you're an automation buff, know that you can also simulate the Word Mail
Merge function from Excel. The idea is fairly simple. You start with a template
that contains bookmarks identifying where each element of contact information will go.

NOTE To see the template that will be used by this code, open the
`MailMerge.docx` document found in the sample files for this book.

With the template set, you simply loop through each contact in your list,
assigning the component pieces of their contact information to the respective
bookmarks.

```
Private Sub MailMergeWithExcel()

'Step 1:  Declare your variables
    Dim wd As Word.Application
    Dim wdDoc As Word.Document
    Dim MyRange As Excel.Range
    Dim MyCell As Excel.Range
    Dim txtAddress As String
    Dim txtCity As String
    Dim txtState As String
    Dim txtPostalCode As String
    Dim txtFname As String
```

```
        Dim txtFullname As String

'Step 2:  Start Word and add a new document
    Set wd = New Word.Application
    Set wdDoc = wd.Documents.Add
    wd.Visible = True

'Step 3:  Set the range of your contact list
    Set MyRange = Sheets("Contact List").Range("A2:A21")

'Step 4:  Start the loop through each cell
    For Each MyCell In MyRange.Cells

'Step 5:  Assign values to each component of the letter
    txtAddress = MyCell.Value
    txtCity = MyCell.Offset(, 1).Value
    txtState = MyCell.Offset(, 2).Value
    txtPostalCode = MyCell.Offset(, 3).Value
    txtFname = MyCell.Offset(, 5).Value
    txtFullname = MyCell.Offset(, 6).Value

'Step 6:Insert the structure of your template document
    wd.Selection.InsertFile "C:\Integration\MailMerge.docx"

'Step 7:  Fill each relevant bookmark with its respective value
    wd.Selection.Goto What:=wdGoToBookmark, Name:="Customer"
    wd.Selection.TypeText Text:=txtFullname

    wd.Selection.Goto What:=wdGoToBookmark, Name:="Address"
    wd.Selection.TypeText Text:=txtAddress

    wd.Selection.Goto What:=wdGoToBookmark, Name:="City"
    wd.Selection.TypeText Text:=txtCity

    wd.Selection.Goto What:=wdGoToBookmark, Name:="State"
    wd.Selection.TypeText Text:=txtState

    wd.Selection.Goto What:=wdGoToBookmark, Name:="Zip"
    wd.Selection.TypeText Text:=txtPostalCode

    wd.Selection.Goto What:=wdGoToBookmark, Name:="FirstName"
    wd.Selection.TypeText Text:=txtFname

'Step 8:  Clear any remaining bookmarks
    On Error Resume Next
    wdDoc.Bookmarks("Address").Delete
    wdDoc.Bookmarks("Customer").Delete
    wdDoc.Bookmarks("City").Delete
    wdDoc.Bookmarks("State").Delete
    wdDoc.Bookmarks("FirstName").Delete
```

```
        wdDoc.Bookmarks("Zip").Delete

'Step 9:  Go to the end, insert new page, and start with the next cell
        wd.Selection.EndKey Unit:=wdStory
        wd.Selection.InsertBreak Type:=wdPageBreak
        Next MyCell

'Step 10:  Set cursor to beginning and clean up memory
        wd.Selection.HomeKey Unit:=wdStory
        wd.Activate
        Set wd = Nothing
        Set wdDoc = Nothing

End Sub
```

Step 1: Declaring the Necessary Variables

In Step 1, you first declare four variables:

- wd is an object variable that exposes the Word `Application` object.
- wdDoc is an object variable that exposes the Word `Document` object.
- MyRange contains the range defining the contact list.
- MyCell is used to pass cell values into the string variables.

Then you declare six string variables. Each of the string variables holds a component piece of information for each contact in the contact list.

Step 2: Opening Word and Starting a New Document

Step 2 opens Word with a blank document. Note that you are setting the `Visible` property of the Word application to `True`. This ensures that you can see the action in Word as the code runs.

Step 3: Setting the Range of the Contact List

Step 3 defines each contact in the contact list. Note that this range only selects the first column in the contacts table. This is because each cell in the range must be passed individually to string variables. Selecting only the first column gives you one cell per row. From that one cell, you can easily adjust your cursor to the right or left to capture the cells around it. The idea is that if you move to the right one space, you will get the value of the next field in that row. If you move to the right two spaces, you will get the value of that field, and so on.

Step 4: Starting Looping Through Each Contact

Step 4 starts the loop through each contact as defined in the range set in Step 3.

Step 5: Assigning Values to Each Component Piece of the Contact's Information

In Step 5, you use the Excel `Offset` method to capture the value of each field in a particular row. You start with the range defined in Step 3 (the first column in the list of contacts). You then use `Offset` to move your cursor a certain number of columns to the right to capture the data in each relevant field. As each field is covered, you assign its value to the appropriate string variable.

Step 6: Inserting the Structure of Your Template

In Step 6, you insert your existing template into the empty document in Word. This is tantamount to copying the structure of your template and pasting it into a blank document.

Step 7: Assigning Values to the Bookmarks

In Step 7, you assign the value of each string variable to its respective bookmark. As you can see in the code, you simply select the bookmark by name, then change the text to equal the value of the assigned string variable.

Step 8: Deleting Bookmarks

The goal in Step 8 is to remove any stray bookmarks. If any bookmarks linger, you will get duplicate bookmarks as the procedure loops through each cell.

Step 9: Inserting a New Document and Looping to Next Contact

At this point in the code, you have created a document for one contact in your list of contacts. The idea now is to create a new blank document so that you can perform the same procedure for the next contact. Inserting a page break effectively creates the blank document. You then loop back to Step 5 where you pick up the contact information for the next row in the list. Then at Step 6, you insert the blank template (complete with bookmarks) into the new page. Finally, you assign values to the bookmarks and clean up. The `For...Next` loop ensures that this cycle is repeated for each row in your contact list.

Step 10: Cleaning Up the Open Objects

In Step 10, you release the objects assigned to your variables, reducing the chance of any problems caused by rogue objects that may remain open in memory.

Integrating Excel with PowerPoint

Many PowerPoint presentations contain data that has been copied from Excel. It's often much easier to analyze and create charts and data views in Excel than in PowerPoint. After those charts and data views have been created, why *wouldn't* you simply copy them into PowerPoint? The time and effort saved by copying directly from Excel is too good to pass up.

This section offers up a few techniques that can help you automate the process of getting your Excel data into PowerPoint.

Creating a PowerPoint Slide with a Title

To help get a few fundamentals down, start simple and automate the creation of a PowerPoint presentation containing one slide with a title. The idea is that you place this code into an Excel module and run it directly from Excel.

Keep in mind that because this code will be run from Excel, you will need to set a reference to the Microsoft PowerPoint Object Library. Again, you can set the reference by opening the Visual Basic Editor in Excel and selecting Tools → References. Scroll down to the entry Microsoft PowerPoint *XX* Object Library, where the *XX* is your version of PowerPoint, and select it.

```
Sub CreatePowerPointSlideWithTitle()

'Step 1:  Declare variables
    Dim PP As PowerPoint.Application
    Dim PPPres As PowerPoint.Presentation
    Dim PPSlide As PowerPoint.Slide
    Dim SlideTitle As String

'Step 2:  Open PowerPoint and create new presentation
    Set PP = New PowerPoint.Application
    Set PPPres = PP.Presentations.Add
    PP.Visible = True

'Step 3:  Add new slide as slide 1 and set focus to it
    Set PPSlide = PPPres.Slides.Add(1, ppLayoutTitleOnly)
    PPSlide.Select

'Step 4:  Add the title to the slide
    SlideTitle = "My First PowerPoint Slide"
    PPSlide.Shapes.Title.TextFrame.TextRange.Text = SlideTitle

'Step 5:  Save the slide
    PPPres.SaveAs "C:\MyFirstPresentation.pptx"
    PP.Activate

'Step 6:  Memory Cleanup
    Set PPSlide = Nothing
    Set PPPres = Nothing
    Set PP = Nothing

End sub
```

Step 1: Declaring the Necessary Variables

In Step 1, you first declare four variables:

- PP is an object variable that exposes the PowerPoint Application object.
- PPPres is an object variable that exposes the PowerPoint Presentation object.
- PPSlide is an object variable that exposes the PowerPoint Slide object.
- SlideTitle is a string variable used to pass the text for the slide title.

Step 2: Opening PowerPoint and Starting a New Presentation

Step 2 opens PowerPoint with an empty presentation. Note that you are setting the Visible property of the PowerPoint application to True. This ensures that you can see the action as the code runs.

Step 3: Adding a New Slide

In Step 3, you add a new slide to the presentation using the Add method of Slide object. Note that when you add a new slide, you'll need to provide two arguments: the index number for the slide and the layout option for the slide. Since this is the first slide in the presentation, the index number is 1. The default layout option enables you to specify which one of many PowerPoint layout options you want to apply to your slide. When you're automating Power Point, it's generally best to use either ppLayoutTitleOnly (when you want a title in your presentation) or ppLayoutBlank (when you don't need a title in your presentation).

Step 4: Adding the Title to the Slide

In Step 4, you store the text for the title in a string variable, then pass that variable to PowerPoint to apply text to the title text frame.

Step 5: Saving the Presentation

Step 5 saves the presentations to the C drive. Note also that you use the Activate method. This sets the focus on PowerPoint, ensuring that is comes into view when the code is done running.

Step 6: Cleaning Up the Open Objects

In Step 6, you release the objects assigned to your variables, reducing the chance of any problems caused by rogue objects that may remain open in memory.

Copying a Range of Cells to a Presentation

Now that you have a good sense of the basic code to create a PowerPoint presentation, you can add some utility and actually copy a range from Excel into PowerPoint presentation. In this example, you are copying a range from the `Chapter11_SampleFile.xlsm` file and pasting that range to a slide in a newly created PowerPoint presentation.

```
Sub CopyRangeToPresentation ()

'Step 1:  Declare your variables
    Dim PP As PowerPoint.Application
    Dim PPPres As PowerPoint.Presentation
    Dim PPSlide As PowerPoint.Slide
    Dim SlideTitle As String

'Step 2:  Open PowerPoint and create new presentation
    Set PP = New PowerPoint.Application
    Set PPPres = PP.Presentations.Add
    PP.Visible = True

'Step 3:  Add new slide as slide 1 and set focus to it
    Set PPSlide = PPPres.Slides.Add(1, ppLayoutTitleOnly)
    PPSlide.Select

'Step 4:  Copy the range as a picture
    Sheets("Slide Data").Range("A1:J28").CopyPicture _
    Appearance:=xlScreen, Format:=xlPicture

'Step 5:  Paste the picture and adjust its position
    PPSlide.Shapes.Paste.Select
    PP.ActiveWindow.Selection.ShapeRange.Align msoAlignCenters, True
    PP.ActiveWindow.Selection.ShapeRange.Align msoAlignMiddles, True

'Step 6:  Add the title to the slide
    SlideTitle = "My First PowerPoint Slide"
    PPSlide.Shapes.Title.TextFrame.TextRange.Text = SlideTitle

'Step 7:  Memory Cleanup
    PP.Activate
    Set PPSlide = Nothing
    Set PPPres = Nothing
    Set PP = Nothing

End sub
```

Step 1: Declaring the Necessary Variables

In Step 1, you first declare four variables:

- PP is an object variable that exposes the PowerPoint Application object.

- PPPres is an object variable that exposes the PowerPoint Presentation object.

- PPSlide is an object variable that exposes the PowerPoint Slide object.

- SlideTitle is a string variable used to pass the text for the slide title.

Step 2: Opening PowerPoint and Starting a New Presentation

Step 2 opens PowerPoint with an empty presentation. Note that you are setting the Visible property of the PowerPoint application to True. This ensures that you can see the action as the code runs.

Step 3: Adding a New Slide and Setting Focus to It

In Step 3, you add a new slide to the presentation using the Add method of Slide object. Note that you are using ppLayoutTitleOnly, ensuring your slide is created with a title text frame. You then take an extra step here and actually set focus on the slide. That is to say you explicitly tell PowerPoint to select this slide, making it active.

Step 4: Copying your Range as a Picture

In Step 4, use the CopyPicture method to copy the target range as a picture. The range being copied here is range A1 to J28 in the Slide Data tab.

Step 5: Pasting the Picture into the Presentation

Step 5 pastes the picture into the active slide and centers the picture both horizontally and vertically.

Step 6: Adding the Title to the Slide

In Step 6, you store the text for the title in a string variable, then pass that variable to PowerPoint to apply text to the title text frame.

Step 7: Cleaning Up the Open Objects

In Step 7, you release the objects assigned to your variables, reducing the chance of any problems caused by rogue objects that may remain open in memory.

Sending All Excel Charts to the Presentation

It's not uncommon to see multiple charts on one worksheet. For example, open the `Chapter11_SampleFile.xlsm` sample file and go to the Slide Data tab. There, you will see a worksheet that contains multiple charts; one for each Region. The idea is that you should be able to automate the process of copying each one of these charts into its own slide.

The following example code does just that. In this code, you loop through each chart in the specified worksheet, copying each and pasting it into its own slide in PowerPoint.

```
Sub CopyAllChartsToPresentation()

'Step 1:  Declare your variables
    Dim PP As PowerPoint.Application
    Dim PPPres As PowerPoint.Presentation
    Dim PPSlide As PowerPoint.Slide
    Dim i As Integer

'Step 2:  Check for charts; exit if no charts exist
    Sheets("Slide Data").Select
    If ActiveSheet.ChartObjects.Count < 1 Then
    MsgBox "No charts existing the active sheet"
    Exit Sub
    End If

'Step 3:  Open PowerPoint and create new presentation
    Set PP = New PowerPoint.Application
    Set PPPres = PP.Presentations.Add
    PP.Visible = True

'Step 4:  Start the loop based on chart count
    For i = 1 To ActiveSheet.ChartObjects.Count

'Step 5:  Copy the chart as a picture
    ActiveSheet.ChartObjects(i).Chart.CopyPicture _
    Size:=xlScreen, Format:=xlPicture

'Step 6:  Count slides and add new slide as next available slide number
    ppSlideCount = PPPres.Slides.Count
    Set PPSlide = PPPres.Slides.Add(SlideCount + 1, ppLayoutBlank)
    PPSlide.Select

'Step 7:  Paste the picture and adjust its position; Go to next chart
    PPSlide.Shapes.Paste.Select
    PP.ActiveWindow.Selection.ShapeRange.Align msoAlignCenters, True
    PP.ActiveWindow.Selection.ShapeRange.Align msoAlignMiddles, True
```

```
     Next i

'Step 8:  Memory Cleanup
     Set PPSlide = Nothing
     Set PPPres = Nothing
     Set PP = Nothing

End Sub
```

Step 1: Declaring the Necessary Variables

In Step 1, you first declare four variables:

- PP is an object variable that exposes the PowerPoint Application object.

- PPPres is an object variable that exposes the PowerPoint Presentation object.

- PPSlide is an object variable that exposes the PowerPoint Slide object.

- i is used as a counter to help loop through the charts in the worksheet.

Step 2: Checking for Charts

Step 2 is an administrative check to ensure there are actually charts in the specified worksheet. If no charts are found, then you exit the procedure with no further action.

Step 3: Opening PowerPoint and Starting a New Presentation

Step 3 opens PowerPoint with an empty presentation. Note that you are setting the Visible property of the PowerPoint application to True. This ensures that you can see the action as the code runs.

Step 4: Starting Looping Through the Charts

In Step 4, you establish how many times you will loop through the procedure by capturing the number of charts in the worksheet. In other words, if there are five charts in the worksheet, you will loop five times. You start the loop with 1 and keep looping through the procedure until you hit the number of charts in the worksheet. The variable i ultimately represents the chart number you are currently on.

Step 5: Copying Your Chart as a Picture

In Step 5, use the CopyPicture method to copy the chart as a picture. The variable i passes the actual chart number you are currently working with.

Step 6: Counting the Slides and Adding a New Slide at the Next Available Index

In Step 6, you add a new slide to the presentation using the `Add` method of the `Slide` object. You will notice that you are using `SlideCount+1` to specify the index number of the added slide. Because you are looping through an unknown number of charts, you can't hard-code the index number for each slide. Using `SlideCount+1` enables you to dynamically assign the next available number as the slide index.

You will also note that you are using `ppLayoutBlank`, ensuring that the newly created slides start with a blank layout. You then take an extra step and actually set focus on the slide. That is to say you explicitly tell PowerPoint to select this slide, making it active.

Step 7: Pasting the Chart into the Presentation and Moving to Next Chart

Step 7 pastes the picture into the active slide, centers the picture both horizontally and vertically, then moves to the next chart.

Step 8: Cleaning Up the Open Objects

In Step 8, you release the objects assigned to your variables, reducing the chance of any problems caused by rogue objects that may remain open in memory.

Converting a Workbook into a PowerPoint Presentation

This last example takes the concept of using Excel data in PowerPoint to the extreme. Open the sample workbook called `WorkbooktoPowerpoint .xlsm`. In this workbook, you will notice that each worksheet contains its own data about a region. It's almost like each worksheet is its own separate slide, providing information on a particular region.

The idea here is that you can build a workbook in such a way that it mimics a PowerPoint presentation; the workbook is the presentation itself and each worksheet becomes a slide in the presentation. When you do that, you can easily convert that workbook into an actual PowerPoint presentation using a bit of automation.

With this technique, you can build entire presentations in Excel where you have better analytical and automation tools. Then you can convert the Excel version of your presentation to a PowerPoint presentation.

```
Sub WorkbooktoPowerPoint()

'Step 1:  Declare your variables
    Dim pp As PowerPoint.Application
    Dim PPPres As PowerPoint.Presentation
    Dim PPSlide As PowerPoint.Slide
```

```
        Dim xlwksht As Excel.Worksheet
        Dim MyRange As String
        Dim MyTitle As String

    'Step 2:  Open PowerPoint, add a new presentation and make visible
        Set pp = New PowerPoint.Application
        Set PPPres = pp.Presentations.Add
        pp.Visible = True

    'Step 3:  Set the ranges for your data and title
        MyRange = "A1:I27"

    'Step 4:  Start the loop through each worksheet
        For Each xlwksht In ActiveWorkbook.Worksheets
        MyTitle = xlwksht.Range("C19").Value

    'Step 5:  Copy the range as picture
        xlwksht.Range(MyRange).CopyPicture _
        Appearance:=xlScreen, Format:=xlPicture

    'Step 6:  Count slides and add new slide as next available slide number
        SlideCount = PPPres.Slides.Count
        Set PPSlide = PPPres.Slides.Add(SlideCount + 1, ppLayoutTitleOnly)
        PPSlide.Select

    'Step 7:  Paste the picture and adjust its position
        PPSlide.Shapes.Paste.Select
        pp.ActiveWindow.Selection.ShapeRange.Align msoAlignCenters, True
        pp.ActiveWindow.Selection.ShapeRange.Top = 100

    'Step 8:  Add the title to the slide then move to next worksheet
        PPSlide.Shapes.Title.TextFrame.TextRange.Text = MyTitle
        Next xlwksht

    'Step 9:  Memory Cleanup
        pp.Activate
        Set PPSlide = Nothing
        Set PPPres = Nothing
        Set pp = Nothing

    End Sub
```

Step 1: Declaring the Necessary Variables

In Step 1, you first declare six variables:

- PP is an object variable that exposes the PowerPoint Application object.

- PPPres is an object variable that exposes the PowerPoint Presentation object.

- `PPSlide` is an object variable that exposes the PowerPoint `Slide` object.

- `xlwksht` is an object variable that exposes the `Worksheet` object.

- `MyRange` is a string variable used to store and pass a range name as a string.

- `MyTitle` is a string variable used to store and pass a title for each slide.

Step 2: Opening PowerPoint and Starting a New Presentation

Step 2 opens PowerPoint with an empty presentation. Note that you are setting the `Visible` property of the PowerPoint application to `True`. This ensures that you can see the action as the code runs.

Step 3: Setting the Ranges for Your Data and Title

In Step 3, fill `MyRange` variable with a string representing the range you want to capture as the slide content. You also fill the `MyTitle` variable with the value of cell C19. The value here will become the title for the slide.

Step 4: Starting Looping Through the Charts

In Step 4, you start the loop through each worksheet in the workbook. The loop stops when all worksheets have been looped through.

Step 5: Copying Your Range as a Picture

In Step 5, use the `CopyPicture` method to copy your specified range as a picture.

Step 6: Counting the Slides and Adding a New Slide at the Next Available Index

In Step 6, you add a new slide to the presentation using the `Add` method of the `Slide` object. Note that you are using `SlideCount+1` to specify the index number of the added slide. Using `SlideCount+1` allows you to dynamically assign the next available number as the slide index. Note also that you are using the `ppLayoutTitleOnly`, ensuring your slide is created with a title text frame.

Step 7: Pasting the Chart into the Presentation and Moving to Next Chart

Step 7 pastes the picture into the active slide, centers the picture horizontally, and adjusts the picture vertically 100 pixels from the top margin.

Step 8: Adding the Title to the Slide

Step 8 passes the `MyTitle` variable to apply text to the title text frame.

Step 9: Cleaning Up the Open Objects

In Step 9, you release the objects assigned to your variables, reducing the chance of any problems caused by rogue objects that may remain open in memory.

Integrating Excel and Outlook

Did you know that you integrate Excel and Outlook every day? It's true. If you sent or received an Excel workbook through Outlook, you've integrated the two programs; albeit manually. In this section, you will discover a few examples of how to integrate Excel and Outlook in a more automated fashion.

Mailing the Active Workbook

The most fundamental Outlook task you can perform through automation is sending an e-mail. In the example code shown here, the active workbook is sent to two e-mail recipients as an attachment. Keep in mind that because this code is run from Excel, you will need to set a reference to the Microsoft Outlook Object Library. You can set the reference by opening the Visual Basic Editor in Excel and selecting Tools → References. Scroll down to the entry Microsoft Outlook *XX* Object Library, where the *XX* is your version of Outlook, and select it.

```
Sub Mail_workbook_Outlook()
'Step 1:   Declare your variables
    Dim OLApp As Outlook.Application
    Dim OLMail As Object

'Step 2:   Open Outlook start a new mail item
    Set OLApp = New Outlook.Application
    Set OLMail = OLApp.CreateItem(0)
    OLApp.Session.Logon

'Step 3:   Build your mail item and send
    With OLMail
    .To = "admin@datapigtechnologies.com; mike@datapigtechnologies.com"
    .CC = ""
    .BCC = ""
    .Subject = "This is the Subject line"
    .Body = "Hi there"
    .Attachments.Add ActiveWorkbook.Fullname
    .Send
```

```
    End With

'Step 4:  Memory cleanup
    Set OLMail = Nothing
    Set OLApp = Nothing

End Sub
```

Step 1: Declaring the Necessary Variables

In Step 1, you first declare two variables:

- `OLApp` is an object variable that exposes the Outlook `Application` object.
- `OLMail` is an object variable that holds a mail item.

Step 2: Opening Outlook and Starting a New Session

In Step 2, you activate Outlook and start a new session. Note that we use `OLApp.Session.Logon` to log on to the current MAPI session with default credentials. You also create a mail item. This is equivalent to selecting the New Message button in Outlook.

Step 3: Building Your Mail Item and Sending

In Step 3, you build the profile of your mail item. This includes the `To` recipients, the `CC` recipients, the `BCC` recipients, the `Subject`, the `Body`, and the `Attachments`. Note that the recipients are entered in quotes, and you separate recipients by a semicolon.

The standard syntax for an attachment is as follows:

```
.Attachments.Add "File Path"
```

In this code, you specify the current workbook's file path with the syntax: `ActiveWorkbook.Fullname`. This sets the current workbook as the attachment for the e-mail. When the message has been built, you use the `Send` method to send the e-mail.

Step 4: Cleaning Up the Open Objects

It is generally good practice to release the objects assigned to your variables. This reduces the chance of any problems caused by rogue objects that may remain open in memory. As you can see in the code, you simply set variable to `Nothing`.

Mailing a Specific Range

You can imagine that you may not always want to send your entire workbook through e-mail. This example demonstrates how you would send a specific range of data rather than the entire workbook.

```
Sub Mail_Range()
'Step 1:  Declare your variables
    Dim OLApp As Outlook.Application
    Dim OLMail As Object


'Step 2:  Copy range, paste to new workbook, and save it
    Sheets("Revenue Table").Range("A1:K50").Copy
    Workbooks.Add
    Range("A1").PasteSpecial xlPasteValues
    Range("A1").PasteSpecial xlPasteFormats
    ActiveWorkbook.SaveAs "C:\Excel_to_be_Mailed.xls"


'Step 3:  Open Outlook start a new mail item
    Set OLApp = New Outlook.Application
    Set OLMail = OLApp.CreateItem(0)
    OLApp.Session.Logon


'Step 4:  Build your mail item and send
    With OLMail
    .To = "admin@datapigtechnologies.com; mike@datapigtechnologies.com"
    .CC = ""
    .BCC = ""
    .Subject = "This is the Subject line"
    .Body = "Hi there"
    .Attachments.Add ("C:\Excel_to_be_Mailed.xls")
    .Send
    End With


'Step 5:  Delete the temporary Excel file
    ActiveWorkbook.Close SaveChanges:=True
    Kill "C:\Excel_to_be_Mailed.xls"


'Step 6:  Memory cleanup
    Set OLMail = Nothing
    Set OLApp = Nothing
```

Step 1: Declaring the Necessary Variables

In Step 1, you first declare two variables:

- OLApp is an object variable that exposes the Outlook Application object.

- OLMail is an object variable that holds a mail item.

Step 2: Copying the Desired Range to a Temporary Excel File

In Step 2, you copy a specified range and paste the values and formats to a temporary Excel file. You then save that temporary file, giving it a file path and file name.

Step 3: Opening Outlook and Starting a New Session

In Step 3, you activate Outlook and start a new session. Note that we use `OLApp.Session.Logon` to log on to the current MAPI session with default credentials. You also create a mail item. This is equivalent to selecting the New Message button in Outlook.

Step 4: Building Your Mail Item and Sending

In Step 4, you build the profile of your mail item. This includes the `To` recipients, the `CC` recipients, the `BCC` recipients, the `Subject`, the `Body`, and the `Attachments`. Note that the recipients are entered in quotes, and you separate recipients by a semicolon.

Here in this code, you specify your newly created temporary Excel file path as the attachment for the e-mail. When the message has been built, you use the `Send` method to send the e-mail.

Step 5: Deleting the Temporary Excel File

You don't want to leave temporary files hanging out there, so after the e-mail has been sent, you delete the temporary Excel file you created.

Step 6: Cleaning Up the Open Objects

It is generally good practice to release the objects assigned to your variables. This reduces the chance of any problems caused by rogue objects that may remain open in memory. As you can see in the code, you simply set variable to `Nothing`.

Mailing to All E-mail Addresses in Your Contact List

Ever need to send out a mass mailing such as a newsletter or a memo? Instead of manually entering each of your contacts' e-mail addresses, you can run the following procedure. In this procedure, you send out one e-mail, automatically adding all the e-mail addresses in your contact list to your e-mail.

```
Sub Mail_To_All_Contacts()
'Step 1:  Declare your variables
    Dim OLApp As Outlook.Application
    Dim OLMail As Object
    Dim MyCell As Range
    Dim MyContacts As Range

'Step 2:  Define the range to loop through
```

```
        Set MyContacts = Sheets("Contact List").Range("H2:H21")

'Step 3:   Open Outlook
    Set OLApp = New Outlook.Application
    Set OLMail = OLApp.CreateItem(0)      OLApp.Session.Logon

'Step 4:   Add each address in the contact list
    With OLMail
        .BCC = ""
          For Each MyCell In MyContacts
             .BCC = .BCC & MyCell.Value & ";"
          Next MyCell
        .Subject = "Chapter 11 Sample Email"
        .Body = "Sample file is attached"
        .Attachments.Add ActiveWorkbook.Fullname
        .Send
    End With

'Step 5:   Memory cleanup
    Set OLMail = Nothing
    Set OLApp = Nothing

End sub
```

Step 1: Declaring the Necessary Variables

In Step 1, you first declare four variables:

- OLApp is an object variable that exposes the Outlook Application object.
- OLMail is an object variable that holds a mail item.
- MyCell is an object variable that holds an Excel range.
- MyContacts is an object variable that holds an Excel range.

Step 2: Defining the Target Range

In Step 2, you point the MyContacts variable to the range of cells that contains your e-mail addresses. This is the range of cells you loop through to add e-mail addresses to your e-mail.

Step 3: Opening Outlook and Starting a New Session

In Step 3, you activate Outlook and start a new session. Note that we use OLApp.Session.Logon to log on to the current MAPI session with default credentials. You also create a mail item. This is equivalent to selecting the New Message button in Outlook.

Step 4: Adding Each Address in Your Contact List

In Step 4, you build the profile of your mail item. Note that you are looping through each cell in the `MyContacts` range and adding the contents (which are e-mail addresses) to the BCC. Here, you are using the BCC property instead of To or CC so that each recipient gets an e-mail that looks as though it was sent only to him. He will not be able to see any of the other e-mail addresses, as they have been sent with BCC (Blind Courtesy Copy).

Step 5: Cleaning Up the Open Objects

It is generally good practice to release the objects assigned to your variables. This reduces the chance of any problems caused by rogue objects that may remain open in memory. As you can see in the code, you simply set variable to `Nothing`.

Saving All Attachments in a Folder

You may often find that certain processes lend themselves to the exchange of data via e-mail. For example, you may send a budget template out for each branch manager to fill out and send back to you via e-mail. Well, if there are 150 branch members, it could be a bit of a pain to download all those e-mail attachments.

The following procedure demonstrates one solution to this problem. In this procedure, you use automation to search for all attachments in your Inbox and save them to a specified folder.

```
Sub SaveAttachments()
'Step 1:  Declare your variables
    Dim ns As Namespace
    Dim MyInbox As MAPIFolder
    Dim MItem As MailItem
    Dim Atmt As Attachment
    Dim FileName As String


'Step 2:  Set a reference to your Inbox
    Set ns = GetNamespace("MAPI")
    Set MyInbox = ns.GetDefaultFolder(olFolderInbox)

'Step 3:  Check for messages in your Inbox ; exit if none
    If MyInbox.Items.Count = 0 Then
    MsgBox "No messages in folder."
    Exit Sub
    End If

'Step 4:  Create directory to hold attachments
    On Error Resume Next
```

```
        MkDir "C:\Integration\MyAttachments\"

  'Step 5:   Start to loop through each mail item
        For Each MItem In MyInbox.Items

  'Step 6:   Save each attachement then go to the next attachment
        For Each Atmt In MItem.Attachments
        FileName = "C:\Integration\MyAttachments\" & Atmt.FileName
        Atmt.SaveAsFile FileName
        Next Atmt

  'Step 7:   Move to the next mail item
        Next MItem
   End Sub
```

Step 1: Declaring the Necessary Variables

In Step 1, you first declare five variables:

- ns is an object is used to expose the MAPI namespace
- MyInbox is used to expose the target mail folder
- MItem is used to expose the properties of a mail item
- Atmt is an object variable that holds an Attachment object
- FileName is a string variable that holds the name of the attachment

Step 2: Pointing to Your Inbox

In Step 2, you set the MyInbox variable to point to the Inbox for your default mail client.

Step 3: Checking for Messages

In Step 3, you perform a quick check to make sure there are actually messages in your Inbox. If there are no messages, you exit the procedure with a message box telling you there are no messages.

Step 4: Creating a Directory to Hold Attachments

In Step 4, you create a directory to hold the attachments you find. Although you could use an existing directory, it's generally best to use a directory dedicated specifically for the attachments you bring down. Here, you are creating that directory on the fly. Note you are using On Error Resume Next. This ensures the code does not error out if the directory you are trying to create already exists.

Step 5: Starting the Loop

In Step 5, you start the loop through each mail item in the target mail folder.

Step 6: Looping Through All Attachments in Each Mail Item

Step 6 ensures that each mail item you loop through gets checked for attachments. As you loop, you will save each attachment you find into the specified directory you created.

Step 7: Moving to the Next Mail Item

Step 7 loops back to Step 5 until there are no more mail items to go through.

Step 8: Cleaning Up the Open Objects

It is generally good practice to release the objects assigned to your variables. This reduces the chance of any problems caused by rogue objects that may remain open in memory. As you can see in the code, you simply set variable to `Nothing`.

Saving Certain Attachments to a Folder

In the previous procedure, you use automation to search for all attachments in your Inbox and save them to a specified folder. However, you will more likely only want to save certain attachments. That is to say, those e-mail attachments that contain a certain Subject for example. In this example, you get a demonstration of how to check for certain syntax and selectively download attachments.

```
Sub SaveCertainAttachments()

'Step 1:  Declare your variables
    Dim ns As Namespace
    Dim MyInbox As MAPIFolder
    Dim Item As Object
    Dim Atmt As Attachment
    Dim FileName As String
    Dim i As Integer

'Step 2:  Set a reference to your Inbox
    Set ns = GetNamespace("MAPI")
    Set MyInbox = ns.GetDefaultFolder(olFolderInbox)

'Step 3:  Check for messages in your Inbox ; exit if none
    If MyInbox.Items.Count = 0 Then
    MsgBox "No messages in folder."
    Exit Sub
    End If

'Step 4:  Create directory to hold attachments
    On Error Resume Next
    MkDir "C:\Integration\MyAttachments\"

'Step 5:  Start to loop through each mail item
```

```
    For Each MItem In MyInbox.Items

'Step 6:  Check for the words Data Submission in Subject line
    If InStr(1, MItem.Subject, "Data Submission") < 1 Then
    GoTo SkipIt
    End If

'Step 7:  Save each with a log number; go to the next attachment
    i = 0
    For Each Atmt In MItem.Attachments
    FileName = _
    "C:\Integration\MyAttachments\Attachment-" & i & "-" & Atmt.FileName
    Atmt.SaveAsFile FileName
    i = i + 1
    Next Atmt

'Step 8:  Move to the next mail item
SkipIt:
    Next MItem

'Step 9:  Memory cleanup
    Set ns = Nothing
    Set MyInbox = Nothing      End Sub
```

Step 1: Declaring the Necessary Variables

In Step 1, you first declare six variables:

- ns is an object used to expose the MAPI namespace.

- MyInbox is used to expose the target mail folder.

- MItem is used to expose the properties of a mail item.

- Atmt is an object variable that holds an Attachment object.

- FileName is a string variable that holds the name of the attachment.

- i is an integer variable used to ensure each attachment is saved as a unique name.

Step 2: Pointing to Your Inbox

In Step 2, you set the MyInbox variable to point to the Inbox for your default mail client.

Step 3: Checking for Messages

In Step 3, you perform a quick check to make sure there are actually messages in your Inbox. If there are no messages, you exit the procedure with a message box telling you there are no messages.

Step 4: Creating a Directory to Hold Attachments

In Step 4, you create a directory to hold the attachments you find. Note you are using `On Error Resume Next`. This ensures the code does not error out if the directory you are trying to create already exists.

Step 5: Starting the Loop

In Step 5, you start the loop through each mail item in the target mail folder.

Step 6: Checking for the Correct Key Words in the Subject Line

In Step 6, you use the `Instr` function to check whether the string `Data Submission` is in the Subject line of the e-mail. If that string does not exist, then you are not interested in the attachment there. Therefore, you force the procedure to go to the `SkipIt` reference (in Step 8). Because the line of code immediately following the `SkipIt` reference is essentially a move next command, this has the effect of telling the procedure to move to the next mail item.

Step 7: Looping Through All Attachments in Each Mail Item

Step 7 loops through the attachments and saves each attachment into the specified directory you created. Note that you are adding a running integer to the name of each attachment. This ensures that each attachment is saved as a unique name, helping you to avoid overwriting attachments.

Step 8: Moving to the Next Mail Item

Step 8 loops back to Step 5 until there are no more mail items to go through.

Step 9: Cleaning Up the Open Objects

It is generally good practice to release the objects assigned to your variables. This reduces the chance of any problems caused by rogue objects that may remain open in memory. As you can see in the code, you simply set the variable to `Nothing`.

Summary

Excel data has a way of touching every application in the Office suite. Excel data is often distributed through a Word document, displayed through a PowerPoint presentation, and even shared using Outlook. Although Access is the most well-suited application to integrate with Excel, these other Office applications also have the ability to integrate with Excel. You can use Excel and Word to create a Mail Merge document. You can automate the creation of an entire PowerPoint presentation directly from an Excel workbook. You can send mass e-mails through Outlook, using nothing more than a list of e-mail addresses in Excel. Use the techniques you learned in this chapter to think about some of the ways you can integrate Excel with the other applications in Office.

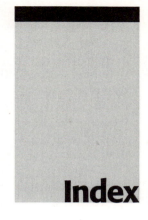

Index